INDIGENOUS MIGRATION
AND SOCIAL CHANGE

INDIGENOUS MIGRATION AND SOCIAL CHANGE

The Forasteros of Cuzco, 1570–1720

ANN M. WIGHTMAN

DUKE UNIVERSITY PRESS
Durham and London ■ 1990

✤ CONTENTS ✤ ✤

For My Parents
David Wightman, Jean Wightman Miller, Melvin J. Miller

✦ PREFACE ✦ ✦

M ORE YEARS ago than I like to remember, I wrote a senior
thesis under the direction of John J. TePaske who very gen-
erously gave me microfilm of documents from his beloved Archivo
General de Indias (AGI) in Sevilla, Spain. I was fascinated by the
descriptions of the Indian community in colonial Peru, but I kept run-
ning across a word related to Indian migration which had no obvious
meaning: "forasteros." When I asked TePaske what it meant, he told me
to go find out.

That search took me to graduate school and to various archives in
Spain and Peru where I pursued my study of colonial Peruvian social
history and those elusive forasteros. In the process I have come to share
TePaske's love for the AGI and Sevilla and have, quite simply, become
addicted to Cuzco, Peru. I also have developed and then discarded
successive definitions of "forasteros" as I moved from the simple meaning of "strangers" to a more sophisticated understanding of forasteros as
foreign-born Indians and their descendants who had migrated to and
had been integrated into existing Indian communities. My analysis of
indigenous migration changed as well: my doctoral dissertation emphasized the importance of migration within the rural zone of the bishopric
of Cuzco; this expanded study recognizes the impossibility of isolating
rural migrants from their urban counterparts. My postdissertation work
is also marked by a broader realization of the significance of indigenous
migration. In my thesis I identified Indian migration as a form of resistance to colonialism. Although I still insist that the forasteros represent a form of resistance to Spanish rule, I also recognize the ironic
consequences of their actions and the painful ways in which indigenous
migration actually facilitated, rather than impeded, the spread of imperial authority. The time frame of my study of Indian migration has
remained the same—1570 to 1720—a period delineated by a combination of demographic and social structures which I will identify more fully
below.

The forasteros of Cuzco are, in any sense of the term, "subject peoples." They were the subjects of an exploitative imperial system; they, like other indigenous peoples under Spanish rule, were the subjects of a process of objectification and definition by negation which led to their being perceived as less than they truly were; they were most often the subjects, rather than the originators, of the bulk of the documentary evidence which purports to describe their historical experience; they are now subject to my own efforts to recover and record that historical experience. I cannot in this book redress all those grievances, undo all that damage, but I have tried to be sensitive to all these constraints in the reading of a document or in the coding of a labor contract and I have tried consistently to emphasize that the major trends I describe are the result of individuals' actions and interactions.

The research which supports this analysis was made possible by dissertation grants from the Social Science Research Council and the Henry L. and Grace Doherty Fellowship Program and by a project grant from Wesleyan University. This book could not have been completed without the generous assistance of the directors and staffs of the Peruvian and Spanish archives. I appreciate all their efforts, but I am particularly indebted to Jorge Olivera O. of the Archivo Departamental del Cusco and to the late Padre Manuel Espejo of the Bishopric of Cuzco, who volunteered to supervise my use of the Archivo Arzobispal del Cusco during the years when it was not officially open to scholars. The interlibrary loan service of Wesleyan's Olin Library under the direction of Steve Lebergott always managed to find the materials I needed.

I am not the only historian of colonial Peru who is indebted to the encouragement, common sense, and integrity of John J. TePaske, but he has remained supportive throughout the years and I am particularly grateful to him. I also want to thank my thesis adviser, Richard M. Morse, and my other professors at Yale—Ursula Lamb, Patricia Otto Klaus, Karen Spalding, and Emilia Viotti da Costa. Scholarship is collaboration, and my work has benefitted greatly from interaction with a number of colleagues. Meeting Irene Silverblatt during my first research trip to Cuzco was a blessing that has only been equaled by her recent move to the nearby University of Connecticut. Along the way, at various conferences and archives, I have had the benefit of comments from and conversations with Peter Bakewell, Alexandra Cook, David Cook, John Kizca, Magnus Morner, Franklin Pease, Deborah Poole, Frank Salomon, Steve J. Stern and T. R. Zuidema. Both the readers at Duke University Press offered helpful suggestions, but I am particularly grateful to Brooke Larson, in part because by identifying herself as one of the readers she made the process more comfortable and comforting. Duke's Dan Ross coped better than I did with the historical conjuncture of a first book and a tenure process.

At Wesleyan University I have experienced faculty colleagueship at its best—friendship, support, and intellectual stimulation that crosses disciplinary boundaries and area studies lines. I am particularly grateful to Richard Elphick and Jeffrey Butler who thoughtfully and carefully read and reread my manuscript, to Carlos Alonso and Diana Goodrich, and to Patricia Hill, Wendy Rayack, and Franek Rozwadowski. Clarence Walker has left Wesleyan for the University of California at Davis but he is still willing to engage in friendly but heated debate over the relationship between race, class, and gender. Having received so much helpful advice and assistance, I must insist even more emphatically than usual that I am responsible for any remaining problems or ambiguities.

A number of people helped in the preparation of the manuscript. Carolyn Macdermott is more my friend than my typist, but I also want to acknowledge her splendid work on the hundreds of pages of tables included in my dissertation. Because of editorial constraints, only the most critical portions of those data are reproduced in this volume and I am grateful to Fran Warren and Karen Kowalski for creating new charts that reduced the information to a more manageable level. Rose Marie Ingalls and Donna Scott remained cheerful and helpful, even when faced with masses of photocopying and repeated requests for Spanish-language printwheels for the laser printer. Ted Bardacke and Jordan Rau proofread sections of the text.

Finally, I want to thank Mal Bochner. The customary phrase—"I couldn't have done it without you"—is alien to the way we see our life together, but we both know that this process was much easier because I was not going through it alone.

Middletown, Connecticut
May 1989

INDIGENOUS MIGRATION AND SOCIAL CHANGE

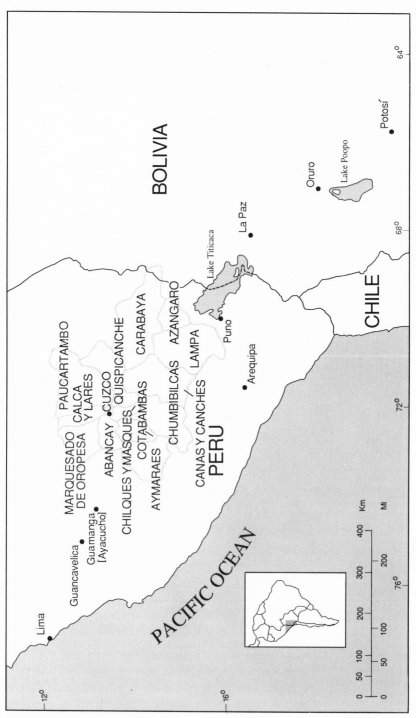

Bishopric of Cuzco c. 1690

❖ 1 ❖ ❖

"Innumerable Indians": Cuzco, 1570

IN OCTOBER 1570 Viceroy Francisco de Toledo—the king's representative and chief executive authority for the vast administrative area known as the Viceroyalty of Peru, stretching from the Panamanian isthmus to Cape Horn—embarked on a five-year tour of the Andean heartland. Traveling slowly into the sierra, Toledo was kept busy issuing a series of reforms and regulations designed to combat the "lawlessness" and "incivility" of the Viceroyalty. Nowhere was he more occupied than in the area surrounding the city of Cuzco, which he reached in June 1571. As he approached the former Incan capital, Toledo rode "a roan horse which was decorated with a beautiful blanket and a gold-trimmed saddle" and he passed under arches "adorned with flowers, birds, and the skins of animals"; as he rode through the surrounding countryside, he passed by "innumerable Indians."[1]

Toledo might have thought that there were "innumerable Indians" in the bishopric of Cuzco, but the local population had dropped drastically since the Spanish conquest, and indigenous patterns of human organization and production had been dramatically altered by the time Toledo arrived to reform colonial government. The process of transformation had not begun with the Europeans' arrival during the 1530s, however, because the Incan state, which had ruled the Cuzco area since before the rapid expansion of the empire in the early fifteenth century, had adapted traditional indigenous institutions and added others in order to solidify control of its central Andean holdings. Pre-Incan society had been divided into kin groups known as *ayllus*, endogamous social units with common ancestry, whose specific membership was determined by a variety of locally generated descent patterns and definitions of "kin." These ayllus were led by *sinchi*, or warriors, a group evolving into a hereditary leadership that oversaw a complicated system of reciprocity in which individuals owed certain responsibilities to other community members and to their ayllus and in which individuals in turn received certain benefits, particularly access to community land and labor assistance. Ayllu members also had the obligation of participating in another expression of ayllu reciprocity, *mita chana cuy*, or labor service on a variety of projects that benefitted the community or its leadership. Special types of services were provided by *mitamaq*, individuals who retained membership in their home ayllu but left its lands to secure commodities available only in different ecological zones, a reflection of the vertical structure of Andean society. Mitamaq remained linked to their home communities through kin ties and through the ayllu's *guarqui*, its ancestral deity.

The Incan adaptations of these Andean institutions served to bind the conquered ayllus to the state, but both the adaptation of traditional structures and the addition of imperial practices altered the basic organization of pre-Incan Andean society. The ayllus were preserved as the basic social unit but the Incas removed some workers, called *yana*, from their kin groups, added new royal ayllus, and imposed administrative units known as "hundreds." The local leadership group was converted into a hereditary leadership sector known as *kurakas*, but imperial envoys were given substantial political powers in the subjugated zones. The concept of reciprocity was extended to include the Incan state, with a new form of communal labor, *mit'a*, and taxes imposed to benefit the empire. The practice of sending colonists to distinct ecological zones to secure specific commodities continued, but under the Incas the *mitmaq* were usually resettled in order to increase the political and military stability of the empire. The Incas allowed local communities to continue their worship of ancestral deities, but forced all citizens of the empire to accept the superiority of the Sun God.

The arrival of the Europeans exacerbated these changes and caused others. The Spaniards were delighted to see those features of Incan society which they could adopt to their own purposes, operating on the theory that conquered peoples could be controlled best through familiar institutions. However, in each case the Spaniards' adoption of Incan institutions substantially changed their structure. Under Spanish control, the ayllu would be redefined, with an increasing emphasis on territoriality rather than ancestry, and the personal-service relationship between the yana and the Inca state would find a much-altered expression in the *yanacona* sector. The kurakas would be incorporated into the system of colonial administration in ways that reshaped their role within indigenous society. The concept of reciprocity would be altered, destroying the balance between ayllu members and between ayllus and the state as the Europeans appropriated for their own profit the Indians' land, goods, and labor service. Tolerance of familiar institutions would not be extended to indigenous religion, which the Spaniards were determined to exterminate. The indigenous peoples of the Andes would not passively accept these assaults on their traditional institutions and they would resent and resist imperial rule, both Incan and Iberian.[2]

Toledo, however, was either unaware of or unconcerned with the subtleties of change within indigenous society. He was much more concerned with the current state of the Viceroyalty and with the ways in which Indians, their leaders, and private settlers were challenging the authority of the Spanish Crown. Toledo's staff had reported that throughout the Cuzco zone "there were many Indians who neither paid tribute nor were supervised by an encomendero or any other person" and the Viceroy himself noted that Cuzco, at an elevation of 11,000 feet, was surrounded by fertile Andean valleys and terraced hillsides, populated by "a great many people of all kinds who wandered idly through the city and towns." He found the indigenous community disorganized, dispersed, and demoralized from the Spanish conquest, the prolonged civil wars between opposing bands of conquistadores (1531–1547), and rumors of an uprising planned by the heir to the Incan Empire, Tupac Amaru. Toledo reported to King Philip II that the indigenous community was being exploited by local landowners and miners, harassed by the colonial judicial system, and deceived by a false religion.[3]

As he had done throughout the sierra, the Viceroy ordered that the Indians of Cuzco be concentrated into organized settlements or *reducciones*, "so that they might become Christians and live decently." To resolve the specific problems he had noted, Toledo regularized and limited the demands that Spanish entrepreneurs could place on Indian laborers, established local courts and officials to protect the indigenous population, and ordered the confiscation of all concealed *guacas*, the objects held sacred in indigenous religion and denounced as "idols" by the Spaniards.[4] Each of these reforms would, over time, have unforeseen consequences that undermined Toledo's original intent: the organization of the indigenous community into reducciones actually stimulated population dispersal and migration; the regularization of indigenous labor created new forms of exploitation which drove Indians to abandon their home communities to seek protection from the Spanish employers who were the targets of the original reforms; the local court systems and officials proved as efficiently predatory as their predecessors; and the campaign to end "idolatry" failed to eradicate traditional religious practices, which were perpetuated and in some ways strengthened by contact with Catholic rituals and institutions. Because of Toledo's actions and their unintended results, the next century and a half would bring a fundamental transformation of the Cuzco region: changes within Indian society and within the legal code would redefine and restructure the indigenous community; integration into the imperial system would transform economic relationships; the imposition of new political institutions and officials would challenge traditional authority lines; and the interaction of indigenous and European values would create a syncretic colonial culture.

The emergence of the social group known as *forasteros*—Indian migrants and their descendants who were integrated into existing communities in the rural zone and within the city of Cuzco[5]—affected every one of these major transformations of traditional society: the presence of forasteros forced the redefinition of community structures and social ties; the migrants' varied economic roles (from wage laborer to private landowner) altered emerging economic patterns; the forasteros' arrangements with local leaders complicated the interaction between traditional authorities and colonial administrators; and the migrants' impact on indigenous religious practices and beliefs exacerbated the conflict between traditional values and Catholicism. Understanding indigenous migration and its impact on social structure, economic activity, political authority, and cultural interaction is necessary not only to accurately represent demographic change but also to understand the broader social and economic transformations of the seventeenth century.

Given recent developments in colonial historiography—particularly in the fields of social history, economic inquiry, and ethnohistory—it should be unnecessary to attack the image of the 1600s as a "Century of Depression," an insignificant interval between the chaos of the conquest and the dislocation of the Borbón reforms.[6] Nevertheless, recognizing the importance of this era has not totally eliminated the image of seventeenth-century Peru as an example of rigid, "classic colonialism."[7]

One of the most serious consequences of this image of the period was to obscure the role of migration in the creation of colonial society, and particularly in the transformation of the indigenous community which Karen Spalding has so aptly labeled *"De indio a campesino."* A decade ago Rolando Mellafe deplored the prevailing "static view of colonial Hispanic American society," reminding scholars that "unless we steadily keep in mind the continuing process of migration in the Viceroyalty of Peru, we can explain hardly any of the major phenomena of change in the family or in the Indian communities." Spalding and Franklin Pease also urged the study of indigenous migration, particularly as an assertive act by Indians who "sought to modify, adapt, avoid, or utilize the institutions imposed by their conquerors, as well as preserve and adapt their own traditions."[8]

Nevertheless, most studies of migration in colonial Peru initially followed Mellafe's own limited format by concentrating on Europeans, Peruvians of mixed racial heritage, and Indians moving from "centers of dispersion" to "permanent areas of attraction";[9] such migration usually involved a parallel transition from traditional to conquest society and from subsistence agriculture to participation in the export economy and its support sectors. Little attention was given to the question of migration within indigenous society or to the role of the forasteros. Too often the complex mechanism of Indian migration was reduced to a simplistic duality of Indians fleeing to areas beyond Spanish control or seeking sanctuary in the employ of private landholders and mineowners.[10] No longer identified as "displaced Indians . . . who usually floated around like hoboes within the confines of the colony," the forasteros were still frequently regarded as marginal to Indian colonial society.[11] Recent research on Indian communities in Upper Peru has contributed to a new understanding of indigenous migration but still emphasizes the impact of the mining communities.[12] In his comprehensive summary of "Demographic and Physical Aspects of the Transition from the Aboriginal to the Colonial World," Woodrow Borah cited the need to analyze the "new socioeconomic forms created by the resettlement of the Indian population," but failed to mention migration within the Indian community or its impact on colonial history. A recent study of major patterns in colonial demography totally ignored indigenous migration.[13] One major theme unites these works: a perception of indigenous migration and migrants as chiefly the result of other developments within colonial history. What I have tried to do is to present the forasteros as a cause as well as a consequence of historical change and to analyze their active role in the transformation of indigenous society under Spanish colonialism.

The failure to recognize the full significance of the forastero sector, which by 1690 was almost half of the population of the bishopric of Cuzco, has obscured another major facet of the Indian response to Spanish rule. Indigenous migration clearly constituted a form of resistance to colonial rule. The vigor with which Spanish administrators sought to control the forasteros indicated the degree to which officials considered unrestricted indigenous migration a challenge to their authority. The size and scope of the forastero sectors, both provincial and urban, represented a potential loss of imperial profits and a possible threat to political and religious hegemony. Yet, paradoxically, some of the consequences of widespread indigenous migration—the redefinition of the kin group and the weakening of communal ties; the indigenous participation in the wage labor force; and the abandonment and subsequent alienation of Indian lands—actually contributed to the expansion of the imperial system in a painfully ironic twist to the theme of indigenous response and resistance to colonial rule. The unintended consequences of an individual's act, whether forastero or viceroy, played a major role in the transformation of the bishopric of Cuzco between 1570 and 1720.

The bishopric of Cuzco during the period from 1570 to 1720 is an excellent locale for such an essential study of the structure and impact of Indian migration. As in most colonial-era research, the availability of documentation influenced the selection of the Cuzco region: the 1690 census of the bishopric is a critical part of the data base for this project. Specific features of the region also contributed to the final choice. Some aspects, such as the Spaniards' efforts to extract labor and goods from the indigenous community, prevailed throughout colonial Peru; other characteristics, such as the impact of the prolonged civil wars and the region's role within the imperial system, distinguished the Cuzco zone from other areas of the Viceroyalty. The Cuzco area was a subsidiary economic zone linked to but not dominated by any of the major growth regions, and the city was an important administrative and transportation center. Within the provinces of the bishopric, Indians were subject to various types of forced labor service with distinct demographic and social consequences, a fact which allows for a comparative approach impossible in other regions.[14] In short, the bishopric of Cuzco was both like and unlike other regions of colonial Peru; studying the Cuzco zone allows for both broad generalizations applicable to other zones and specific conclusions emphasizing the area's unique history.

This study begins in the 1570s during the administration of Viceroy Francisco de Toledo (1569–1581), but the emphasis on Toledo's tenure is not intended to disparage the significant developments of the immediate postconquest era.[15] Rather, this period has been chosen because of the imposition of Toledo's complex bureaucratic system which regularized Indian labor and tribute obligations, prohibited unauthorized resettlement within indigenous society, and formalized the procedure through which an individual's legal status and community identity were determined by birthplace. The logical endpoint for an analysis of that system is the decade following the pan-Andean epidemic of 1719–1721, which devastated the Cuzco area and forced a readjustment of colonial administrative policy and a redefinition of the individual Indian's social position, with legal status and community membership dependent on access to resources of production, not birth.

Ironically, the period so clearly defined by specific chronological events can best be studied through a distinctly unchronological approach. I have therefore adopted a structure which, like the term "forastero," needs some elucidation. This chapter introduces the bishopric of Cuzco in the 1570s, explaining why this particular area and period were selected. Chapter 2 establishes a roughly chronological framework for the themes which follow by presenting a history of migration policy through two parallel lines of analysis: viceregal administration and local reaction and resistance. In chapter 3 I discuss motives for Indian migration and profile the forastero population, suggesting a new approach to the region's demographic history and a restructuring of basic patterns in colonial demography. In chapter 4 I examine the impact of indigenous migration on community structures and linkages within the rural zone; chapter 5 emphasizes parallel changes within the city of Cuzco. Chapter 6 discusses the ways in which rural and urban indigenous migration altered both the traditional and colonial relationships of production. In chapter 7 I conclude the study and complete the 1570–1720 cycle by returning to the scene set at the beginning of the work.

The impact of these fundamental structural changes within the indigenous community was not, of course, confined to the period from 1570 to 1720. Rather, the emergence of a forastero sector and the redefinition of the indigenous community constituted an initial, critical phase in the prolonged, to date incomplete, transformation from caste to class in

Andean America.[16] This original alteration of the traditional community was both a result and a cause of the economic changes which concurrently necessitated the dislocation of the preconquest population and facilitated the reassimilation of the Indian migrants.[17] A systematic examination of the composition and activities of the forastero sector will, I hope, shatter any remaining stereotypes of Indian migration and will provide a focal point for understanding the complex, diverse, and ultimately mobile society of seventeenth-century Peru.

✛ 2 ✛ ✛

"The Indian Towns Have Been Deserted . . . but the Indians Have Not Disappeared": The Failure of the Reducciones

C OLONIAL AUTHORITIES did not have to be convinced of the significance of indigenous migration. But they would have been surprised—perhaps even appalled—at any analysis which so emphasized migration over other aspects of the "Indian problem." Successive viceroys and their staffs recognized that migration threatened the economic viability and social order of Peru but reacted to indigenous migration within the broader context of the confusing and contradictory policies which sought simultaneously to protect and to exploit the Indian. Particular proposals to stabilize the Indian population were adopted not because they might effectively control Indian migration but because they would generate the least conflict with local-interest groups. Colonial administrators were unable to see the human dimension of the problem or to understand that migration was a cause as well as a consequence of complex changes within Indian communities.

Throughout the colonial period, the size and stability of the "Republic of Indians" was a matter of grave concern for colonial administrators who sought to maintain the indigenous communities for the purposes of regulating and Christianizing the population, facilitating the extraction of goods and services, and concentrating the available work force. Alarmed by the rapid postconquest depopulation of the sierra, colonial authorities sought to stabilize the indigenous communities by concentrating Indians into *reducciones*, or settlements, and by identifying individuals as *originarios*, or native-born members of kin-groups with distinct territorial affiliations. The inherent inequalities in the *reducción* system imposed by Viceroy Francisco de Toledo in the 1570s only stimulated Indian migration, and the inability of that system to reincorporate migrants who remained within Indian society led to the distinct status of the forasteros. The sporadic attempts of colonial viceroys to stop Indian migration through redefinition of legal obligations and social status were repeatedly counteracted by their immediate successors, whose erratic policies actually stimulated further movement. Refusing to recognize the failures of the reducción system, the Crown clung to the Toledo structure and perpetuated the originario-forastero dichotomy throughout the seventeenth century. Not until the demographic crisis of the 1720s did the Crown undertake a comprehensive reorganization and redefinition of Indian society which recognized the importance and the impact of sustained indigenous migration within colonial Peru.

The conflict between theory and practice which characterized Spanish-American colonial administration also dominated migration policy, in which the tension was between the ideal of a strictly controlled Indian community concentrated in reducciones and the reality of widespread indigenous movement. Regulations governing Indian migration usually reflected the individual initiative of frustrated colonial officials rather than Hapsburg imperial policy. The extensive reforms proposed by the Duque de Palata in the 1680s occurred both in spite of and because of weaknesses in peninsular administration. Although some of the eighteenth-century Borbón reforms had a direct impact on Cuzco's Indian population, the policies implemented in the 1720s did not respond to a change of dynasty in Spain but rather to local conditions and crises resulting from more than a century of unchecked indigenous migration.[1]

THE REDUCCIÓN DEBATE

The initial contact between the indigenous populations of the Americas and the *conquistadores* inevitably produced a demographic—and human—disaster: unprecedented Indian mortality rates from transferred diseases, accompanied by rapid and massive population displacement. The few remaining Caribs and Taino Arawaks fled the larger islands of the Spanish Main for more remote archipelagoes; the former subjects of the Aztec Confederation "developed a dangerous tendency to drift away from their villages" as soon as their provinces were conquered by the Europeans; and thousands of Indians fought, died, or fled at Pizarro's penetration of the Andean sierra.[2] Speaking of this population displacement, Nicolás Sánchez-Albornoz has described the "chaotic shuffling around of men, institutions, and ideas that took place during the early days of Spanish domination."[3] Certainly some of the most frequently shuffled institutions and ideas applied within the New World were those concerned with the maintenance and management of the Indian population. On the theoretical level, the question of the nature of the Indian would ultimately lead to the Great Debate, whose impact is still visible in the confrontation of the Black Legend and the White Legend and in the perpetuation of dangerous and offensive stereotypes.[4] On a more practical, immediate level, the concern for nurturing the indigenous population would produce a series of alternative schemes to protect and simultaneously to exploit the Indians, schemes whose failures have their ramifications in the current repression and depression of the *campesino* community of the Andean sierra. Nicolás de Ovando, the first viceroy in the Spanish colonies, was sent to Santo Domingo in 1502 with specific instructions to care for the Indian population and to compensate for the abuses of Cristobal Colón and Francisco de Bobadilla. Three hundred years later viceroys in Mexico and Peru were still being commanded to stabilize the Indian community and to correct their predecessors' errors.[5]

In the Viceroyalty of Peru the general patterns of depopulation and dislocation were intensified by the particular circumstances of the conquest and the subsequent civil wars.[6] The rapid changes in colonial administration produced conflicting Indian policies, but most early governors were united in their disapproval of any proposed relocation of the indigenous population to areas favored by European settlers: the viceroys "held that Spanish cities should be founded wherever there was a dense native population and, therefore, that European immigrants should be urged to settle in such cities." The policy was discredited throughout the 1560s and totally abandoned in 1572 with the arrival in Peru of Francisco de Toledo, who "held that the native labor force should be concentrated in those regions that because of favorable opportunities for economic exploitation had already been settled by Europeans; in other words, Indians should be settled where Spanish entrepreneurs could use this labor."[7] Although Toledo cited other justifications for the resettlement of the Indians of Peru—chiefly the need for an ordered political life and the importance of regular religious instruction—the Europeans' access to indigenous labor remained his chief concern.

The Spanish policy of reducción, of concentrating population resources by resettling groups of Indians into new settlements or reducciones, was not created by Francisco de Toledo. Emphasis on urban life and the political autonomy of the *cabildo,* or town council, were characteristic of Iberian colonial expansion and the belief that Indians should also be organized into towns dates from the early colonial period. The Catholic church was the first advocate of Indian reducciones and a consistent supporter of the resettlement program. The linkage between congregation and Christianization was clearly expressed in 1538, when Charles V reminded the Audiencia of Guatemala that "it is just and expedient to concentrate the Indian population of this province, so that they may be taught the doctrine of our holy faith."[8]

The further benefits of reducciones were expressed in two *Cédulas Reales,* issued in 1551, which would provide both the impetus and the justification for the Toledo reforms. In the first royal decree the governor of Tierra Firme was instructed that Indians should be removed from the private service of Spaniards who had usurped official control and that these Indians "should be brought together in one or more towns where they can live and prosper and be taught the doctrine of our holy Catholic faith."[9] The second ordinance, which would be restated five times in the next two decades, established the legal basis for all future reducciones by mandating "that the Indians be reduced to towns and that they not live dispersed, isolated by the mountains and hillsides, deprived of all spiritual and worldly good." Officials throughout the Indies were commanded "to secure the concentration, settlement, and Christianization of the Indians with caution and moderation."[10] Although the legal basis for reducciones had been established by the 1550s, few settlements were organized in the Andean area, and fewer still in the Cuzco zone.[11] Colonial bureaucrats seemed much more concerned with the growing number of *mestizos* who, they told the King, "wander aimlessly, committing idolatry and other crimes and sins—fornication and adultery, theft and murder." In 1555, Charles V responded with an order "that these children of Spaniards be gathered into towns, and saved from their evil ways."[12]

By the mid-sixteenth century, this image of the reducción as an antidote to idleness and idolatry was increasingly popular among royal officials who sought to blame the economic vulnerability of the colonies on "the Indians of these provinces . . . a lazy people who will not work, whose idleness is the reason for the current shortages of food stuffs."[13] In his *Gobierno del Perú* (1567), Juan de Matienzo synthesized the complaints of colonists when he denounced the Indians: "for them there is no tomorrow; they are satisfied with fulfilling their needs for a week and will work no more than is necessary in order to eat and drink that week. They hate work and love idleness, alcohol, drunkenness, and idolatry; while drunk, they commit mortal sins with women. They obey their superiors willingly and therefore it is necessary to rule them, govern them, and make them work—to keep them from idleness and sin."[14] To combat these problems and to secure the economic survival of the vice-royalty, Matienzo suggested that reducciones be established throughout Peru: "Among the other responsibilities of your majesty . . . is that of teaching the Indians to live in civil order so that they can more easily be instructed in our sacred Catholic faith, which is our chief goal; and thus any provision that the Indians be reduced to towns is just and righteous."[15] Matienzo never had the opportunity to effect a massive resettlement of the Indian population, but the generally favorable response to his *Gobierno del Perú* certainly facilitated the acceptance of the later Toledo reducciones. Guillermo Lohmann Villena feels that Matienzo probably contributed to the Toledo reforms in a much more specific way: several key provisions of the Matienzo proposal, most notably that male Indians between the ages of eighteen and fifty should be taxed, appear in the Toledo *ordenanzas,* or regulations.[16] More importantly, both Matienzo and Toledo used practical experience and legal precedent in formulating their resettlement schemes, a combination that explains some of their identical conclusions, such as the belief that the Indian population should be concentrated in new settlements and should serve labor duty in environments similar to their home communities. In the 1530s Francisco de Jeréz thought that the Spaniards first became aware of the dangers of rapid changes in altitude when "some of the horses caught cold" in the ascent to Cuzco, but Europeans themselves certainly were not immune to the effects of the dramatic climatic variations within the sierra valleys. Nor could the Spaniards ignore the illness and high mortality rates among Indians subjected to drastic environmental changes. In 1541 Carlos V proclaimed "that Indians from cold climates not be taken to warmer regions nor the opposite be allowed." This policy was reaffirmed throughout the colonial period, but when employers and *encomenderos* complied with the law, they were usually motivated by concern for the health of their enterprises, not of the Indian laborers.[17]

Another, less concrete circumstance can help to explain the similarities between the *Gobierno del Perú* and the Ordenanzas de Toledo: both authors were facing the challenges of the 1560s, "a decade of exciting uncertainty"[18] regarding the fate of New World settlements. During this period political theorists and bureaucrats in Spain and America realized that the survival and prosperity of the colonies depended on the effective preservation, control, and exploitation of the indigenous community.

The obvious need for fundamental reform was complicated by the failure of familiar institutions to halt the rapid depopulation of the Andes. In their attempts to govern the American colonies Spanish monarchs repeatedly had adapted and transplanted into the New World a structure which had functioned well within the Iberian kingdoms: the *mesta*, the *consulado*, the *capitán general*, the *Hermandad*, and the *Audiencia* all had distinct peninsular and ultramarine manifestations. The two institutions most concerned with the governance of the Indians of Peru, the *encomienda* and the *corregimiento*, also were Old World in origin. The encomienda, as instituted in Reconquest Spain, was a grant of economic reward and political authority, with implicit territorial control of a recently subdued area. In the Americas the encomienda entailed the "rights to the tribute and labor of the subjects of certain chiefs (casiques), not to the Indians who lived in a certain territory."[19] Within Castile, the *corregidor* was an urban official, a position created by the crown to counterbalance the political and financial power of the nobility. In Peru the first corregidores did serve in the urban centers, but the corregimiento was soon extended to the countryside on a provincial basis, with corregidores appointed to administer the Indian population, to collect taxes, and to oversee the *mita* labor draft.[20]

Robert G. Keith's excellent analysis of the relationship between the encomienda, corregimiento, and *hacienda* emphasizes that the success of both the encomienda and the corregimiento depended on the survival of the indigenous community. Keith has shown clearly that the corregimiento was instituted in response to the failure of the encomienda to maintain the core units of Indian society and therefore to preserve the revenue base and labor force of the colonies.[21] The corregimiento was somewhat more successful in protecting Indian communities, chiefly due to its explicit guarantee that Indians would retain their lands, but not even the implementation of the corregimiento could halt Indian depopulation and migration, particularly not in the Viceroyalty of Peru. The preservation and control of the Indian population demanded the consideration of broader, bolder alternatives and the appointment of a determined and dynamic administrator.

THE TOLEDO REDUCCIONES

Francisco de Toledo was the most famous—and the most controversial—viceroy of Peru. Although some of his biographers have virtually deified this competent and creative colonial administrator, his contemporaries denounced Toledo more often than they praised him. Less than one-fourth of his *residencia,* or judicial accounting of his tenure in office, has survived; nevertheless, the remaining documentation is larger than the entire proceedings conducted against many of his successors.[22] His detractors and admirers would agree, however, that during Toledo's twelve years as viceroy (1569–1581) he permanently altered the economic base and social organization of Peru, particularly through the resettlement, reorganization, and exploitation of the indigenous population.

In a memorial to Philip II, Toledo recounted his arrival in Peru, his perceptions of the viceroyalty, and his determination "to visit personally all this kingdom." During this five-year *visita general* Toledo repressed an Incan revolt against Spanish authority and reshaped the lives of the Indians of the sierra. Toledo arrived in America with "the Christian education, conversion, government, and preservation of the Indians" as his chief concern. During his journeys through the sierra, Toledo wrote, he became convinced "that there was no conceivable way that the Indians could be educated in the Catholic faith or could live in a civilized and Christian way while they continued to dwell in the fields and farmlands, the mountains and hills where they were dispersed and hidden, fleeing from contact or communication with Spaniards."[23] Denouncing the Indians who "wander aimlessly and lazily, full of vice and practicing idolatry," Toledo decided "to travel throughout the provinces, accompanied by inspectors whose chief aim was to gather and to resettle the Indians in towns located at the most appropriate sites."[24]

These "appropriate sites," in accordance with the shift in official policy, would be areas of proven or potential economic benefit to the Crown. Indians would be relocated in proximity to the mining zones, particularly Potosí and Guancavelica, and in the agricultural valleys of the sierra. Throughout these regions indigenous communities—generally defined by Toledo as all Indians who recognized the authority of a particular *kuraka*—were to be moved en masse to the nearest designated locale, which might or might not be an existing population center. Several kin-groups might be united to achieve the desired labor pool, which varied in size from region to region. These new units, called *repartimientos*, would be resettled in carefully enumerated towns; each resident would be identified by name, age, sex, and civil status on an official *padrón*, or census list. Thereafter, these Indians and their descendants were to be known as *originarios*, or native-born Indians, of their reducción towns, and Indian identity was to be defined as and determined by a unity of ancestry and residence.[25]

Once resettled and recounted, Indians were liable for varying degrees of taxes, goods, and labor services. A universal per capita tax was assessed against all *tributarios*, male Indians between the ages of eighteen and fifty; in some communities widows who were heads of families also paid this tax. Repartimientos were also assessed certain quantities of specific goods, based on local custom or pre-Toledo obligations to the state or to individual Spaniards.[26]

In addition to standardizing tribute obligations the Toledo reforms also instituted compulsory labor service for most tributarios. (Kurakas and their principal assistants were exempt from the requirement that adult male Indians spend two of every fourteen months in mita labor.) Although some form of labor draft existed for every repartimiento, the mita's chief purpose was to assign Indians to mine labor: the *mita de minas*. Communities in sixteen provinces were ordered to send Indians to Potosí; tributarios from eleven more provinces would labor at Guancavelica. In theory, one-seventh of the adult males in the Indian reducciones would constantly be on active mita duty, most of them in the mining zones of the sierra.[27]

To emphasize the ostensible goal of the reducciones—the conversion of the Indians—the repartimientos were organized into *doctrinas*, or parishes, composed of a principal town and one or more annexes. Although a priest might not be present on a permanent basis, each town would have a church, with attendant Indian *sacristanes*, or wardens. Political control of the parish officially was vested in the Indian *alcaldes*, or mayors, and the cabildo, or town council, but the kurakas, whose hereditary leadership was the focal point of the reducción system, were powerful figures within the new communities, with special privileges and parallel responsibilities.[28]

The systematic establishment of Indian communities based on traditional leadership patterns was complicated by the great number of Indians who did not recognize the authority of a kuraka or who already had been removed from indigenous society into *yanacona* status. The complex nature of the yanacona has inspired a series of definitions which accent distinct aspects of their socioeconomic position. Some scholars have emphasized the hereditary aspect of yanacona status and have adopted the early Spaniards' practice of calling yanaconas "slaves" or "semislaves"; others have cited the personalized lord-worker relationship governing these "serfs" or "quasiserfs"; still others have emphasized the minimal wages mandated by Spanish law, a feature critical to one definition of yanacona as "a vagrant proletariat."[29] None of these interpretations conveys the anomalous position of the yanaconas of colonial Cuzco, a transitional social group which was neither a caste nor a class.[30] By law, yanacona status could only be conferred by birth; in practice, any other Indians engaged in similar economic activities could assume that identity.

The position of the yanacona in colonial society was based on the role of the Incan *yana*—a social group characterized by a special, inherited relationship of service and subordination to the state, as personified in the emperor or the local elite.[31] The actual duties and the origin of the yana sector varied greatly, but whether the servitors were from the heartland or the frontiers of the empire, whether they were artisans, weavers, or personal body servants, important characteristics united all yana: they were removed physically and structurally from their ancestral communities, exempted from formal mita service, and alienated from their kin-groups.[32] The special status of the yana and the emergence of a social sector defined solely by economic function indicate that Incan social structure was undergoing significant change at the time of the Spanish conquest.[33]

The Iberians were quick to recognize the utility of yana status: "of all the Inca institutions, the *yana* were one of the very few to be taken over by the Europeans. The latter must have been delighted to discover an existing servile group to supplement the 'souls' granted them through their *encomienda;* in the process many a man was proclaimed a *yana* who had never been one in Inca times."[34] The term "yana," recorded as "yanacona" by colonial officials, was initially applied to the indigenous allies or servants of the conquistadores; the concept was quickly expanded by peninsular authorities to include all Indians who "because they love the Spaniards, voluntarily live with them and serve them."[35] In pre-Toledo Peru this supposedly voluntary submission developed into a form of uncompensated, forced labor—deplored but tolerated by the Crown, which soon followed the conquistadores' lead in rewarding soldiers and settlers with grants of yanaconas to supplement Indian laborers hired or acquired by force. Writing in the 1560s, Juan de Matienzo urged an end to these grants and suggested that all yanaconas not under direct European control be resettled at Potosí.[36]

Viceroy Francisco de Toledo did not relocate all yanaconas in the mining zones, but in the 1570s he did deal with the issue of the vagrant, unsupervised Indians by distinguishing between *yanaconas de españoles*, those with Spanish employers and exempt from mita duty, and yanaconas recognizing no authority but the King's, the *yanaconas del Rey*. Yanaconas de españoles whose employers could provide proof of legal labor allocations retained that status. All other yanaconas were taxed, subjected to mita duty, and resettled into standard reducciones, with those in colonial cities assigned to urban parishes. Because social status was hereditary, both yanaconas de españoles and yanaconas del Rey were carefully enrolled in *padrones*, or registers, often under the general category of "yanaconas."[37]

The simplistic division of indigenous society into originarios and yanaconas reflects the two basic assumptions on which Toledo had based the reducciones: the system which he had designed to halt a dramatic and drastic decline in the Indian population depended chiefly on the interrelated techniques of social stabilization and natural reproduction. Toledo had assumed that a resettled Indian population would reproduce itself, maintaining the size of the labor pool, meeting mita demands, and eliminating the need for frequent, costly *revisitas*, or reevaluations, financed by the Indian community.[38] Instead, concentrating the indigenous community into reducciones increased exposure to epidemics, intensified European demands for goods and services, and led to a dramatic population decline. Less than ten years after the implementation of the Toledo settlements, an unidentified informant wrote Philip II that "many of the Indians have died in the mines, in other labors, or from the recurrent epidemics; others have fled to escape their labor and tribute obligations."[39]

As early as 1597 the Indians of Maras, Cuzco, were requesting a recount of their official population and a reduction of the related mita demands. As their corregidor reported, "they claim that they are too heavily burdened and that they supply many more tributario laborers than the legal one-seventh assessment; therefore they ask a reduction in their obligations."[40] The Indians' petition was denied. In theory, only infrequent revisitas should be needed to correct minor injustices in taxation and mita demands; in practice, only constant reassessments could have kept a community's obligations consistent with demographic and economic reality. The Cuzco-area towns of Vellille and Chamaca, both in the province of Chumbibilcas, were initially organized and taxed during Francisco de Toledo's 1572 visit to the sierra. The first reevaluation of these communities, issued on June 27, 1599, was still the official basis for treasury accounts as late as 1629. Although there may have been an intervening, post-1629 visita, the next recorded retaxation occurred in 1652. This statement of community obligations remained in effect from 1652 to 1728, a period in which the region's population fluctuated dramatically.[41] Tribute records from other Cuzco towns follow this same pattern.

The infrequent revisitas of their communities forced Indians to rely heavily on a process of redress of grievances through appeal to royal officials. In a paradoxical and self-defeating move early seventeenth-century viceroys, particularly the Príncipe de Esquilache, reduced the salaries of the *protectores*—the colonial officials who served as the Indians' advocates in the appeal process—because of a decline in mining income and tax revenues due to the diminished population and depressed replacement rate.[42]

Because Toledo also assumed that Indian status would be hereditary, and virtually immutable, he had defined only two main categories of Indians: tributarios and yanaconas, the latter term being understood to include both the yanaconas del Rey and the yanaconas de españoles. This inflexible system could not incorporate the new Indian subgroups emerging in response to the immediate impact of the reducciones and the long-term adjustment to colonial rule. Chief among these groups were the *forasteros*. Technically, forasteros were individuals living outside their reducciones who were exempt from mita service but still legally members of their home community. In practice, forastero migrants and their descendants negotiated a wide range of relationships with established indigenous communities and assumed a variety of social identities.[43]

The anomalous position of the forasteros resulted from contradictory definitions of Indian identity, which stimulated migration and encouraged relocation within indigenous society. The Spaniards' failure to apply consistent and compatible criteria of social differentiation created a multiplicity of legal identities, with varied obligations to the state. The initial separation of tributarios and yanaconas, according to an individual's acceptance or rejection of the local kuraka's authority, appeared to divide indigenous society by political allegiance and to reaffirm traditional leadership patterns within the Indian communities. The subsequent definition by degree of obligation to the state—in which yanaconas del Rey were assessed the same taxes and mita service as tributarios—contradicted this original distinction, and the mita-exempt status of the yanaconas de españoles became an obvious reason for Indians to desert their home communities.

The most serious structural flaw in the reducción system, however, was its rigid definition of tributario status. Within the new settlements, all Indians were affiliated with hereditary kin-groups, which were assigned specific lands for the use of their members. By assuming a fixed unity of kinship and territoriality, two potentially conflicting rather than necessarily complementary principles of social organization,[44] Toledo intended to stabilize indigenous society. However, his inseparable linkage of kin membership, territorial affiliation, and obligation to the state provided the greatest impetus for Indian migration: because individuals who resettled within indigenous society owed tribute and labor through their ancestral kin-group, whether or not they currently resided within its communal lands, Indians had the strongest possible motive for abandoning their reducciones.

ADMINISTERING THE REDUCCIONES

Enforcement of the Toledo regulations entailed the relocation of over 1,500,000 people under an inflexible, idealistic system which ignored the structure of indigenous society, attacked the autonomy of traditional communities, and shattered individual lives. In the Cuzco area, the site of one of the most important preconquest American cities, resettlement was not characterized by the sudden emergence of a primary urban core. Rather, the reducción system had its greatest impact in the rural areas, with the establishment of new towns whose compact and regularized format contrasted sharply with what Toledo called "the disorder in which Indians lived before resettlement . . . on cliffs or in ravines and valleys inaccessible to a priest on horseback or even on foot."[45]

Contrary to the program's intent, the announcement and implementation of the reducciones caused an immediate increase in Indian migration. Spanish counselors underestimated the Indians' attachment to their ancestral lands, and many of the tributarios and yanaconas simply abandoned the reducciones "to return home."[46] The cost of the Toledo *visita*, both the burden of supporting the viceroy's entourage and the later charges for administrative services, intensified this movement. In 1572, at the start of Toledo's journey through the sierra, local kurakas were already complaining that "since the beginning of the inspection ordered by Don Francisco de Toledo, we have been treated very badly. We have been abused by the imposition of these reducciones and our Indians have fled because they were forced to abandon their houses and their lands against their will."[47] Treasury officials supported the kurakas' assessment of the impact of the visitas: "the Indians are at present totally exhausted with the work of moving to the reducciones and with the demands for food and other services from the inspectors and resettlement officials."[48] One resident of Lima estimated that it would take the Indians six or seven years just to pay for the cost of the visita.[49]

Members of Toledo's own government, including the *fiscal*, or crown attorney of the High Court of Lima, who had accompanied the viceroy through the sierra, thought that the taxes and labor obligations were excessive: "it seems to me that the Indians have been very heavily burdened with a greater duty than they can possibly bear; the inspectors with whom I have spoken are also of this opinion."[50] The assessment of varying amounts of goods was denounced as an inequity among Indian communities which, over time, would stimulate migration. The Toledo regulations, in general, recognized no local economic conditions which might affect a community's ability to pay tribute. At least one colonial bureaucrat thought that this policy would force Indians into the personal service of Spaniards, stimulating illegal migration, "since of necessity they will have to hire themselves out or look for other work so they can pay these taxes, because very few Indians can earn these sums in their home communities, except in the few repartimientos where there are mines, or textile workshops."[51] Although some colonists considered the standardized tribute demands a decided improvement, others emphatically opposed the viceroy and his reforms. Writing in 1572 at the inception of the reducción program, the chaplain of the cathedral of Cuzco bitterly denounced "Don Francisco de Toledo and his administration, which has brought ruin to the Church as well as the Spaniards and Indians; the day that he entered these lands, he began to destroy them."[52]

Not all the opposition to the reducción system can be attributed to the impact of its implementation or to the flaws in its structure: the new Indian policy contradicted and was undermined by both practice and legal precedent. Indians had previously been allowed to change residence without penalty, providing that they had fulfilled all current obligations, and a series of royal decrees had proclaimed "that the Indians may exchange one place of residence for another."[53] Reminding his viceroy that the Catholic monarchs had desired "that the indigenous peoples be treated as subjects and vassals of Spain," Charles V had issued an "Ordinance allowing the Indians to live wherever they desire and permitting them to move from one town to another."[54] In 1583, even as the reducción system was being implemented throughout the Spanish colonies, a Cédula Reál reaffirmed Indian mobility, providing "that all Indians who wish to move from one town to another go to populated and settled areas, where care can be taken with their religious education; and that they indicate their destination before they depart from their current residence." Local officials were convinced that Indians would claim the rights specified in this cédula and would use this freedom of movement to relocate in areas where, free from the influence of a Catholic priest, they could practice their "idolatrous customs." In spite of this opposition, the King defended his earlier pronouncements.[55]

Additional statutes dealing with Indian migration further weakened the system established by Toledo. Indian women who had borne children of Spaniards were allowed to follow or to accompany these men anywhere in the Spanish empire, bringing their children, who might otherwise be considered potential tributarios. Two early seventeenth-century cédulas allowed for legal relocation within Indian society: married women were required to live in their husbands' villages "even if the husband is absent, or has fled," but widows could return to their home communities; and children of abandoned or unmarried Indian women could claim the same privilege. A third Cédula Reál guaranteed "that Indios forasteros shall not be given to encomenderos or pay tribute but shall do as they please." Designed specifically to exempt only those Indians who had migrated to Chile, this decree could be quoted in the defense of forasteros throughout the Viceroyalty of Peru.[56] In an attempt to legitimize a movement which they could not control, Toledo's successors granted numerous relocation permits which prohibited the forced return of individual migrants with "prolonged" residency in their new communities.[57] Any of these ordinances could be used to prevent or, minimally, to delay the forced return of a migrant to his reducción.

Legislative confusion and bureaucratic delay contributed to the failure of the Toledo settlements, but the structure of the reducciones, specifically the conflicting definitions of Indian status with varied tribute and labor obligations, were the chief cause for the extensive violations of the system. Certainly corruption was not unique to colonial Peru or to the Andean area, where John Murra has identified a parallel "attempt to 'hide' a number of citizens for personal profit and power" among Incan administrators.[58] The Toledo reforms, however, were particularly vulnerable to manipulation because the per-capita basis for tribute and mita assessments led Indian leaders to underreport their base population. Royal regulations stipulated heavy penalties for such deceptions, insisting that "the kuraka who hides any potential tributario must be suspended from his post . . . and the Indian involved in this fraudulent practice will be given two hundred lashes, will have his hair cut short [a sign of punishment and disgrace] and will be condemned to the mines."[59]

The simplest way to block the collection of taxes, whether with the intent of minimizing community obligations or maximizing personal profit, was to "misplace," lose, or alter community records. In 1608 kurakas of the Cuzco repartimiento of Omacha, Chilques y Masques, probably had the tacit support of the local corregidor when they attempted to reduce their official obligations by claiming that twenty-four tributarios cited in an earlier padrón had died; when the viceroy ordered these Indians returned to the tax rolls on the advice of the corregidor's lieutenant, the kurakas and the corregidor lost a substantial source of private income. Kurakas also occasionally submitted padrones which, a parish priest charged, "listed only Indians over the age of fifty and their young sons, so that those Indians who by law should pay taxes and serve mita duty were not included."[60] By the early seventeenth century, when migrants had become a substantial presence in some communities, local leaders had found another way to harass royal officials and to maximize private incomes: "in concealing the presence of forasteros, the kurakas are the accomplices of the corregidores and the priests, all of whom want more Indians subject to their private authority."[61] The most common and effective way of defrauding the royal hacienda and the mita de minas was to identify Indios tributarios as yanaconas de españoles. Repeated royal decrees insisted that local officials verify all claims for yanacona status, but administrators were unable or unwilling to control the movement of tributarios into the yanacona sector.[62]

The conflicting definitions of yanacona status, the abuses of corregidores, kurakas, and individual Spaniards, and the resulting decline in the Indian population were all cited by Luis de Velasco (1596–1604), the first viceroy to acknowledge openly the failure of the Toledo system:

> The reducciones which Don Francisco de Toledo established in the Andean provinces are in ruin, because so many Indians have died; some have fled to avoid the mita de minas or the personal service to which they are assigned, and others have left to escape the abuses of the corregidores, parish priests, and kurakas, who are their worst enemies; still other Indians have fled to private estates, where the owners protect them by claiming that they are yanaconas. . . . Also, the Indians hide in mountains and isolated pastures, where they can not easily be discovered.[63]

Few other royal officials were so candid about the collapse of the fabled reducciones, but by the end of the sixteenth century Philip III was aware of what had been obvious to every royal official in the Viceroyalty of Peru: "that many of these provinces and Indian communities are depopulated, and the loss continues." Reminding his administrators "that the Indians must not wander without supervision, but rather must live in their homes and villages," the King ordered the enforcement of the Toledo reducciones: "I charge you and order you to be very attentive to the Indians and to their preservation, doing whatever may be necessary for the survival of the reducciones."[64] In 1602 another cédula commanded the members of the High Court of Charcas to locate and to repatriate the more than six thousand Indians who had abandoned their reducciones in Tucuman.[65] Finally, in 1604 Philip III issued a comprehensive order "that the Indians who have been resettled not live outside of their established reducciones" under any circumstances.[66]

The King's commands met with little compliance in Peru, where the impossibility of enforcing the reducciones was obvious to colonial authorities. Throughout the seventeenth century indigenous migration was regarded as an inevitable consequence of the Toledo system. The serious attempts of viceroys Montesclaros, Salvatierra, and Palata to stabilize indigenous society by altering the structure of the Toledo settlements would be frustrated by their successors' policies or interference from Spain. This sporadic pronouncement and reversal of administrative reform actually stimulated even more Indian migration and ultimately destroyed the Toledo reducciones.

The first comprehensive efforts to save the reducciones through radical reform were initiated by Juan de Mendoza y Luna, Marqués de Montesclaros (1607–1615), who attempted to revitalize the settlements and the mita de minas by restricting the forastero population and by challenging the number of Indians claiming yanacona status. On his arrival in Peru, Montesclaros found "the mines of Guancavelica in disrepair, with the viceroyalty desperately in need of mercury."[67] He immediately launched an exhaustive inquiry into the state of the mines, winning at least temporarily the approval of the residents of Guancavelica, who wrote their King that of "those who have ably governed these colonies, none of the former viceroys has had the insight and understanding of Don Francisco de Toledo and the Marqués of Montesclaros."[68]

It is doubtful whether Montesclaros would have appreciated the comparison to Toledo. While recognizing that many of the mines suffered from a lack of capital or inefficient management, the new viceroy quickly identified a critical labor shortage as the main problem and had no hesitation in blaming the original Toledo ordenanzas for the crisis. Montesclaros did not question Toledo's motives in establishing and defining yanacona status. He did argue, however, that the practice of assigning yanaconas to certain sites and the parallel custom of reducing the yanaconas' obligations were unjust to Indians and detrimental to the mita de minas. Furthermore, Montesclaros contended, subsequent viceroys had carelessly issued numerous *licencias de yanaconas*, permits for individual Spaniards to acquire the personal service of Indian laborers, resulting in an excess of Indian workers on private estates and an acute labor shortage in the mines. Montesclaros did not criticize Luis de Velasco for reaffirming the rights of yanaconas, nor did he (or could he) reproach the King for issuing a series of conflicting and confusing decrees extending those rights to all yanaconas. Instead, Montesclaros denounced the practices of post-Velasco viceroys, and particularly their policies regarding Indian labor.[69]

Moving cautiously at first, Montesclaros continued to issue licencias de yanaconas, allowing Spaniards "to acquire voluntary laborers for their haciendas" but "with the stipulation that these Indians be released to serve their regular mita duty." When he became aware of the ways in which these permits, and especially the clauses regarding mita labor, were being exploited, Montesclaros immediately halted the practice because, as he wrote in his memoirs, "once the system was implemented, the flaws were obvious in that the owners of the haciendas were able to acquire yanaconas in an even more devious way: using these provisions to secure Indians on mita service by showing the signature of the Viceroy to kurakas who were easily deceived. Not all of these Indians knew how to read, and even those who were literate were not given time to examine the provisions carefully."[70]

To prevent such abuses and to increase production at both Guancavelica and Potosí, Montesclaros proposed an amended version of the Toledo reducciones. Certainly he would attempt "to enforce and to repopulate the reducciones established by Don Francisco, [appointing] several inspectors, just as my predecessors have done." However, he suggested several changes in the customary reducción techniques: first, that corregidores admit no new forasteros into their jurisdictions; second, that forasteros who refused to return to their home communities be subjected to the mita demands of their place of residence; and third, that all yanaconas be counted and then reallocated to private estates on the basis of need, "and afterwards, I will remove the surplus laborers, reducing the allocation of yanaconas, who will be resettled in traditional reducciones or new towns."[71]

Montesclaros achieved some limited success with his two-part plan to control and to exploit the forastero sector, a plan he believed was much more effective than trying to relocate these migrants: "I preferred to order all Corregidores that they admit no additional forasteros into their jurisdictions and that they satisfy mita obligations with the migrants who had settled in those districts."[72] His instructions to the corregidores were explicit: "You will force all the Indios forasteros who at present live in these towns . . . to return to their towns and their reducciones with their families and their belongings; you will not allow that they remain in their present location, unless they pay tribute to their home communities and satisfy all their other obligations; if they do not return to their reducciones, you will force the forasteros to comply with the mita and tax demands of the Indios originarios of these towns. Let there be no exemptions!"[73] The Montesclaros policy so increased the rate of mita compliance that almost fifty years later the Conde de Alba repeated Montesclaros's instructions to his own corregidores in a futile attempt to regain the efficiency of that earlier administration.

Montesclaros was much less successful with his most controversial proposal, the reassignment of the yanaconas. Although he completed a fairly comprehensive survey of all licencias de yanaconas, Montesclaros was still awaiting government approval of his reallocation plan when he left office in 1615.[74] His successor, Francisco de Borja y Aragón, Príncipe de Esquilache (1615–1621), neutralized the impact of the Montesclaros reforms by returning to the original Toledo system and by restricting the role of the *protectores de naturales* and other Indian advocates.

The *hacendados* and *obraje* owners who relied on yanacona labor and who had campaigned actively against Montesclaros and his reforms must have been delighted with the appointment of the Príncipe de Esquilache; corregidores and kurakas who profited from the illegal contributions of forastero Indians must also have been relieved. Abandoning Montesclaros's schemes to control forasteros by making it impossible for them to avoid labor obligations, Esquilache returned to the practice of depending on the *originario* Indian population for the fulfillment of mita quotas. The general inspection he ordered certainly sounded like a comprehensive one. All Indians were to be recorded on official padrones, "and those who have abandoned their towns and reducciones should be returned to them, removing the Indians from the estates, farms, mines, pastures, and other places where they have been living, and allowing no exemptions whatsoever." Not even the yanaconas on Spaniards' estates were safe from resettlement: "you must remove from the haciendas all yanaconas, even those who have been there for many years, whom the Spaniards have settled on their estates to farm the fields and tend the herds."[75] However, Esquilache undermined, or sabotaged, these reforms by neglecting to provide enough *visitadores* and by depending on local officials and Indian kurakas for census data. This reliance on kurakas was particularly confusing because Esquilache considered their greed—not depopulation, not the excesses of corregidores, not the demands of private employers—to be the real cause of Peru's economic crisis and social instability: "the failure of the mita and other labor services is not due to Indian mortality, but rather to the reluctance of the kurakas to apprehend those Indians who have fled their reducciones. These Indians are left alone in remote and isolated sites, so that the kurakas may collect from them sums which exceed their legal tribute obligations and may exploit them in other ways."[76]

When Esquilache sailed from Peru in 1621, he departed convinced "that the kurakas are responsible for the destruction of the reducciones."[77] Why, then, would he entrust his major effort at population and labor reform to those individuals who would be most likely to effect the least possible change? Probably Esquilache, and the Council of the Indies, recognized the necessity of placating the powerful interests who had been irritated by Montesclaros's attacks on yanacona labor. Two important decrees issued in Madrid on October 10, 1618, at the mid-point of Esquilache's tenure as viceroy, reveal a desire to appease, or minimally not to antagonize, Spanish entrepreneurs.

The first cédula stipulated that "Indian infidels" from the frontier areas who had recently been converted to Catholicism "are not subject to mita service . . . [but] it is proper that they begin to learn the value of labor, becoming reconciled to earning wages and to work."[78] Clearly, one way for these Indians to "earn wages" was in the employ of hacendados or obraje owners.

The second provision, titled "That the Indians employed on estates should not be considered Yanaconas," actually permitted that those Indians "have as their official reducción the hacienda where they have been working."[79] Although this highly irregular "resettlement" did not automatically entail yanacona privileges, it facilitated the assumption of such rights. Esquilache had probably urged formal articulation of this policy, which closely paralleled his earlier instructions to the Corregidor of Carangas: "if you are able to ascertain that any Indians have been absent from their repartimientos or provinces for more than ten years and that they have been enrolled in the communities in which they now live or that they have been yanaconas on the estates where they now reside for the entire time, you may allow them to work in those sites, and to pay tribute in their repartimiento and pueblos."[80] Although Esquilache quoted the *Ordenanzas de Toledo* to support this policy, Francisco de Toledo had created the ten-year rule to correct errors in the original visitas, not to facilitate the incorporation of forasteros into local communities. The provision that Indians who had paid no tribute for ten years be reclassified as yanaconas was intended to generate royal revenues from yanaconas del Rey, not to transfer their allegiance and service to private landowners.

By expanding and systematizing his predecessors' practice of issuing individual permits to migrants with prolonged residency in an adopted community, Esquilache legitimized a new, intermediary social group within indigenous society: Indians with the tribute obligations of originarios and the labor exemptions of yanaconas de españoles. Rather than stabilizing indigenous society, Esquilache's policy stimulated forastero relocation by creating an alternative form of tributario status linked to migration. When he left office in 1621, Esquilache was still requesting additional instructions concerning "all those Indians [who] flee their reducciones."[81]

The next serious attempt to restrict Indian migration and to resolve the conflicting definitions of Indian status and obligation was the general numeration and reassessment ordered by García Sarmiento de Sotomayor, Conde de Salvatierra (1648–1655). By the mid-seventeenth century the Council of the Indies was fully aware of the colonists' resistance to the enforcement of the reducciones and the King cautioned Salvatierra to select his agents carefully;[82] in the past, visitadores had often sold their commissions to hacendados or mineowners, who had obvious personal reasons for not executing viceregal instructions.[83]

Salvatierra immediately initiated a general inspection and relocation, but he made one important policy decision which would nullify all his efforts: citing the Cédula Reál of 1618 and the policies of the Príncipe de Esquilache, Salvatierra decreed that any migrant who had lived ten or more years in a new community should be allowed to remain there, exempt from mita labor, so long as he fulfilled his tribute obligations. Throughout Peru the response was swift and angry. Indian kurakas maintained that any exemption to resettlement would legitimize virtually all migrants because of the ease with which the minimum residency rule could be invoked.[84] Hacendados, pleased with the recognition of some of their claims to yanacona service, nevertheless complained that the directive would rob them of newly acquired laborers. The clergy protested that the spiritual state of the Indians (and the church's income) would deteriorate "because if they are free of the mita when absent from their reducciones and subject to its demands when returned to their towns, of course they will flee again . . . to the lands of the Infidels." The most irate objections, however, came from those who would be most directly affected by Salvatierra's decision: the miners at Potosí claimed that "because so many Indians can meet this requirement . . . the enforcement of this law will mean the ruin of the mita."[85] Faced with substantial opposition within the colonies and hampered by insufficient support from the Council in Sevilla, Salvatierra abandoned his renumeration efforts.

Caught in the bureaucratic chaos caused by the announcement and then the reversal of Salvatierra's revisita policy, corregidores of provinces with high mita demands were desperate to fill their quotas. As early as 1630 corregidores from regions such as Cuzco, which had been most affected by Indian migration, had begun to forcibly repatriate individual forasteros from their jurisdictions.[86] In 1654 the corregidor of Pacajes, a sierra province subject to the mita de minas, gave his nephew the credentials of a "judge of the reducción" and sent him to Arica, on the Pacific Coast, to locate natives of Pacajes who could be sent to Potosí. Overcoming substantial resistance from local authorities, the nephew seized more than 120 Indians, some because they had been born in Pacajes and others because "their fathers were originarios of that province." The corregidor of Arica, the protector de naturales, and the viceroy all were furious because the Indians had been "born and raised in that jurisdiction, settled in the region for more than fifty years"; furthermore, the nephew was accused of confiscating the Indians' money, clothing, and herds, valued at twenty thousand pesos. An irate Conde de Salvatierra issued a general order, reminding his corregidores, "I ordered that no Indian be disturbed if he had been living in his current community for more than ten years." In a decision that would influence Indian migration policy for the rest of the century, the Audiencia of Lima announced on October 22, 1654, that the viceroy should nominate a representative to review the dispute and to resettle in Pacajes those Indians who had been in Arica less than ten years. All other Indians who had been relocated by the overzealous nephew were to be returned to the coast. The Corregidor of Pacajes was rebuked for exceeding his authority and was assessed a stiff fine.[87]

THE PALATA REFORMS

The failure of the Audiencia of Lima to support the corregidor of Pacajes virtually terminated all efforts to enforce the Toledo reducciones on the provincial level; Esquilache's reversal of the Montesclaros reforms and the chaotic policy shifts of the Salvatierra years discouraged future viceroys from attempting broader revisions in the laws governing Indian communities, tribute, and labor. Indians were still legally identified by birthplace or ancestral community, but the erosion of the Toledo reducciones made those designations virtually meaningless. The disruptive effects of the forastero migration would continue to be the subject of prolonged debate, but little action, for the next twenty-five years, until the arrival in Peru of Viceroy Melchor de Navarra y Rocafull, Duque de Palata (1681–1689).

Palata wrote the King that Peru was in a state of disaster, "with all the towns so destroyed and depopulated that it seemed the area had been ravaged by constant wars and plagues, which are the daggers which slay the most prosperous and populated kingdoms."[88] By the 1680s the crisis was so acute that the Archbishop of la Plata suggested abandoning the mita and condemning "all Indian criminals to the mines . . . for four, six, or ten years, depending on the offense."[89] The parish priest in Anta, Abancay, had no such dramatic remedy for the depopulation of the sierra. Reviewing his twenty years in the bishopric of Cuzco, the priest could only lament the continuous disappearance of his Indian parishoners, "and although we have tried to return them to this town, with official decrees from various royal governors, we have had little success."[90]

Palata, too, had little faith in the reducción system because of "the facility with which the Indians change residences, disappearing into the cities and hiding beyond the reach of the kurakas' authority . . . in order to escape their obligations."[91] After observing the size and scope of Indian migration in the viceroyalty, Palata concluded that "the mita has been the cause of the ruin of the reducciones, not the reason for the lack of Indians."[92] Although reminiscent of peninsular officials' claims that there were sufficient Indians in Peru to support the demands of the export sector, the Duque's evaluation emphasized that the location rather than the size of the Indian community was the key factor in the economic survival of the colony, "since the kingdom can not be saved by the strength of its main cities if the rest of its territory lies weak and abandoned." On August 21, 1683, the Duque de Palata wrote the King and the Council of the Indies, informing them that he had decided on a total reassessment of the Indian community of Peru.[93]

Denouncing "the impossibility of returning the Indians to the reducciones they have fled," Palata abandoned the shell of the Toledo reducciones. Henceforth, Indians would be identified by residence, not native community. Both originarios and forasteros would be required to meet standardized tribute and mita demands. To minimize wage labor at the mines, Palata increased the mita allocations to Potosí and Guancavelica. Most significantly, Indians could no longer easily escape the mita de minas by migrating within the viceroyalty, because Palata expanded the number of contributing provinces and included laborers on private haciendas and "volunteers" at the mines in the labor draft. All *mitayos* would be carefully monitored to ensure their return home and to eliminate illegal relocations in the mining zones.[94]

Palata's efforts to halt migration and to identify Indians by residence and not by ancestral community were not new concepts. In 1643 the Corregidor of Potosí had suggested that "those Indians called forasteros who escape the mita . . . by moving from one town to another be forced to serve labor duty wherever they are living."[95] Several other programs proposed by colonists contained similar provisions. The Palata reforms, however, marked the first such suggestion by a Peruvian viceroy who seemed unusually determined to force compliance.

In October 1683 the viceroy authorized a general numeration, reclassification, and *retasa,* a reassessment of the tribute and labor obligations of the Indian community. In his 1687 *Aranzél de jornales,* a comprehensive schedule of labor and wage regulations, Palata virtually rewrote the colony's labor codes, chiefly by recognizing and taxing existing modes of production and patterns of Indian labor. Both pronouncements rocked the viceroyalty. In the sierra, where the new regulations had their greatest potential for disrupting the economic status quo, traditional enemies united to denounce the *Aranzél.* Hacendados, miners, and obraje owners vilified the provisions which would force their workers to serve mita labor. Clerics deplored the severity of the assessments against forasteros and predicted that more migrants would flee to the "heathen" frontier zones.[96] The bishop of Cuzco insisted that the only people to benefit from the Palata decrees were the corregidores who would maximize their salaries "not only by listing forasteros as originarios but also by claiming the taxes of any travelers in the district." Kurakas in the sierra complained that they could not possibly control every Indian who happened to be in their towns on the day of the numeration: "regarding the tribute payments, both the former kurakas and the present leaders testify that they can fulfill their previous assessment, although with great effort; but they can not remit the sums due from the forasteros who have disappeared since the last general numeration because they know neither their names nor their current location."[97]

As the King wrote to the Conde de la Monclova a decade later, "after the provisions of mita and tribute were published throughout the thirty provinces involved, there were severe problems with enforcement, due to the resistance of some bishops and many corregidores and kurakas, who maintained it was impossible to organize the mita or to collect tribute."[98] The King was displeased by charges of fraud and incompetence in the renumeration process, in which some Indians "were counted in two or three towns because the Corregidores were only concerned with rapidly finishing their inquiries." In 1685 the King demanded a full report from Palata and announced a moratorium on the enforcement of the retasas, "temporarily suspending approval of the general numeration of the Indians until we receive reports of its impact."[99] A moratorium was hardly necessary. The panic within the colony was caused by the announcement, not the enforcement, of the Palata reforms. Not all provincial padrones had been submitted by 1685; several reports had been returned to their authors for corrections, additions, or certifications by parish priests. Corregidores were accused of intentionally omitting vital information, especially the province and repartimiento of each forastero. In exasperation, Palata wrote the King that his corregidores were either "criminals or idiots."[100]

These bureaucratic delays hampered renumeration and retaxation throughout the bishopric of Cuzco. By 1691 retasas had been issued for all four area provinces which sent Indians to Potosí—Azángaro, Canas y Canches, Lampa, and Quispicanche—but for only one of the provinces in the mita to Guancavelica: Angares. In the other Cuzco provinces local officials reported that "not one reassessment has been issued." Incredibly, "in the province of Abancay, no census had been conducted; no lists had been submitted." When the corregidores of the provinces in the mita de Potosí were questioned about implementation of the new retasas, they responded unanimously that the Palata instructions were difficult to follow and the new regulations were impossible to enforce. The Corregidor of Quispicanche ridiculed the entire procedure by reporting that in his province, with an estimated population of thirteen thousand Indians, he had located only one Indian living on a private estate and the hacendado had refused to let the visitador enter that Indian's name on an official padrón.[101]

Faced with growing royal opposition and universal noncompliance within the Viceroyalty, Palata summoned the Tribunal de Cuentas in 1689 to debate the continuation of his reforms. Tribunal members immediately suggested that if Palata did not wish to conduct an entirely new general numeration with more realistic criteria, "he could issue a general order throughout the viceroyalty, ordering the suspension of the new mita and tax laws until the Government had decided what approach to take; in the interim the corregidores and kurakas would comply with the existing community assessments."[102] If the Duque remained determined to enforce the new retasas, the tribunal implored him to recognize the recent increase in Indian migration and to cut in half the official population figures and obligations of the forasteros. Even though this arbitrary decrease "might be unfair and might disrupt the Indian communities," the tribunal considered this preferable to strict enforcement, which would only exacerbate the situation. The viceroy reluctantly agreed. On July 21, 1689, he issued an *acuerdo*, or agreement "that the assessment of each repartimiento or town be reduced by one-half the tribute assigned those Indians who were listed as forasteros or yanaconas in the last census."[103] The mita obligations of these forasteros were later reduced to 40 percent of the retasa figures, but all other regulations remained intact.[104]

These regulations would barely survive their author's departure from Peru. When Melchor Portocarrero y Lasso de la Vega, Conde de la Monclova (1689–1705) replaced the Duque de Palata in 1689, the new viceroy initially announced his intention of continuing his predecessor's efforts. Although Monclova would later claim that he had never seen the Cédula Reál of 1685 which suspended the retasas,[105] his early enthusiasm probably reflects the Crown's hopes that the necessary renumeration of the Indian community could be accomplished without the controversial and contentious Duque de Palata.

Less than six months after his arrival in Peru, however, Monclova realized that it would be necessary to alter the Palata decrees in order to preserve the Indian communities. The new viceroy appeared shocked by the severity of the Palata program and the demands of mita labor. In a letter written to the King soon after his arrival in Peru, Monclova expressed his surprise at finding "that the mita to Potosí is considered necessary in this kingdom, because I come from New Spain, *where there are no such mitas* and where there are rich and extensive mineral deposits." Although the mita might be necessary in Peru, Montesclaros argued that "whether he be an Indian or a member of a stronger people, any man will suffer more ill effects from one month of forced labor than from one year of voluntary wage labor; if this is true, think of the added impact of being sent to distant provinces!"[106] Wage labor was much more "just and Christian"; it also guaranteed a stabler work force than the mita to Potosí, which "has repeatedly and consistently failed to meet labor demands, no matter what anyone says."[107] With these justifications, Monclova initiated a systematic attack on the Palata regulations, slashing the number of Indians assigned to the mita at Potosí from 2,850 to 1,360. During the next year he issued a series of individual decisions and decrees which were united in the comprehensive *Aranzél de 27 de abril del año de 1692.*[108] The *Aranzél,* which was immediately circulated throughout the sierra, denounced and dismantled the Palata program, directly repudiating each of the Duque's reforms. Once again, the Toledo reducciones were to be enforced throughout Peru, and Indians were to be divided into originarios and forasteros. Originarios could appeal for a reassessment of their obligations. Forasteros who were not resettled in "home" communities would not be subjected to increased tax demands or to mita labor; instead, migrants would pay tribute at the reduced rate of four pesos, the amount assessed yanaconas. To maximize the use of wage labor, Monclova reduced the number of mitayos and raised the wages of the "voluntary" Indian laborers, thereby encouraging permanent relocation in the mining zones.[109]

The Monclova program was quickly and gratefully accepted throughout the colony. On December 10, 1692, royal officials at Potosí wrote the King that they had abandoned even token enforcement of the Palata regulations because "The Conde de la Monclova resolved that the forasteros should remain—as they always have been—exempt from the mita."[110] Three months earlier the Bishop of Lima had pronounced a final epitaph for the Palata program: "although at the time of its formulation the plan was considered an absolute necessity for the relief of the Indians, the efficient collection of royal tributes, and the reorganization of the mita . . . the results were absolutely the opposite of these goals."[111] Rejecting the Duque's reforms, peninsular and colonial officials returned to the badly battered and much amended Toledo reducciones. Indians would continue to be identified as natives or descendants of natives of a particular town, not as current residents of a repartimiento.

The Indians of the sierra could not and did not wait passively for a resolution of the official appeals. During the Palata numeration thousands of forasteros fled their adopted communities; many of those who were listed on the new padrones disappeared soon after the visitadores departed. Tributarios who had clung to their home communities were then faced with increased demands, calculated from the inflated population figures; when the forasteros fled, originarios and hacienda workers followed.[112]

In 1689 the bishop of Cuzco estimated that six years after the survey of his jurisdiction, less than one-third of the forasteros and yanaconas counted by the corregidores remained in their parishes.[113] Although some of the decline was due to a 1687 epidemic of smallpox, most of the discrepancy arose because of fraudulent padrones and because "no care had been taken to insure that the newly-enrolled forasteros would stay in their towns; as soon as the new lists were compiled, these Indians migrated to other regions."[114] Rather than stabilizing indigenous society, the Palata renumeration and regulations had inadvertently stimulated Indian migration. As in the Montesclaro-Esquilache era, the imaginative reforms of a competent but controversial viceroy had been thwarted by his successor's surrender to the combined opposition of colonial bureaucrats, Spanish entrepreneurs, and Indian kurakas who profited from the increased Indian migration which threatened the economic survival of the Peruvian colonies.

CONTINUED RELIANCE ON THE REDUCCIONES MODEL

Despite the obvious failure of the Andean reducciones, the Crown considered the feasibility of expanding the system to organize non-Indians into similar settlements. In 1609 Philip III wrote to the Marqués de Montesclaros, explaining, "I want to know all the possible merit in this matter: if it would be worthwhile for you to carry out the reduction of all the mulatos, zambos, blacks and mestizos; if it could be done easily; what the format and location of the settlements should be; what taxes we could collect; and if it would be possible to form a labor pool for the mines of Potosí."[115] Although these communities were never established, the royal authorities did extend the Indian reducciones throughout South America. The 1618 decrees which established the model for Indian towns in Paraguay and the Río de la Plata cited the Peruvian reducciones approvingly. In 1703 the Council of the Indies proposed that the Indian population in the Kingdom of Chile be organized into formal reducciones; the bishop of Chile thought this would be "easy."[116]

In part, the Crown clung to the reducción format because successive colonial administrations doggedly insisted that proper enforcement of the Toledo regulations could solve the crisis within the Indian communities. The viceroys' intransigence can be attributed to a variety of factors. The logistical requirements and bureaucratic complications of moving hundreds of thousands of Indians were daunting; so, too, was the prospect of attacking the vested interests of miners, hacendados, and obraje owners. In 1634 when the Council of the Indies proposed severe penalties for any Spaniard or Indian who provided lands or other assistance to forasteros, the viceroy Conde de Chinchón urged moderation "because so many are concerned in this matter, it could evoke more than the usual opposition." None of the proposed reforms seemed potentially more successful than the existing system. Furthermore, the corregidores, clerics, and kurakas who would be charged with enforcing new regulations could not be depended on "because everyone wants Justice, but in someone else's jurisdiction."[117] Ultimately, though, the Toledo structure prevailed because of an attitude of caution and the bureaucratic inertia that characterized most Spanish colonial administration. Ever conscious of the impending ordeal of their final residencias, viceroys rejected innovation or even reform for the security of a system which, although obviously ineffective, had the attractions of precedent and permanency. Most viceroys of Peru would probably have agreed with the Marqués de Guadalcázar (1622–1629) who urged that his successor, the Conde de Chinchón (1629–1636), not act precipitously upon his arrival in Peru. The Marqués was fully aware of both the desirability and the political peril of reforming the system: "The ordenanzas of Viceroy Don Francisco de Toledo have much authority in this Kingdom, and His Majesty has ordered that they be generally obeyed, even though time has brought many changes so that it would be better to rework the system; but as you now enter the government, it would be better not to make any innovations in these regulations until, having more experience, you can consult with the King on the different aspects of this matter."[118] Few Peruvian viceroys would try to "make any innovations." Even during the brief periods of the Montesclaros and Palata reforms, the official policy remained one of Indian control through the return of individuals to their home communities. The Corregidor of Cotabambas in 1593 was interrogated about his enforcement of Indian reducciones; his counterpart in Andaguaylas, in 1715, faced the same question. Each man would say that he had done his best to enforce the *Ordenanzas de Toledo*.[119]

This pattern of official denial of a migration problem and continued insistence on the value of the reducciones had obvious ramifications in the Cuzco area, where the large migrant population placed unusually heavy stress on the Toledo system. At the subordinate administrative level, however, the tensions were between viceroys seeking to avoid the responsibility for the continued decline of the Indian population and corregidores defending their conduct. In 1595 royal officials complained bitterly of the high number of forasteros in the rich Urubamba valley; by 1607 bureaucrats in Lima had denounced the total breakdown of the Cuzco reducciones: "In some regions and provinces—particularly those of the bishoprics of Cuzco and Charcas—there is at present as great a need of resettlement as there was at the time when Viceroy Don Francisco de Toledo completed his reducciones, because these are now so altered that the Indians have returned to their previous condition."[120]

Meanwhile, area corregidores were denying that they had any problems controlling the Indian population. In 1593 the Corregidor of the province of Cotabambas insisted "there are no Indians absent from their reducciones" in this province because "at the time of the Toledo inspection, we made and completed our reducciones and they have not been weakened or altered."[121] Sixteen years later his successor would still insist "that in this jurisdiction, the Indians always remain in their reducciones." The later incumbent, however, admitted that "because a few Indians were missing" he had toured the province, and had dispatched letters ordering resettlement.[122] Throughout the 1620s the number of corregidores admitting to some problems with the reducciones increased as the demands from Lima became stronger and more specific. In 1628 corregidores were reminded that "in fulfillment of the obligations of your office, you are required to resettle all the Indian men, women, and children who . . . have fled, removing them from the control of whatever individuals have them so that the Indians may pay their taxes and comply with the mitas and other duties assigned to them."[123] Corregidores were now compelled to admit that perhaps they had not been totally successful in implementing the reducción orders. As Captain Gabriel Parragas y Rojas confessed, "I sent many kurakas and leaders after the Indians who had fled their communities, so that the absentees might be brought to their towns and reducciones. In some instances, this was accomplished."[124]

On September 15, 1633, the cabildo of Cuzco made public a viceregal order in which the Conde de Chinchón demanded that all area residents comply with his previous decree that Indians be returned to their home communities regardless of temporary residence or employment. Following this general order, which extended responsibility to private employers as well as to all local officials, corregidores were more willing to admit the failure of the reducciones in their area and to attribute that failure to the interference of individual Spaniards and Indian leaders.[125]

Relieved of final responsibility for the failure of the reducciones, convinced that any review of their management of Indian settlements would be a mere formality, and freed to pursue their own private interests, Cuzco area corregidores would be less than enthusiastic about the sporadic and potentially effective reforms proposed by the ablest of colonial viceroys.

The need for such reforms rose dramatically after a series of *composiciones de tierras*, or sales of Indian land judged vacant and confiscated by the Crown in the 1630s and 1640s. This practice both stimulated further migration and precluded widespread resettlement by alienating Indian lands from the forasteros' home communities. The councilor of the city of Cuzco, in a testimonial written April 21, 1632, recognized the dangers of these composiciones, which declared unoccupied Indian lands to be the property of the Crown, available for purchase by private individuals: "selling the lands which today are judged vacant because of the absence of Indians, may shut the door on the comprehensive reducción so necessary to the survival of these provinces; this will be impossible with the loss of community property and the absent Indians will despair of ever returning to their towns, because of this lack of arable lands."[126]

The Cuzqueños repeated a theme common in mid-century assessments of the continuing crisis within the Indian community: "in Peru, there is no lack of Indians who could easily be returned to their ancient reducciones, to fulfill the assigned obligations of taxes and mita labor."[127] Colonists were also beginning to contradict the officials in Lima and to insist that no comprehensive reducción effort could succeed. Few of the individuals who studied the issues of Indian population and labor would have agreed publicly with Captain Juan Serrano de Almagro that "even if the reducciones could be enforced, they should not be."[128] Throughout the seventeenth century, however, an increasing number of the reports sent to the Council of Indies in Sevilla contained proposals designed to replace rather than to reenforce the reducciones.

Virtually every one of these proposals opened with a recognition of the scope of indigenous migration and a call for a general renumeration of the Indian population. Rather than summarizing local totals, visitadores were to provide a complete profile of each adult male Indian. One colonial bureaucrat, true to his training, provided a possible formula for the data to be collected: "So-and-so, tribute paying Indian, native of such-and-such a town in such-and-such an ayllu in the encomienda of Don So-and-so in such-and-such a province and corregimiento; son of so-and-so; found in this town, farm, or estate, where he was living with his children: so-and-so and so-and-so."[129] Once this information had been compiled, "these census lists should be sent to a judge . . . and from them, a map should be made of all the provinces involved, returning to each province, town, and ayllu all the Indians on the lists who belong in those jurisdictions; and a separate list should be made for each corregimiento where Indians with mita and tribute obligations are found."[130] After carefully calling for such a strictly enforced general reducción, most petitioners virtually proceeded to rewrite the *Ordenanzas de Toledo* by allowing for a number of exemptions which eliminated the conflicting claims on forasteros and precluded effective relocation of the Indian population. If Indians could not be returned to their home communities, they would be assigned to any town within their native province; however, individuals who could not identify their parents, remember their home communities, or provide any relevant information, would be allowed to remain in their places of residence. Any forasteros who had developed "a genuine love" for their new communities would also be allowed to stay, providing they developed an equal affection for those communities' mita and tribute obligations. Mita quotas would thereafter be based on one-seventh of the existent, not the official, population. Migrants to colonial cities would be allowed to reside in urban parishes. Forasteros who had settled in mining zones, particularly the Cerro de Potosí, would be organized into communities, taxed, and subjected to mita labor in the mines where they now worked "voluntarily." A resident of Buenos Aires suggested supplementing those Indian miners with slaves from the illegal slave trade already flourishing in the Río de la Plata basin. One colonial bureaucrat thought Indian labor alone would be sufficient because when new, equitable mita and tribute assessments had been completed Indians would voluntarily rejoin their home communities, "many of them returning from their present sanctuary in the land of the infidel, once word of this great relief reaches them."[131]

Some of these plans were minutely detailed; some were vague suggestions that the King "rely on [the author's] good will"; others were a strange blend of cynicism and naïveté. The Buenos Aires citizen who suggested that the Church conduct the new census mistrusted the clergy and devised a complex system of penalties, including defrocking, to insure the priests' accurate compliance; nevertheless, he was sure this process was the perfect way to identify and to enroll all of Peru's Indians because "they would never tell a lie to their priest."[132] No matter what their tone or content, however, the varied proposals originating in seventeenth-century Peru all reached the same conclusions: that Indian migration was inevitable and irreversible and that the only way to minimize the damage to the Crown and the colony was to revise the structure of the reducciones so as to exploit all forasteros, including those who attempted to pass as yanaconas, at their current place of residence.

Throughout the seventeenth century the Crown and the Council of Indies continued to reject this interpretation, following their policy of Indian control through the Toledo resettlements. Incredibly, some royal officials insisted that the reducciones had functioned effectively and efficiently through the administration of the Conde de Chinchón (1629–1639). The Council of the Indies adopted the position that Indian migration was a recent phenomenon which could be handled speedily by correct application of the Toledo ordenanzas and the subsequent royal decrees.[133] These assumptions were reflected in the King's reproachful Reál Cédula of 1637, directed at the Conde de Chinchón: "although I have previously charged you by different decrees . . . that you should comply by all possible means, I still feel I must order you and command you . . . to reduce the Indians of these provinces to their settlements."[134] Chinchón tried to explain his noncompliance in a Memorial to the King: "Enforcing a general reducción is absolutely necessary; but if at first there are no apparent difficulties, in the process there are many great obstacles and the work seems useless because the results do not endure."[135] The Conde's successor, Pedro de Toledo y Leiva, Marqués de Mancera (1639–1648), expressed himself more succinctly: "It is easy to issue dispatches, orders, and resolutions, but difficult to enforce them." In spite of Chinchón's and Mancera's protests, the King repeated the command to effect a general reducción to the Conde de Salvatierra (1648–1655), demanding "the resettlement of all the Indians who have left their original reducciones."[136]

Minutes from a 1651 session of the Council of the Indies explain the Crown's insistence on enforcing the Toledo regulations. In the margin of a copy of one Limeño's proposal, Juan de Solórzano Pereira, the famous seventeenth-century jurist, scribbled his conviction that "the reducciones are necessary and that . . . the fugitives and forasteros absent from their settlements should be returned to them." Although it might be expedient to allow some of these migrants to stay in their new towns where "they shall perform their labor service as if they were originarios,"

Solórzano supported none of the colonists' suggestions to utilize Indian labor more effectively by abandoning or altering the Toledo system. He denounced a proposal that all forasteros be seized and sent to work in haciendas, obrajes, or mines for the benefit of the royal treasury: "it is not just, nor possible, nor acceptable. How can anyone propose or even suggest to a King as holy and as pious as ours (may God guard his majesty) that he should make so much money from the sweat and the labor of those miserable Indians?"[137] The key to Solórzano's opposition is the phrase "so much money." Neither Solórzano nor any other counselor objected to extracting a "fair and just" profit from the Indies and the Indians, but royal officials remained convinced that simply satisfying the established tribute and labor demands through enforcement of existing reducciones would achieve that goal.

The Council of Indies maintained that position throughout the seventeenth century. In spite of sporadic attempts at reorganization, such as the Montesclaros and Palata reforms, the official definition of Indian society retained a structure of differentiation by ancestral community. This originario-forastero dichotomy continued in law, but not in practice, as sustained Indian migration increased the size of the forastero sector and the forasteros' reincorporation into established communities produced new, extralegal forms of social identification. When the conflict between the rigid structure of the Toledo reducciones and the incessant mobility of Indian society was finally resolved in the early eighteenth century, the solution was prompted not by a change of policy in Madrid but by an unprecedented demographic and economic crisis in the Peruvian sierra.

THE EPIDEMIC OF 1720 AND THE REDEFINITION OF INDIAN STATUS

The viceroyalty had not yet recovered from the aftershock of the Palata renumeration when a deadly epidemic identified only as *fiebre*, or fever, swept through the Andes, killing a minimum of 300,000 Indians. The anonymous chronicler of the *Anales del Cuzco* recorded a total of 80,000 fatalities in the bishopric, including 20,000 within the city, where the fiebre was first reported in April 1720.[138] The priest noted a particular vulnerability among "the wretched Indians" and thousands of Indians fled the region in a vain attempt to outrun the disease as it was carried northward toward Trujillo, probably by some of these same migrants. The impact of the epidemic on Cuzco, as described by the chronicler, was devastating: "who can describe exactly the deplorable condition of Cuzco and the surrounding provinces? There are no words which can exaggerate this disaster, and there are so many tears to mourn it."[139] The epidemic brought economic ruin to the sierra, where "almost all the homes are vacant and the herds without keepers; the farms lie fallow and the mines stand idle." The labor shortage was so acute that the mita de minas was suspended and some Cuzco hacendados had to sell their estates because of a lack of Indian labor. Observers agreed that the drop in production and the scarcity of basic foodstuffs were due entirely to the loss of Indian workers.[140]

A decline in the Indian population produced a decline in royal revenue as well. The Crown suspended all tribute payments until six months after the epidemic had passed through the provinces; subsequent obligations were assessed according to the number of Indians actually living in a repartimiento, not according to the total present during the last visita.[141] New padrones were compiled in 1723 after the epidemic had ended and retasas were issued to every province in the bishopric of Cuzco in the late 1720s.

These new padrones and retasas resembled those compiled for the Duque de Palata in that all Indians were to be listed, "originarios as well as forasteros . . . without exempting the yanaconas." However, for the first time a critical distinction was made between migrants who had been incorporated into the community and transients. "Forasteros con tierras," those with access to land, would remit their share of the goods included in the community's established obligations and would be taxed at the originario rate of about five pesos per year. Transients would pay only four pesos, to be collected in advance of the tax period.[142] Henceforth, access to economic resources, not ancestry, would determine an Indian's legal identity and obligations. This redefinition of community membership eliminated one major flaw in the Toledo structure: territorial affiliation had superseded kin-group membership as the primary criterion for stratification within indigenous society.

This startling departure in colonial policy was apparently enacted without the traditional preliminary inquiries and debates; the change also was apparently implemented without the vehement opposition usually voiced by at least one of the economic and political interest groups within Spanish society. The demographic and economic devastation of the sierra, which threatened the survival of the viceroyalty, provided the impetus for a comprehensive reevaluation of indigenous society, directed by Viceroy José de Armendáriz, Marqués de Castelfuerte (1724–1736).

The general retasa conducted in the bishopric of Cuzco in the late 1720s did not end Indian migration in the region, as litigants in late-eighteenth-century disputes lamented their inability to control the Indian population.[143] However, the devastating epidemic and resulting labor shortages of the 1720s did force royal officials to reevaluate the structure of indigenous society and to alter the legal composition and obligations of Indian communities. Ironically, after one hundred years of tortuous and conflicting administrative reforms and retractions, the eighteenth-century redefinition of the Indian community did little more than to formalize changes that had already occurred within indigenous society, largely in response to widespread Indian migration.

❖ 3 ❖ ❖

"Those Who Have Left Their Native Towns for Others": The Forasteros of Cuzco

To MOVE through the mountains and the valleys of the Peruvian sierra is an exhilirating but exhausting experience. The stark verticality and abrupt precipices of the imposing peaks form at once the majesty and the menace of the Andes. For the native of the high sierra, the rugged terrain and treacherous climate can make the briefest passage perilous. For the valley-dweller or lowlander, the transition to the upper altitudes can be devastating: sudden effort is impossible; sustained exertion, debilitating.

Prolonged residency or permanent relocation within the region requires much more than the obvious physiological acclimatization. In an area where geographic barriers and seasonal isolation effectively sever ties to home communities, migrants face the total disruption of economic activity, social linkages, and cultural context. In the colonial period—when legal identity, social position, and access to resources were determined by birthplace—the consequences of migration within indigenous society were even more disastrous. Yet throughout the colonial era, particularly during the seventeenth century, thousands of Indians traded the security of their traditional communities for freedom from their tax and labor obligations to contribute to the demographic and social transformation of the indigenous community under Spanish rule.[1]

The Spanish conquest of the Incas stimulated the earliest cycles of population dispersal and relocation within Andean America, but throughout the colonial period widespread Indian migration was sustained by a variety of factors. The most important impetus for migration was the indigenous community's forced integration into the European economy. The varied features of that economic integration, particularly the type of labor service owed to the state, created distinct regional

45

demographic trends within the Cuzco zone. The city of Cuzco attracted many migrants, but many more remained within rural indigenous society, leading to the emergence of a new social group—the *forasteros,* or foreign-born, newcomers and their descendants who were assimilated into established communities, forming a stable and significant sector of the Indian population. In the Cuzco area these forasteros were the key factor in the irregular depopulation of the sierra and in the regional demographic fluctuations which reflect the impact of sustained indigenous migration and characterize the bishopric's unique demographic history.

MOTIVATIONS FOR MIGRATION

Europeans blamed the initial dislocation of the Andean population on the breakdown of local political control and the end of Incan restrictions on travel. The chronicler Hernando de Santillán estimated that by 1560 one-third of the Indian community was on the move, partly in response to a new sense of physical mobility. Some Spaniards believed that this migration represented a flight from Christianity, but the Indians probably were fleeing from the violent conflict and economic crisis caused by the European conquest of the sierra. During the brutal and devastating civil wars between conflicting bands of conquistadores and the Crown, thousands of Indians abandoned the lower valleys of the Andes.[2] Writing in the 1560s, the Spanish jurist Juan de Matienzo lamented the depopulation of the sierra, particularly the areas adjacent to the former Incan storehouses and fortifications, where whole communities had disappeared "for fear of the Civil Wars."[3] Those Indians who did not flee the opposing armies might actually be forced to accompany them; Indian *kurakas,* or chiefs, of the conquered areas assigned bearers and servants to European soldiers, who immediately removed these retainers from their home communities.[4]

The Spaniards carried with them another motivation for Indian migration: disease. Throughout the colonial period, the indigenous population—undernourished, overworked, and lacking natural immunities—was decimated by periodic epidemics of European maladies.[5] Migration rose dramatically when Indians tried to escape the early plagues of measles (1531), typhus (1546), influenza (1558–1559), and smallpox (1585–1591). During the seventeenth century intermittent outbreaks of diphtheria, measles, and smallpox continued to ravage the viceroyalty.[6]

The provinces of the bishopric of Cuzco were hard hit by these epidemics, and the Indian population was particularly devastated. In 1577 the *cabildo*, or town council, of Cuzco reported that "at present there are many sick Indians in the parishes" and voted to try to procure some medicines for their relief.[7]

During the 1580s "an infinite number of Indians and Creoles reportedly died, more in the city of Cuzco than elsewhere" from repeated, related epidemics of smallpox and influenza.[8] In 1614, when the former Inca capital had the dubious honor of bestowing its name on the particularly virulent "Cuzco Diphtheria Epidemic," the cabildo sought public contributions for the Indian hospital.[9] Similarly, the smallpox epidemic which peaked in 1692, "the first to affect a [demographically] recovering Andean population,"[10] struck the Indians of Cuzco early and brutally in 1687.

None of these previous crises, not even the smallpox attacks of the 1580s, was as devastating as the pan-sierra epidemics of smallpox and influenza of 1719–1721.[11] The bishopric of Cuzco, where one wave of the epidemic originated in 1720, lost more than half of its total population; most of the area's eighty thousand victims were Indians. Thousands more fled the region, spreading the disease northward in a vain attempt to escape contamination. When four hundred people died of pleurisy in Cuzco in 1726, the memory of the earlier disaster stimulated a fresh wave of migration.[12]

Natural, as well as epidemiological, disasters forced Indians to leave their home communities in the Cuzco area. That region, like much of the Andes, suffers alternately from an abundance or a scarcity of rain; the drought of 1592, which, the cabildo of Potosí lamented, produced "a notable and unprecedented sterility" from Potosí to Cuzco, was only the first during the colonial period. In 1657, for example, the Indians of the province of Aymares complained bitterly of "great scarcity because of the severe droughts."[13] The seismic disturbances which shook the sierra with threatening series of small, recurring tremors and devastating earthquakes were another stimulus to Indian migration. The powerful quake which destroyed much of the city of Cuzco in 1650 produced an immediate wave of Indian movement into the countryside, in part because the indigenous community lived in poorly constructed, vulnerable dwellings.[14] The priest compiling the bishopric's *Anales del Cuzco* reported that the earthquake of 1707 produced another type of migration: scores of Indians, including "various witches," convened at the epicenter Indian town of Capi, Cotabambas, to prevent aftershocks by practicing "all sorts of superstitious rites, even idolatry."[15] The ecclesiastical hierarchy was convinced that this movement would perpetuate heresy.

The Church's intolerance was another strong impetus for migration. Many Indians who clung to traditional religious practices abandoned their home communities during the intensive religious campaigns of the early colonial period. Periodic *visitas*, inspections designed to identify and prosecute heretics, further stimulated Indian migration. The special relationship between a deity and its dwelling place in traditional Andean culture produced two opposing types of migration: Indians accused of heresy were forcibly relocated in distant towns in order to destroy local cults; and, more commonly, Indians who had been resettled under the control of Catholic priests fled to sites sacred in indigenous religion.[16]

The main cause of Indian migration, however, was the impact on the indigenous community of its incorporation into the Spanish colonial system and the world economy. The harsh demands of the mineral export sector and supporting agricultural production drove Indians to trade the security of their home community for freedom from tribute and labor obligations. Although the development of a Spanish economy and depopulation are not inseparable,[17] the nature of economic activity in the Peruvian sierra—mineral production and large-scale hacienda cultivation—demanded the use of Indian labor and the alienation of indigenous land. Throughout the bishopric of Cuzco, the imperial system designed to maximize the extraction of goods and services for European markets produced a variety of interrelated migration patterns.

One major reason for migration was the rapid depletion of community resources due to conflicts in the sierra, the extraction of tribute and, above all, the loss of Indian lands. During the conquest and the civil wars invading armies had seized the foodstores and livestock of Cuzco-area communities; throughout the colonial period Spaniards traveling the Andean highways could demand shelter, meals, and transport from local pueblos.[18] Other communal assets, such as the two thousand sheep bequeathed to the town of Horunillo, Lampa, by a conscience-stricken Spaniard, were confiscated by royal officials or Indian kurakas.[19] The regularization of Spanish demands for goods into formal tribute payments spurred Indian migration, especially after the 1570s, when Viceroy Francisco de Toledo commuted most assessments to cash payments. The Crown's seizure and sale of Indian land temporarily relieved a community's tax burden but permanently impaired its members' ability to meet further demands; in 1681 a royal decree acknowledged that thousands of Indians had fled "because of the burden of paying taxes and the towns are depopulated."[20] Because the Crown granted Indians lands on a per capita basis, this migration intensified the alienation of Indian holdings, particularly in the 1630s and 1640s when the King ordered a series of *composiciones de tierras*, inspections and forced sales of Indian lands judged vacant or abandoned.[21] By the mid-1650s the systematic attacks on Indian community assets which had begun during the conquest of the sierra had resulted in a powerful and irreversible force for Indian migration.

The alienation of community lands was both preceded by and intensified by the chief stimulus for Indian migration: the constant demand for indigenous labor in the haciendas, the mines, and the personal service of European and Indian elites. Official condemnation of the use of Indians as private servants began soon after the conquest of Cuba, when the King prohibited Spaniards from taking Caribbean Indians on expeditions to the Central and South American mainlands because individuals threatened with such voyages were abandoning their home communities. In 1539 Charles V was particularly incensed to discover that many Spaniards had carried Peruvian Indians to Panama, where indigenous labor could not possibly be needed for a conquest expedition.[22] Throughout the sixteenth and seventeenth centuries *Cédulas Reales*, or royal decrees, proclaimed "that the Indians should be free, and not subject to involuntary service," and prohibited the forced relocation of Indians, but with little success.[23] For example, in both 1618 and 1681 royal decrees were issued prohibiting the removal of Indians from the provinces of the Río de la Plata to the Andean sierra.[24] Throughout the colonial period Indians migrated to escape illegal demands on their labor. In 1611 a Lima resident reported that thousands of Indians had fled their settlements because of "their great fear of personal service"; at the end of the century Cuzco Indians were still leaving their homes to avoid the abuses of local elites.[25] Many of these Indians were resisting domestic service or forced agricultural labor, but at least some Indians fled because of conditions in the *obrajes*, or textile workshops. This sweatshop labor was so brutal that it was used (illegally) by *corregidores* to punish Indians who failed to meet tribute payments.[26]

Indians detested their service in the households and obrajes of the colonial elite, but they despised and feared above all the *mita de minas*, the labor draft to the silver mines at Potosí and to the mercury mines at

Guancavelica. According to regulations established by Viceroy Toledo, male Indians between the ages of eighteen and fifty were required to work two months of mita labor, followed by twelve months of rest; in theory, one-seventh of the adult male Indian population would always be working for employers with official access to mita laborers. Indians subject to a local agricultural mita could be assigned to estates near their home communities, but Indians subject to the mita de minas were dispatched to the mining zones.[27] The mita de minas was the chief cause of Indian migration from the provinces supplying labor to Guancavelica and Potosí, and throughout the sixteenth and seventeenth centuries the rapid depopulation of these provinces intensified the demands on the remaining residents, further stimulating migration. In 1689 the parish priest of Pachaconas, Aymares, complained that "the Indians who go [to the mines] never return because since they are so few, they scarcely rest eight months before they are obliged to serve mita duty again and because of this severity and because of the low pay . . . they flee and go to the Andes and the lands of the Infidels."[28]

The Indians clearly were aware of the dangers of mining at Potosí, as the local *Protector de Naturales*, the appointed advocate for the indigenous community, wrote in 1582: "The Indians must descend to the depths of the mines with obvious risk to their lives; after they have emerged sweating and with hardly any sign of life, the greatest relief that they have is to sit down on a cold rock and eat fewer than a dozen kernels of corn, while the wind chills them to the bone, from which they die."[29] The mercury mines at Guancavelica inspired even greater horror and resistance. A mid-seventeenth-century report on Indian labor revealed that "the Indians fear the labor at the mine of Guancavelica so much that many mothers maim their infant sons in the arms or legs so that when they are older, they will be exempt from that duty."[30] Parents who mutilated their children were aware of the conditions at Guancavelica, where thousands of Indians died "because of the lack of air and the danger of the dust that rises, which is fatal when combined with the hot smoke of the lamps and the vapor; after three or four successive mitas, disease [mercury poisoning] and death are inescapable."[31] By 1626 the cabildo of Cuzco was lamenting the drastic depopulation of the province of Cotabambas because "most of the Indians have died at the mines of Guancavelica and others have fled, fearing this duty."[32] Few of those Indians who survived their turn at the mita de minas returned to their home communities, in part because of economic opportunities in the mining zones. Entire families went to the mining zones with the designated adult male worker and remained there after his shift had been completed, working in the processing pits or the small-scale agricultural sector created to supplement the shipments of food from the major production centers. Indians who did return to their home communities often found that their lands had been seized by Spaniards, taken by neighbors, or occupied by migrants from other communities.[33]

A new motive for Indian migration appeared during the mid-seventeenth century: the *repartimiento de bienes* or *repartimiento de mercancías*. Through the repartimiento, merchants, royal officials, and kurakas conspired to relieve the oversupplied Peruvian markets flooded by contraband European goods smuggled through Buenos Aires.[34] Merchants arranged with corregidores to dispose of unsold commodities by distributing them at highly inflated prices to Indians who were barely able to pay for basic necessities; the value of these "purchased" goods was then deducted from the indigenous communities' small cash reserves or individuals' salaries. Indians leaving for the mita de minas were considered particularly desirable "customers" because officials in Potosí or Guancavelica would guarantee payment from mita wages.[35] This form of debt peonage produced widespread migration and, in the opinion of the *Audiencia,* or High Court of Lima, was the main reason for the suffering of the Indians during the late seventeenth century. Resentment of the repartimiento de bienes led to the assassination of the Corregidor of Carabaya, Cuzco, in 1726 and was a major factor in the pan-sierra rebellions of the late eighteenth century.[36]

The repartimiento de bienes was just one way, although an important one, in which colonial administrators used their power for personal profit. The imposition of imperial economic and political systems created new positions of authority over the indigenous community, such as the corregidor and the parish priest, and amplified the traditional role of the Indian kurakas, whom the Spaniards also called *caciques* or *casiques.* All of these officeholders could abuse their substantial powers to exploit Indians. Women, in particular, were the victims of these attacks, and one of the chief reasons for the migration of female Indians was sexual abuse by their corregidores or priests.[37] Although not subject to mita service, women were forced to work as Spaniards' domestic servants or to weave cloth for their corregidores to sell at Potosí.[38] Men and women compelled to cultivate the priests' and corregidores' private lands were sent to their estates elsewhere in the viceroyalty.[39] One priest was accused of abusing and destroying an entire Indian village when "one day in a drunken fit he burned down some houses in the town of Totopón and the owners fled to the mountains, where they gathered and built new homes."[40] Spaniards, including the Bishop of Cuzco in 1635, preferred to think that "the abusive rule of the Indian kurakas is one of the main reasons for the destruction of Indian towns."[41] Certainly, Indian authorities were not immune to the temptation to profit from their positions, and the kurakas had the double advantage of exploiting not only the residents of their jurisdictions, but also migrants seeking sanctuary there as well.

Of course, some of these Indians had migrated for purely personal reasons: because colonialism offered new opportunities for changing their physical environment, social position, or economic status; because migration meant ending an unhappy relationship or avoiding an arranged marriage;[42] or simply because they wanted to move. There would be some Indian migrants who profited from the lighter tasks of wage workers who settled in the mining areas after their mita duty, some who preferred to work for individual entrepreneurs in haciendas and urban centers, and others who wanted no contact whatsoever with any European. In all of these cases, and in the varied ways in which Indians reacted to the imposition of European rule, there appears an undeniable assertion of individual choice, tempered by the confines of the colonial system. David Brading and Harry E. Cross have asked of the mita to Potosí, "Was it so dangerous as to drive a man to desert his ayllu [kin-group] and abandon his lands?"[43] Behind the history of Indian migration there lies another question: because participation in the colonial economy meant death or separation from kin-members or probable loss of ancestral land, why should Indians accept this alienation from their traditional communities on any terms but their own?

DEFINING THE FORASTERO SECTOR

Indians who chose migration were not always called "forasteros"—foreigners, or strangers. During the turmoil of the conquest period the term "forastero" might be accompanied, or replaced, by another: *yanacona* or, as the Spaniards simplistically defined the concept, "servant."[44] During the 1570s, however, Viceroy Francisco de Toledo divided the indigenous community into two clearly defined major categories: yanaconas and *originarios*, or native-born members, of carefully organized Indian settlements.[45] Thereafter, the word "forastero" had a clearer meaning—"stranger," specifically, "outsider" or "migrant to the community from elsewhere."[46] As migration continued throughout the sixteenth and seventeenth centuries, and as indigenous society adjusted to that movement by developing a variety of ways to assimilate individuals or groups of migrants, the term "forastero" became increasingly associated with Indians who had been successfully reincorporated into existing communities. Although reports from the colonies differed concerning the extent to which forasteros contributed to the taxes and labor quotas of their home communities, bureaucrats agreed that the *indios forasteros* of seventeenth-century Peru were a stable sector of indigenous society, "those who have left their native towns for others, where they are unknown, and there they are called forasteros."[47] In some instances entire towns were repopulated by forasteros, who acquired the name, but not the legal obligations, of the community.[48] One key way of determining whether or not non-native Indians were forasteros who had been integrated into their new community was to see if they owned their own homes. The parish priest of San Cristóbal, Cuzco, emphasized that the Indians who had migrated into his district "also have houses of their own and these Indians are called *forasteros.*"[49]

Former migrants retained the name "forasteros" regardless of the length of their residence in new communities and regardless of their degree of assimilation; a variety of documents indicates that Spanish authorities, native-born Indians, and migrants themselves used this concept. Consistent with the caste structure of indigenous society, in which group identification and social position were hereditary attributes, the forastero category included the descendants of original migrants who had not married into originario *ayllus.* Some Indians with mixed originario and forastero ancestry also claimed the title "forastero." In 1648 the Corregidor of Cañete condemned this classification system when he blamed the economic ruin of his province on "the Indios forasteros in this jurisdiction, by which it is understood that although they were born here, they pay no tribute, recognize no legal residence or encomendero, comply with neither mita nor personal service, because their fathers or grandfathers or other ancestors left their homes and came to this area many years ago."[50] The corregidor's assessment of Indian contributions is obviously a defensive one, but his account of the hereditary nature of forastero status is corroborated by additional seventeenth-century reports. In 1690 all twenty-four Indians in the town of Alcopaya, Aymares, "although born in this very town, are known as forasteros because they send their tribute to the towns where their ancestors were originarios."[51] The same distinction applied in other communities throughout the bishopric of Cuzco, even though "all these Indians have established families and have lived here many years."[52]

By the late seventeenth century the legal distinction between originario and forastero had been complicated by functional definitions of Indian status, which reflected the linkages between assimilated migrants and their new communities. A report prepared for Viceroy Duque de Palata (1681–1689) complained that Toledo's initial originario-forastero dichotomy had not allowed for alternative social groups resulting from prolonged Indian migration; the viceroy condemned this migration "which has gone on for so long that there has emerged a second type of forasteros, those who are called *yernos* [sons-in-law] and *sobrinos* [nephews], sons of forasteros and native-born women."[53] Not all forasteros were linked by blood to established Indian communities, and in the Cuzco area the familial terms "yernos" and "sobrinos" were supplemented by other phrases used to describe assimilated migrants. Seventeenth-century colonial authorities very carefully distinguished the *forasteros revisitados*, those "who live in their respective ayllus because their ancestors were born here and were integrated into these communities," from the "*forasteros advenedisos* and other recent arrivals who at present are found within the ayllus but leave at will."[54]

In spite of increasing differentiation between assimilated and unassimilated migrants, forasteros retained the legal and social status of hereditary members of their original communities. Even though they were not presently residing in their ancestral lands, forasteros remaining within Indian society were linked to their kin-groups. In contrast, the *vagabondos* or, simply, *vagos*,[55] who congregated in colonial towns and mining centers or "wandered through all the provinces of this kingdom without permanency in any,"[56] had severed their ties with traditional Indian communities. Although there undoubtedly were some Indians among these transients, Magnus Mörner has identified the majority of the vagos as *castas*, individuals of mixed racial inheritance, chiefly "a frustrated type of *mestizo*," unsuccessful within established colonial society.[57] The Crown defined these "Spanish vagrants" and "sons of Spaniards" as non-Indians and barred them from entering the Indian villages. Repeated royal decrees ordered that the vagos be settled in towns of their own and forced to "earn a living at some respectable employment."[58] Transients who resisted were exiled to the Philippines or to frontier garrisons in Florida and northern Mexico.[59]

The designation "indios vagos" did not appear in Cuzco-area documentation until the mid-seventeenth century, when the composiciones de tierras—the confiscation and sale of "vacant" Indian lands—had reduced the established communities' ability to accommodate forasteros. By 1661 the Crown had become very concerned with "the Indians who wander aimlessly through the countryside . . . because their lands have been taken from them and sold."[60] Most colonial bureaucrats recognized that these indios vagos made up a distinct category.[61] A parish priest, compiling census material for the bishop of Cuzco in 1690, identified the originarios and forasteros in his district and then explained: "The Indians who have been listed unaccompanied by the names of their home communities are called vagrants, because today they are in this town and province and tomorrow they will be elsewhere. Many Indians named in the most recent census have since died and others have fled, so that this parish is now much smaller."[62]

During the late seventeenth century this transient sector of the Indian population of Cuzco was twice threatened by taxation: first, when the Viceroy Duque de Palata initiated a renumeration of the entire Indian community, and again in 1689, when Bishop Don Manuel de Mollinedo y Angulo ordered a census of the fourteen provinces under his jurisdiction. The announcement of the Palata census was followed by increased migration, particularly among unassimilated Indians; during the later effort, the second within five years, the rest of the transient population abandoned the bishopric of Cuzco, leaving only the established forasteros.[63]

The size of that forastero sector and its importance within Indian society were key factors in the Crown's decision to abandon the originario-forastero dichotomy after the devastating plagues of the 1720s produced economic ruin and acute labor shortages throughout the sierra. The new legal distinctions continued to emphasize ancestry, but allowed for variations within this hereditary status which reflected the migrants' relationships with their adopted communities. Henceforth, *forasteros con tierra*—assimilated migrants, or the descendants of migrants, with access to local lands—would be treated as native-born Indians and would be called originarios or *sobrinos de originarios*. Membership in this new category was explicitly linked to access to community resources: regulations specified that only "the forasteros in town who hold houses and lands free of charge, in their own right or through their wives" were included.[64] The terms "forasteros," "*forasteros sin tierra*," and "vagos" were now used synonymously within indigenous society to designate transients who had no linkages to land.[65] The evolution of new forms of forastero assimilation had forced a redefinition of social distinctions and a reformulation of Indian identity in which access to the means of production, not ancestry, was the final determinant of status within indigenous society.

This distinction between the assimilated forasteros and forasteros sin tierra identifies the origin of the landless transient population which would form the basis of the wage labor and *colonato* sectors of the eighteenth century. An essential element of the colonato system, in which landowners "compensate their farm workers, wholly or partially by letting them have the usufruct of small plots of land,"[66] is the availability of a landless labor force. The changes within Indian society that led to certain groups being denied access to land were an important preliminary step in generating that work force. The eighteenth-century economic contraction of the viceroyalty coincided with a recovering Indian population, intensifying the pressure on community lands, reducing the number of Indians who could be reincorporated into indigenous society, and forcing those without access to land to become hacienda workers or tenant laborers. Magnus Morner believes that "the scarce evidence that is available suggests that the Andean Colonato institutions came into being" during this period.[67]

Morner and other scholars have linked the hacienda labor force of the late eighteenth century to the migrant community, but have failed to recognize variations of the originario-forastero dichotomy which redefined community membership on the basis of access to resources and produced a landless, unassimilated migrant sector. The forasteros they cite are definitely forasteros sin tierras, not the established forastero population which was reincorporated into Indian society during the late sixteenth and seventeenth centuries.[68] The landless, highly mobile Indian transients, not the assimilated migrants and their descendants, were the "foreign" Indians who played a crucial role in the outbreak of indigenous rebellions throughout the sierra in the late 1700s.[69] The forastero sin tierra, not the forastero, is "the symbol of as well as a significant factor in the great changes that shook the Viceroyalty" in the late eighteenth century.[70] For most of the colonial period the forastero community consisted chiefly of those migrants who had been reassimilated into indigenous society and their descendants; these forasteros are the focus of this study.

The late seventeenth-century *relaciones,* or reports, of the parish priests in the bishopric of Cuzco provide an unusual opportunity to identify and to examine the assimilated migrant population later identified as forasteros con tierras. In the aftermath of the 1685 Palata census many of the unassimilated Indians fled the area. During the smallpox epidemic of 1687 the remaining transients abandoned the bishopric, leaving chiefly the established forasteros to be enrolled in the comprehensive numeration conducted by the Church in 1689–1690.

In July 1689 Bishop Don Manuel de Mollinedo y Angulo responded to a royal demand for an official census of the Andean sierra by circulating a pastoral letter requesting detailed demographic and economic data from each of the 125 parish priests in the fourteen provinces of the bishopric of Cuzco. Although reports began arriving in Cuzco during the first week of August 1689, the large number of responses outstanding forced the bishop to issue a series of admonitory follow-up letters in March 1690. During July of that year the last reports reached Cuzco and the bishop requested and received the accounts of the city's parishes.[71]

The demographic profile compiled from these relaciones shows a diverse and widely distributed forastero population. Forasteros were firmly established in every province of the bishopric of Cuzco and in two-thirds of the local *doctrinas,* or parishes. These parishes with forasteros accounted for 72 percent of the provinces' total Indian population of 113,565. Forastero representation varied widely, ranging from 6 to 100 percent of individual parishes. Provincial summaries, skewed by the varied number of data entries, show percentages of forasteros ranging from 15.2 to 100, but most provincial totals were clustered between 40 and 50 percent, dramatic evidence of the impact of the colonial system in decimating and dislocating the indigenous population. High concentrations of forasteros were reported in the provinces along the Cuzco-Puno corridor, the route to Upper Peru, indicating that mita workers traveling through the region on their way to or from the mining center of Potosí had relocated in the Vilcanota River valley. The province of Abancay, a regional administrative and transportation center, contained a large forastero group. The Marquesado de Oropesa and the province of Calca y

TABLE 3.1. Forasteros in the Indian Population: Bishopric of Cuzco, 1690

Provinces in Mita Service to:	Doctrinas Reporting Forasteros	Percentage of Provinces' Population	Forasteros— Percentage of Adult Males	Forasteros— Percentage of All Indians
Guancavelica	25 of 40	63.3	32.7	21.3
Potosí	28 of 43	65.8	40.9	64.0
Paucartambo Coca Fields	3 of 6	73.0	100.0	100.0
Local Employers	29 of 36	82.9	58.2	42.0
Totals	85 of 125	72.0	50.3	43.6

Lares, adjacent to the city of Cuzco, had strong forastero sectors resulting from the extra-urban movement which occurred when lands in the depopulated countryside were occupied by Indians born in colonial cities.[72]

Division of the Cuzco area into labor zones based chiefly on mita obligations reveals a different distribution pattern for the forastero population, as shown in table 3.1. Four of the bishopric's provinces dispatched laborers to the silver mines at Potosí; three more provinces sent workers to the mercury deposits at Guancavelica; and in six other provinces Indians performed varied duties for local employers. In the remaining province of Paucartambo, service in the coca fields was a distinct form of local mita, linked to the mineral export sector through the high consumption of coca at Potosí.[73]

The established forastero population was largest in Paucartambo, where the brutal labor in the coca fields had devastated the originarios, producing total replacement by forasteros. Although the other provinces with local mita service also showed a uniformly strong forastero sector, distribution varied within the labor zones of the mita de minas. Fewer forasteros were found in the region which sent Indians to Guancavelica, perhaps because migrants hesitated to move into areas subject to this most feared mita duty. The unusually high percentage of forasteros in the provinces with mitas to Potosí can be explained by the influx of migrants into an area which had lost much of its originario population to the mines or to flight from the mita. Throughout the seventeenth cen-

TABLE 3.2. Breakdown of Originario and Forastero Populations by Town and Rural Sectors

Provinces in Mita Service to:	Total Parish		Originario		Forastero	
	Town	Rural	Town	Rural	Town	Rural
Guancavelica	85.9	14.1	91.1	8.9	73.7	26.3
Potosí	76.9	23.1	99.3	0.7	67.4	32.6
Paucartambo Coca Fields	12.1	87.9	—	—	12.1	87.9
Local Employers	53.9	46.1	97.6	2.4	3.6	96.4

tury entrepreneurs in Potosí relied increasingly on the "voluntary" or "rented" workers who congregated at the site; forasteros resettled in those Cuzco provinces which sent laborers to Potosí would therefore be less likely to be forced into mita duty than forasteros in the areas serving Guancavelica, where the higher mortality rates and poorer working conditions precluded the development of a wage labor force to compensate for the lack of originarios. Many of the forasteros in the Potosí zone could also find employment in the subsidiary agricultural sector which developed in the surrounding provinces.

Ironically, the forasteros generally settled in areas of economic opportunity where the dangerous working conditions and state demands for labor which had removed the originario population were not so severe as to threaten assimilated migrants. However, other local factors affected the distribution patterns within doctrinas. An initial appraisal of the division of the Indian population into those living in towns and those inhabiting outlying lands indicated that the majority of the forasteros— 65.8 percent—were in the rural sector, with 34.2 percent in towns; for the originarios the figures were 3.7 percent and 96.3 percent, respectively. The towns showed an overwhelming originario majority of 72.4 percent, but forasteros, with a 27.6 percent representation, were still a strong presence in these doctrinas. The rural sectors showed a dramatic reversal and polarization of these groups: 5 percent originario versus 95 percent forastero.[74]

Resolution of the town-rural composition data into labor zones, however, provides a clearer image of forastero distribution, as seen in tables 3.2 and 3.3.[75] In the provinces subject to a mita de minas the majority of the forastero population lived in towns; only in the agricultural zone of

TABLE 3.3. Composition of Provincial Parishes by Originario and Forastero

Provinces in Mita Service to:	Total Population		In Town		Rural Sector	
	Percent-age of Origi-narios	Percent-age of Fora-steros	Percent-age of Origi-narios	Percent-age of Fora-steros	Percent-age of Origi-narios	Percent-age of Fora-steros
Guancavelica	70.5	29.5	74.7	25.3	44.9	55.1
Potosí	29.8	70.2	38.5	61.5	0.9	99.1
Paucartambo Coca Fields	0	100.0	0	100.0	0	100.0
Local Employers	53.5	46.5	96.9	3.1	2.8	97.2

Paucartambo and in the parishes with local labor duty did the forasteros reside chiefly in the rural sector (table 3.2). The data on parish composition show a greater variation of forastero presence in towns, but clearly the forasteros, who continued to dominate the rural sector, played a stronger role in towns within provinces subject to the mita de minas (table 3.3). These figures demonstrate that not all resettled migrants were located on the fringes of established Indian communities. In areas where the originario population had been most affected by the demands of the mining export sector, the forasteros had been assimilated into existing Indian towns; in some parishes, forasteros had totally replaced the originarios.[76]

This broadly distributed forastero sector had a slightly higher percentage of males (48.6) than the parallel originario group (45.2) or the total Indian population (44.3).[77] An initial review of provincial totals appears to follow this general gender distribution pattern, but a closer examination of the gender ratios within the originario and forastero sectors, by labor zone, reveals some interesting deviations (see table 3.4). The provinces with mita to Guancavelica, the most dreaded labor duty, show a much lower male presence, particularly among the originarios, the only group legally obligated to perform mita service, of whom only 39 percent are males; the corresponding forastero figure is 51.1 percent. The provinces with mitas to Potosí show a similarly low male originario sector, 38.8 percent, and a higher male forastero figure of 41.3 percent.

TABLE 3.4. Indian Population by Sex

Provinces in Mita Service to:	Total		Originario		Forastero	
	Male	Female	Male	Female	Male	Female
Guancavelica	36.0	64.0	39.0	61.0	51.1	48.9
Potosí	43.7	56.3	38.8	61.2	41.3	58.7
Paucartambo Coca Fields	n.a	n.a.	n.a.	n.a.	n.a.	n.a.
Local Employers	48.4	51.6	48.0	52.0	49.3	50.7
Totals	44.3	55.7	45.2	54.8	48.6	51.4

Both areas are in sharp contrast to the much higher and demographically standard figure of 48 percent males in the native-born population of those provinces with only local labor duties. Individual parish reports reflect these provincial patterns: the doctrina with the highest male representation, 66 percent, was Amaybamba y Quillabamba, Vilcabamba, an isolated region which owed only local labor service; the lowest representation of males, 19 percent, was in the parish of Aquira, Cotabambas, which sent its mita laborers to the mercury mines at Guancavelica.[78]

This disparity can be explained in part by gender-specific selection factors affecting male originarios: men were subject to the mita de minas and other health conditions which produced higher mortality and migration rates. Interpretation of the gender balance of the forastero population is, however, more complicated. In both zones with a mita de minas the proportion of males among the forasteros is higher than among the originarios; in the area subject to the mita to Guancavelica the forasteros' male/female ratio approaches the demographic norm of parity, which is also achieved in those provinces without mine labor service. The Guancavelica data indicate that in the provinces with the most onerous labor duty, forasteros increased the proportion of males in the general population and redressed the imbalance in gender ratios among the originarios.

The higher percentage of males among the forastero population should not, however, be interpreted to mean that the assimilated migrant population was composed primarily of male Indians who intermarried with originarios. The forasteros incorporated into existing Indian towns and those located in rural areas showed almost identical gender ratios.[79]

Throughout the bishopric the forastero sector displayed an average family size and a child-adult ratio higher than those of the originario group.[80] The data on gender ratios therefore show that assimilated migrants of both sexes and, more importantly, the descendants of those migrants were a permanent feature of the bishopric of Cuzco, including those provinces where a mita de minas might otherwise have been expected to destabilize the male sector.

A combination of qualitative and quantitative evidence indicates that many, if not most, of the forasteros settled in the bishopric of Cuzco had originated elsewhere in the bishopric. Despite some officials' claims that Indians had fled to areas beyond Spanish control, more candid observers stated that forasteros had resettled in neighboring communities or provinces and various reports from the Cuzco area in the mid- and late seventeenth century confirm this impression.[81] In one case of extreme short-range mobility a forastero community was formed in the 1640s when natives of the parish of Pampamarca, Aymares, moved into lands belonging to its ecclesiastical annex, Colca, because a composición de tierras in Pampamarca had left several families landless. These Indians immediately built a church in Colca, as a sign of their independence from Pampamarca; when the building was destroyed in the 1660s the forasteros built another "in order not to be returned to Pampamarca, where they are originarios." Thirty years later the descendants of these original migrants were clearly identified as the forasteros of Colca.[82]

Although most migrants did not resettle quite so close to their home communities, colonial authorities believed that Indians from neighboring jurisdictions had a higher chance of successful assimilation in Cuzco-area provinces.[83] Evidence supporting this theory can be found in the *conciertos*, or labor contracts, recorded in the notarial registers of Cuzco. Thirty-four of the seventy-four contracts negotiated during the period from 1630 to 1699 involved natives of area provinces willing to relocate within the provinces of the bishopric; an additional twenty-six laborers were identified as natives of the city itself. Only thirteen Indians committed to resettlement were from outside the bishopric, and the majority of these workers were from the nearby jurisdictions of Huamanga and Arequipa. Forty-one of these contracts involved short-term labor in the coca fields of Paucartambo, a depopulated area in which any migrant who survived the length of his coca service could easily resettle.[84]

The most reliable sources for information concerning the home communities of migrants are parish registers of an individual doctrina, such as Yucay, Marquesado de Oropesa, where the presence of a clearly identified *ayllu forastero*—kin-group of foreigners—distinguishes assimilated Indians of foreign descent from transients in the community.[85] An analysis of the ancestry of resident forasteros and parishoners whose children were baptized in Yucay during the period from 1675 to 1735 shows that an overwhelming number of the reincorporated migrants, 97 percent, had origins in the bishopric of Cuzco. Most of these forasteros with ties to other Cuzco provinces traced their ancestry to the Marquesado de Oropesa and the adjoining provinces of Calca y Lares. Many Yucay residents were linked to the neighboring towns of Urubamba, Ollantaytambo, and Guaillabamba.[86]

The preceding profile of the forastero population demonstrates that this stable sector of indigenous society in late-seventeenth-century Cuzco was, in general, the product of short-range migration from Indian communities within the bishopric or from the city of Cuzco itself. The forastero population had a balanced gender distribution and an average family size and child-adult ratio which exceeded those of the originario group. Forasteros were an established presence throughout the bishopric, particularly in provinces subject to the mitas to Potosí and Paucartambo. Although most forasteros lived in rural areas, a significant minority had been incorporated into existing Indian towns whose originario population had been reduced or totally destroyed by the demands of the mita de minas.

THE DEMOGRAPHIC IMPACT OF THE FORASTERO SECTOR

The population data accumulated for this study of the forasteros, particularly the census of 1690, reflect the importance of the migrant sector and indicate that accepted patterns in colonial demographic history must be reevaluated, with particular attention to the discrepancy between the official and the actual Indian populations, and then must be modified to recognize variation by region and economic structure. This reassessment must begin with the traditional interpretations of the size of the indigenous community of colonial Peru. Estimates of the population of the Incan Empire vary widely, but N. David Cook's carefully documented analysis places the preconquest population of Peru at approximately nine million; by 1620, the population had fallen to about 600,000.[87] The earliest population profiles for the seventeenth century claimed that following this initial rapid fall, the Indian community en-

TABLE 3.5. Indigenous Population of the Bishopric of Cuzco: Selected Years, 1561–1754

	Total (Including City of Cuzco)	Provincial Totals
1561	267,000	—
1586	400,075	—
1628	321,484	—
1652	97,478	—
1690	121,887	113,565
1725	—	96,793
1754	127,988	119,003

DATA SOURCES:

1561—Silvio Zavala, *La encomienda indiana*. Madrid, 1935, p. 324.*

1586—Angel Rosenblat, *La población indígena y el mestizaje en America*. Buenos Aires, 1954, p. 84, from Juan Canales Albarrán, Descripción de todos los reinos del Perú, Chile, y Tierra Firme, 1586, BNE, 3178, f. 15.*

1628—Antonio Vázquez de Espinosa, *Compendium and Description of the West Indies*. Washington, D.C.: Smithsonian Institution, 1942, pp. 703–20.*

1652—*Anales del Cuzco, 1600–1750*, f. 118.

1690—AGI, Lima 471. Padrón del obispado del Cuzco, 1690. See Appendix II.

1725—ANP, Tributos. Legajos 1 and 2, Cuadernos de las provincias del obispado del Cuzco.

1754—Memorias de los Virreyes que gobernaron el Perú durante el tiempo del colonaje español. Vol. IV, Apendice, pp. 7–15.

*Cited in Noble David Cook, "La población indígena." Cook states that the increase in the 1561–1586 period is due to "the inclusion of part of the northeast zone of Arequipa" (p. 87).

tered a period of steady, consistent decline until the rapid decrease of the early eighteenth century, when the pan-Andean plagues decimated indigenous society. In recent years the scholars who articulated this model have amended it to allow for regional demographic variation, but the model must be further adjusted to allow for intervening periods of population maintenance or recuperation and to permit an analysis of demographic variation by economic zone.[88]

Population totals for the bishopric of Cuzco contradict both the traditional pattern of continuous demographic decline and the assumption that the lowpoint of the indigenous population in the 1720s was the

TABLE 3.6. Indigenous Population of the Provinces of the Bishopric of Cuzco: Selected Years, 1628–1754

Province	1628	1676	1690	1725	1754
Abancay	17,070	23,700	13,734	11,323	12,276
Aymares	44,957	12,400	9,540	5,149	11,276
Azángaro	—	—	8,712	10,302	11,543
Calca y Lares	—	—	6,009	2,953	—
y Vilcabamba	—	—	6,982	—	3,906
Canas y Canches	—	—	12,229	13,527	12,785
Caravaya y Sangabán	—	—	4,940	—	6,540
Cotabambas	29,552	—	6,954	5,362	7,423
Chilques y Masques	—	—	11,759	4,007	7,839
Chumbibilcas	23,160	—	6,434	6,174	8,145
Lampa	—	15,200	9,390	14,978	9,072
Marquesado de Oropesa	—	10,500	5,226	3,625	3,497
Paucartambo	4,631	—	4,668	4,819	7,141
Quispicanche	21,779	—	12,997	14,574	17,560
Totals—14 provinces			113,565	—	119,003
Comparative Totals—					
12 provinces			107,652	96,793	—
11 provinces			101,643	93,840	108,557

DATA SOURCES:

1628—Antonio Vázquez de Espinosa, *Compendium and Description of the West Indies*. Washington, D.C.: Smithsonian Institution, 1942, pp. 703–20. Cited in Noble David Cook, "La población indígena."

1676—AGI, Lima 306, No. VI. Visita que el Dor. D. Manuel de Mollinedo, Obispo del Cusco del Consejo del Rey N.S. hizo en el año de 1676.

1690—AGI, Lima 471. Padrón del obispado del Cuzco, 1690. See Appendix II.

1725—ANP, Tributos, Legajos 1 and 2, Cuadernos de las provincias del obispado del Cuzco. Data manipulation based on conversion figure generated by internal data in Legajo 2, Cuaderno 21, ff. 1–34. Ratio of 2.6729/1; dependent population/tributario. See below.

1754—Memorias de los Virreyes que gobernaron el Perú durante el tiempo del colonaje español. Vol. IV, Apendice, pp. 7–15.

result of a sharp and dramatic fall (table 3.5). Data from the Cuzco region display a variety of provincial patterns (table 3.6) and indicate two possible population nadirs within the Indian community, the first in the mid seventeenth century, the second after the plague of 1719. The 1652 figure of 97,478, an undifferentiated total of the bishopric's parishioners

TABLE 3.6–2. 1725 Population Totals

Province	Tributarios	Total Population
Abancay	3,083	11,323
Aymares	1,402	5,149
Azángaro	2,805	10,302
Calca y Lares	804	2,953
Canas y Canches	3,683	13,527
Cotabambas	1,460	5,362
Chilques y Masques	1,091	4,007
Chumbibilcas	1,681	6,174
Lampa	4,078	14,978
Marquesado de Oropesa	957	3,625
Paucartambo	1,312	4,819
Quispicanche	3,968	14,574
Total	26,354	96,793

DATA SOURCES: ANP, Tributos, Cuadernos de las provincias del
obispado del Cuzco.

Abancay	Legajo 1, Cuaderno 7, ff. 60–67.
Aymares	Legajo 1, Cuaderno 7, ff. 36–39.
Azángaro	Legajo 1, Cuaderno 6, ff. 79–92.
Calca y Lares	Legajo 1, Cuaderno 6, ff. 149–56.
Canas y Canches	Legajo 2, Cuaderno 21, ff. 1–34.
Cotabambas	Legajo 1, Cuaderno 6, ff. 133–40.
Chilques y Masques	Legajo 1, Cuaderno 13, ff. 144–55.
Chumbibilcas	Legajo 1, Cuaderno 6, ff. 116–28.
Lampa	Legajo 1, Cuaderno 6, ff. 57–78.
Marquesado de Oropesa	Legajo 1, Cuaderno 7, ff. 90–96.
Paucartambo	Legajo 1, Cuaderno 7, ff. 79–82.
Quispicanche	Legajo 1, Cuaderno 6, ff. 116–28.

over "the age of confession," (probably seven years old) is a minimal figure, but compensation for an infant population subject to high mortality rates would not greatly alter the relative position of the data entries or explain this apparent mid-seventeenth-century recovery. Moreover, the value of the 1652 data is undercut by the more detailed provincial and parish totals shown in tables 3.6 and 3.7, which do not demonstrate a general pattern of decline, recovery, and subsequent decline. Input from over three-fourths of the bishopric's ninety-one provincial parishes show

TABLE 3.7. Comparison of Available Parish Population Data for 1676 and 1690

Provinces in Mita Service to:	1676	1690	Percentage of Change	Parishes* Reporting: 1676–1690
Potosí	35,900	25,838	−28.0	27 of 43
Azángaro	9,400	7,542	−19.8	7 of 9
Canas y Canches	6,000	2,379	−60.3	3 of 11
Lampa	15,200	9,390	−38.2	13 of 13
Quispicanche	5,300	6,527	23.2	4 of 10
Guancavelica	16,900	14,073	−16.7	25 of 29
Aymares	12,400	9,540	−23.1	16 of 16
Cotabambas	4,500	4,533	0.7	9 of 13
Local Employers	43,200	23,514	−45.6	17 of 19
Abancay	23,700	13,734	−42.1	9 of 9
Calca y Lares	9,000	4,554	−49.4	4 of 6
Marquesado de Oropesa	10,500	5,226	−50.2	4 of 4
Total	96,000	63,425	−33.9	69 of 91

Data entries and subtotals are found in appendix II, tables IIB1–8.

*This column indicates the number of parishes for which data are available in both census years, compared with the number of parishes in the province in 1690. The figures are, of course, based only on those parishes for which comparative materials are available.

an overall population decline of 33.9 percent in the period from 1676 to 1690[89] (table 3.7).

The 1690 data, more reliable and more specific than the 1652 figures, show that the official Indian population of the bishopric of Cuzco reached its lowpoint much earlier than has been believed. Applying the average rate of forastero representation in 1690 to just those parishes which definitely contained forasteros yields a maximum of 82,367 originarios.[90] The contribution of forasteros to local labor and tribute obligations varied widely, but the economic dislocation and labor shortages resulting from the declining originario population were obvious throughout the Cuzco area, particularly in the late seventeenth century.[91]

The substantial forastero sector is the main reason for the apparent, but deceptive, stability of the total Indian population between 1690 and 1725. The relatively small decline of approximately 10 percent between the data figures of 1690 and 1725 is remarkable, considering the record mortality rates of the 1719 to 1721 period. Contemporary observers believed that between forty thousand and eighty thousand Cuzco Indians died in the epidemics; the acute labor shortage paralyzed the regional economy. At a time when official reports stated that the bishopric had lost over half of its Indian population, the data show a low demographic decline that cannot be explained by however many transients reentered the region after the plague abated in the early 1720s. Rather, the apparently small population loss can be attributed to the nature of the population enrolled in each survey: the assimilated forasteros, who appear in the church's 1690 count of the actual Indian population, represent not a new but a newly counted population block in the official 1720s surveys. The 1690–1725 comparison, which also supports previous assertions that the migrants profiled in the earlier census were assimilated forasteros, reveals the discrepancy between the actual and the official sizes of the indigenous community.

Throughout the sixteenth and seventeenth centuries Cuzco officials were aware of this gap between the official and actual populations, but they could provide no accurate assessment, or even estimate, of the size of the growing migrant sector. Officials were reluctant to recognize the migrants within their jurisdictions and few of the sporadic renumerations of individual communities distinguished between the native-born originarios and the newcomers.[92] The data generated by these surveys were inconsistent and incomplete; usually just the originarios, who were the only Indians legally liable for a community's tax and mita assessments, were included.

The disparity between official and actual population figures, which intensified demands on the remaining originario population, produced some contradictory and ludicrous bureacratic policies. In 1617, at the same session in which the cabildo of Cuzco deplored the decline of the Indian population, its members selected a special envoy to Spain who would plead for more labor allocations to city residents because of the many Indians who were "everywhere" in the nearby provinces.[93] The Duque de Palata expressed his awareness of the discrepancy in population data by advising the King in 1683 "that the Indian towns have been deserted . . . but the Indians have not disappeared."[94] Colonists complained that the entire administrative structure had a vested interest in deliberately hiding the extent of forastero assimilation: "the caciques for their part are the accomplices of the Corregidores and priests in hiding the newcomers and are interested in having even more subjects in their jurisdictions."[95]

Although contemporary historians have not intentionally minimized the extent of the forastero movement, they have not fully recognized the number and role of the assimilated migrants, particularly in the seventeenth century; nor have they effectively analyzed the impact of migration within Indian society as a factor in the decline of the official Indian population. Scholars have cited a number of factors related to the demographic disaster of the conquest period: the "homicide" theory, which "embraces a wide variety of offensive actions against the Indian masses"; the loss of will to survive; the economic and social readjustment; and, of course, disease.[96] During the postconquest period some Indians entered the officially "white" population; thousands of other Indians, including potential tribute payers and mita workers, escaped into the legal haven of mestizo status.[97]

None of the standard demographic theories, however, has given sufficient attention to migration within indigenous society and the development of the assimilated forastero sector as reasons for the reported depopulation of the Andean region. Sánchez-Albornoz has written that "depopulation for which there is a large amount of evidence, was less than census records would suggest, since no one will ever know how many Indians fled beyond the reach of encomenderos and corregidores."[98] That aspect of Indian migration is, however, distinct from those Indians who stayed *within* "the reach of encomenderos and corregidores" but were consistently and consciously omitted from census records. Continuing this interpretation of Indian migration as flight from established indigenous society, Sánchez-Albornoz states that "from a demographic point of view, flight and isolation did not favor reproduction to the same extent as life in a stable society."[99] The forasteros of Cuzco did *not* flee Spanish control, nor did they live in isolation, and the data on town-rural distribution, family size, and child-adult ratio prove that assimilated migrant groups were an important factor in the biological recuperation and reproduction of the Indian population. In the bishopric of Cuzco these forasteros were a key factor in regional demographic fluctuations, which reflect the impact of sustained migration, and in the irregular depopulation of the sierra, which contradicts the prevailing models in Peruvian demographic history.

A NEW MODEL FOR THE DEMOGRAPHIC HISTORY OF COLONIAL CUZCO

A comprehensive analysis of population size, rates of decline, and forastero presence and distribution reveals distinct demographic histories for the major labor zones of the bishopric of Cuzco which contradict and modify the unilateral decline patterns of the prevailing models (tables 3.1, 3.2, 3.3, 3.6, 3.7). In the province of Paucartambo, in which work site and mita zone coincided, the population declined rapidly until the early seventeenth century but thereafter remained constant, at approximately 4,700 Indians. This level was maintained only through the continuous infusion of workers from other regions who remained in Paucartambo after their labor in the coca fields. In 1690 these assimilated forasteros were 100 percent of the sector identified by origin and 73 percent of the province's total population. The discrepancy between actual and official population was potentially highest in this region due to the disappearance of the originario sector and the strong forastero infusion, but a variety of labor relationships secured sufficient Indian workers and obscured the need for a general renumeration and reassessment. The assimilated forasteros made some contributions in the form of payments to the clergy, but in Paucartambo no real attempts were made to reevaluate or to enroll the current population.

In the regions with mita service to local employers the indigenous population declined more slowly in the early and mid-seventeenth century because of lower mita-related mortality and emigration; in some instances the population actually rose through natural increase and immigration, an intermittent recovery which contradicts the established models of uniform and unilateral decline. In spite of periodic labor shortages the discrepancy between the actual and official populations was not critical until the late seventeenth century, when these provinces showed the sharpest rate of decline, in part because the smallpox epidemic of 1687 affected the closely settled originario population more harshly. This region also contained a strong forastero sector which had never been subject to the mita de minas. The Palata reform proposals of the 1680s, which could have forced those Indians with ancestry in mining zones to serve in Potosí or Guancavelica, generated additional population loss through these forasteros' flight.

The provinces with mita service to the mines experienced a rapid decline in the early 1600s, which had abated somewhat by mid-century; as a consequence of the earlier depletion, these areas suffered relatively fewer losses in the 1676–1690 period. Nevertheless, the initial decline in the originario population created a persistent labor shortage, as evidenced by the constant failure of colonial officials to meet labor quotas. The provinces with mita duty in Guancavelica remained in decline, but the population of the area with service to Potosí rose in the 1690–1725 period, in part due to the same circumstances which were responsible for the higher representation of forasteros in that area: the concentration of population and resources in the Cuzco-Potosí corridor and participation in the subsidiary agricultural sector of the Vilcanota-Puno zone.

The different demographic patterns of provinces subject to local service or to the mita de minas can be seen clearly by close examination of three provinces, one from each labor zone: Abancay (local); Aymares (Guancavelica); and Azángaro (Potosí) (table 3.8). The population of Abancay increased 38.8 percent in the 1628–1676 interval, before decreasing dramatically in the 1676–1690 and 1690–1725 cycles, at rates far greater than those of the other two provinces. The Aymares population declined throughout these three subperiods, but at a decreasing rate of change. In Azángaro, where the 1628–1676 decline was probably similar to the decline of 40.3 percent of the other Potosí provinces, the 1676–1690 decrease of 19.8 percent was the smallest cited, and the 1690–1725 period showed a population increase of 18.2 percent.

The general trends of forastero representation are also obvious in the profiles of these three provinces. Abancay contained a strong forastero sector of 40.9 percent, while Azángaro and Aymares displayed the high and low extremes of forastero presence in mita de minas provinces: 100 percent and 15.2 percent, respectively. The former figure reflects the reluctance of forasteros to resettle in areas subject to the mines at Guancavelica; the latter is skewed by the one-input sample, but the comparable figure for all Potosí provinces, 64 percent, indicates the higher forastero presence related to the wage labor and subsidiary economic activity at Potosí. In both mita de minas provinces a majority or near majority of the forasteros resided in towns; only in the provinces with local mita labor and higher originario concentration were forasteros concentrated in the rural area.

TABLE 3.8. Comparison of Provinces from Major Labor Zones

	Abancay Local Mita	Aymares Guancavelica	Azángaro Potosí
Percentage of Total Population Change			
1628–1676	38.8	−72.4	n.a.*
1676–1690	−42.0	−23.1	−19.8
1690–1725	−17.6	−8.7	18.2
Percentage of Forasteros in the Population	40.9	15.2	100.0**
Percentage of Those Forasteros in Town	0.0	64.3	46.6

*Comparative rates for other Potosí provinces: −40.3.
**Based on one data entry. For all provinces to Potosí, the comparable figure is 64.0.
Data sources appear on tables 3.1, 3.2, 3.3, 3.5, and 3.6.

The distinct profiles of regional labor zones and the general seventeenth-century population nadir in the bishopric of Cuzco amend the established models of colonial demographic history and challenge the inherent assumptions concerning the nature of indigenous migration. The impact of Indian migration and forastero assimilation on the population structure of the bishopric is clear. Indians migrated for a variety of reasons, the most important being the impact on indigenous society of incorporation into the colonial economic system. Rather than fleeing to areas beyond Spanish control, migrants were reincorporated into indigenous society wherever their immunity as non-originarios enabled them to exploit the economic opportunities caused by the decimation of the native-born population, even in zones subject to the mita de minas. Most migration was the result of short- and medium-range relocation within the bishopric, including an important urban-to-rural outflow. The forasteros—the original assimilated migrants and their descendants—were a stable sector of indigenous society, comprising as much as one-half of the total sedentary population and displaying balanced family and gender distribution patterns. These forasteros clearly differed from transients; the distinction between forasteros con tierras and forasteros sin tierras developed within indigenous society and was formalized by changes in colonial administrative policy in the 1720s.

The size of this established forastero sector created a tremendous disparity between the actual and official Indian populations, intensifying the demand on the remaining originarios, stimulating further out-migration, and causing periodic labor shortages throughout the Cuzco area. The reassessment of Indian migrants and their reincorporation into official population totals following the epidemics of 1719–1721 lessened the official population loss throughout that period of dramatic demographic decline and actually increased the size of the available *tributario-mitayo* pool by the early eighteenth century.

Within these general demographic parameters, areas of the bishopric of Cuzco showed specific patterns of growth and decline, reflecting the labor obligations of the distinct zones' originarios. Areas subject to the different types of mita displayed chronologically distinct emigration and immigration fluctuations; the size, structure, and distribution of the forastero sector varied as well. Even within the broad category of provinces with mita duty to the mines, the demographic histories of provinces sending laborers to Guancavelica differed sharply from those of provinces with mita obligations to Potosí. Clearly, "those who have left their native towns for others" played a key role in the demographic transformation of the bishopric of Cuzco between 1570 and 1720.

❖ 4 ❖

"El Ayllu Forastero": Migration, Community Structure, and Community Identity

THE SIZE and scope of indigenous migration fundamentally altered the structure and composition of the basic unit of social organization within Andean society—the traditional *ayllu*. Other factors, such as imperial resettlement policies, new political and religious institutions, and Spanish demands for goods, lands, and labor, affected specific aspects of the ayllu's autonomy, redefining or restricting key functions. By the early eighteenth century the traditional ayllu had been transformed from a kin-group whose members enjoyed inherited rights to community lands and labor assistance into an imperial administrative unit, composed of all residents of a given area who were not necessarily linked by familial ties. In many ways the administrative policies of the 1720s which officially redefined ayllu membership reflected changes which had already occurred within indigenous society as the ayllus developed alternative forms of social identification. This structural transformation is epitomized by the emergence of the *ayllu forastero*—literally, a kin-group of strangers.

Although the resiliency and resistance of the ayllus played a key role in the perpetuation of indigenous culture, the structure and function of the ayllu changed dramatically under Spanish rule. One particular aspect of colonial Indian culture—social differentiation within indigenous society—was deeply affected by the impact of migration on the surviving ayllus. Identification by ayllu membership or affiliation continued throughout the colonial period, but the loss of originarios and the influx of forasteros had a devastating impact on community structure and ties. Although indigenous migration initially helped preserve particular aspects of preconquest society, it ultimately contributed significantly to the transformation of the traditional ayllu.

74

The pre-Incan Andean ayllus had already been substantially altered by their incorporation into the empire of Manco Capac and Pachacuti. The expansion of Incan control and the emergence of distinct social groups within the empire had initiated a process of differentiation by degree of obligation to the state. This incipient transformation from a "tribal-communal" to a "tribal-tributary" society, from an egalitarian to an hierarchical order, was interrupted by the arrival of the Europeans, who superimposed their own structure onto the traditional communities.[1] Throughout the colonial period social identity and access to economic resources within Indian society would, by law, continue to be determined by kin-group membership. However, the impact of the colonial system on the ayllus, chiefly the reassimilation of thousands of indios forasteros, reshaped the traditional Andean communities so that membership in some ayllus was determined by access to the means of production. The emergence of the forastero sector and its reincorporation into indigenous society were not the final step in the transformation of Andean social organization. However, they do constitute the initial, critical cycle in the prolonged transformation from caste to class in Andean America.

THE DEVELOPMENT OF THE AYLLU

That transformation was once obscured by early scholars' emphasis on the "seemingly great survival value" and "singular tenacity and stability" of the ayllus.[2] Because of the tremendous adaptability and endurance of communal life, the first analyses assumed a continuity of internal structure and function, a thesis which achieved its extreme expression in a definition of the ayllu as "the fundamental social group common to all Andean societies, great and small, ancient and modern."[3] Other definitions of the ayllu also drew heavily on observations of contemporary ayllus[4], an approach that has been emphatically renounced by Karen Spalding, who argued for a definition of the ayllu based on historical evidence, not one derived by observations of modern communities. Citing Indian myths, colonial dictionaries, and other documentary evidence, Spalding concluded that in the sixteenth century "any group whose members were regarded as 'of the same kind' could be called an ayllu."[5] This sense of unity and linkage has been interpreted by scholars in vastly different ways that emphasize specific economic, political, or cultural features of the ayllu. George Kubler's perception of the community as "the repository and the unit cell of Quechua 'culture'" contrasts sharply with Nathan Wachtel's image of "an endogamous core group which gathers together a certain number of lineages, with collective possession of a clearly identified territory."[6] The current understanding of the ayllu as "formally an endogamous lineage claiming descent from a common ancestor," the basic unit of Andean indigenous society, represents the latest and best attempt to simplify and to reconcile the confusing and contradictory definitions which once prompted Bernard Mishkin to question the validity of "that mysterious, almost unidentifiable concept—the ayllu."[7]

Judging from the controversy surrounding the nature and origin of the ayllu, Mishkin may be right to suggest abandoning the concept. The pre-Incan ayllu, and particularly its internal structure and its patterns of descent, have been the subject of such contradictory and complementary studies that it would be easier, if facile, to adopt the legendary Aymaran belief that "the various ayllus emerged from caves, mountain peaks, lakes, and rivers."[8] It is impossible here to resolve the issues of the origin and nature of kinship linkages and it is unnecessary to do so in order to identify the most important characteristic of the pre-Incan ayllu: linkage through common ancestry which conferred access to communal property and reciprocal labor assistance. Common land holdings not only provided the means of subsistence but also symbolized ayllu unity. Kin ties were also implicit in the individual's right to claim labor assistance through the system of reciprocity, in which each ayllu member owed varying types and amounts of services to others by virtue of their common affiliation. Such reciprocity within a community was paralleled by understandings between ayllu groups.[9]

The rights and obligations of members of pre-Incan ayllus were exemplified in the duties of the *mitmaq*—rotating groups of Indians living in different, vertically defined, ecological zones for the purpose of securing resources not available at the home community. While supplying this vital service, the mitmaq retained full ayllu status, and lands allocated for the support of their households were cultivated by the remaining residents.[10]

Community members owed additional labor services to the headman, whose chief duties included the administration and allocation of ayllu lands. The relationship between these headmen and the *kurakas*, or chiefs, some of whom could command the allegiance of more than one ayllu, was a complicated one. An ayllu was theoretically governed by all adult male members; administration was in the hands of temporary, designated officials, such as the headman or the *sinchi*, an elected wartime leader. Expanding ayllu size, increased economic activities, or constant regional political tension led to the emergence of a permanent hereditary leadership whose position would be amplified and solidified under Incan rule.[11]

When Manco Capac, legendary founder of the Inca Dynasty, marched down the banks of the Vilcanota River to take control of the valley of Cuzco, he found the area occupied by three indigenous ayllus. In a series of fierce battles the Inca, his brothers, and his sisters defeated the Hualla, the Sawasuay, and the Alcahuiza and established his capital city.[12] In their rapid expansion throughout the Andean sierra, later Inca conquerors continued to subjugate native communities by adapting and adopting for imperial use the existing social and political structures. The eleven royal ayllus created for the families of emperors were organized on traditional Andean kin-lines of patrilineal descent from a common ancestor.[13] The Inca converted the emerging kuraka elite into a powerful, hereditary leadership which transmitted commands, supervised labor services to the state, and maintained order. Mitmaq became the model for imperial colonies founded to protect strategic locations or to replace rebellious populations who were moved to securer regions of the empire. Even the formation of the *yana* labor group, customarily identified as an Incan innovation, may be considered an attempt to reconstruct on the imperial level the personal-service relationship between the headman and his community.[14]

The Incas recognized the traditional ayllus as the basic units of social organization throughout the sierra but significantly altered the structure and function of these communities. Although the ayllu retained some of its pre-Incan characteristics—principally the communal allocation of resources and reciprocity of labor—its essential consanguineous nature was threatened by the Inca practice of relocating conquered communities or concentrating local populations into villages.

Other imperial practices further weakened ayllu autonomy. The Inca system of "hundreds" divided the population into new administrative groups independent of ayllu structures: the *pachaka* (groups of 100 tributary households), the *waranga* (groups of 1,000 households), and the *hunu* (groups of 10,000 households). Enforcement of the comprehensive Inca code of justice took precedence over local mores. Universal recognition of the seniority of the Sun God demanded the subordination of a community's own deities.[15]

Once the superiority of the state had been established, however, ayllus were granted substantial local authority. In the new villages and towns, ayllus were assigned to specific neighborhoods or to housing compounds governed by the traditional leadership. Although politically subordinated to Incan administrative units, the ayllus retained responsibility for key functions, such as the military draft.[16] Local social customs or religious practices which did not conflict with Inca law or doctrine were allowed to continue.

Most significantly, the ayllus maintained control over marriage, which continued along established endogamous lines. Although no betrothal could be regarded as binding until certified by the imperial government, the selection of marriage partners remained an internal process conducted in accordance with local customs.[17] This self-determination of community membership through regulation of marriage was the main defense against the external pressures threatening to transform the ayllu from a kin-group with common ancestry into a village with communal lands.

Control over ayllu membership also was important because access to land continued to be achieved through community affiliation. However, the Incan conquest resulted in a fundamental change in the concept of property because the community was alienated from its lands even though it retained hereditary access to those lands through the labor of community members. The seventeenth-century Spanish historian Bernabé Cobo described this process: "When the Inca settled a town, or reduced one to obedience, he set up markers on its boundaries and divided the fields and arable land within its territory into three parts, in the following way. One part he assigned to Religion and the cult of his false gods, another he took for himself, and the third he left for the common use of the people. . . ."

According to Cobo, "The third part of the land, assigned to the people according to the division above, was in the manner of commons, it being understood that the land was the property of the Inca, and the community only had the usufruct of it."[18] Community members paid their reciprocal obligations to the state through labor on the fields allocated for the support of the Inca emperor and the gods. Cobo explained that "the labor of sowing and cultivating these lands and harvesting their products formed a large part of the tribute which the taxpayer paid the king."[19] Additional tribute was extracted in the form of *mit'a*, compulsory services for the benefit of the state, *Tawantinsuyu*, which John Murra claims were regarded as a natural outgrowth of *mitachanacuy*, a specific form of inner-community labor exchange.[20] Despite the profound changes in the nature of property and reciprocity, local economic activity continued to be conducted and understood in the traditional context of access to land and labor assistance through ayllu membership.

THE AYLLU UNDER SPANISH RULE

The arrival of the Spaniards and the drastic reordering of the Andean economy challenged, and in some instances destroyed, the continuity of ayllu functions. The Spaniards claimed the land assigned to the Inca and the Sun God for their King and Church and divided local communal lands into private holdings, further transforming the nature of property. The demand for goods as well as services altered distribution patterns as contributions to the state took precedence over local needs. Changes in relationships of production led Indians into new fields, such as *obraje* labor in textile workshops. Forced compliance with the expanded mit'a, now called *mita*, violated established patterns of reciprocity and effectively eliminated inner-community work assistance; the distances traveled by participants in the *mita de minas* to Bolivia further reduced the ayllu's control over member labor. Incorporation into a cash economy altered the Indians' perceptions of the value of goods and services and frequently required their participation in the market system or their employment as wage laborers.

From the earliest years of this transformation, the ayllu was identified, and valued, as a convenient unit for organizing the extraction of goods and services from Indian society. The sixteenth-century chronicler Pedro Sarmiento de Gamboa gave the most common Spanish interpretation of indigenous social organization when he listed the names of "ten tribes or *ayllus*, which means among these barbarians 'lineages' or 'parties'."[21] The Spaniards realized that members of an ayllu shared kin ties, but were unaware of the exact nature of the relationship involved. Nor did the Europeans understand that the ayllu's ability to conduct its rapidly contracting economic activities would be affected by changes in its internal organization.

The ayllu's control over its diminished resources was further complicated when the Spaniards altered traditional power relationships by imposing new layers of authority and by modifying the preconquest position of the kuraka. The new administrative offices in the civil and ecclesiastical sectors created opposing centers of power within Indian communities. However, patterns of traditional authority survived, parallel to the official system, limiting the effectiveness of the new positions and insuring that power was held by individuals with legitimate rights. Village elders were elected to the new *cabildo de indios*, the town council composed of the *alcalde* (or mayor), his assistants, and the town constables; guardians of traditional deities doubled as sacristans of the local church.[22]

In addition to establishing new leadership positions, the Spanish authorities maintained the preconquest authority of the kurakas, expanding their role to include the collection of cash tribute payments and the organization of the expanded mita system. These duties made a kuraka personally responsible for his community's obligations to the state. With the added advantage of inherited claims on ayllu goods and services, the local leaders enjoyed tremendous economic opportunities which, at least initially, outweighed the risk of bankruptcy and imprisonment for debt.[23]

Economic power and social prestige made the *cacigazgos*, or chiefdoms, highly coveted positions. Spanish law awarded these posts to Indians who could prove direct patrilineal descent from at least three generations of kurakas, a policy that occasionally barred legitimate claimants from communities where local practice differed from the norm.[24] Enforcement of the rule of primogeniture led to complicated court battles in situations that would never have arisen under the less rigid traditional succession practices; the need to replace an incompetent official with his younger brother could simply have been avoided by awarding the title to the more competent man in the first place.[25] The disruption of traditional authority patterns and the assault on ayllu autonomy were particularly severe in the Cuzco area. As the administrative capital of Andean Peru, the city was the site of intensified Indo-European interaction, which caused the most drastic drop in Indian population in the sierra. Increased disease transference, rapid alienation of Indian lands, and the ravages of the civil wars all contributed to the shrinking size and internal dislocation of Cuzco ayllus.

Imperial regulations also affected the size and composition of ayllu membership by diminishing the importance of kinship ties. The late-sixteenth-century Toledo *reducciones,* or settlements, subdivided larger ayllus and separated communities which previously had been closely linked in reciprocity. These reducciones were a severe blow to ayllu autonomy, but the end of endogamous marriage patterns had much graver consequences for Indian society. Reduced ayllu populations and church regulations restricting marriage between blood relatives soon forced many Indians to seek partners from outside their home communities. Although a majority of the ceremonies performed during the late seventeenth-century in the parish of Yucay, Marquesado de Oropesa, followed the traditional patterns, a substantial minority of Indians married outside their ayllus.[26] The certification of marriages had become the province of the Catholic Church, allowing for marriage contracted without community approval or knowledge. Clergy conducting ceremonies involving a forastero were expected to solicit a "license of liberty to marry" from the migrant's parish priest, but seventeenth-century church regulations required no proof of family or ayllu consent:

> for the marriage of indios forasteros, if the betrothed came from within twenty leagues surrounding the vicarage, an order must be sent to their own priests, so that they may publish the banns of marriage and upon receiving certification that there exists no impediment, the Indians shall be married by the priest in whose jurisdiction they currently reside. But if the betrothed Indians are natives of sites more then twenty leagues distant, it is necessary to receive proof of their freedom to marry and having verified the report, a license will be issued, so that the priest in whose jurisdiction they currently reside may marry them.[27]

In 1695 the incumbent of Curaguasi, Abancay, was rebuked by the ecclesiastical council of Cuzco because he had married two foreign-born Indians without asking for their priests' permission. Church authorities were not concerned that the couple had eloped because a village elder had tried to arrange a traditional match between the woman and his son.[28] The primary issue for the Church was compliance with canon law, not ayllu autonomy.

Although the form and function of the traditional Andean ayllu changed greatly during the colonial period, ayllu membership remained the most important means of social differentiation within the indigenous community; the hierarchical ranking of ayllus by age, wealth, or other local criteria superseded the imposed *reducción* structure. Ayllu designations disappeared from documentation *not* because indigenous society had abandoned its internal structure based on membership in or affiliation with an ayllu, but because royal officials considered ayllu identification unimportant. In spite of regulations demanding that workers be identified by ayllu, *parcialidad,* and town, the bureaucrats administering the mita were satisfied if "the Indians name their provinces and repartimientos, even though they omit their ayllus, which are the least important."[29] In a report prepared for the 1690 ecclesiastical census the parish priest of Urubamba, Marquesado de Oropesa, failed to identify his Indian parishioners by ayllu affiliation; other documents compiled that same year show that allocation of land for individual use was conducted by Urubamba's kurakas according to the local ayllus' *libros de repartación,* official lists of the ayllus' members.[30] Other population summaries prepared for the 1690 census reflected the persistent divisions of local Indians into "parcialities, which in their language are called ayllus." At the end of the colonial period Indians still regarded themselves as members of ayllus.[31]

Membership in these ayllus, however, was no longer solely the result of birthright. The composition of ayllus had altered substantially, due to confrontation with the colonial system and internal and external pressures resulting from the loss of ayllu members and the appearance of social groups not present in traditional Andean society—groups which were permanently relocated in local communities without necessarily belonging to those communities' established ayllus: *yanaconas,* particularly those in service to private individuals; forcibly resettled mitmaq; and assimilated forasteros. All of these groups initially contributed to the preservation of indigenous society by remaining within the Indian sector, and some supported local ayllus with goods and labor assistance; ultimately, however, they threatened the solidarity and the survival of local ayllus which were forced to accept the presence of nonmembers on traditional ayllu lands.

THE YANACONA AND THE MITMAQ

The first of these social groups, the yanacona sector, grew steadily throughout the colonial period. By the mid-seventeenth century there were an estimated 25,000 yanaconas in the Viceroyalty of Peru. Some were *yanaconas del Rey,* who had been formally enrolled in reducciones, but many were *yanaconas de españoles,* working on the private estates of

Europeans or the Indian elite, where they enjoyed reduced taxation and exemption from labor service.[32] The impact on the mita was disastrous. Officials at Potosí did not hesitate to attribute their labor shortages to the yanaconas, "who are particularly responsible for this damage because they have voluntarily chosen this lazy status [*yanaconaje*] and they are lost to the mita."[33]

Francisco de Toledo had hoped to control the size of the yanacona sector by strictly limiting yanacona de español status to Indians who could document their claim to that right. He and his successors failed miserably, their efforts resisted by Spaniard and Indian alike.[34] Not all yanacona labor was voluntary, as seen in the passionate appeal for help received by the bishop of Cuzco in 1705 from one Indian who complained that "my employer has held me in his power and in servitude since my birth, more than twelve years ago, simply because my parents were his yanaconas and I was born on his hacienda." Nevertheless, most available documentation indicates that Indians actively sought yanacona status.[35]

The problem was particularly acute in the Cuzco area, where Toledo had originally identified an unusually high yanacona presence and where the rapid growth of the haciendas, which sought yanacona labor, was sustained throughout the seventeenth century. The documentation available in the city's notarial archives is not indicative of the total size of the yanacona sector, because the contracts negotiated in the urban labor market were probably the last resort of landowners coping with local labor shortages. However, these agreements contain valuable information about a labor relationship so universally understood that the brief job description "to serve as a yanacona" was sufficient to express the functions and responsibilities of both the employer and the laborer involved.[36]

The specific provisions of the yanaconas' contracts display a uniformity lacking in those of other agricultural workers, particularly with regard to average duration (both mean and mode), additional proof of the regularity of this occupation. The only yanacona contracts covering less than twelve months of service were signed before 1650, indicating that the alienation of community lands during the widespread forced sales of the 1630s and 1640s may have regularized as well as expanded this labor sector. Average wage rates for yanaconas were the highest in the agricultural sector, perhaps reflective of greater or more varied demands. More yanaconas also received cash advances, although at a lower proportion of total wages. The frequency of such advances—from 80 to 88 percent—

suggests a high potential for these labor agreements to evolve into a form of debt peonage, particularly where the total compensation was prepaid. Although most agricultural workers were guaranteed food and clothing at their employers' expense, yanaconas were more likely to receive these commodities. The most important distinction in the yanaconas' contracts, however, was the increased availability of land for personal use, particularly after 1650.[37]

The yanaconas' special relationship with the land played a critical role in changes within the sector during the seventeenth century. Although the inclusion of Indians in land transfers or wills was outlawed in 1601, yanaconas were often "recommended" to new landowners or "commended" to beneficiaries' care.[38] The system was open to obvious abuse, but offered the yanacona some security through protection from the mita and access to land. The *composiciones de tierras* of the 1630s and 1640s, which limited the traditional communities' capacity to absorb newcomers, intensified the yanaconas' dependence on their employers' resources. By the late 1680s, when the Duque de Palata attempted to reform the colonial labor system, "yanacona" had acquired a new connotation and the relationship of service to a landowner had been transformed into one of affiliation with his land. In 1680 a Reál Cédula emphasized that "those who are called yanaconas . . . voluntarily have tied themselves to the charcas and the haciendas in the countryside."[39] The title "yanacona" was first modified by and then replaced by the adjective *agregado,* or attached, emphasizing the linkage of laborer to land. In a parallel development the number of yanaconas agregados receiving plots of land as part of the compensation specified in labor contracts increased throughout the late seventeenth century. In Palata's 1687 *Aranzel* of labor regulations, agregados were guaranteed access to land as a condition of employment.[40] The severe labor shortage following the plague of 1720 initiated a new stage in the development of yanaconaje, as landowners consistently and explicitly offered both access to land and protection from mita and taxation as incentives to all workers. By the late eighteenth century most of the Indians working on haciendas had assumed these features of yanacona status.[41]

The increasing security and stability of yanacona status has usually been considered a strong impetus to Indian migration, but the relationship between these two important features of colonial society is more complex than generally depicted. The initial linkage of yanaconas and migration was made in 1560 by Juan de Matienzo when he wrote that "there are in this kingdom other Indians called yanaconas because they or their parents left the settlement or province of their birth to live with and to serve Spaniards." Subsequent observers have accepted and amplified Matienzo's observations, so that physical relocation in a distant region has become an almost mandatory feature of any definition of "yana" or "yanacona."[42] Traditional analyses have consistently identified yanacona service on a Spaniard's estate as the principal—or even the only—destination of Indian migrants remaining within the rural zone. The hereditary status of yanaconas has been minimized or ignored, so that "uprooting, flight, [and] forced migration" have been identified as the origin of the yanacona sector of the seventeenth and eighteenth centuries.[43]

Equating yanaconas and migrants is too simplistic an approach to the complex relationship of these two sectors. The reduced obligations of the yanaconas were a strong impetus for relocation and the growing number of Indians who illegally assumed yanacona status contained many migrants who had abandoned their reducciones. But to claim that yanaconas severed all linkages with their kurakas or ayllus is too strong; to insist on the physical separation, typical of the conquest era, rather than social or spiritual alienation, is to ignore the diversity of linkages within indigenous communities.

A 1653 survey of yanaconas and mita laborers on a Spaniard's estate near Quiquijana, Quispicanche, demonstrates that yanacona status did not always entail severing ties with home ayllus. Fifteen Indians worked on the estate: nine *mitayos* from the local ayllus and six yanaconas. Three of the yanaconas were from the city of Cuzco, two from the nearby town of Oropesa, and one from Quiquijana. All six of the yanaconas recognized the authority of kurakas from their home communities; the originario of Quiquijana clearly retained his ayllu identification and remained under the jurisdiction of the same kuraka who governed the mitayos from his kin-group.[44] Nor did yanacona service require permanent removal to an hacienda: although the potential for debt peonage increased in the late seventeenth century, most of the contracts governing yanacona labor covered specific, limited time periods, and on the coast of Peru "*yanacona* usually meant an agricultural laborer hired by the year."[45] Recognizing this type of yanacona status, some colonial authorities believed that new yanaconas had altered little more than their physical appearance, "changing their traditional clothing and adopting that of the yanaconas."[46] Although the authorities failed to comprehend the significance of this transition from traditional to colonial culture, administrators were probably correct in assuming that some yanaconas were living in the vicinity of their original reducciones. Rather than being simply the consequence of Indian migration, the growth of the yanacona sector must also be seen as an alternative to migration: a compromise which enabled originarios to maintain some linkages with their home ayllus while engaging in temporary wage-sector employment, or which allowed locally assimilated forasteros to accumulate cash to satisfy their adopted communities' demands.

In contrast to the varied and ambiguous status of individual yana-conas, the mitmaq—the descendants of Indians sent from one locale to another on a seasonal or permanent basis—retained a distinct, collective identity which isolated them from neighboring ayllus. In pre-Incan Andean societies these colonists resided temporarily in ecological zones which supplied resources unavailable in their home environment, re-taining their ayllu membership and inherent rights to land and labor as-sistance.[47] Under the Incan Empire this temporary service was adapted and expanded into permanent relocation for the *mitimas*, with whole families removed from their ayllus in order to serve the state.[48] Soon after the Spanish conquest the chronicler Pedro Cieza de León identi-fied two main reasons for forced resettlement: frontier defense and pacification of subjugated areas. The first and less significant category consisted of soldiers in garrisons on the eastern slopes of the Andes; the latter group, the relocated settlers, played a critical role in the Incan attempt to stabilize and unify the empire. To establish political control and ensure the loyalty of the recently subdued regions, the Incas ordered the removal of whole communities and their replacement by a similar number of families from the center of the empire. These mitimas usually severed their ties with home ayllus and accepted the political authority of new local rulers.[49]

Some of the mitmaq appear to have continued the pre-Incan practice of securing specific commodities, but for imperial rather than local distribution: expanding the cultivation of maize to supply high-altitude communities was one such mitmaq function. Individual ayllus were allowed to continue their traditional patterns of resource procurement only with the approval of imperial authorities. Under the Incas the designation "mitmaq" was not applied to Indians on this temporary service. The Spaniards, however, interpreted the word to mean trans-ported or moved as well as to designate "newcomers" or "outsiders."

During the pre-Toledo period these terms were frequently applied to any Indian physically separated from an ancestral ayllu.[50] In a major misinterpretation of preconquest practices the Europeans considered all mitmaq to have been permanently removed from their ayllus and officials defined these Indians as natives of their place of residence. In the mid-sixteenth century hundreds of mitmaq fled to their home communities from assigned settlements in the vicinity of Amaybamba, Vilcabamba, a strategic Inca outpost in the Urubamba River valley, but the creation of the reducciones would outlaw such large-scale returns.[51]

In the 1570s Francisco de Toledo resettled both temporary absentees and permanent mitmaq into repartimientos, or administrative units, near their current residences, not their home communities. Indians in these sectors and their descendants were labeled "mitmaq" or "mitimaes" as reported by Bernabé Cobo, the seventeenth-century historian: "To all of these people who . . . had remained in the lands where we find them, we also give now the name of *mitimaes* without distinguishing them from the first ones, the only people that were *mitimaes* at the time of the Incas."[52] Establishing these temporary mitmaq far from their home was a strong and immediate impetus for illegal Indian migration; in addition, the practice created subgroups within the reducciones which were alienated from their important kin-based networks. The permanent mitmaq settlers and their descendants were also isolated from local ayllus. Although cultural homogeneity had been a major goal of the Incan settlements, Cobo reported that Incan mitmaq had been permitted to retain "the dress, emblems, and symbols" of their home communities. In 1653 Cobo recorded that "this custom has been preserved up to the present time, for even now on the basis of the aforementioned things, we can distinguish between the natives of each town and the mitimaes."[53]

Other observers attested to the perpetuation of the mitmaq sector and its distinct role within indigenous communities. In 1621 Viceroy Príncipe de Esquilache stated that the mitmaq were "considered to be strangers by the other Indians"; to support this opinion, Esquilache cited one example of contrasting mitmaq and originario customs: "The distinction is most actively maintained, and can be seen in the difference with which they build their chimneys, more accurately called stovepipes, because the Mitmaq decorate theirs with a hanging, curved design and the originarios use an erect, straight one."[54] Tax records compiled by Spaniards in the 1580s demonstrate the original distinctions between mitmaq and the originarios of Nasca; mid-seventeenth-century petitions initiated by Indians provide additional, explicit evidence of the durability of mitmaq identification. Both the kurakas of the "repartimiento of the mitmaq de Guadachirí, settled in the town of Santa Cruz de Guamantambo," and "Diego Napa Guaraca, kuraka of the mitmaq Indians of Andaguaylas, settled in the town of Pampaconba, Abancay," regarded themselves and their followers as discrete sectors within their local communities.[55] Although forcibly resettled mitmaq were probably more numerous and more important during the early colonial periods, they remained an intrusive presence in Indian villages throughout the seventeenth century.

THE AYLLU FORASTERO

The presence of the mitmaq and the yanaconas was a clear threat to local ayllus' authority and autonomy. However, the most significant changes within the traditional Indian community occurred through the reintegration of the thousands of *indios forasteros* who wanted to remain within indigenous society. These migrants were reintegrated into Indian society through a variety of community-determined mechanisms. If the newcomers were descendants of mitmaq colonists or ayllu members separated from the community by Spanish resettlement regulations, the adjustment would be a relatively simple one. Incorporation of unrelated Indians who sought communal identification, access to land, and labor assistance was a more complicated process, as migrants forged links with original residents through marriage into existing ayllus, submission to local kurakas, or the development of an ayllu forastero.

The simplest way for a migrant to join an established community was to marry into the ayllu, with the approval of its elders. As the spouse of a local resident or as a *sobrina/o* (niece/nephew-in-law) of an ayllu, the newcomer was guaranteed access to depopulated or abandoned community lands. The male forastero's position with respect to tribute and mita demands was an ambivalent one and depended on a variety of factors, chiefly the amount of his new ayllu's obligations, the distance from his home community, and the personality and persistence of all the kurakas involved. Migrants who thought that they had found sanctuary in another Indian community could be forced to flee again if their arrangements with local officials were disrupted.[56]

In return for access to land and relative economic security the immigrant had to acknowledge the inherited authority of local kurakas and elders and to accept a subordinate position within the ayllu. In a society where traditional leadership lines had been bent but not broken, few sobrinos ever achieved the position of *mandón*, or ruler, held by Don Diego de Rojas, who married into the severely depopulated ayllu of Andamarcas, San Juan de los Sancos. Any forastero designated a kuraka might have been chosen for totally nontraditional reasons. A kuraka's inability to meet tribute obligations or failure to satisfy mita quotas was punishable by imprisonment and confiscation of personal property. As a parish priest explained in 1689, "there is no Indian who wants to be kuraka, because of the problems to be faced in the fulfillment of the different obligations; and the corregidores and their assistants force the richest Indian to take this office, to serve as kuraka of these ayllus, even though he may not be an originario of the town."[57]

The newly created political offices were also usually held by originarios, but forasteros served as alcaldes in the depopulated town of Paucarcolla and filled all administrative positions in communities where migrants had totally replaced native-born Indians. Church posts offered more possibility for advancement, and some talented migrants earned recognition as *cantores*, or musicians.[58]

Individuals who resented these restrictions, or who could not or would not marry local residents, obtained direct access to land through share-cropping, rental, or purchase. After the forced sale of "vacant" Indian lands in the 1640s severely limited the capacity of established ayllus to accommodate migrants on community lands, the most secure and comprehensive method of reintegration was through membership in an ayllu forastero. The notation "ayllu forastero" after an Indian's name has usually been interpreted as indicating ignorance of the individual's home community; subsequent references to groups of migrants have lacked details of their origin, structure, or function. However, an analysis of parish records from Yucay, Marquesado de Oropesa, shows that Yucay's ayllu forastero was an artificially created but self-perpetuating social group which, during the course of the seventeenth century, acquired or developed the economic, social, and political functions characteristic of the transformed Indian ayllu under Spanish colonialism. The emergence of this "kin-group of strangers" was a major development in the redefinition of ayllu membership and represents an advance in the transition from caste to class in Andean society.

The forasteros who settled in the vicinity of Yucay in the late sixteenth and early seventeenth centuries were initially unincorporated migrants who rented lands from established ayllus and paid fees to parish priests for the administration of sacraments, in compliance with standard church regulations concerning non-native residents.[59] Local kurakas, who preferred to rent vacant land to Spaniards or *mestizos* with higher social and legal status, made no effort to link the forasteros to their community. The parish priests of Yucay, involved in continual jurisdictional disputes with their counterparts from the neighboring village of Urubamba, organized the forasteros under the leadership of a special *alcalde de forasteros*, who guaranteed that migrants would attend—and pay for—catechism classes and mass. In 1618, arguing for the unity of physical and spiritual authority, the clergy of Yucay sought and received from the ecclesiastical council of Cuzco a pronouncement barring the parish priest of Urubamba from entering the disputed lands.[60]

Under the leadership of the alcalde de forasteros (a post rapidly subordinated to the cabildo de indios, or town council, of Yucay) the migrants were increasingly incorporated into local religious, political, and economic life. By the mid-seventeenth century changes in the relationship between the native-born Indians of Yucay and the forastero community had given the latter all the features of an established ayllu. In addition to the alcalde, senior councilors were elected for the forasteros by the same cabildo de indios which chose other local officials. The mayor and his assistants were recognized by the provincial *corregidor*, who bestowed on them the distinctive *varas*, or staffs, symbolizing their authority.[61] Increasing church revenue through enforced attendance at mass was no longer the alcalde's chief duty. Instead of paying the fees usually charged non-originarios for specific religious services, the Yucay forasteros made regular contributions to the priests' salaries, which were administered by the Marqués de Oropesa.[62] His Excellency's agents collected additional cash from the forasteros; payments to village kurakas increasingly had been diverted to meet community obligations and by 1650 were recognized as tribute, not rent.[63] Forasteros participated in the local labor draft and public work projects, helping to maintain the bridge at Guayllabamba.[64] By 1653, when the current incumbent of the parish of Urubamba reopened the jurisdictional dispute, the well-organized forastero community of Yucay was exercising the major functions of the ayllu under the Spanish imperial system: control of the local political structures; maintenance of order; regulation of labor and collection of goods for state and church; determination of access to land; and participation in mita and communal labor.

The renewal of litigation was marked by reams of redundant testimony and wild countercharges. The parish priest of Yucay was accused of neglecting his duties because of illness; his partisans filed more lurid charges against the incumbent of Urubamba: kidnapping the alcalde de forasteros, administering the sacraments covertly to Yucay residents, and directing parishioners to steal the bodies of Yucay's dead for burial in Urubamba.[65] Echoing the framework of the 1618 decision, the Urubamba incumbent maintained that the obraje of Quispiguanca and the farmlands of Paca and Chichobamba were within the jurisdiction of his parish; he claimed all resident forasteros or descendants of forasteros as his parishioners. Determining actual physical boundaries was complicated by the Marqués de Oropesa's attempts to emphasize his own seniority in the province by outlawing traditional ceremonies that identified the ravine dividing the two villages: "when they went to the town of Urubamba, the mayors of the villa of Yucay carried their staffs erect until they came to the stream; and there they left their staffs, and entered without them into Urubamba; and the mayors of Urubamba, when they went to Yucay, left their staffs in their houses."[66] The reenactment of this ritual and the close inspection of community records proved conclusively that the disputed farmlands had been incorporated into Yucay in 1627. Witnesses testified that not only were the lands in question originally the property of the ayllu Paca, Yucay, but that the Indians residing in Paca and Chichobamba were completely distinct from those in the obraje because "the indios forasteros who farm those plots, in contrast to the indios forasteros in the obraje . . . have always acknowledged the church of this villa of Yucay as their parish."[67]

The priest of Urubamba continued to press for jurisdiction over two groups of Indians: residents in the obraje which he had been serving on a regular basis, and natives of Urubamba who had moved to Yucay and had joined the forasteros or other ayllus.[68] The 1655 mandate of the Cuzco officials was a compromise: the clergy of Urubamba could continue to administer the sacraments to obraje workers, but all Indians permanently settled on the disputed lands were to be considered parishioners and members of Yucay.[69]

Due to the confusing and conflicting ayllu status of short-range migrants, the complex problem of the Urubamba-born residents of Yucay was the subject of extensive litigation. In successive appeals continuing into the eighteenth century the Urubamba clerics switched tactics, claiming that the determination of physical territory was irrelevant because spiritual authority took precedence over secular jurisdiction.[70] The Yucay priests were perfectly willing to support this theory but asserted that the Indians in question were members of their own physical and religious community.[71] When the ecclesiastical council of Cuzco announced that spiritual membership would be the deciding factor in determining a parish's official size—and its priest's salary—the incumbent of Yucay had only to present his official registers, complete with periodic certification by visiting bishops of Cuzco.

Within these parish records information about each ayllu was recorded separately. The entries pertaining to the established ayllu forastero were clearly distinct from those concerning transient indios forasteros. The ayllu forastero was a cohesive, self-perpetuating unit; most ayllu forastero males inherited rather than acquired their ayllu identification and a majority of marriages involving ayllu forastero grooms entered this group.

The ayllu forastero did absorb some foreign-born Indians, but most of these migrants married into other groups, primarily the yanacona sector. The desirability, or necessity, of acquiring land and labor assistance through advantageous marriages was reflected in the fact that no foreign-born male residing in Yucay married a foreign-born female. Consistent with village patterns, the inner-marriage rate for the ayllu forastero members was high, although not at the level of other Yucay ayllus.[72] The lower inner-ayllu marriage rate and the parallel tendency of foreign-born Indians to marry into other ayllus may indicate that the ayllu forastero members had a slightly lower status within their community. Kinship groups within a village were often ranked by age or wealth,[73] and the recently formed ayllu forastero of Yucay would score low in both categories. Conversely, the figures could merely be reflecting a sex-ratio imbalance, with a surplus of females in the older ayllus. Neither interpretation detracts from the obvious significance of the administrative powers, economic activities, and labor obligations of the ayllu forastero, the artificially created ayllu which had acquired a structure and function identical to those of the established Yucay kin-groups.

THE FORMATION OF COLONIAL INDIAN CULTURE

The ayllu forastero of Yucay represents the most dramatic and significant changes that occurred when the added pressure from extensive Indian migration led to the development of alternative forms of ayllu affiliation and the redefinition of community membership as a function of an individual's access to local resources. The presence of assimilated migrants, mitmaq, and yanacona generated new forms of social identification and status within Indian communities.[74] Because this social system was clearly affected by both indigenous tradition and by Spanish laws and attitudes, it represents the syncretic fusion of indigenous heritage and Spanish influence that created colonial Indian culture. An analysis of that cultural transformation is not the purpose of this study, which assumes the emergence of a context in which " 'being an Indian' meant not just the place in the colonial social hierarchy assigned to them by Spanish laws and regulations . . . [but also] a way of living, a way of looking at the world and defining one's place in it."[75] Instead, this study seeks to identify the role of migration in the formation of colonial Indian culture and in the European-Indian interaction essential to the process.

The study of the transformation of indigenous culture has changed radically since 1960, when Frank Tannenbaum summarized the prevailing model of a total separation of the Indian and the European: "Between these two races no effective means of understanding . . . was ever found. They met as billiard balls do on a billiard table. They met but did not penetrate."[76] Four years later Henry Dobyns condemned this approach, which "assumed Indigenous Community culture to be a unitary and an Indian culture, surviving largely intact from preconquest times." Dobyns's argument did not immediately prevail; that same year Marvin Harris advocated an extreme, opposing interpretation of total acculturation, particularly with regard to religious practices, arguing that "to talk about aboriginal survivals in this context is clearly out of the question."[77] Yet less than a decade later, Andeanists *were* talking about "aboriginal survivals" in that context; the debate over cultural separation versus total assimilation had focused rapidly on the survival of preconquest values and practices. Rather than parallelling Robert Ricard's work by describing a "Spiritual Conquest of Peru," scholars emphasized the Peruvian Indians' subversion of conquest culture and Catholicism. Participants in the Symposium on Ideology and Religion held in Lima in 1977 concentrated almost exclusively on identifying the extent and impact of surviving indigenous religious thought and rituals, ranging from polytheism to cannibalism. Irene Silverblatt's recent work both extends and amends this analysis by depicting cultural resistance as the most persistent and most effective challenge to Spanish colonialism and by identifying Indian women as the main force within that movement. Today most Peruvianists have moved to an appreciation of the survival of indigenous values, the irregular and selective adaptation of Spanish norms, and the syncretic fusion of European and indigenous cultures into colonial "Indian culture."[78]

Tannenbaum's analysis failed to allow for the development of colonial Indian culture, discrediting his image of European-indigenous relations, but another of his suppositions—that when an Indian "survived and lived in his own community, he remained an Indian in his ways and attitudes"[79]—has retained significant support. Some scholars have qualified, but not seriously quarreled with, the implicit assumption that minimal contact with Europeans or their Hispanicized agents was the surest guarantee of the survival of indigenous culture;[80] others have approached the study of cultural interaction by postulating varied stages of assimilation.[81] Despite recognition of these different rates of change and despite the emphasis given to distinct aspects of the acculturation process, the causal relationship between Indian-European contact and cultural transformation has never been severely challenged or discredited.

Within this established framework of acculturation studies, the Indians who remained in rural communities appear as a force for the perpetuation of traditional Andean culture, particularly when contrasted to the impact of the movement of Indians to urban centers. However, the forastero presence altered the traditional structure of local communities, threatened the survival of indigenous religious practices, and contributed to the diffusion of European culture.

The significance of Indian-European contact was recognized by colonial authorities who attempted to limit interaction between the two societies by isolating Indians in reducciones. The "republic of Indians" was to remain distinct from the "republic of Spaniards." Access to Indian villages was granted only to the parish priest and to the provincial corregidor, the chief agents of the Spaniards' efforts to "civilize" the indigenous population through carefully monitored exposure to European culture.[82]

The most famous example of this authorized Indian-European contact, as well as the most obvious attempt to alter traditional culture was, of course, the campaign to convert the Indians to Christianity. However, the Spaniards employed other, more selective, techniques to Hispanicize sectors of indigenous society. The deliberate creation of an intermediary political elite alienated from both the conquering and conquered cultures was not unique to colonial Peru or to the Spanish empire, but the Jesuit school for kurakas' sons founded in Cuzco in 1620 was considered one of the most successful of these efforts. Its graduates, however, were not always a source of stability within their home communities. Writing to the King in 1635, the bishop of Cuzco denounced the school's former pupils who "become totally Hispanicized, so that upon returning to their homes they are demons; instead of dressing as Indians, they imitate rich Spaniards." Because of the subsequent flight of Indians forced to fund this extravagant behavior, the bishop suggested abandoning the program. Despite his opposition, throughout the seventeenth century the Jesuits continued to train future kurakas, scribes, interpreters, and other government functionaries, fostering the selective assimilation of the Indian elite and providing a new source of social and economic mobility for a few talented Indian males.[83]

The impact of this deliberately created *ladino*, or Hispanicized, elite was minimal when compared to the unregulated interaction resulting from demographic developments and Indian migration: the size and mobility of the mestizo group, which included Indians escaping into *casta*, or mixed-blood status; the movement of Indians to colonial cities and the important urban-to-rural counterflow; and the presence of the forasteros, which appeared to be a factor in the preservation of Indian society but actually fragmented ayllu unity and weakened the survival of traditional cultural practices, particularly indigenous religion. The growing mestizo population, whose influence on the Indian community was bitterly deplored by colonial authorities, was the most obvious if not the most important example of this increasing Indian-European contact. Both the "frustrated type of mestizo" described by Morner and the "culture broker"—the agent of cultural interaction and exchange depicted by Eric Wolf—served as intermediaries in this process.[84] Throughout the colonial period an increasing number of Indians escaped into the legal sanctuary of mestizo status, whether through genetic heritage, phenotypic attributes, or the deliberate adoption of clothing and occupations reserved for persons of mixed blood. Many of these mestizos retained their ties to home communities or attempted to reside in other Indian parishes, judging by the frequency with which the King issued cédulas stipulating that only Indians should live in Indian towns. Throughout the colonial period mestizos who sought leadership positions within Indian communities had to be restricted by repeated royal decrees barring castas from such posts. Despite these prohibitions the mestizo population, particularly the transient sector, played an important and widely recognized role in the interaction of Hispanic and indigenous cultures.[85]

The impact of another form of migration, the resettlement of urban Indians in rural zones, has been overshadowed by the emphasis placed on indigenous migration to colonial cities. However, a broad, previously undetected urban-to-rural movement allowed for significant cross-cultural exchange. Some of this interaction resulted from the relocation of originarios from rural zones who had resided temporarily in a city. During the seventeenth century many of these migrants entered the provinces of the bishopric of Cuzco. The irregularity of the data pool precludes an accurate assessment of the total number of transients who were present in Cuzco long enough to negotiate labor contracts which required resettlement within the region, but this work force was one source of urban-rural interaction, particularly in the province of Paucartambo.[86]

A distinct and more important conduit for the spread of Hispanic culture—urban natives who relocated in rural parishes—can be identified through the use of ecclesiastical records. Almost one-half of the assimilated forasteros whose children were baptized in Yucay, Marquesado de Oropesa, between 1675 and 1734 were originarios of Cuzco. Although the proximity of Yucay to the city may have intensified this presence, Cuzco natives resettled in other areas of the bishopric. A 1645 survey of adult male originarios of the various ayllus in the urban parish of Santiago, Cuzco, showed that only 40 percent were living in the parish. Of Indians listed as being "outside" of Santiago, almost half were residing within the provinces of the bishopric; a few were working on unidentified *estancias*, the rest were living "in the homes of Spaniards," probably in Cuzco. This migration of urbanites to the depopulated countryside spread Hispanic norms and customs as the forastero presence initially delayed yet ultimately facilitated the transformation of traditional Andean cultures into colonial Indian culture.[87]

THE FORASTEROS' ROLE IN CULTURAL TRANSFORMATION

The presence of these urbanites was less of a trauma for the local Indian communities than the continued loss of originarios and the assimilation of forasteros. The impact of male-specific mortality and migration rates, particularly in the provinces subject to the mita de minas, created a dramatic imbalance in the sex-ratio of the originario population. A colonial bureaucrat reported that in these areas women served as local political leaders, "carrying the traditional staffs of authority and administering justice." Although this assumption of power has been regarded as a reversal of sex roles, new evidence of the preconquest political activities of Andean women indicates that the demographic imbalance of local communities offered women the opportunity to reclaim traditional political rights lost under the colonial administrative system.[88]

The imbalanced sex distribution among the originario population may also have strengthened surviving Indian cultural values and practices. Silverblatt has stated that "from the indigenous point of view, women became identified as the upholders of Andean culture and thus as the defenders of pre-Columbian lifeways." This perception was the result of the impact of colonization on indigenous women, as described by Silverblatt: "Defined by Europeans as being by nature more susceptible to demonic forces—forces which in the colonial context were equated with any and all indigenous practices and beliefs—Andean women, because of the male bias of colonial economic, political, and religious institutions, tended to turn to those traditional practices which were interpreted by the colonial regime as diabolic."[89] Silverblatt argues that many Indian women fled to the *puna*, the high tablelands beyond European control, where they attempted to reconstruct traditional social relations; within the established reducciones, however, Indian women became "the legitimate, albeit underground, representatives of Andean society."[90] Their assertion of traditional Andean indigenous cultural values would have a greater impact in communities subject to the mita de minas, where gender-specific mortality and migration created a predominantly female originario population. In this instance the outflow of Indian migrants, generally a factor in cultural transformation, produced a retention, rather than a loss, of traditional values.

The imbalanced sex-ratios resulting from male-specific mortality and migration rates also had an impact on family structure within Indian communities. Mita workers and migrants were often accompanied by spouses and children, but when a family was separated the ayllu identification of its members, particularly the children, could be the subject of prolonged litigation.[91] The Spaniards were quick to denounce and to deplore the impact of Indian migration on Christian marriage and the nuclear family, but Europeans were less able to grasp the significance of the loss of kin-group ties and communal lands. The royal official who blamed forastero migration on the loss of community resources spoke of the Indians' *raices,* or roots, in a purely economic context and suggested that other lands could replace fields that had been sold to Spaniards.[92] Neither he nor other colonial administrators could understand the Indians' sense of loss at the alienation of ancestral holdings. Europeans were also incapable of realizing that the funeral rites conducted for ayllu members departing for the mita were a lament for the spiritual death of an individual separated from the community as well as a recognition of the dangers of service in the mines and obrajes: "the order to go . . . frightens the Indians much more than any of the severe punishments they have received for their sinful conduct. The wives and mothers begin to mourn the death of their husbands and sons the moment that the men are condemned to this hardship."[93] The loss of community resources and members was part of a general contraction of ayllu linkages and activities—not necessarily a shift from "kin-group" to "elementary family" but rather "the disappearance of many functions of the wider ties of kinship," which left individuals isolated and bewildered.[94]

The spiritual void and sense of alienation were also felt by forastero migrants, who had to face the added strain of hostility from the decimated originario sector. Irregular rates of originario loss and varied economic opportunities determined the relative ease with which migrants were welcomed into existing Indian communities, but the relationship between originario and forastero remained a delicate one.[95] The perpetuation of the "forastero" identification for descendants of the original migrants was indicative of this tension. Bautista Saavedra saw the Indians' insistence on an originario-forastero distinction as an antagonistic assertion of ayllu strength and a reaffirmation of ayllu unity: "the forastero—the extraneous member in this territorial-based clan—is a sign of the resurrection of the fictitious ancestor of the ancient kin group." Rollando Mellafe considers the terms "indio forastero" and the rarer, pejorative *"indio fugado"* (fugitive Indian) and *"indio intruso"* (Indian trespasser) to be symptomatic of the native-immigrant conflict, which "came to be normal from the second half of the seventeenth century onward." This tension was obvious in 1672 when members of the repartimiento of los Hacas, Guamalies, complained bitterly of local employers' attempts to satisfy seasonal labor demands by establishing a permanent forastero colony "awarding them our lands and making them local residents, which has seriously hurt our community." When an elder of Uripa was stabbed in 1703, members of the repartimiento continued to insist that the assailant had been an indio forastero residing in the area, even after an investigation by the corregidor of Andahuaylas determined that a Spaniard had been the perpetrator.[96]

Nowhere was the distinction between originarios and forasteros more obvious, nowhere did Indian migration contribute more to the transformation of Andean culture, than in its impact on traditional religious thought. Preconquest religious practices had been centered in the kingroup, and the postconquest efforts to Christianize the indigenous population, because of Church emphasis on communal structures, intensified this identification of religion and community.[97] The forasteros' ambivalent relationships with local ayllus complicated the interaction of the distinct social networks and religious alliances encountered within the same territorial community.

This support for the local community was particularly important in Andean America because of the close relationship between ayllu membership, kin-group linkages, and ancestor worship. Each pre-Incan ayllu "had an ancestor, real or imaginary, in the totem, *guarqui*, which took the form of an animal or inanimate object, or natural phenomenon, such as a puma, rock or lightning."[98] These local guarqui, more commonly called *guauqui* or *huauqui*, were the object of intense spiritual devotion, even after the imposition of Incan rule required the kin-group to acknowledge the superior power of the Sun God. Each Incan emperor selected his particular guauqui to serve as companion, oracle, and object of veneration for his descendants. For the local and the royal ayllus, the term "guauqui" encompassed both the spirit and the object in which it was incarnated. Because a portion of the community's resources was consecrated to the use of each guauqui—to support its custodians and to supply corn and cloth for ceremonial functions—the bond between the ancestral spirit and the ayllu's lands was a particularly strong and significant manifestation of internal kin-group linkages. Through this relationship the concept of the guauqui had expanded to comprehend the deity, its physical representation, and its sacred lands or dwelling place. The Spaniards were unaware of the triple significance of the guauquis, which they called *guacas*, and denounced the Indians' worship of "idols and demons." In its determined effort to achieve "the extirpation of idolatry in Peru," the Catholic Church emphasized the identification and confiscation of the guacas, a procedure thwarted by the complexity of the concept, which enabled Indians to identify sacred sites rather than specific physical manifestations of a deity or to substitute insignificant stones or carvings for genuine guacas.[99]

Ironically, the Church's effort to preserve the local Indian community by excluding other Europeans and by enforcing the Toledo reducciones perpetuated the communal bases in which ancestral worship and adoration of guacas flourished. Entire towns protected the guacas and their adherents, as Indians holding political and religious offices in the new colonial bureaucracies were intimately involved in the re-creation of traditional authority lines and the perpetuation of indigenous religions. Parallelling the Crown's use of Catholicism as an instrument of social and political control within Indian society, kurakas encouraged local cults and evoked the sanction of ancestral guacas in order to consolidate power within their villages.[100] Sacristans concealed guacas within parish churches, constructed shrines on traditionally sacred lands, and participated actively in the varied techniques which applied a facade of Spanish Catholicism over indigenous rituals, such as the extended celebration of Corpus Christi which masked the Indians' commemoration of the summer solstice.[101] The missionaries' commitment to using indigenous languages extended the use of Quechua beyond its role in the Inca Empire and allowed for the memorialization of preconquest deities and myths. As one colonist observed, "Quite often the Indians have surnames in which they commemorate the ancient fables and traditions of their ancestors by incorporating the names of their heroes."[102] Astute parish priests realized that the coca, corn, and *cuy* brought to Catholic churchyards were traditional offerings to the dead, but more than one cleric was fooled and considered these gifts proof that "the Indians are most observant in their spiritual obligation to the dead; almost every day they cover the tombs with bread, corn, chili peppers, potatoes, and other small contributions from the little they have with no other purpose than the prayer which the priest will say over each of these graves."[103]

The obligation to ayllu ancestors and the communal structure of indigenous religion, exemplified by this veneration of burial grounds, constituted a key deterrent to migration. The importance of a specific physical territory to the concept of the guaca held Indians to home communities in the face of strong pressures for migration. In the opinion of one seventeenth-century priest, Indians who remained in parishes subject to the mita de minas did so "for love of their town." Colonial authorities recognized the significance of this linkage by stipulating that the "most obstinate" sinners be forced to "live in a town distant from the shrines" of their guacas.[104]

Under the reducción system the religious significance of ancestral lands also became a powerful motive for Indian migration. Clerics warned that "much of the danger of idolatry also comes from the Indians' conduct on finding themselves reduced in convenient towns, where a priest may have them in his charge to educate them and to administer the sacraments; many of the Indians have fled these areas, returning to locations from which they were originally removed, the traditional sites where they have their guacas and shrines."[105] Other communities compensated for their alienation from sacred lands by designing pilgrimage routes, ostensibly to Christian shrines, which coincided with preconquest ceremonial progressions to major guacas. In a more obvious example of the interaction of migration and indigenous religious practices, thousands of Indians fled to the frontier regions in order to satisfy what one Lima priest denounced as their "disgusting tendency toward idolatry." Silverblatt argues that this migration, particularly among women, was the key factor in the perpetuation of traditional beliefs, rites, and social relationships.[106]

If flight to areas beyond Spanish control contributed to the perpetuation of traditional Andean religion, migration within established Indian society had the opposite effect, as forasteros were systematically excluded from the continued observance of preconquest practices. The linkage between communal deities and political control which enhanced the power of kurakas had less impact on assimilated migrants. The veneration of ancestral graves and sacred lands received less support from forasteros. The care and adoration of guacas were dominated by originarios of the ayllus involved, and rituals were carefully preserved by the selective participation of successive generations of native-born worshipers.[107]

In his seventeenth-century account of the "campaign against the infidel," the famous Visitor General Pablo Joseph de Arriaga indicated the isolation of the forastero sector. Arriaga offered explicit advice on how to conduct an inspection: Indians should be questioned closely about their neighbors' piety; residents of one village should be interrogated about idolatry in adjacent parishes. Nowhere does Arriaga suggest consulting the forasteros, whose rivalry with originarios might lead to betrayal of a local guaca.[108] This experienced investigator considered the forastero to be unaware of or excluded from the originario network.

The failure of forasteros to participate in local rituals or to perpetuate their own cults is implicit in the documentation from the campaigns against idolatry: no forastero appears as either a defendant or a witness in any of thirty lengthy investigations of heresy charges conducted in the bishopric of Cuzco during the seventeenth century.[109] The failure of the local cults to incorporate the increasingly predominant forastero sector would ultimately weaken the survival of traditional religious thought and practices in the strongest and most subtle instance of the impact of Indian migration on the transformation of indigenous culture.

The forasteros' isolation from originario rituals was indicative of their more profound separation from both their ancestral ayllus and the established reciprocity patterns of their adopted villages. The presence of assimilated migrants in established Indian communities, ostensibly a factor in the perpetuation of traditional Andean culture, was instead a conduit for the Indian-European interaction essential to the formation of colonial Indian culture. Indian migration, plus the presence of yana-conas and mitmaq, played a key role in the weakening of kin-group ties and the redefinition of the ayllu.

That traditional Andean ayllu—a kin-group whose members were guaranteed access to land and labor assistance—had been modified on its inclusion into the Inca Empire to conform to the structure of the state, but had retained its essentially consanguineous character. More drastic changes in ayllu organization and activity occurred under Spanish domination, with its reorientation of the regional economy, manipulation of inherited leadership patterns, and usurpation of ayllu authority. Partly in response to imperial regulations but chiefly in response to pressures within indigenous society, the ayllus evolved new forms of membership and social relationships. By the time the administrative reforms of the 1720s redefined community membership in terms of access to local lands, the ayllu had already begun the profound internal transformation from a kin-group with a common ancestry to a village with communal lands, an important initial step in the progression from a caste to a class society. This process would be further affected by indigenous migration to colonial urban centers, which produced a shift in loyalty and affiliation from kin-group to occupational sector, another important force in the transformation of indigenous society under colonial rule.

❖ 5 ❖ ❖

"Residente en Esa Ciudad":
The Urban Migrant in Cuzco

CUZCO IS a beautiful city. All of the tour books say this, especially those which tell the reader what airplane seats to select in order to get the best view as the pilot makes a sharp, banking turn before landing and travelers get their first view of a mosaic of white-walled houses with the claypipe roofs, which are so characteristic of the city that municipal housing authorities require all construction—even the Swiss chalets in the development Barrio Magistral—to include the distinctive roofing. But the city *is* beautiful, especially when approached by foot from the hillside parish of San Cristobal or by the twisted road from the Pisac River valley as travelers huddled on an open flatbed truck first glimpse and then lose the city and its outlying villages through shifting mountain views. It is impossible to fully describe the impact of this trip, particularly if you are returning at sunset after a day at the ruins in Pisac. As you approach the city, Cuzco exudes a magical mythical presence.

Those lucky enough to be in Cuzco have always felt that presence. Whether as a link to the Incan civilization or as a place where employment can be found, the city continues to attract both tourists and workers. In the colonial period thousands of Indians came to Cuzco—to earn a living, to escape the *mita*, to resolve personal problems. In doing so these migrants contributed in special ways to the transformation of indigenous society and added a new component to the social dynamics of Cuzco.

THE FORASTEROS OF CUZCO

As the Incan capital, Cuzco had held a special importance for subjects of the empire. Because Cuzco was the site of key Incan cere-

monies, the city's population swelled regularly for celebrations such as
Inti Raymi, which marked the summer solstice. Participants viewing
Cuzco for the first time must also have felt the fascination of this city,
this sacred space. The seventeenth-century Spanish historian Bernabé
Cobo conveyed a sense of the city's importance when he observed that
"In the middle of them [the Inca lands] was the royal city of Cuzco like
the heart in the middle of the body."[1] The city was the political and
religious core of the Incan state, the administrative center for the sprawl-
ing empire and the fixed point of orientation for the solar observations
critical to Incan calendars and ceremonies. For some of the empire's
subjects this core was rotten. Conquered populations forcibly resettled
in the Cuzco zone, sons of regional leaders virtually held hostage at
schools in the capital, and worshipers of local deities whose images had
been removed to Cuzco for "safekeeping" would have regarded the city
with loathing rather than awe.[2]

The Spaniards' initial responses combined both disgust and respect:
disgust at the temples and the beliefs of the city's residents and respect
for its ferocious defenders. Entering Cuzco in 1533, Pedro Pizarro
admired the fortress of Sacsayhuaman: "a very strong fort surrounded
with masonry walls of stones and having two very high round towers . . .
[with] . . . stones so large and thick that it seemed impossible that human
hands could have set them in place," yet he deplored "the people who
were in this city of Cuzco and the vices which they had."[3] Some of
Pizarro's contemporaries were kinder to the Incan capital. Pedro Cieza
de León thought that "Cuzco had great style and worth; it had to have
been founded by remarkable people."[4]

None of these opinions affected the formal founding of the colonial
city of Cuzco in October 1534.[5] In many ways Europeans were forced to
establish a city there. Creating a Spanish city on the stone foundations of
the Incan capital had tremendous symbolic importance. Moreover, Pizarro wanted a city at Cuzco for the same reasons the Incas did. The site
was conveniently located for administering the Vilcanota and Urubamba
River valleys and the region was strategically important. Of course, for
the Spaniards, "strategic" had a different connotation: the Incas had
fortified Cuzco and its provinces, particularly those toward the east, to
defend their empire; the Spaniards settled in the Cuzco zone to exploit
theirs. Ruling Cuzco and its environs gave them fertile lands, access to
Indian labor, and control of major supply routes to the mining zones at
Guancavelica and Potosí.

Although the city never regained the preeminence it had held under the Incas, Cuzco prospered throughout the colonial period because of its agricultural wealth and its role in supplying commodities to the mining zones. The expanding European control of productive lands and the indigenous sector's growing involvement in the market economy increased agricultural production and exports. When markets in the mining zones were threatened by shifting trade patterns, regional distribution networks emerged. The city's economy was characterized by steady expansion rather than by the boom-bust cycles of the mining zones, but this pattern of regular growth was violently disrupted in the mid-seventeenth century.[6]

On Thursday, March 31, 1650, a massive earthquake struck Cuzco. The compiler of the *Anales del Cuzco* declared that according to some of the bishopric's priests the quake had lasted the time required to pray "two creeds"; other observers, perhaps more frightened, claimed that they had said three; more secular observers commented that the quake lasted about fifteen minutes. Cuzqueños were terrified and "everyone ran in confusion through the plazas and streets without knowing where to go; men did not protect their wives nor women their children, but everyone tried to escape alive." In spite of desperate attempts "to appease the wrath of God," the tremors and confusion continued, with panicked residents crying that "the Day of Judgment was at hand." For the next five weeks serious aftershocks hit Cuzco; lesser temblors terrorized the population until January 1651.[7]

The *Anales* stated that thirty people were killed in the first devastating quake. Other sources reported that "fewer than ten Spaniards" and "about one hundred Indians" had perished but luckily "no one of importance" had died. Casualties were lower during the aftershocks, in part because much of the Indian population abandoned their badly constructed housing in the poorer neighborhoods and camped at the outskirts of town. Some left the area permanently. The 1650 disaster is not the sole reason that the indigenous population of the bishopric dropped from around 321,000 in 1628 to roughly 97,000 in 1652, but postquake migration was a factor in the decline. Damage estimates ranged from 3.3 to 6 million pesos. Although local officials wrote that "all the city is in ruins and there are grave losses in the province[s]," the major reports sent to Lima and Spain emphasized the losses suffered by the city's elite. A lengthy report on earthquake damage presented specific estimates for the damage to public buildings, church property, and

269 private homes and then commented in general terms on the condition of the Indians' houses. Local priests seemed more concerned that Indians were taking advantage of an emergency ruling that enabled them to marry without posting banns and paying fees.[8]

Most of the damage reports emphasized the destruction of elite-owned property; the debate over disaster relief was also focused chiefly on elite concerns. Claiming that the surrounding Indian towns had been decimated, the city's *encomenderos* petitioned the crown to extend their rights to Indian labor for at least another generation in order to realize the full value of their original grants. This request was denied, although the Council of the Indies agreed to pay particular attention to specific petitions. More importantly, the Crown suspended the collection of taxes for six years and contributed a portion of its other revenues to rebuilding the city's churches, convents, and hospitals.[9] These royal concessions spurred the reconstruction and revitalization of the city. Residents rebuilt their homes and newcomers joined the expanding economy.

Periods of economic growth such as the postquake recovery attracted migrants to the city but Cuzco had always been a target for migration, especially among the indigenous population. Although not all Indian migration was voluntary—in 1654 hundreds of Indians from the province of Quispicanche were forcibly settled in the urban parish of San Gerónimo—many migrants came to Cuzco by choice.[10] Before the Spanish conquest Cuzco had offered economic and social advancement through specialized service to the Inca Empire. During the colonial period the city represented not only economic opportunity but also escape from oppression in the countryside. In the period before the Toledo reforms Indians charged with conveying tribute to Cuzco and other colonial cities stayed in the urban centers. After Toledo's regularization of the mita, Cuzco attracted Indians fleeing from labor in the mines. In the late seventeenth century a perceptive priest noted that Cuzco had grown in direct contrast to the areas subject to the *mita de minas*. He complained that many Indians had fled to the city from his parish, San Pedro de Aquira, Cotabambas, which sent laborers to the mercury mines.[11]

Although he may have erred by insisting that all his missing parishioners were in Cuzco, the priest was right on one point: migration from the provinces of its bishopric was a key factor in maintaining the city's population, which was approximately eleven thousand by the end of the seventeenth century.[12] Throughout this period most of the migrants entering the Cuzco labor force—77 percent—were from the provinces surrounding the city. An additional 9.7 percent were from the adjoining bishoprics of Guamanga and Arequipa. The largest blocks of migrants from outside the Central Sierra were from Upper Peru and the La Plata region, 3.9 and 4.4 percent, respectively (for further information, see tables IB and II).[13]

Of course, not all of these individuals settled in Cuzco. Some returned to their homes, some joined other indigenous communities in the rural zone, and some moved on to another colonial city or mining zone. Colonial observers clearly understood the difference between the phrases "presente" and "residente en esa ciudad." The former was applied to an individual appearing in Cuzco at a particular recorded moment, perhaps to file a grievance with the authorities, and the latter described forasteros residing in the city. Parish priests supplying data for the 1690 ecclesiastical census of the city differentiated between the "unstable Indians" and the settled forasteros who owned homes or had joined households in Cuzco.[14]

Because of the priests' careful distinctions, the established *forasteros* of Cuzco can be isolated from the transients, who in 1690 composed 7.7 percent of the total Indian population identified by origin and 16.2 percent of the foreign-born population. That same census revealed that 47.4 percent of the city's Indian population was foreign-born. Adjusted for the transient presence, the established forastero sector represented 39.6 percent of Cuzco's total Indian population identified by origin and was an important part of the city's Indian community.[15]

THE MIGRANTS IN THE CITY

To judge from colonial administrators' comments forasteros were more than a significant minority of the Indian population total: they were overrunning the city. Officials blamed migrants for the labor shortages in the rural zones, particularly in the mita to the mines, and wanted urban migrants returned to their home communities. Throughout the colonial period successive viceroys attempted, and failed, to return urban forasteros to their reducciones.

The resettlement efforts failed, in part, because of general administrative chaos and contradictory population control policies.[16] In the cities, however, another confusing practice complicated efforts to regulate forasteros. Colonial administrators undermined their own resettlement programs by issuing a series of decrees allowing urban migrants to become permanent residents, immune to repatriation and exempt from the obligations of their home communities. This practice of changing legal status and mita-tribute obligations through permanent relocation in a city—a continuation of the medieval European principle which Henri Pirenne summarized as *Stadtluft macht's frei*—was one of the strongest attractions for migrants to urban centers. Forasteros who could prove that they had lived in a city for at least ten years were free from resettlement and free from the tribute and labor demands of home communities. Any Indian threatened with return to a rural *reducción* could appeal, based on this policy. Whether or not the migrant was an established urban resident, the lengthy court process could delay, or prevent, relocation.[17]

Colonial administrators thought that urban migrants were much too free in another sense: free from the supervision of their *kurakas* and the guidance of their parish priests and free to commit crimes in the city. Although one official claimed that forasteros were victimized by the colonial justice system, administrators thought that most migrants were potentially dangerous criminals.[18] Whether or not Cuzco's forasteros actually were a majority of the underclass is uncertain. As Gabriel Haslip-Viera has written, "lawbreakers, beggars, and the unemployed made a conscious effort to avoid the census takers."[19] Forasteros appear as both plaintiffs and defendants in criminal cases conducted in Cuzco during the seventeenth century, but it is impossible to say whether or not they do so disproportionately to their presence in the general population.

One factor that might have led to more frequent court appearances for migrants was the tension between native-born Cuzqueños and newcomers. In 1664 Diego Guaman Topa, a tailor who had migrated to Cuzco from the town of Urcos, Quispicanche, began working in the shop of Miguel Hilaguita, a Cuzco tailor, with the understanding that Guaman Topa's work would be kept separately and paid separately from other projects in the store. Despite Hilaguita's assurances that Guaman Topa's materials would be safe, the shop was robbed one night. Only Guaman Topa's work was stolen. After a thorough investigation Hilaguita was arrested and released on his promise to replace the missing goods. When Hilaguita refused to comply, Guaman Topa asked that the Cuzco Indians who had stood surety for Hilaguita's behavior, including an elder of the parish of San Sebastián, return Hilaguita to the city jail.

Two years late Guaman Topa had to repeat that request. The originario-forastero tension that pervades this court case indicates that one reason forasteros were so often involved in litigation was their vulnerability in the city.[20]

Migrants might also have been subjected to regular judicial processes more frequently because they were isolated from kin who could help them resolve family tensions without recourse to litigation. Furthermore, although urban migrants had escaped the authorities from their home communities, they were subject to others. Both of these factors are obvious in case studies from the *causas matrimoniales*, or marital litigation, from the archives of the bishopric of Cuzco. In 1646 Diego Quispe, a migrant to Cuzco, was accused of bigamy when the mother of his second wife charged that the first wife had not died, as Quispe claimed, but was living in the countryside. At his mother-in-law's insistence, Quispe was arrested. During the course of the ecclesiastical investigation the mother-in-law, Ana Sisa, confessed that "while out of [her] mind, drunk, and angered at [her] son-in-law because he mistreated [her] daughter" she had deliberately lied to her parish priest; the first wife was indeed dead. Sisa asked for freedom for Quispe and forgiveness for herself. Both were granted, but Sisa was severely rebuked and told that she should leave the couple alone. The court felt that this family quarrel should have remained a private one and resented the involvement of Church authorities in a domestic dispute.[21]

The causas matrimoniales also reveal that Church officials were concerned about another way in which forasteros could become free—from previous marriages. Indians who married in their home communities and remarried in Cuzco appeared frequently in ecclesiastical court proceedings.[22] So did Cuzco residents whose spouses had fled to the countryside. In one particularly plaintive document from 1698 Maria Ana Sisa, who had been searching for her absent husband, asked Church officials to save her from the workshop where she had been imprisoned when her husband convinced local authorities that she was not his wife but a troublemaker. The ecclesiastical *cabildo*, which had encouraged and authorized her search, launched a full investigation which was complicated by the fact that both Sisa and her husband, Juan Poma, had been migrants to Cuzco and had originally married without the permission of their home communities' parish priests. Almost a year after the initial petition had been filed the cabildo ordered that Poma be stripped from the waist up, paraded through the city, and given 100 lashes; he was also sentenced to work two years at a local convent. Furthermore, the cabildo decreed that the two marriages he had contracted since leaving his first wife were nullified and he was forced to live with Sisa, who had been released from the workshop.[23]

Partly at the urging of concerned ecclesiastical authorities and partly in response to kurakas' claims that urban migrants were avoiding their tribute obligations, colonial authorities tried to reestablish traditional authority lines among the loosely knit groups of *indios vagabondos*—or drifters—found in colonial urban and mining centers. In some cases migrants were forced to live in a particular parish or a town adjacent to the city; in others, colonial administrators tried to create new communities among migrants.[24]

The most detailed instructions for migrant resettlement were developed for the mining zones and nearby cities. Less than thirty years after the establishment of the Toledo reducciones and mita system, Viceroy Luis de Velasco reported the failure of his predecessors' attempts to stabilize Indian society and to insure a steady labor force for Potosí.[25] In his initial response to Velasco's complaints Philip III ordered the colonial authorities to repopulate the mining areas: "Choosing appropriate and healthy locations, you should establish settlements of Indians where they can be gathered to live in organized towns, and can have religious instruction, health care, and all other necessities so that upon seeing the benefits of this labor the Indians will come [to the mines] so readily that it will not be necessary to bring others from more distant communities."[26]

In the second phase of this effort the king responded to Velasco's suggestion that "voluntary" laborers remaining at the mines after the completion of required mita duty should be organized into new ayllus with lands and leaders of their own. A Reál Cédula, dated May 26, 1609, commanded officials "to settle all necessary Indian laborers in the district of the mines of Potosí, by which means you can utilize those Indians who voluntarily want to live in this neighborhood as well as those who at present are found working at Potosí and other mines; and to all these Indians who of their own free will come to these towns, you will give lands, which you will find for them in the district of each mining site, so that the newly congregated Indians may farm them and prosper."[27] Members of the new reducciones were to sever all ties with their home communities, effectively forming the bases for new kin-groups: "and to establish order within these settlements, a census shall be taken of all the Indians present, so that if one leaves his new residence, he may be returned and punished: and afterward, the Casiques shall be informed and threatened with severe penalties, that they might admit into their towns none of the natives [who had been relocated]."[28] In compensation the resettled Indians would pay less tribute, "and among other privileges, they will be excluded from all other labor drafts, and will not have to serve the mita to the mines for a period of six years."[29] If this concession failed to reconcile a sufficient number of Indians to permanent residence at the mines, officials at Potosí could draft Indians from remote provinces to populate these new towns.[30]

In spite of these royal decrees the Velasco plan was never implemented. Nor did colonial authorities succeed in enforcing any of the numerous seventeenth-century commands to resolve the problems of depopulation and the related labor shortage by creating new communities or by arbitrarily assigning individual migrants to existing groups. Thomas M. Davies's claim that "thousands of new [ayllus] were created on the lands given to Indian curacas" exaggerates the achievements of local officials. However, control of the indigenous population through modified ayllu structures remained the model for all such efforts to establish new, viable reducciones.[31]

In Cuzco authorities employed another technique to replicate traditional authority lines among *vagabondos*. Spanish administrators appointed group leaders, such as Don Andrés Ygnacio Auquieare, "Head Kuraka and Captain of Forasteros" in mid-seventeenth-century Cuzco, whose public position and access to migrant laborers led to his private employment as chief administrator of extensive Spanish-owned estates.[32] Appointed Indian leaders such as Don Andrés were influential figures in the complicated relationships between local kurakas, Spanish administrators, church officials, and private employers, but neither these individuals nor the artificial communities created for the indios vagabondos represent a significant development in the transformation of the Indian community. A much more important force for change was the migrants' participation in the urban economy, particularly their integration into the wage labor force.

THE CONCIERTOS DE TRABAJO

In spite of their reputation for lawlessness, immigrants to Cuzco were incorporated into the city's European economy in productive ways—entering the labor market, joining the wage labor force, acquiring property, and participating in the market economy. Some of the migrants were successful. A will filed in 1715 for the estate of a woman originally from the province of Chilques y Masques listed cash, personal possessions, and only a few debts. However, many migrants never amassed enough property to justify the expense of writing a formal will.[33] A more representative depiction of the lives of Cuzco's forasteros requires a broader form of documentation than an occasional last testament, ecclesiastical litigation, or criminal investigation. The *conciertos*, or labor contracts, found in the notarial records of colonial Cuzco supply this documentation.

The historical record contained in these labor contracts presents different information than the data compiled for a general occupational census of the type analyzed by Patricia Seed in her study of race, occupation, and social status in Mexico City.[34] Because certain occupations, such as day laborer, do not appear in the Cuzco contracts and because the sample is drawn solely from the indigenous sector, these conciertos are not the best source for a discussion of the coincidence of race and class in seventeenth-century Cuzco. However, the contracts are the best source for an analysis of major migration patterns and the role of the forasteros in urban society.

Throughout the colonial period foreign-born residents, transient laborers, and native Cuzqueños negotiated hundreds of labor contracts that form a rich data source for a study of urban labor patterns. Foreign-born workers arranged a majority of these contracts, forming 60 to 70 percent of the work force throughout the seventeenth century. Within this foreign-born category, migrants from the provinces of the bishopric of Cuzco consistently outnumbered those from other regions of the viceroyalty, especially in the late seventeenth century.[35]

The analyzed contracts, which are described in detail in appendix I, can be simplified into four main labor categories: agriculture (9.5 percent); transportation (48.8 percent); the service sector (30.9 percent); and skilled trades (10.2 percent) (tables IB and IC). These categories reflect not only specific occupational groups but also major migration patterns. The transportation workers, a category dominated by the foreign-born workers, were a highly mobile work force whose presence in Cuzco was followed by travel to other colonial urban or mining centers. The agricultural workers represent an urban-to-rural outflow as a combination of city natives and migrants present in Cuzco accepted relocation within the bishopric, at least for the duration of their contracts. The service sectors include a relatively balanced group of foreign-born and native workers who would definitely be residing within the city. Few foreign-born skilled craftsmen entered the labor markets, but those who did were also committed to staying in Cuzco.[36] Each of these sectors had distinct characteristics which the conciertos depict in detail.

TRANSPORT WORKERS

The transportation workers, a majority of all contractees from 1630 until 1670, represent the clearest example of labor outflow from the city of Cuzco. Three-fourths of all Indians agreeing to work outside the city and its bishopric joined packtrains to Lima, La Paz, or Potosí; most of the drivers with unspecified destinations probably worked these well-established routes. During the late seventeenth century, however, shifting commercial patterns within Spanish America led to the "meridionalization" of colonial trade and a sharp rise in the volume of contraband goods entering the Upper Peruvian mining areas from Argentina and Chile through Tucumán and Arica.[37] The proportionate drop in the legitimate Cuzco-Potosí trade created a sharp fall in the number of muleteers hired in Cuzco, and their presence in the labor market declined drastically.

The shift in colonial markets also produced a change in the origin of mule drivers in the Cuzco labor pool. Throughout the 1600s, 60 to 75 percent of the transportation workers hired in Cuzco were born outside of the city, but the internal composition of that group varied, with natives of the bishopric assuming a greater role. In the early decades of the seventeenth century a sizeable proportion of transportation workers were natives of more distant areas of the viceroyalty (tables IF and II). The later drop in long-distance commerce, the loss of the valuable Potosí markets, and the increased demand for goods in the Cuzco area contributed to the rise of local markets and an increase in regional trade. During the seventeenth century the percentage of transport workers born outside the Cuzco zone fell from 29 to 14 percent; and natives of the provinces of the bishopric rose from 23 to 67 percent of all transport workers as convoys along relatively shorter routes, such as the one linking Cuzco to Abancay, attracted a growing number of Indians who could meet their need for a cash income without traveling to Upper Peru.

Changing market patterns affected the destinations and origins of transport workers, but one feature remained constant: whether engaged in long-distance hauling to Lima, La Paz, or Potosí, or employed on shorter routes within the Cuzco zone, muleteers left Cuzco without the promise of return work. Mateo Hillva, a muleteer born in Guarocondo, Abancay, who had migrated to Cuzco and married, expected to return to the house he had purchased in the parish of Santa Ana.[38] For most Indians, however, employment as a muleteer included accepting the possibility of permanent migration. Although some workers undoubtedly secured employment back to Cuzco, only two muleteers joining convoys to Lima or to the Potosí area were guaranteed return trips.

AGRICULTURAL WORKERS

The agricultural workers hired in the city also agreed to leave Cuzco, but for temporary resettlement in the rural zone. Some of these workers would return to Cuzco; others would continue to work for private employers or move into depopulated lands. Throughout the seventeenth century more than half of these agricultural workers were natives of the provinces of the bishopric; an additional 20 percent were migrants from other regions in the viceroyalty. Four of the sixty-one workers whose contracts gave specific destinations agreed to travel to Lima or to Upper Peru for their new employers. The rest were hired to work within the bishopric, chiefly the province of Paucartambo.[39]

The destination distribution for agricultural workers is definitely affected by a 1646–1647 data cluster of Indians contracting to harvest coca in the province of Paucartambo. With the exception of the 1640s total, the agricultural workers were a consistent 4 to 8 percent of the work force, recruited to compensate for local labor shortages or hired by Spaniards and Indian elites residing in Cuzco. The steady recourse to urban labor pools demonstrates not only the interaction between rural and urban labor systems but also the constant demand for labor which could not be secured in the countryside. Occasionally that need was acute. The recruitment of forty-one coca workers during the mid-1640s was a response to a severe crisis in the mita labor draft and emphasizes the role of the urban labor market in supplementing the official labor system.

The cultivation and ceremonial use of coca were important features of preconquest Andean culture. Consumption was theoretically restricted to the nobility and religious leaders, but Incan subjects also enjoyed coca. The sixteenth-century chronicler Pedro de Cieza de León noted that "the Indians relish sucking roots, twigs, and grasses" and that coca was popular throughout the Andes. According to Cieza, the Indians always carried coca leaves between their teeth because with coca "they were not affected by their hunger and they felt fresh and strong."[40]

The Spaniards were quick to recognize the profits in coca production and to generalize its use. By the 1540s coca was being sold in Potosí, where it remained a valuable commodity throughout the colonial period because, as Cieza had noted, it enabled Indian miners to endure longer shifts under brutal conditions. In the late seventeenth century coca was still in demand in the mining zones.

Much of the coca shipped to Potosí was grown in the province of Paucartambo where, a parish priest reported, "the hot and humid land is perfect for planting coca."[41] However, the climate was not perfect for the Indian laborers. From the beginning of the colonial period, officials recognized that coca cultivation was dangerous and debilitating labor. Because of high mortality rates, Francisco de Toledo attempted to regulate Indian labor in the coca zones; because of high profits, growers constantly violated those regulations. Toledo's original decrees, incorporated by the town council of Cuzco into its 1573 "statement on Indian labor," were explicit: no one could seize an Indian worker's blanket in order to cover coca plants; no Indians could be forced into coca labor, even if they were promised a salary for this work; no Indians should be given cash advances for coca work, even if they indicated that they were accepting the money voluntarily. Most importantly, because so many of the laborers who worked in the coca fields became ill and died, no Indian "could be kept in those provinces for more than twenty-four working days."[42] Toledo's regulations on coca labor, like many other provisions of his *Ordenanzas*, were never effectively enforced in spite of repeated decrees issued by later viceroys, such as the Príncipe de Esquilache.[43] Because coca labor was so brutal, producers in the Cuzco area could not rely on the local mita and turned to the urban labor market to hire additional workers.

The contracts negotiated for coca workers in the Cuzco labor market systematically violated the major provisions of the Toledo regulations. Two-thirds of the contracts exceeded the twenty-four-day work cycle and almost half of the contracts were longer than two months, the standard mita obligation. Reflecting the dangers of coca cultivation, the laborers received higher wages than other agricultural workers. Salaries ranged from ten to twenty-two pesos per month, with an average rate of fifteen pesos. In direct violation of the Toledo regulations, all of the forty-one workers recruited from 1646 to 1647 received large advances. Five had been paid their entire salaries and another nineteen workers had received at least half of their earnings. Given these debts, plus the distance and expense in returning from Paucartambo, many of these workers probably stayed in the province after the expiration of their contracts, either signing new conciertos or working under a form of debt peonage. At least two of the workers heading for Paucartambo in 1646 intended to stay: both Miguel Quispe and Pedro Suarez stipulated in their contracts that their wives were to accompany them to new homes in the coca zone.[44]

THE SERVICE SECTOR

In contrast to the more mobile transport and agricultural workers, service-sector employees stayed in the city of Cuzco. Some of these workers were native Cuzqueños; others were migrants seeking new jobs and new lives in the city. Throughout most of the seventeenth century the service categories consistently showed a majority of urban-born workers, with a substantial minority from the surrounding provinces. Very few migrants from other regions of the viceroyalty entered this employment sector; similar jobs were available in other urban centers and the salary range for service work was not high enough to stimulate long-distance migration.[45] Data from the 1680s indicate a surge in migrant service workers coinciding with the rise of that sector within the Cuzco labor market in response to both the city's delayed recovery from the devastating earthquakes of the 1650s and the general population recovery of the late seventeenth and early eighteenth centuries. In the late seventeenth century the service sector became the largest employment group as the shift in markets affected the transport sector.[46]

Almost all of these service-sector employees settled in Cuzco. In November 1683 Sebastián Tucra agreed to serve Don Juan Antonio de Sanabría "in his house and also outside of this city," but Tucra's employer was a lawyer who journeyed regularly between Cuzco and Lima and the travel clause was an unusual one for a service-sector contract. Tucra's contract is unusual in another sense: it was negotiated for a male Indian. Not surprisingly, 81 percent of the service-sector workers were women. A few married couples signed joint contracts, usually combining cooking duties for the wife and unspecified "service" for the husband; in two cases married couples migrating to Cuzco from the bishopric found employment together in service jobs. However, almost all of the women in the service sector acted in their own right, with few of the contracts coded for the woman's marital status and fewer still bearing the obligatory statement on a married woman's contract that she was acting "with her husband's permission."[47] Yet another feature of Tucra's contract is unusual: he was a migrant from the town of Quiquijana, Quispicanche, and most of the males entering the service sector were urban natives who, like Tucra, were employed as personal servants. A few males worked as "bakers" or "pastry makers," jobs which paid more than the "cook" classification dominated by women, but most males were hired to "serve in the house" or simply "to serve" the employer.[48] Such jobs failed to attract migrants from the bishopric or the exterior, who moved into the more attractive transport sector.

Some of the male-dominated, higher-paying jobs were closed to women, but service-sector employment offered some opportunities for women, particularly for women migrants. Of course, newcomers could be exploited. In 1668 Maria Ynquillay, a migrant to Cuzco, agreed to work as a cook and laundress for Doña Micaela de Salasar. Ynquillay was to receive food and new clothes and sandals each year of the six-year contract. She was paid no salary.[49]

Most women workers earned cash wages, working in a variety of occupations. The most frequently documented job, if not the most common occupation, was wet nurse.[50] Indian women cared for the children of Cuzco's Spanish and Indian elite, for the children of slaves, for the children of widowers and married couples, and perhaps even for their own children: a number of children—"orphans, left at the door of the house"—were the subject of contracts arranged between Indian women and Spaniards. In addition to their salaries, wet nurses usually received food and clothing and explicit instructions to care for the child "with all caution and cleanliness, without cohabitating with any man." This restriction applied even to married women. When Josepha Mallqui, a migrant from the town of Guaillabamba, Marquesado de Oropesa, agreed to care for the infant son of Ygnacio Bernardo de Quiróz, she promised to "have nothing to do with her husband or any other man."[51]

As in many colonial cities, women played a major role in food production and distribution. In Cuzco women were particularly active in making *chicha*, a fermented corn beverage. Chicha was frequently made and consumed within Indian households, but a number of women made chicha for the local market, usually as the employee of a Spaniard who paid their wages, furnished supplies, and kept most of the profits. Some of the workers were paid according to the amount of chicha sold; others received a flat wage. *Chicheras* usually were hired individually, but one mother-and-daughter pair agreed to produce and sell chicha for a Cuzco entrepreneur with the added stipulation that they be allowed to drink some of their product.[52]

Although some formal guild structure may have existed among food producers in other colonial urban centers, no such linkages appear among the Cuzco chicha workers. Their contracts show none of the uniformity that marked the skilled tradesmen's agreements. More importantly, only 5 percent of these contracts were guaranteed by an individual with the same occupation, a key feature of guild membership.[53]

THE ARTISANS

A formal guild structure did govern the skilled trades in Cuzco, a small but active economic sector. The seventeenth century was a period of growth and expansion for the artisan sector throughout the viceroyalty, in part because Indian craftsmen moved from producing traditional goods to participating in the urban craft market. During the later part of the century the Cuzco skilled-trade groups grew, surpassing their 6 to 8 percent representation in the pre-1680 labor force (table IC). Throughout the colonial period craft guilds controlled "small scale production for largely inelastic markets," ideal conditions for the formation and perpetuation of guilds. Although guild regulations were tightest in larger cities such as Potosí or Lima, the guild structure in cities such as Cuzco carefully regulated production and membership.[54]

The local guilds' control of trade is seen in the origins of their members: a majority of skilled craftsmen were originally from the city of Cuzco and the provinces of the bishopric (table IL). The possibility of acquiring or practicing a skilled trade provided economic opportunities for urban residents of all ages and encouraged the urban migration of adult males. Few craftsmen arrived in Cuzco from other regions of the viceroyalty. One who did, Felipe Guanca, a carpenter originally from Zuli, Omasayo, might have regretted the move: the severe master carpenter who hired Guanca stipulated that if he did not finish his work on time he would have to work Sundays and holidays.[55] The low rate of long-distance migration among skilled craftsmen was not due to Cuzco working conditions, however. Skilled workers could generally find employment in their home communities and local masters were able to control local production by excluding foreign-born artisans.

Although Cuzco women may have played an important role in artisan production, they do not appear in the formal contracts governing artisan work. Lyman Johnson has argued that throughout colonial Spanish America "wives and daughters became skilled assistants, even though they had no direct link with a guild and received little recognition or compensation." If, as Johnson believes, "[a]rtisanal production, in this sense, was family production," family participation was largely unrecorded. Only one woman appears as a contractee in the conciertos governing Cuzco artisan production. In 1707 a "maestro curtidor," owner of a tannery, hired "Lucas Corimanya and his wife" to scrape hides in his shop. The wife's name was mentioned nowhere in the contract.[56]

Women were active, however, in negotiating the *conciertos de aprendís*, or contracts creating apprenticeships, which determined future guild membership. Between 1600 and 1719 a total of ninety-four such agreements were signed: fifty-three negotiated by adult Indians and forty-one arranged for young Indian males (table IP–1). The overall majority of self-negotiated contracts obscures an interesting trend: a significant increase in the proportion of family-arranged agreements in the post-1690 period. Because few such contracts state the occupation of the family member negotiating the apprenticeship, it is unclear if access to skilled trades was increasingly restricted to young relatives of trained craftsmen, but the contracts do indicate that during the late colonial period skilled craftsmen were more carefully controlling membership in their guilds.[57]

Each of the forty-one arranged conciertos was negotiated for the apprentice by a family member, with an overwhelming 92 percent initiated by one or both parents. Mothers signing alone accounted for 44 percent of the agreements, but only three documents satisfied notarial regulations stipulating that female contractees be identified by civil status and that married women be required to demonstrate their husbands' approval of any litigation.[58] Any speculation concerning the relationship between place of origin and household structure is complicated by the failure of the notaries to indicate home communities for 32 percent of the contractees involved (table IP–2).

A majority of all apprentices with identified origins—53.9 percent—

came from the provinces of the bishopric and most trainees entered the skilled trades; individuals with both these characteristics formed the largest data subgroup, 29 percent of the total sample (table IP–2). Data totals for the different types of apprenticeships follow this pattern of origin and distribution but vary greatly with respect to the identity of the individual negotiating the contract, especially among the apprentices from the city and from the non-Cuzco regions of the viceroyalty. These two groups are evenly represented among the self-negotiated apprentices, but within the family-arranged sector the Cuzqueños vastly outnumber the Indians from the exterior and equal those from the archbishopric (tables IP–1 and IP–2).

The possibility of entering a craft guild stimulated short-range migration of individual male Indians born within the bishopric who migrated to Cuzco, especially during the pre-1680 period of guild formation and consolidation. In the later decades of the seventeenth century an increasingly rigid guild structure gave membership preference to urban residents, who may have been children or acquaintances of guild members.

MIGRANTS AND THEIR FIADORES

The increasingly cohesive nature of guild organization is also apparent in the artisan contracts with *fiadores*, or guarantors. Because the fiador was liable for any damages resulting from the worker's violation of the contract, the relationship between guarantor and contractee was necessarily one of confidence and mutual obligation.[59] Of the artisan contracts signed in the city of Cuzco during the mid- and late seventeenth century, 81 percent involved a craftsman standing surety for another craftsman's work. Several of the craftsmen negotiated a type of contract called *Concierto y Obligación*, in which artisans working on the same job guaranteed each other's compliance. Twelve percent of the craftsmen, chiefly migrants from the bishopric, depended on other Indians from their hometowns to guarantee their work; only 3 percent relied on family members as fiadores.[60]

Guild affiliations obviously superseded kin linkages and family ties, but the skilled-trades sector could, by definition, be expected to show a high rate of shared-occupational fiadores. Moreover, in preconquest society certain occupational groups had been separated from their home communities by the Incas. During the colonial period, however, the shift in identity from kin-group to occupational sector was obvious even in nonskilled occupations.

For Indians outside the formal guild structure the importance of ayllu linkages was threatened by relocation within Indian society and weakened by migration to urban centers. Some Indians who moved to colonial cities minimized or severed their ties with ancestral kin-groups, as seen by an examination of the fiadores for labor contracts from the nonartisan sectors, which show that although no formal guild structure existed among these sectors of Cuzco, these groups were shifting their identity from kin-group to occupational sector.

Conciertos involving muleteers, who would be entrusted with valuable animals and equipment, showed the highest rate of guarantors: approximately one-third of these contracts were cosigned by fiadores. About one-fifth of the service-sector workers, particularly wet nurses who would care for the employers' children, found fiadores for their agreements.[61] Within these broad categories no clear patterns indicate which workers' contracts would most likely include guarantors. In April 1664 two Cuzco natives signed contracts to work for the same packtrain leader, at the same salary, and with the same supplemental remuneration, chiefly clothing and supplies. Pedro Vayamay agreed to serve for one year and received an advance of thirty pesos, one-fourth of his yearly salary. Lazaro Pulido, who was heavily in debt, signed up for three years and was advanced most of his projected earnings, 300 of 360 pesos. Only one contract was guaranteed: Vayamay's. Another native Cuzqueño pledged to assure Vayamay's compliance and stood surety for the much smaller advance in salary.[62] Apparently, employers sought fiadores whenever possible but accepted workers whose contracts could not be guaranteed.

Because natives of the city and the bishopric's provinces were more likely to have kin-members or acquaintances in Cuzco, their contracts had a higher rate of fiadores. However, the selection of those fiadores shows a variety of contractee-guarantor relationships and the data summarized on table IN–2 contain significant internal variation.

The percentage of workers choosing a kin-member for this important role varied inversely with the distance between the home community and the city of Cuzco; in contrast, the percentage of laborers choosing a fiador with the same occupation, even a non-Indian, rose directly with the scope of migration. Logically, most native-born Cuzqueños, 58.5 percent, chose family members to guarantee their labor contracts; 15.1

percent chose a kuraka or an Indian elder, indicating that traditional authority lines remained strong among urban natives. Although 22.6 percent of the city natives found fiadores within their occupational sector, only 7.5 percent of these urbanites had guarantors whose sole link with the contractee was a shared occupation (table IN–2).

Indians with origins outside the bishopric displayed a markedly different data pattern which reflects the distance between their birthplaces and Cuzco: only 20 percent selected family members as guarantors. The foreign-born contractees were also clearly isolated from traditional indigenous authority lines. None of their contracts was guaranteed by a kuraka or an elder. Most of the contractees with origins outside the bishopric—66.7 percent—found guarantors within their occupational sector. Within this category, contractees had developed occupational linkages which replaced family and village ties: 26.7 percent of the foreign-born contractees were involved in mutually guaranteed contracts, where the fiador and laborer were both contracting to work in identical occupations for the same employer; another 26.7 percent of these agreements linked laborers to fiadores with the same regional origin as well as occupation. Both of these categories were dominated by muleteers from the provinces of the Río de la Plata, a group whose high-mobility employment would foster such internal cohesion.

The relationship between migration and a shift in identification from kin-group to occupational sector is particularly important with respect to originarios from the towns and provinces surrounding Cuzco, workers who conceivably could maintain closer ties with their ancestral communities. Approximately one-third of the bishopric's residents relied on family members to secure their contracts and another 28.4 percent chose fiadores from their home communities, dominating that classification with 61 percent of the entries. Another 10.5 percent of the laborers born in the bishopric were sponsored by traditional authority figures, kurakas or elders, who may or may not have been from the laborer's home community. Nevertheless, 28.5 percent of the bishopric's residents selected guarantors from within their occupational sector and a majority, 55.1 percent, of all contracts guaranteed by a coworker were initiated by laborers born in the bishopric (table IN–2). The importance of participation in the urban Hispanic economy and its role in the transformation from caste to class is clear: even in those instances where traditional relationships could conceivably be utilized, a substantial number of

Indians chose to rely on linkages within their occupational sector rather than their family or home community.

The data on fiadores show that some migrants to urban sectors severed ties with their home communities, becoming more closely integrated into colonial urban culture. However, the contracts also show that many migrants to urban centers maintained contact with their families and their hometowns, allowing for the greater diffusion of European values.[63] The urban migrants' role in the creation of colonial culture united them with their counterparts who relocated within the rural zone. Although at first glance the mechanisms of cultural interaction and change generated by urban and rural migration seem to contrast sharply, the processes are clearly interrelated and the impact, accelerated cultural change, is the same. In the rural zone resettled migrants could conceivably reinforce indigenous folkways and contribute to the perpetuation of preconquest norms and values. However, the presence of resettled urban natives, the exclusion of forasteros from local religious ceremonies, and the cultural isolation of different social groups such as the yana and the mitmaq weakened the traditional culture of the rural zone. The urban forasteros showed a higher assimilation rate and were more directly involved in the Indian-European interaction which stimulated the formation of colonial culture.

In the political realm migration had a similar impact. Relocation in the rural zone appeared to slow change within indigenous society, but both the rural and the urban forasteros ultimately altered traditional authority patterns. In the countryside the presence of familiar figures in new positions of power and the migrants' submission to local kurakas perpetuated preconquest authority lines, but these were challenged by the need to reincorporate forasteros and to devise new relationships between migrants and local authorities. In the urban zone the forasteros' relative freedom from home communities, their participation in new ways of resolving disputes, and their exposure to new positions of power, such as government-appointed leaders, weakened traditional authority lines.

In the area where migration had the greatest impact, altering forms of social interaction leading to the redefinition of the community, developments within the urban zone were more dramatic and more easily detected than change within the rural sector. In the city inherited ayllu identification was being superseded by the emergence of urban guilds, the creation of occupational linkages, and the increased emphasis on the nuclear family, in part because of Spanish law and in part because of migrants' isolation from broader kin-ties. Change in the countryside was more subtle, with ayllu autonomy threatened by Spanish control of marriage patterns and challenged by the presence of new social groups and by the reincorporation of forasteros.

In both the rural and the urban zone migration patterns produced new definitions of community, new social linkages, and new patterns of interaction which contributed to the prolonged progression from a caste to a class society. Although the processes at times seem isolated or contradictory there is one area in which the combined impact of urban and rural migration is clear: indigenous migration played a key role in the transformation of relationships of production, perhaps the most complex and complicated transformation of the indigenous community under Spanish rule.

❖ 6 ❖ ❖

"Trabajar por un Año": The Migrants' Role in the Transformation of Production Under Spanish Rule

THE EXPERIENCES of the urban worker and the rural *forastero* varied greatly, but they faced one common, fundamental challenge. Whether they were forasteros and their descendants in the countryside or established urban residents active in Cuzco's labor market, all migrants faced the most serious consequence of leaving their *ayllus:* isolation from ancestral community resources, particularly land and labor assistance. Because of their vulnerability, migrants were often forced to participate directly and actively in the colonial economic system. By doing so, they played a major role in the transformation of production from the preconquest system of reciprocal exchange emphasizing communal benefit, to the colonial system of imperial extraction emphasizing private profit. Some of the migrants' actions appeared to reinforce traditional structures but, ultimately, migrant economic activity served to further rather than to frustrate the formation of the imperial system.

The migrants' particular destinations formed the specific dynamic of their participation in the colonial economy. Some relocated in cities and mining zones, where they served a private employer or participated directly in the export economy. Others settled within traditional rural society and established linkages with local communities or landowners. The first generations of forasteros which negotiated these linkages were the most vulnerable, but their descendants were also subjected to exploitation, particularly when land or tribute was in dispute. All of these migrants evolved alternative ways of obtaining access to resources of production and compensating for lost community land and labor assistance. Migrants attained land by entering existing ayllus or renting or purchasing property. They articulated new labor relationships, including some which parallelled the structures of ayllu reciprocity and others which demanded alternative forms of labor organization, weakened the official *mita* system, and ultimately led to a wage labor force. From their labor and their land migrants earned the cash they needed to guarantee their welcome in new communities, to compensate the ones they had abandoned, or simply to survive.

Because migrants had severed ties to their ayllus they were vulnerable but they were not, as some authors have claimed, marginalized from the colonial economy.[1] Instead, their vulnerability forced migrants to participate actively and directly in both community-based production and the wider imperial system. The social groups related to indigenous migration—the established forasteros of the city and bishopric of Cuzco and the wage labor sector represented by the urban contract workers—were deeply involved in the major transformations in production during the colonial period: participation in a cash economy; individualization of landholding and alternative concepts of property, part of a long-term transformation of property from a relationship to a commodity; and the creation of alternative labor relationships, leading over time to the emergence of a wage labor force.

To argue that migrants alone were responsible for these changes would be simplistic. Cuzco-area migrants were part of a wider colonial economy and were affected by changes within that broader context: particularly, the decline in mining production which shifted market patterns in the late seventeenth century, and the growth of hacienda-scale agriculture which demanded the transfer of land from communal to individual holdings through the forced sale of Indian lands. Moreover, many *originarios* chose to participate actively in the colonial system without leaving their home communities. However, what some regarded as opportunities were for most migrants necessities, and the relationships which evolved to incorporate forasteros into the productive sector epitomize and elucidate basic changes in the transformation of production under Spanish rule.

THE MIGRANTS AND THE CASH ECONOMY

When migrants left their ayllus they lost access to land and labor assistance, but their most immediate need was for money. Fleeing the tribute and mita obligations of their home communities increased the migrants' dependence on cash: they were still liable for tribute payments and they needed cash for basic necessities. Migrants to towns and mining centers needed it to secure housing and food; forasteros resettled in the rural zone needed it to gain access to land; workers who figure in the urban labor market at Cuzco needed it to survive until they found a job.

This need was part of a wider participation in the cash economy, which must be the subject of further detailed studies, particularly of the rural zone. The Incan state had demanded and allocated goods and services within a regionally based reciprocal network, but the Spaniards extracted tribute, in cash as well as goods and labor, to be removed from the local community. Because of these fundamental differences, mechanisms of exchange and conceptualizations of value altered dramatically during the colonial period, but the documentary evidence of these transformations is suggestive rather than conclusive. Recent studies have discredited earlier ones, which maintained that Indians never saw cash or that all Indians who participated in the market economy did so reluctantly or without profit, but much more work must be done on this important feature of the colonial system.[2] Clearly, however, when migrants left their home communities to avoid tribute payments or to earn money for taxes, they ultimately increased both their own and their communities' participation in and dependence on the cash economy.

The major way in which migrants participated in the market economy was, of course, as wage laborers, and the migrants' acceptance of low-paying jobs reflected their need for the food and clothing guaranteed by their contracts. In the countryside migrants needed money, or the promise of compensation through future produce or labor service, in order to secure access to land. The documentary notation that forasteros "rented" land does not always mean that they paid cash because forasteros often compensated the originarios by a combination of money, labor assistance, or crops, which were particularly valuable in two ways: communities unable to remit taxed goods in kind, even in years of famine, could be charged their cash value, as calculated by the *corregidor* or his staff at highly inflated prices, and forastero products would reduce this assessment; and towns near Cuzco or other market centers could sell their goods, including the forasteros' contributions, to meet their cash obligations. Some forasteros sold their crops directly to Cuzco consumers, playing an important role in the city's food supply, but the *kurakas* of urban parishes levied their own illegal assessments against the vendors.[3]

Indigenous communities needed these contributions from forasteros because individuals' acts influenced broader structural changes and the migrants' actions threatened the ayllus they had abandoned. Toledo's *reducción* program and the regularization of tribute had increased imperial demands on Indian society, and the infrequency of retasas to compensate for dead or absent community members intensified those demands. By the 1590s the community assets which had been used to meet shortfalls in tribute were exhausted and kurakas who could not collect from *ausentes*, absent ayllu members, needed forastero contributions to alleviate the burden on the diminished originario population. The Toledo regulations allowed communities unable to satisfy their mita quotas to remit part or all of their labor service in goods or money, and in order to substitute cold cash for warm bodies they were forced into the market economy. In Cuzco an unusually high rate of commuting labor service to cash intensified the indigenous role in the cash economy. By the 1720s most Cuzco-area communities participated directly in the market economy or depended on the participation of forastero tenants.[4]

THE FORASTEROS AND TRIBUTE

The degree to which those communities could rely on forastero contributions and remittances from absent members to meet tribute payments varied greatly, depending on the migrants' distance from their ancestral communities, the nature of those communities' obligations, their precise relationship with local forasteros, and the persistence and personality of all the officials involved. The confusion over the migrants' role in tribute collection started with the collection process itself: everyone knew that these Indians were supposed to be paying some kind of tribute somewhere but no one was sure exactly how much tribute should be sent where. The basic principle behind Indian tribute, as articulated by Charles V in 1523, was that "it is just and reasonable that Our pacified and obedient Indian vassals should serve Us and give tribute in recognition of Our sovereignty and labor which they owe Us as vassals." In 1539 this principle was applied to *mitimaes*, who were ordered to pay taxes in the communities where they resided, and the Toledo regulations established taxes for originarios and *yanaconas*. Because tribute paid in goods required access to land, Toledo demanded only cash payments from Indians living outside their reducciones, a group he considered to be an insignificant segment of the Indian population.[5]

Subsequent royal regulations, however, produced a contradictory and confusing series of tribute regulations concerning these Indians absent from their home communities. Indians working for Spaniards were required to pay tribute to the Crown, but the regulations said nothing about Indians employed by any other ethnic group. Under special exemptions issued in the 1580s, *indios forasteros* who had settled near mines could not be forced to pay tribute or provide labor for their *encomenderos* until the extent of their contributions in the mining zone was determined. This provision hoped to increase the number of such forasteros who were "each more valuable than twenty tributarios."[6]

As migration rose during the late sixteenth and early seventeenth centuries, so did the debate over the forasteros' tribute obligations and the originarios' liability for taxes of ausentes. In repeated letters and cédulas monarchs demanded to know if communities were receiving tribute from their absent members. In 1628, recognizing the extent of the revenues lost through indigenous migration, Philip III ordered "that taxes shall be collected from Indians who live outside of their reducciones" but neglected to explain exactly how this was to be accomplished. At the same time the Indians living within those reducciones were not to be held responsible for the tribute of deceased or absent community members; nor were the remaining originarios liable for mita labor owed by "absent, fugitive, or dead" ayllu members.[7]

The regulations were confusing, but their administration was chaotic. The King might forbid making communities pay the taxes of absent members, but the royal officials who conducted post-tenure investigations of corregidores and fiscal officers were much less lenient and held administrators responsible for the amounts stipulated in the most recent tribute assessments of their provinces. "Most recent," however, meant neither "current" nor "accurate" and the gap between the recorded and actual populations placed a heavy burden on the remaining community members, who were forced to remit the full sum specified in outdated tax levies. Frequent *revisitas,* or reassessments, were necessary to keep community obligations consistent with the declining indigenous population, but few were conducted. In the 1650s Aymares Indians were being assessed taxes from *padrones,* or lists of tributaries, dating from the late 1500s. In 1660 one-third of the *repartimientos* in the province of Quispicanche were paying tribute based on Toledo's population counts. At the close of the colonial period most Cuzco communities were subject to the revisitas of the 1720s, but in the province of Chilques y Masques the 1684 obligations were enforced.[8]

Not all colonial officials thought infrequent revisitas were a bad idea. Toledo believed that Indians entering the tributary age bracket would compensate for dead contributors still listed on ayllu rolls, but even if the deceased did outnumber the new members he thought that the community, which had to bear the heavy revisita costs, would save by paying the higher assessment. When revisitas were taken either forasteros or ausentes or both might be included and the distorted tributary count would not give a true picture of a community's resources or ability to pay. Colonial officials recognized these problems but were reluctant to reduce a community's obligations because they agreed with Viceroy Montesclaros that the kurakas were "eager to hide tributaries and very clever at doing so," in spite of severe penalties for compiling fraudulent padrones in order to minimize taxes.[9]

Cuzco-area kurakas were also eager to hide the presence of forasteros who contributed to their adopted communities' tribute obligations through payments of cash and produce, which technically were not tribute payments. Some forasteros willingly assumed the tribute obligations of totally depopulated towns in return for access to communal lands, but direct tribute payments by groups of forasteros were rare. Until the 1720s, when forasteros with access to land were ordered to pay tribute in their community of residence, local kurakas were not permitted to collect taxes from forasteros without formal authorization from the kurakas of the forasteros' ancestral ayllu, and such agreements were unusual. When the author of a 1725 report stated that forasteros with lands would pay taxes in their communities of residence "as they have been doing," he was referring to the informal payments arranged within local communities, not to any systematic state collection. In 1730, when the communities of Cavana and Cavanilla, Canas y Canches, were subject to reassessment, local forasteros explained that "from time immemorial" they had "paid half their taxes to the kurakas from their ancestral towns and half to the kurakas from Cavana and Cavanilla" under the name of "pasture fees" or "rent." The kurakas sought to justify this arrangement by explaining that "this procedure had been customary throughout the Viceroyalty with all forasteros who had not been incorporated into another town or ayllu," but there is little evidence to support the extent of their claim.[10] Such explicit and publicly proclaimed agreements between forasteros and kurakas undoubtedly existed, but they were the exception, not the norm.

The majority of forastero contributions were informal and illegal;

some were also involuntary. Writing in 1690, the parish priest of Nuñoa, Lampa, claimed to be appalled at abuses inflicted on the forasteros by greedy kurakas, but the most clearly documented instances of forastero abuse were committed by the clergy, whose salaries were based on the number of originarios within their parishes. In 1656 forastero women living in Saraya, Aymares, complained to a visiting inspector that they had been forced to weave cloth which their priest sold at a local market, but the clergy were most often accused of exploiting forasteros by charging fees to administer the sacraments. Claiming that clerical salaries covered services to only the originario population, priests assessed forasteros yearly fees and charged sums for administering specific rites: not surprisingly, the clergy were particularly successful at getting forasteros to pay extra for burials. In at least some towns forasteros got more than rituals for their money. In 1682 a royal official at Potosí complained that for a fee of one peso per year for catechism and sacraments, parish priests would shield forasteros from their kurakas. In response to a 1680 Cédula Reál, the Duque de Palata had ordered that the money a priest received from forasteros should be deducted from his official salary, but this regulation was never fully enforced and forasteros continued to pay fees to Cuzco-area priests, including the incumbent of Andarapa, Andahuaylas, who was the subject of a formal inquiry in 1716.[11]

Officials who sought to control clerical abuses and to regularize forastero contributions would have welcomed a more systematic investigation of all the priests', kurakas', and corregidores' demands on migrants because enforcing tribute regulations was one of the major administrative problems of the colonial period.[12] In scores of inquiries and *residencias* everyone responsible for collecting the forasteros' tribute maintained that they had done everything possible to collect tribute from Indians absent from their reducciones in spite of the interference of "interested parties" such as private employers, including some who hid Indians from tribute collectors and others who claimed that they had paid their workers' tribute to the appropriate kurakas.[13]

The collection of ausentes' tribute was most successful in the rural zone, especially in areas where the forastero sector was the result of short-range migration. Throughout the seventeenth century kurakas in rural Cuzco communities managed to locate some ausentes and to collect their taxes. During the 1690 census of the bishopric of Cuzco, priests from a dozen rural parishes reported that the forasteros living in their jurisdiction paid taxes to their home communities. In two of these same parishes kurakas also pursued absentee *tributarios*, "collecting their taxes, mita [labor], personal services, and all their other obligations." Residents of Guaquirca, Aymares, were allegedly so impressed with the kurakas' diligence that they refused to reveal the location of absent family members.[14] Most of these energetic kurakas were from communities within provinces not subject to the *mita de minas*, where reduced labor demands had produced short-range migration and a lower percentage of absentees, enabling the kurakas to find missing community members.

Diligent kurakas might pursue ausentes in the rural zone, but urban ayllu leaders seem to have been much less enthusiastic about locating missing members. Some Cuzco kurakas collected their ausentes' taxes by dispatching agents into the countryside, such as the envoy from the parish of Belén who left the city in 1633 "to collect the tribute of several ausentes" and was "resting at roadside" when he was almost caught in a violent confrontation between forty Indians from the towns of Surite and the local *hacendado*'s employees. After witnessing this incident the envoy "went on his way to find the forasteros in order to collect their taxes." As the number of ausentes grew, however, such collection efforts were less successful. In 1690 the number of adult males missing from the parish of San Blas was greater than the number present in the city, but the kurakas collected taxes from only a few of the absentees.[15]

Urban kurakas might have been compensated by informal arrangements with forasteros residing in their districts, but most migrants to the city of Cuzco were protected by special regulations governing the urban zones and generally escaped tribute demands.[16] By the end of the seventeenth century few of the forasteros who were such a sizeable presence in Cuzco were concerned with their tribute obligations. Of the hundreds of labor contracts involving migrants, only three specified that the Indian's wages would include current tribute payments; two more *conciertos* stipulated that the cash advance would be applied to pay back-taxes.[17] Forasteros in both the urban and the rural zones had much more urgent uses for their money.

THE MIGRANTS' SEARCH FOR LAND

One of the migrants' main uses for cash was to secure access to land, the chief concern of the vast majority of forasteros relocated within the rural zone. By the mid-seventeenth century most of these forasteros were descendants of individuals who had negotiated linkages with established communities in the years between the Toledo reducciones and the forced sale of Indian lands in the 1630s and 1640s, a period when the rapidly declining population had created available lands within Cuzco-area ayllus. Forasteros obtained land in a variety of ways, all of which emphasized an individual relationship with land and the people who controlled it. This privatization of property was in sharp contrast to preconquest communal systems of production in which the ayllu held the hereditary right to work lands whose title was vested in the Inca.[18] Within that system access to land had been an inherited right but for forasteros it became a negotiated relationship. The first generations of forasteros secured land; subsequent generations defended it; all were dependent on it.

The two most direct and most secure ways to gain access to land were through marriage into an existing ayllu or through outright purchase. Marriage to ayllu members generally conferred access to community lands and migrants became as secure, or as vulnerable, as their new communities. Direct purchase represented another form of security. Although always subject to title disputes, enterprising forasteros could amass substantial property. Few were as successful as Juan Gaspar Canqui, an immigrant to Guayallate, Cotabambas, whose estate of 400 to 500 llamas and extensive pasturelands was the subject of conflicting claims advanced by two priests on behalf of themselves and their parishes. However, many forasteros did purchase small plots of land which they worked either independently or in cooperation with nearby ayllus.[19]

Such holdings definitely offered more security than rented lands, where tenants were subject to a local kuraka's will and to interference from Spanish authorities. Most Cuzco-area forasteros were forced to rely on tenuous agreements with local kurakas who used the rental income to enrich their private holdings or to meet their ayllu's tribute obligations. When challenged by ayllu members or by Spanish authorities, the majority of the kurakas claimed that they had used the funds for community needs, and in some cases rental income did pay tribute obligations or local priests' salaries. In Tinta, Canas y Canches, forastero tenants lived intermingled with originarios and helped pay their ayllu's taxes. However, at least one Cuzco-area ayllu resented the forasteros' presence and claimed that its kurakas had supplemented their incomes by allowing forasteros to rent lands needed by originarios. In 1648 these complaints by the Indians of Checacupe and Pitomarca, Canas y Canches, were substantiated in a formal inquiry by the royal treasury.[20]

The forasteros involved in the Checacupe and Pitomarca dispute would have been as eager as the accused kurakas to avoid such an investigation because Indians occupying another ayllu's lands had little protection under colonial law. In 1634 Viceroy Conde de Chinchón warned the King that granting forasteros vacant lands would cause more resentment than was usually provoked whenever land was redistributed in the colony, and subsequent royal demands for "just" land allocations to Indians said nothing about protecting forasteros.[21] Their presence might complicate the *composiciones*, but lands were technically unoccupied if they were not occupied by native-born members of the community. The community and the forasteros had little recourse if colonial judges declared those lands forfeit.

In February 1629 a *juez de comisión*, a visiting land inspector, arrived in Ollantaytambo, Calca y Lares, to ascertain if certain lands sought by a Spanish Cuzqueño were unoccupied and therefore subject to sale on behalf of the King. Neither the kuraka of Ollantaytambo nor any of his assistants appeared at the formal hearing. Instead, the judge was confronted by forasteros who testified that they had been renting the fields from village authorities who used the cash for ayllu tribute payments. The witnesses claimed that "nothing is known of the ownership of these lands, other than that they are claimed by the Indians of this town and that in order to help pay the taxes, the local *casique* [kuraka] rents them [to migrants]." The judge immediately evicted the residents "because they are forasteros and not native-born" and relocated several Indian holdings to "better sites," thereby consolidating all vacant lands. Over two hundred *topos* of "rich land for wheat and corn" were sold cheaply to the Spaniard who had filed the original inquiry.[22]

Forastero tenants who organized as a subunit of a local ayllu and gave titular allegiance to local kurakas were better protected by and more closely incorporated into established communities, primarily because of the cash and goods they contributed toward tribute demands. These migrants also played an important role in power struggles between rival communities, such as those between the towns of Combapata and Checacupe, Canas y Canches.[23] In a hotly contested dispute the kurakas of both towns claimed title to lands farmed by indios forasteros who recognized the leadership of and paid tribute to the kurakas of Combapata. When colonial authorities awarded title to the community of Checacupe the *principales*, or elders, of that community agreed "that the said indios forasteros should be allowed to live on the lands they now inhabit and plant and cultivate them in their traditional way, so long as the authority of the Indians of Combapata, which the forasteros had previously recognized, henceforth be vested in the Indians of Checacupe."[24] Once the forasteros had accepted this stipulation and also had promised to transfer rent payments, the regional juez de comisión allowed the former migrants to remain on the lands, ignoring the precedent set in Ollantaytambo twenty years earlier.[25] Perhaps by the mid-seventeenth century Spanish officials had realized the impossibility of dispossessing all such forastero groups; more probably the lower value of these potato fields or the absence of a waiting buyer dissuaded the judge from embarking on the tedious confiscation proceedings. In any case, the compromise temporarily prevented the alienation of these Indian lands, alleviated tensions within the region, and insured the security of the organized migrant group, which remained in possession even though the community of Combapata appealed and litigation continued through the 1670s.[26]

CONFLICTS OVER INDIAN LANDS

That the Canas y Canches dispute continued in litigation is hardly surprising. Land-tenure cases were among the most hotly contested within the colonial judicial system, and the rising value of land and the shrinking assets of indigenous communities provoked bitter disputes.[27] Migration complicated the debates over land inheritance and titles in ways which were reflected in the courts throughout the seventeenth century.

The forasteros' access to land depended on changing concepts of property and the widespread transfer of communal land into private hands. In the Cuzco zone land passed into individual control in various ways. Property identified as belonging to the Incan emperor, state, or gods could be confiscated and granted to Spanish settlers. Because Cuzco had been the Incan capital this justification was frequently cited in court cases, as in 1571 when a Spaniard claimed territory in Quispicanche because "these were the Inca's lands." Members of the Indian elite could use Spanish inheritance laws to claim extensive property. The reducción system had calculated a community's total holdings on a per capita basis and some individuals claimed private title to community lands. Kurakas claimed as their own the allocations of absent or dead community members. Local communities resisted this alienation of Indian lands, but the process begun with the conquest of the sierra continued throughout the colonial period.[28]

Indian communities frequently lost land through *composiciones de tierras,* the inspections and seizures of land declared to be vacant and therefore subject to resale in the name of the King. By 1600 frequent composiciones had transferred extensive lands in the Cuzco zone to private individuals, chiefly Spaniards who were part of the growing hacienda sector. In 1611 the *cabildo* of Cuzco awarded grazing lands to a Spaniard who claimed that the fields had never been cultivated, even under Inca rule.[29] Such attacks on Indian land accelerated during the early 1600s, a period of rapid expansion of the haciendas, large landed estates based on private holdings and developing in direct opposition to the interests of the indigenous community. During this period the declining Indian population was used as an excuse to confiscate Indian lands and resell them to the very haciendas whose previous encroachments had deliberately weakened the Indian communities.[30] In a rather ironic twist a Spaniard urged that Indian lands be seized and sold because the fact that the same amount of land had held so many more Indians before the Europeans' arrival was proof that the Indians no longer required such extensive holdings. A similar argument was advanced in 1619 by a parish priest who urged that local Indian lands be sold because the Indian population had radically declined and the lands were vacant. If the population should recover, the priest continued, there would be sufficient unoccupied lands available throughout the region.[31]

Not all colonial officials were so optimistic or so blind to the multitude of informal arrangements governing Indian lands, particularly the ways in which forasteros had secured access to land in the period between the establishment of the Toledo reducciones and the composiciones of the 1630s and 1640s. Leaving office in 1639, Viceroy Chinchón warned his successor to proceed carefully with the composiciones because many of the areas reported to be vacant were not, and it would cause him "no little trouble" if so much property were confiscated and resold that future generations of Indians, both originarios and forasteros, lacked land. Neither the Marqués de Mancera nor subsequent viceroys followed Chinchón's advice. The composiciones of the 1640s were extensive and the periodic inspection and confiscation of Indian land continued to transfer communal assets to private owners throughout the seventeenth century.[32]

Indians bitterly resented the loss of their lands and contested both individual titles and composiciones de tierras.[33] Forasteros figured in such disputes in two major ways: as individuals involved in private land-transfer cases or as pawns in the increasing alienation of Indian land through composiciones de tierras. Migrants involved in this process of privatization of land appear infrequently in the court records and figure chiefly as claimants to property they no longer occupied. In one case a forastero settled on disputed lands vigorously defended his title against an originario's claims, but the majority of disputes involving migrants concern property rights in their ancestral communities. Residents in Cuzco, some of whom owned substantial assets in the city, continued to claim property in home communities and went to court to defend those holdings. In one very complicated case, members of an ayllu originally based in Quiquijana, Quispicanche, who had been forcibly relocated in the urban parish of San Gerónimo, sued to recover lands sold by their kurakas years before. Their first claim, filed in 1630, was against a migrant to the Quiquijana area who had purchased several topos of community land. More than twenty years later the Cuzco residents initiated proceedings contesting the titles of additional ayllu lands that had been awarded to a Spaniard and to the widow of a local kuraka who had taken possession of the property after paying the community's tribute debts.[34]

The conflicting claims of Indians absent from their reducciones and local leaders who wanted to allocate the absentees' lands to other Indians occasionally were addressed, if not resolved, in court. In 1673 an Indian who claimed his prolonged absence was actually due to mita labor resisted his kuraka's efforts to allow other Indians to farm his assigned lands in his ancestral community. When the originarios of San Andrés de Hatuncolla, Lampa, returned home from mita service they discovered that their lands had been occupied by residents of a neighboring parish.[35] Migrants also went to court to prevent exactly that kind of unwanted intrusion by disposing of contested holdings in their home communities, perhaps without the knowledge of the current occupants or local kurakas. Such transactions usually involved urban residents who had inherited the land but had no intention of returning home to live on it. Occasionally the community contested these actions, claiming that the land belonged to the ayllu, and migrants responded in lengthy and bitter proceedings.[36]

Migrants were much less active and assertive in court cases challenging the *visitas* and composiciones de tierras, even though these proceedings were a major threat to the relationships between forasteros and local ayllus. Occasionally forasteros were the target of eviction hearings like the ones described above or were named as participants in illegal seizures of land linked to confiscation hearings. In many cases possession of the property was the deciding factor and Spaniards coveting Indian fields would hire migrants to occupy land in order to prove that its owners had abandoned it. However, forasteros were usually cited in composición hearings simply to show how disputed tracts had previously been used or how their sale would affect a community's future.[37]

Although litigation of contested lands continued throughout the seventeenth century, the damage to indigenous society was immediate and irreversible. After the composiciones de tierras of the 1630s and 1640s Indian communities were increasingly unable to absorb migrants. Some ayllus were even unable to accommodate members returning from mita duty.[38] Moreover, the composiciones stimulated a new wave of indigenous migration by both dispossessed forasteros and originarios.

In a Cédula Reál of September 24, 1648, the King recognized that the composiciones de tierras had increased indigenous migration and had thrust many Indians into private service, but he attributed these results to fraudulent allocations which had deprived native-born Indians of legitimate holdings. Viceroy Salvatierra agreed that the presiding judges were at fault but another colonial observer blamed the new landholders who forced local *mitayos* to work "as slaves . . . on the lands where they were born, causing them grief and anguish" so that they ran away. The situation might be improved, he wrote the King, if a cédula were issued forbidding mita Indians from working on lands which their community had once owned. Such a decree would "console" the Indians for the loss of their lands.[39] In at least one case authorities had already sympathized with the dispossessed Indians. Hacienda owners in the province of Quispicanche were denied agricultural workers from four nearby Indian towns because these communities were the source of the owners' newly acquired holdings.[40] Indian kurakas deprived of forastero tenants were concerned with another form of "grief and anguish": originarios who faced heavier tribute burdens without forastero assistance were abandoning their communities. Writing in 1690, the Protector de Naturales de Lima informed the King that the alienation of Indian lands was the major cause of Indian migration and mita labor shortages because whole communities had been uprooted during the composiciones de tierras of the 1630s and 1640s.[41]

MIGRATION AND THE LABOR FORCE

Although the Protector emphasized the impact of the composiciones, mita labor shortages linked to indigenous migration began before the extensive loss of Indian lands in the 1630s and 1640s. Toledo had declared that Indians not residing in their home communities would be exempt from mita duty—a provision which stimulated Indian migration and undermined the entire mita labor system from its inception.[42] The mita crisis which preoccupied colonial authorities—labor shortfalls in the mita de minas to Potosí—appeared during the late sixteenth century. But this most troubled mita system was also the most successful at evolving alternative practices to resolve labor shortages. By the mid-1650s the situation at Potosí had been stabilized while other mita systems continued to face severe shortages.[43] Labor demands within Cuzco provinces which did not serve Potosí had already engendered a variety of alternative labor relationships, but after the 1640s an increasingly regularized wage labor force emerged as the composiciones precluded migrant resettlement in rural zones and the expanded hacienda sector required a larger labor force than could be supplied through the established mita.

The mita system, particularly the mita de minas to Potosí, was a source of constant aggravation to its administrators throughout the colonial period. Officials were clearly most concerned with the mita de minas to Potosí. Scattered demands for Indian labor on private agricultural estates could not compare to the concentrated pressure from Potosí's royal officials and miners. However, the discrepancy between the official and the actual populations created by sustained indigenous migration affected the general tributary pool within the bishopric of Cuzco, not just the population in provinces subject to the Potosí mita.

This discrepancy can be seen most clearly in an analysis of the size of the *tributario-mitayo* sector, the male Indians between the ages of eighteen and fifty who were obligated to pay taxes and to participate in the labor draft. The data in table 6.1, drawn from two Cuzco provinces,

TABLE 6.1. Comparative Tributario Populations

| Repartimiento | Previous Retasa | | Tributarios 1720s | Percentage of Change |
	Date	Tributarios		
Province of Chumbibilcas				
Vellille	1652	189	111	−41.3
Chamarca	1652	89	101	13.5
Colquemarca	1653	145	164	13.1
Quinota/Llusco	1653	151	179	18.5
San Tomas	1653	105	138	31.4
Cotaguasi	1680	63	221	250.8
Achambi	1680	25	69	176.0
Livitaca	1698	126	282	123.8
Alca	1698	92	201	118.4
Province of Canas y Canches				
Sicoani	1604–1606	407	288	−44.0
Tinta	1627	404	393	−2.7
Cangalla	1655	32	29	−9.4
Pichigua	1657	518	533	3.0
Langui	1659	141	186	31.9
Checasupa	1670	92	345	275.0
Corpoaque	1672	42	168	300.0
Cacha	1675	192	176	−8.3
Checacupa/Pitomarca	1683	149	227	52.3
Yauri	1706	69	252	265.2

DATA SOURCES:
Chumbibilcas—ANP, Tributos, Legajo 1, Cuaderno 6. Tasas y Tributos del Cuzco, Provincia de Chumbibilcas, ff. 116–28.
Canas y Canches—ANP, Tributos, Legajo 2, Cuaderno 21. Retasa del tributo de la Provincia de Canas y Canches, ff. 1–34.

show the most recent assessment of the labor pool, the basis for mita demands on the individual parishes, as compared to the actual number of tributarios present in the parishes during the population surveys of the 1720s; the table also states the date of each parish's preceding assessment, demonstrating the irregularity and infrequency of official renumerations. The last column of table 6.1 is not meant to indicate a direct increase or decrease between the two discrete figures, but rather

TABLE 6.2. Comparison of the Number of Tributarios in the Provinces with Mita Service to Potosí

Province	1685	1690	1725
Azángaro	3,433	1,902	2,805
Canas y Canches	4,718	2,670	3,683
Lampa	4,569	2,050	4,078
Quispicanche	2,381	2,837	3,968
Totals	15,101	9,459	14,534

FIELD:

   1685—all tributarios, originarios, and forasteros (per Palata)
   1690—all tributarios, originarios, no forasteros
   1725—all tributarios, originarios, and forasteros

DATA SOURCES:

   1685—AGI, Charcas 271, Libro V. Libro del Señor Duque de Palata, 1690, ff. 211–11V, 219V–20, 297–97V, 306V–7.
   1690—AGI, Lima 471. Padrón del obispado del Cuzco, 1690. Data entries, conversion figures, and subtotals in Appendix II.
   1725—ANP, Tributos.
      Azángaro, Legajo 1, Cuaderno 6, ff. 79–92.
      Canas y Canches, Legajo 2, Cuaderno 21, ff. 1–34.
      Lampa, Legajo 1, Cuaderno 6, ff. 57–78.
      Quispicanche, Legajo 1, Cuaderno 6, ff. 3–35.

to show the variation between the official and actual tributario populations as defined in the 1720s reevaluations, which included established forasteros in the labor pool. Although a few individual parishes show a decline in that sector most of the parishes display a substantial growth in the available labor force. Throughout the seventeenth century the mita shortages were due to a decline in the originario-tributario-mitayo sector, not to a universal drop in the category of males aged eighteen to fifty.[44]

This discrepancy was obvious in the provinces with mita duty to Potosí, where the forasteros' ability to escape mita duty was a key element in mita shortfalls, as shown in table 6.2. The redefinition of the tributario-mitayo sector for the 1720s count actually expanded the mita labor pool throughout a period of disastrous demographic decline. In 1690 only originarios were identified as tributarios; in 1725, as in 1685, male *forasteros con tierra* were also included. The forastero representation

TABLE 6.3. Forasteros in the Tributario-Mitayo Sector, 1685 and 1725

Province	1685		1725	
	Base N	Forasteros	Base N	Forasteros
Azángaro	3,433	49.9	2,805	45.7
Canas y Canches	4,718	46.2	3,683	27.0
Lampa	4,569	22.9	4,078	39.3
Quispicanche	2,381	35.3	3,968	19.1
Totals	15,101	38.3	14,534	31.9

FIELD:
1685—All potential tributarios and mitayos, originarios and forasteros, per Palata
1725—All tributarios and mitayos, originarios and forasteros

DATA SOURCES:
1685—AGI, Charcas 271, Libro V, ff. 211–11V; 219V–20; 297–97V; 306V–7.
1725—ANP, Tributos.
 Azángaro, Legajo 1, Cuaderno 6, ff. 79–92.
 Canas y Canches, Legajo 2, Cuaderno 21, ff. 1–34.
 Lampa, Legajo 1, Cuaderno 6, ff. 57–78.
 Quispicanche, Legajo 1, Cuaderno 6, ff. 3–35.

in the labor pool in 1685 was higher than that of 1725, but both tributario groups were approximately one-third forastero (table 6.3). In the earlier census the Duque de Palata was thwarted in his attempts to incorporate forasteros into the labor pool of their place of residence; in the later survey established forasteros with access to land would be included in local mitas. The 1720s redefinition of the Indian community—the identification of an individual by access to resources instead of by ancestry—had a substantial impact on the official labor pool and helped lessen the discrepancy between the official and actual tributario-age sectors.[45]

That redefinition was, of course, of no help to the royal officials faced with labor shortages almost from the moment Toledo instituted the mita system. In the mining zones of Upper Peru, however, employers could draw on an alternative labor pool composed of migrants and former mita laborers who remained in the area. This wage labor might be more expensive than mita labor, but workers were available and their salaries could be paid in part by cash remissions from the communities whose failure to meet mita quotas had caused the shortages. Some of that cash undoubtedly came from forastero payments for access to land; some came from community members who had resettled in the mining zones. At Potosí indigenous migration and its impact on the mita de minas had a key role in the emergence of alternative labor forms which perpetuated the mita de minas by compensating for shortfalls and making it unnecessary to totally abandon the forced labor draft. In the mining town the Spaniards established at Oruro the entire Indian population was of foreign-born ancestry and, Ann Zulawski has argued, provided a more permanent and disciplined wage labor force.[46]

The impact of migration on mitas other than the mita de minas could not be resolved by the creation of a permanent labor pool and the influx of cash payments for missing workers. The Guancavelica mines were never able to attract enough migrant labor or to retain enough former mitayos to compensate for the high mortality rates associated with mercury mining. Because of health factors the few "voluntary" Indian laborers at Guancavelica in the mid-seventeenth century were only permitted to work the equivalent of one mita turn per year, precluding the development of a permanent wage labor force. In 1615 a visiting inspector informed the Council of the Indies that mercury production would stop within three or four years without major renovations in both the mines and the mita system. In 1619 mita compliance was temporarily increased through the efforts of visiting inspector Juan de Solórzano, but by mid-century severe shortages had reduced mercury production drastically and in 1695 Viceroy Monclova reported that he could ship no more mercury to Mexico because less than one-fourth of the necessary mitayos had reported to Guancavelica.[47]

The nonmining mita labor drafts in effect throughout the bishopric of Cuzco, which chiefly assigned Indians to *obraje* workshops and to agricultural production, were also characterized by persistent labor shortages. In the face of recurring labor shortages landowners used a variety of coercive measures to secure labor. In 1650 Cuzco's Protector de Naturales denounced a local hacendado for seizing Indians and forcing them to work "as if they were slaves," but explicit accusations of such practices were rare. Landowners were more frequently denounced for violating the Toledo regulations by trying to include Indian laborers in property transfers, in effect selling workers with land.[48]

Indigenous communities and private employers also tried to meet these shortfalls in various legal ways, some of which replicated or paralleled preconquest practices and others which represented dramatic changes in labor patterns. Migrants figured prominently in these new labor relationships, all of which differed from the pre-Incan practices based on reciprocity within and between kin-groups and from the Incan adaptation and expansion of that reciprocity network. However, some of the emerging labor relationships more closely resembled the precolonial practices. Individual migrants who married into established ayllus and their descendants who remained within those ayllus were subject to the local kurakas' right to demand both community labor assistance and participation in the state system. Within these ayllus preconquest kin-ties and labor reciprocity survived, although affected by the colonial system as described earlier in the discussion of the ayllu under colonial rule. Individuals or groups of forasteros who rented lands from other Indian communities might pay for that access to land by labor assistance on communal labor projects, but there is no evidence that these forasteros served mita duty as replacements for ayllu members. Members of the *ayllu forastero* of Yucay—and presumably those of other similarly constituted forastero communities—reconstructed the labor practices of the traditional ayllus, as modified to fit the colonial system, including assisting with local mita projects.

Participation in the wage labor market represents the greatest departure from preconquest labor patterns, not merely because the commodification of labor altered traditional reciprocity patterns but also because much of that participation in wage labor, particularly in cities and mining zones, involved new areas of economic activity and new forms of production and exchange. The numerous obrajes, or textile workshops, within the bishopric of Cuzco represented another new form of economic activity. Cuzco was one of the most important production zones within the viceroyalty and a major exporter of cloth to Upper Peru, particularly in the eighteenth century. The obrajes also represented a new form of exploitation of the indigenous population. Varying in size from small units to large workshops with up to a thousand laborers, Cuzco obrajes, particularly the workshop at Urcos, Marquesado de Oropesa, were unhealthy and uncomfortable workplaces and Indians were often forced into obraje labor.[49]

Crown policy governing obrajes was confusing and contradictory. Francisco de Toledo had approved mita labor allotments to obrajes, but in subsequent cédulas the Crown alternately restricted and then restored Indian obraje laborers. According to repeated decrees issued between 1601 and 1670, Indians were not to be sent involuntarily to obrajes or held there against their will, but colonial officials continued to grant mita allotments to obraje owners who often forcibly imprisoned laborers—former mitayos, women, and children—when the mita draft did not arrive. Few descriptions of obrajes specifically identified forastero workers, but in 1649 an inspection of an Abancay obraje revealed a number of "voluntary" Indian workers from nearby communities.[50]

THE INDIVIDUALIZATION OF LABOR

Although the obrajes, mining zones, and urban centers might provide the most obvious contrast to preconquest production patterns, the most profound changes occurred within the rural zone, where the demands for cash and the privatization of property led to the articulation of new labor relationships within a traditional production sector. The emergence of a landless agricultural wage labor force, in large part due to the alienation of indigenous land and sustained indigenous migration, was characterized by an increasing reliance on the definition of labor relationships through colonial state structures, particularly formalized contract labor, which superseded traditional relationships. Francisco de Toledo had approved the principle of Indian wage labor and subsequent viceroys had upheld the Indians' right to seek private employment. However, Toledo had insisted that such individual arrangements must not take precedence over community needs: Indians who entered private service would be required to return home to serve mita duty even if they had to violate contracts to do so.[51] In spite of his intentions the period from 1570 to 1720 saw the preeminence of private contracts over community obligations, the rise in the individualization of labor relationships, and the commodification of labor. The state emerged as the definer and regulator of labor relationships, and the individual became the key labor unit in the colonial economy in spite of the continuation of a mita system which demanded the labor of ayllu members to meet the obligations of the community as a whole. Because of their impact on the mita and their high participation in the wage labor force, migrants played an important role in the individualization and commodification of labor.

In spite of this growing emphasis on individual economic activity officials continued to enforce the shared nature of community obligations whenever communal responsibility served state purposes, particularly in the collection of tribute and the assessment of mita labor quotas. When convenient to the state, preconquest ties were perpetuated in postconquest practices, such as the special status granted surviving members of the Incan nobility and the belief that individual ayllu members shared the responsibility for community debts.[52]

Within this shifting balance of communal and individual responsibilities the role of the kuraka was an ambivalent one. Although the Toledo system emphasized the shared nature of tribute and labor obligations the state consistently held kurakas personally responsible for their communities' failure to pay taxes or meet mita quotas, even in the early eighteenth century when the fiscal and labor resources of most Cuzco-area communities had been exhausted. More importantly, the state acted to restrict the kuraka's control of non-mita Indian labor. Labor conciertos from the pre-Toledo period show that Cuzco-area kurakas served as intermediaries between Indian laborers and Spanish employers by negotiating contracts for members of their communities. In April and July 1571 the kurakas of several Cuzco repartimientos arranged for groups of Indian men, "healthy and able to work—no boys or old men," to haul cargo to Potosí. After the mita was established the cabildo of Cuzco reaffirmed the corollary regulation that no kuraka would be allowed to allocate the labor of Indians from his community to private employers. The state retained the right to an individual's labor as part of the community's obligation and the individual retained the right to negotiate private contracts, but the traditional intermediary was isolated from private labor relationships. Agents were allowed to negotiate with Indians on behalf of their employers, but kurakas could no longer fill that role. Cuzco officials also moved to restrict the kurakas' influence by taking control of informal but long-standing agreements between kurakas and landowners.[53]

Some of the symbolism of personalized labor relationships was deliberately continued but within an official context which emphasized the colonial state's control of the definition and articulation of labor relationships. In January 1609 when the repartimiento of Pitic Caica y Guasac was awarded to Don Gaspar Osorio, an Indian belonging to the repartimiento was taken by the hand and given to Don Gaspar. The individual who performed this symbolic transfer was the Corregidor of Cuzco. The contract which perhaps best epitomizes the transformation of preconquest communal landholding and labor reciprocity was one recorded in 1666 in which an Indian agreed to work as a wage laborer on the private estate of his own kuraka.[54]

Not all the labor contracts signed by Cuzco Indians were as dramatic as this one and not all the individuals working as wage laborers signed formal contracts. In spite of the fact that the persistent failure of local mitas led to greater reliance on contract wage labor and altered traditional labor patterns, not all of these new relationships can be detected. Seasonal labor, reflecting ecological factors and preconquest patterns of production, continued within the rural sector but was rarely mentioned in the documentation. These workers would have been part of the transient migrant labor force, distinct from the established forasteros, or seasonal laborers who agreed to work part-time on their own initiative or as part of a community effort. Many individuals who engaged in wage labor while remaining within their home communities simply do not appear in the records. Workers may have been hired through informal agreements or illegally, through local kurakas.[55]

Luckily a number of contracts survive which give details of the increasingly regularized rural wage labor force which developed with sustained indigenous migration and grew rapidly in the aftermath of the composiciones of the mid-seventeenth century. Occasionally these contracts show a sudden surge in employment dictated by a particularly acute crisis in the local agricultural mita, as occurred in Paucartambo during the 1640s. The urban labor market was also used by employers seeking workers for general agricultural labor and their contracts demonstrate the transformation of agricultural labor within the bishopric of Cuzco.[56]

The data from these contracts show that the demand on the Cuzco labor market for agricultural workers to supplement local mita allocations rose after 1640, an increase that cannot be explained solely by the sources or sampling techniques. During the decades of the 1630s through the 1660s most of these agricultural workers were foreign-born and chiefly from the provinces of the bishopric, reflecting the extensive composiciones de tierras in the Cuzco area. Most of these workers were classified vaguely as "laborers" and "yanaconas"; only the herders had specific duties. The major distinction among these rural laborers was the degree of supplemental remuneration contained in the individual contracts. Yanaconas were more likely to receive allocations of food and clothing, indicating a continuation of the more personalized linkages originally associated with yanacona status. Although the sample sizes are small, they indicate that yanaconas also had a slightly greater access to land. More importantly, these agricultural workers' conciertos, particularly the yanacona contracts, show an increasing regularization of labor relationships with only the herders' contracts showing variations in duration and wages which may reflect seasonal factors. The laborers' and yanaconas' conciertos with few exceptions show regularized contract lengths and wage rates indicating a formalization of these labor categories.[57]

This rural wage labor force was also characterized by early indications of the debt peonage system which would emerge fully during the eighteenth century. Almost all of the agricultural workers hired through the urban labor market received substantial advances on their wages, particularly those workers headed for the coca fields in Paucartambo. A number of the advances granted to Indian laborers in other sectors far exceeded the wages stipulated in their contracts and almost guaranteed their continued indebtedness. The clearest example of this trend was a two-year contract for a migrant who was to be paid forty pesos per year as a muledriver. His employer advanced him fifty pesos to pay half of a personal debt and promised to make the second payment at the end of the muleteer's second year of service. At the end of the contract period the worker would still be indebted to his employer and would probably have to extend his contract on unfavorable terms. Another migrant accepted a four-year contract at a salary far below the average wage for muleteers in return for a substanial cash advance which included his employer paying for unspecified "damages" the worker had caused. Several Indians were committed to working for employers "until [their] debts are paid." These rather vague contracts rarely included the rate at which labor was to be credited toward the debt or explain how the worker would be supplied food and clothing, omissions which obviously could lead to perpetual indebtedness. Although these contracts are few in number, similar but informal relationships undoubtedly occurred throughout the region. Significantly, the majority of the contracts which indicate the formation of a debt peonage system date from the 1660 to 1700 period, a time when the constriction of migrants' other opportunities, most notably a decline in their access to land, would have forced them into these dependent positions.[58]

The migrants' vulnerability to coercive labor practices reflects the greater vulnerability of Indians who had lost access to the land and labor resources of their ancestral communities. The need to compensate for that loss drove migrants into the colonial economy and integrated them into the local and export production sectors. In some ways forasteros were more deeply involved in the colonial economy then originarios.

Migrants to the cities and mining centers obviously engaged in new forms and relationships of production and although some forasteros in the rural zone undoubtedly minimalized their contact with both originario communities and the colonial state, many forasteros participated directly and indirectly in the very systems of tribute collection and labor service which they had fled their home communities to avoid. Some consequences of indigenous migration—particularly the concentrated labor force at Potosí and the availability in Cuzco of workers who could compensate for periodic shortfalls in local mitas—strengthened aspects of the colonial system. This urban and rural wage labor force represented a dramatic departure from precolonial labor relationships and contributed to the alienation of labor from land, a key aspect in the transformation of production under Spanish rule.

❖ 7 ❖ ❖

"Because All the Indians Have Died": Cuzco, 1720

THE SEVENTEENTH-CENTURY chronicler Guaman Poma de
Ayala claimed that Francisco de Toledo died brokenhearted
after being recalled to Spain in disgrace in 1581 to confront royal
officials critical of his administration. Had he been able to revisit the
bishopric of Cuzco in the 1720s Toledo would have encountered an
equally distressing situation: the system which he had devised to concentrate the indigenous population into stable communities and to regularize labor services and production had yielded almost the opposite of
the desired results. Although colonial officials blamed the devastating
plague of 1720 for the bishopric's acute labor shortages and declining
tribute revenues, the current crisis was symptomatic of broader fundamental weaknesses within the reducciones. Throughout the seventeenth
century erratic administration, contradictory imperial policies, and the
actions of all sectors of society, particularly of the indigenous population,
had significantly transformed the Toledo settlements.[1]

Toledo had designed the reducciones as an administrative network of
stable towns, but the forced relocation of the indigenous population had
resulted in widespread migration. Indians had left their reducciones for
a variety of reasons, the most important being the impact of incorporation into the colonial economic system, a process centered in and epitomized by the Toledo reducciones. Whole communities had been abandoned and although some had been repopulated by migrants others lay
in ruin. Different demands by the state, and particularly the nature of
labor service, produced different patterns of indigenous migration with
regional variations in the size, structure, and distribution of the migrant
sector. Even within the category of provinces with mita duty to the mines,
the impact was not identical: the demographic histories of provinces
subject to the mita to Guancavelica contrast sharply with those of provinces subject to the mita to Potosí. However, these varied migration

patterns did have a common impact on indigenous society and altered it
in ways which might well have broken Toledo's heart.

The system which Toledo hoped would demographically stabilize the
indigenous community created conditions which led to the decline of the
official population and the administrative, if not the physical, disappearance of a large sector of the population. Migration was the main
reason for the discrepancy between the official count and the actual size
of the indigenous population, particularly the tributary pool. The Toledo
regulations designed to minimize the number of yanaconas under individual Spaniards' control had instead created incentives for migration
into private service, increasing the size of the yanacona sector. Toledo's
provisions covering the few individuals who were temporarily outside
their home communities had stimulated migration so that this small
sector—the forasteros—had become a majority in some Cuzco-area
provinces and a substantial minority in others. The forasteros of 1720
were not the isolated individuals Toledo had envisioned. Forasteros were
a stable, well-established sector of indigenous society, the result of
short- and medium-range migration within the bishopric, including an
urban-to-rural outflow. Forasteros also differed sharply from transients.
A clear distinction between the incorporated migrant and the landless
laborer had developed within indigenous society and was formalized by
administrative policy in the 1720s.

Toledo's efforts to regularize labor and production had proved to be as
unsuccessful as his efforts to stabilize the indigenous community. Widespread resistance to the mita, Toledo's major attempt to regularize state
control of labor, generated a variety of labor relationships, not just the
initial adjustments made when the mita was imposed but also the regularization of agricultural wage labor, the emergence of an urban wage
labor force, and the intensification of other mechanisms of labor control,
such as debt peonage. The efforts to guarantee Indians access to land
and to link local production to the colonial economy through regularized
tribute demands led to the individualization of property. The subsequent
alienation of indigenous land, intensified by the composiciones de tierras, was a major factor in the destruction of the reducciones and the
increase in the forastero sector throughout the sierra.

The forastero sector grew irregularly within the bishopric of Cuzco
but the period of greatest migration occurred between the imposition of
the Toledo reducciones and the reform efforts of the Duque de Palata.[2]
The period of greatest migrant reincorporation into indigenous soci-

ety—as represented by the established forasteros sector—occurred between the Toledo reducciones and the composiciones de tierras of the mid-seventeenth century, which severely limited the ability of traditional communities to absorb newcomers on indigenous lands. The greatest impact of indigenous migration, represented by both the established forasteros and the *forasteros sin tierra* of the emerging wage labor force, was felt in the late seventeenth and early eighteenth centuries when royal officials were forced to recognize the migrants' role in the transformation of indigenous society and the creation of the colonial economy.

Migration was always a challenge and a danger, but between 1570 and 1650 Indians seeking integration into indigenous society had much greater opportunities. The drop in the originario population, due to a variety of factors including disease, famine, low reproduction rates, and migration, meant that migrants could find homes on lands still controlled by indigenous ayllus which would welcome their contributions to tax and mita obligations. In the countryside forasteros were able to negotiate a wide range of relationships with Indian towns, private landowners, and colonial administrators. Although production in the major mining centers began to drop in the early seventeenth century and although the mita quotas were not always met, the number of Indians working as wage labor in the mining zone provided enough labor so that colonial officials tolerated the presence of assimilated forasteros on originarios' lands and accepted a variety of private labor relationships, particularly yanacona status.

After 1650 new migrants and even established forasteros faced new challenges and dangers within a context of constricting opportunities and options as the consequences of indigenous migration, particularly the originarios' removal from community lands and the shortfalls in the mita de minas. The composiciones de tierras reduced the Indian communities' ability to absorb newcomers and in some instances even removed established forasteros from lands they and their ancestors had occupied for decades. The drop in mining production, particularly at Potosí, created two other tensions: at the mining zones Indians had fewer economic opportunities; in the countryside officials who blamed the mines' drop in productivity and profitability on the failure of the mita sought to enforce the labor obligations of forasteros with ancestry in provinces subject to the mita de minas. Although wage labor certainly predates the 1650s, Indians with limited options in the contracting colonial economy began to participate more actively in contract wage labor, frequently under conditions which led to debt peonage.

Although one of Toledo's successors praised him as "the man who foresaw everything possible,"[3] even Toledo could not have predicted that the indigenous response to his efforts to stabilize the Indian population would create alternative forms of ayllu identification and redefine community structures. This transformation was not solely the result of the Toledo reducciones and indigenous migration, but these early developments represent an essential reformulation of ayllu structure and social identity. Moreover, the emergence of groups without community-dependent social identities, such as the wage labor sector and the urban migrants, contributed to the general, as yet incomplete, structural transformation of the Andean world from a caste to a class society.

Indigenous migration also represented a major form of Indian resistance to Spanish rule but resistance through migration had unintended and ironic consequences.[4] Forasteros who relocated within rural communities might seem to be affirming indigenous lifeways but migrants played a key role in the spread of Hispanic norms and the formation of colonial culture. The forasteros' occupation of lands kept those lands within the indigenous sector, but having to develop new forms of access to land changed concepts of property and undermined communal holdings. Migrants might escape the mita de minas but often only by participating in new forms of labor relationships which were even less compatible with traditional reciprocity patterns. Although individual migrants might appear to be perpetuating indigenous norms and rejecting imperial rule, their actions advanced the colonial system and facilitated the formation of colonial society. Neither Francisco de Toledo nor any other participant in the process could have predicted the full impact of indigenous migration or the unintended and ironic consequences of individual resistance to imperial rule.

✤ GLOSSARY ✤ ✤

ausentes: a general term applied to any Indians not living in their home ayllus

ayllu: the basic unit of Andean social organization; originally an endogamous group with belief in common ancestry, the ayllu was greatly transformed by its incorporation into both the Incan and the Spanish empires

cédula reál: a royal decree

composición de tierras: an official proceeding through which Indian lands were judged to be vacant, were confiscated by the crown, and were sold to or awarded to private individuals

concierto de aprendís: contract creating an apprenticeship

concierto de trabajo: a labor contract

encomienda: a royal grant entitling the holder to commodities produced by an Indian community

fiador: an individual who guaranteed completion of another's contract

forasteros: Indians and their descendants who left their home ayllus and were integrated into indigenous society through a variety of relationships with established communities

forasteros con tierra: in the 1720 renumeration, Indian migrants and the descendants of migrants who had secured access to lands

forasteros sin tierra: in the 1720 renumeration, Indians who did not have secure access to land

kuraka: the leader of an ayllu or other Indian community

mit'a: under the Incas, a form of labor service to the state, understood within the broader context of traditional reciprocity

mita: the Spanish system of compulsory labor

mita de minas: the labor draft to the mining zones, particularly Guancavelica and Potosí

originarios: Indians living in the ayllu of their birth

reducción: a concentrated settlement of Indians from various ayllus, established by the Spanish government in order to more effectively control, exploit, and convert the indigenous population

retasa: a renumeration of an Indian community, with a reassessment of its tax and labor obligations

tributarios: generally, male Indians between the ages of eighteen and fifty who owed taxes and labor service to the Spanish crown

yana: under the Incas, a group of Indians and their descendants who were removed from their home communities in order to provide personal service to the empire and its elite

yanacona: under the Spaniards, Indians and their descendants who were linked by special service relationships to private individuals

✤ APPENDIX I ✤ ✤

Labor Contracts from the Notarial Records

The climate of the Peruvian sierra and the durability of *papel sellado* deserve much of the credit for the survival of pre-1750 documentation concerning local and regional activity in the Cuzco zone. The *Archivo Departamental* has never been sufficiently funded or staffed, and current efforts are directed at preserving and organizing materials from the republican era.[1] The physical condition and irregular classification of the valuable notarial records are important factors affecting the use of this particular data source.

Plans for using a standard sampling technique were thwarted by the condition of the data and the varied frequency of documents relating to the Indian population. Occasionally a volume listed in the archival index would actually be no more than a few loose sheets; more frequently the choice of notarial records finally analyzed was determined by the absence or presence of relevant materials. Fortunately a number of volumes, particularly those in the period from 1640 to 1720, contained *registros de indios*, sections of litigation initiated exclusively in the name of Indians. These registros were the richest data source and contributed to the increased sample size for the years 1630 to 1680. Volumes without registros de indios were carefully examined for any documents initiated by Indians. If no registro existed and if no litigation involving Indians appeared, another volume was selected. The occasional use of more than one data source per given year resulted from the archive's division of a single register into distinct protocols or the unexpected appearance of multi-year entries in a single sample volume, such as 94A–284, which contained scattered entries from 1705 to 1733. The eight-page list of specific volumes consulted is not reproduced in this volume but is available from the author; individual contracts cited in the text are accompanied by a full citation.

Examination of 206 notarial registers from the period 1560 to 1735 identified 1,167 *conciertos*, or contracts, which were coded for type of labor to be performed, terms of the contract, and gender, origin, and destination of worker (tables IB and IC). An additional 94 agreements creating apprenticeships were similarly analyzed (table IP). Both types of contracts were examined for data on the *fiadores*, or guarantors, and their origin, occupation, and relationship to the contractee (tables IN and IP).

Not all of the contracts supplied detailed information for all data categories. Although the length of employment was always explicitly stated, many contracts merely indicated that a worker would be paid "at the regular rate" or would receive "the usual supplies."[2] Only the documents relating to agricultural workers and wet nurses—occupations involving irregularly supervised labor on employers' property or direct contact with their children—consistently provided specific details of wages, cash advances, and supplemental remuneration such as access to land, guaranteed health care, and allotments of food and clothing. Several of the wet nurses' contracts contained special clauses describing the care to be given the child or demanding that the wet nurse abstain from sexual intercourse for the duration of her employment.

Due to the high number of these wet nurse contracts women dominated the personal/domestic service and the foodstuffs production/sales categories (500s and 600s). However, females were virtually excluded from all other job classifications: agriculture (100s), transportation (300s), construction (700s), skilled crafts (800s), and the arts (900s). All ninety-four of the apprentices to master builders, craftsmen, and artists were males, as were the seven Indians in the miscellaneous state/church employee (400s) grouping. Three of these contractees were hired to work at the Cuzco jail, three others collected charity offerings throughout the bishopric, and one assisted the priests at the cathedral. Two special contracts in which Indian leaders agreed to secure workers for private employers were not coded for the general analysis of the conciertos.

All of the preceding job categories were subdivided by origin of the Indian laborer (tables IB and IC). Each urban parish and province of the bishopric was coded separately, with generalized groupings to facilitate city and area totals. The Viceroyalty of Peru was divided into areas reflecting geographic and administrative divisions: Lima and its environs; coastal and northern Peru; Andean Peru; Argentina, Chile, and Southeast Bolivia. Indian towns lacking complete provincial or regional identification were located by consulting Cosme Bueno's *Geografía del Perú Virreinal* and the 1690 census of the bishopric of Cuzco.[3]

Of the 1,167 labor contracts a definite majority, 83.4 percent, dated from the period of January 1, 1630, to December 31, 1689. Generalizations and conclusions drawn from these entries are therefore the most reliable. The smaller samples for the 1690s, 1700s, and 1710s are proportionately less useful. The extremely small samples from the pre-1600 period, the 1600s, the 1610s, 1620s, 1720s, and 1730s reduce the significance of these data entries and related percentages. The deteriorated condition and low number of registros limited the availability of pre-1630 materials. The data fall in the later years, however, is probably due to the disruptive impact on the urban labor market of the pansierra plague of the 1720s. The twenty-five registers examined for the period from 1720 to 1729 comprise the highest decade total, but only two registros contained relevant documentation. The ninety-three *conciertos de aprendís,* or contracts creating apprenticeships, analyzed for this study are also concentrated in the 1630 to 1719 period.

The conciertos and conciertos de aprendís signed in the city of Cuzco during the seventeenth and early eighteenth centuries yield a variety of data on job descriptions and distribution, periodic crises in the labor market, regional economic patterns, changing family relationships, and growing professional identification. The detailed information from these valuable notarial documents contributes significantly to the analysis of Indian migration and its impact on the urban labor markets and formal mita system of colonial Peru.

TABLE IA. Labor Contract Coding: Origins

100s City of Cuzco
110 Santa Ana
120 Belén
130 San Blas
140 San Cristóbal
150 San Gerónimo
160 Hospital de Naturales
170 San Sebastián
180 Santiago
190 Unspecified
199 Specifically says "residente en el Cuzco," not included in summations of Indians born in the city

300s and 400s Provinces in the Bishopric of Cuzco
310 Abancay
320 Aymares
330 Azángaro
340 Calca y Lares
350 Canas y Canches
360 Caravaya
370 Cotabambas
380 Chilques y Masques
410 Chumbibilcas
420 Lampa
430 Marquesado de Oropesa
440 Paucartambo
450 Quispicanche
470 Vilcabamba
490 Unspecified, within the bishopric

500s Lima and Environs
600s Andean Peru
700s Coastal and Northern Peru
800s Argentina, Chile, Lower Bolivia
900s Unknown, Unspecified
990 Outside of the city of Cuzco, but unspecified
999 City of Cuzco and unspecified area outside of city limits

On the Following Charts
C = City of Cuzco
B = Area of the Bishopric
E = Exterior
U = Unknown

TABLE IB–I. Labor Contracts: Distribution by Labor Group and Origin (labor groups defined on p. 158)

Labor Group		100	300	400	500	600	700	800	900	Totals
Decade	Origin	x	x		x					xx
pre-1600	C				4					4
	B									0
	E	1	2		3			1		7
	U	1			3					4
Total		2	2		10			1		15
1600s	C				1					1
	B	1					1			2
	E									0
	U									0
Total		1			1		1			3
1610s	C		1							1
	B		0							0
	E		2							2
	U		2							2
Total			5							5
1620s	C									0
	B		2							2
	E		2		1			1		4
	U					7	1			8
Total			4		1	7	1	1		14
1630s	C	2	17		8		1		1	29
	B	1	15		7	1	1	1		26
	E	1	13		1	1		2		18
	U		5		3				1	9
Total		4	50		19	2	2	3	2	82

TABLE IB–2. Labor Contracts: Distribution by Labor Group and Origin

Labor Group		100	300	400	500	600	700	800	900	Totals
Decade	Origin	x	x		x					xx
1640s	C	15	43	1	14	1	11	2		87
	B	23	40		12	1	10	2	1	89
	E	11	29							40
	U	1	12		2	1				16
Total		50	124	1	28	3	21	4	1	232
1650s	C	2	17		11	11	3	1		45
	B	3	50		10	1	3			67
	E	2	8			1	1			12
	U	1	4		3	2				10
Total		8	79		24	15	7	1		134
1660s	C	5	48	2	27	3	2	4	6	97
	B	8	93		15	7	6	1	1	131
	E	5	28		6	0			2	41
	U	4	11		7	8	1		1	32
Total		22	180	2	55	18	9	5	10	301
1670s	C	3	13		14	2	3			35
	B	6	36		10		5	4	1	62
	E		5		1			1		7
	U		3		4	1				8
Total		9	57		29	3	8	5	1	112
1680s	C	1	12	1	21		3		3	41
	B	3	24	2	28		1			58
	E	1	6		2				1	10
	U		1		2					3
Total		5	43	3	53		4		4	112

TABLE IB–3. Labor Contracts: Distribution by Labor Group and Origin

Labor Group		100	300	400	500	600	700	800	900	Totals
Decade	Origin	x	x	·	x					xx
1690s	C	2	8	1	15	1	2		1	30
	B	2	5		13					20
	E		1		1					2
	U	1			3		1	1	2	8
Total		5	14	1	32	1	3	1	3	60
1700s	C		2		15		2	1	2	22
	B	2	3		10		4	1	1	21
	E		1		1				1	3
	U	1			9	1				11
Total		3	6		35	1	6	2	4	57
1710s	C		1		11		1	1	2	16
	B	2	3		7			1		13
	E		1							1
	U								5	5
Total		2	5		18		1	2	7	35
1720s	C		2							2
	B									0
	E									0
	U		2							2
Total			4							4
1730s	C									0
	B		1							1
	E									0
	U									0
Total			1							1

TABLE IB-4. Labor Contracts: Distribution by Labor Group and Origin

Labor Group	100	300	400	500	600	700	800	900	Totals
Origin									
C	30	162	5	143	18	28	9	15	410
B	51	271	2	113	10	31	10	4	492
E	21	98	0	16	2	1	5	4	147
U	9	38	0	38	20	3	1	9	118
Totals	111	569	7	310	50	63	25	32	1,167

TABLE IC–I. Labor Contracts: Labor Group and Origin by Percentages

Labor Group		100	300	400	500	600	700	800	900	Totals	
Decade	Origin										
pre-1600	C									27	
	B									0	
	E									47	
	U									27	
Total		13	13		67			7			1
1600s	C									33	
	B									66	
	E									0	
	U									0	
Total		33			33		33				*
1610s	C									20	
	B									0	
	E									40	
	U									40	
Total			100								*
1620s	C									0	
	B									14	
	E									29	
	U									57	
Total			29		7	50	7	7			1
1630s	C									35	
	B									32	
	E									22	
	U									11	
Total		5	61		23	2	2	4	2		7
1640s	C									38	
	B									38	
	E									17	
	U									7	
Total		22	53	*	12	1	9	2	*		20

*Less than I percent.

TABLE IC-2. Labor Contracts: Labor Group and Origin by Percentages

Labor Group		100	300	400	500	600	700	800	900	Totals	
Decade	Origin										
1650s	C									34	
	B									50	
	E									9	
	U									7	
Total		6	59		18	11	5	1			11
1660s	C									32	
	B									43	
	E									14	
	U									11	
Total		7	60	1	18	6	3	2	3		26
1670s	C									31	
	B									55	
	E									6	
	U									7	
Total		8	51		26	3	7	4	1		10
1680s	C									37	
	B									52	
	E									9	
	U									3	
Total		4	38	3	47		4		4		10
1690s	C									50	
	B									33	
	E									3	
	U									13	
Total		8	23	2	53	2	5	2	5		5
1700s	C									39	
	B									37	
	E									5	
	U									19	
Total		5	11		61	2	11	3	7		5

*Less than 1 percent.

TABLE IC–3. Labor Contracts: Labor Group and Origin by Percentages

Labor Group		100	300	400	500	600	700	800	900	Totals	
Decade	Origin										
1710s	C									46	
	B									37	
	E									3	
	U									14	
Total		6	14		51		3	6	20		3
1720s	C									50	
	B									0	
	E									0	
	U									50	
Total			100								*
1730s	C									0	
	B									100	
	E									0	
	U									0	
Total			100								*
Total:	C									35.1	
pre-1600	B									42.1	
to 1740	E									12.6	
	U									10.1	
Totals		9.5	48.8	0.6	26.6	4.3	5.4	2.1	2.7		

*Less than 1 percent.

TABLE ID−1. Foreign-Born Workers as a Percentage of Occupation Groups

Labor Group		100s	300s	500s/600s	700s/800s/900s	Totals
pre-1600	B					
	E	100	100	43	100	64
	TOTAL	100	100	43	100	64
	[N	1	2	7	1	11]
1600s	B	100		50		67
	E					
	TOTAL	100		50		67
	[N	1	0	2	0	3]
1610s	B					
	E		67			67
	TOTAL		67			67
	[N	0	3	0	0	3]
1620s	B		50			33
	E		50	100	100	67
	TOTAL		100	100	100	100
	[N	0	4	1	1	6]
1630s	B	25	33	44	33	36
	E	25	29	11	33	24
	TOTAL	50	62	55	66	60
	[N	4	45	18	6	73]

B = Migrant from Bishopric
E = Migrant from Exterior

TABLE ID-2. Foreign-Born Workers as a Percentage of Occupation Groups

Labor Group		100s	300s	500s/600s	700s/800s/900s	Totals
1640s	B	47	36	46	50	41
	E	22	26			19
	TOTAL	69	62	46	50	60
	[N	49	112	28	26	215]
1650s	B	43	67	32	38	54
	E	29	11	3	12	10
	TOTAL	72	78	35	50	64
	[N	7	75	34	8	124]
1660s	B	44	55	38	36	49
	E	28	17	10	9	15
	TOTAL	72	72	48	45	64
	[N	18	169	58	22	267]
1670s	B	67	67	37	71	60
	E		9	4	7	7
	TOTAL	67	76	41	78	67
	[N	9	54	27	14	104]
1680s	B	60	57	55	12	55
	E	20	14	4	12	9
	TOTAL	80	71	59	24	64
	[N	5	42	51	8	106]

TABLE ID-3. Foreign-Born Workers as a Percentage of Occupation Groups

Labor Group		100s	300s	500s/600s	700s/800s/900s	Totals
1690s	B	50	36	43	0	38
	E		7	3	0	4
	TOTAL	50	42	46	0	42
	[N	4	14	30	3	51]
1700s	B	100	50	38	50	46
	E		17	4	8	6
	TOTAL	100	67	42	58	52
	[N	2	6	26	12	46]
1710s	B	100	60	39	20	43
	E		20			3
	TOTAL	100	80	39	20	46
	[N	2	5	18	5	30]
1720s	B		0			0
	E		0			0
	TOTAL		0			0
	[N		2			2]
1730s	B					
	E		100			100
	TOTAL		100			100
	[N		1			1]
Total	B	50	51	41	42	47
	E	21	18	6	9	14
	TOTAL	71	69	47	51	61
	[N	102	524	300	106	1,042]

TABLE IE–I. Percentages of Migrants Entering an Occupation Group

Labor Group		100s	300s	500s/600s	700s/800s/900s	N
pre-1600	B					0
	E	14	28	43	14	7
	TOTAL	14	28	43	14	7
1600s	B	50			50	2
	E					0
	TOTAL	50			50	2
1610s	B					0
	E		100			2
	TOTAL		100			2
1620s	B		100			2
	E		50	25	25	4
	TOTAL		67	17	17	6
1630s	B	4	58	31	8	26
	E	6	72	11	11	18
	TOTAL	4	64	23	9	44
1640s	B	26	45	15	15	89
	E	28	72			40
	TOTAL	26	53	10	10	129
1650s	B	4	75	16	4	67
	E	17	67	8	8	12
	TOTAL	6	73	15	5	79
1660s	B	6	71	17	6	131
	E	12	68	15	5	41
	TOTAL	8	70	16	6	172
1670s	B	10	58	16	16	62
	E	0	71	14	14	7
	TOTAL	9	59	16	16	69

B = Migrant from Bishopric
E = Migrant from Exterior

TABLE IE−2. Percentages of Migrants Entering an Occupation Group

Labor Group		100s	300s	500s/600s	700s/800s/900s	N
1680s	B	5	43	50	2	56
	E	10	60	20	10	10
	TOTAL	6	45	45	3	66
1690s	B	10	25	65	0	20
	E	0	50	50	0	2
	TOTAL	9	27	64	0	22
1700s	B	9	14	48	28	21
	E	0	33	33	33	3
	TOTAL	8	17	46	29	24
1710s	B	15	23	54	8	13
	E	0	100	0	0	1
	TOTAL	14	28	50	7	14
1720s	B					0
	E					0
	TOTAL					0
1730s	B		100			1
	E					0
	TOTAL		100			1
Totals	B	10	55	25	9	490
	E	14	67	12	7	147
	TOTAL	11	58	22	9	637

TABLE IF. Origin of Transport and Service Sector Workers: Selected
Decades, by Percentages

		Transport		Service Sector	
	Origins	300s	N	500s/600s	N
1630s	C	38		44	
	B	33		44	
	E	29		11	
			45		18
1640s	C	38		54	
	B	36		46	
	E	26		0	
			112		28
1650s	C	23		65	
	B	67		32	
	E	11		3	
			75		34
1660s	C	28		52	
	B	55		38	
	E	17		10	
			169		58
1670s	C	24		59	
	B	67		37	
	E	9		4	
			54		27
1680s	C	28		41	
	B	57		55	
	E	14		4	
			42		51
Totals	C	30		52	
	B	52		43	
	E	18		5	
			497		216
Total N as percentage of all sector entries			93.2		86.7

TABLE IG–I. Service Sector Jobs by Gender

Labor Group		500s Women	500s Men	500s Totals	600s Women	600s Men	600s Totals
pre-1600	c	1	3	4			
	b	0	0	0			
	e	0	3	3			
	u	1	2	3			
	TOTAL	2	8	10			0
1600s	c	1	0	1			
	b	0	0	0			
	e	0	0	0			
	u	0	0	0			
	TOTAL	1	0	1			0
1610s				0			0
1620s	c	0	0	0	0	0	0
	b	0	0	0	0	0	0
	e	0	1	1	0	0	0
	u	0	0	0	0	7	7
	TOTAL	0	1	1	0	7	7
1630s	c	7	1	8	0	0	0
	b	3	4	7	1	0	1
	e	0	1	1	1	0	1
	u	3	0	3	0	0	0
	TOTAL	13	6	19	2	0	2

c = Born in Cuzco
b = Migrant from Bishopric
e = Migrant from Exterior
u = Origin Unknown

TABLE IG–2. Service Sector Jobs by Gender

Labor Group		500s			600s		
		Women	Men	Totals	Women	Men	Totals
1640s	C	12	2	14	1	0	1
	B	9	3	12	1	0	1
	E	0	0	0	0	0	0
	U	2	0	2	1	0	1
	TOTAL	23	5	28	3	0	3
1650s	C	7	4	11	8	3	11
	B	7	3	10	1	0	1
	E	0	0	0	0	1	1
	U	3	0	3	2	0	2
	TOTAL	17	7	24	11	4	15
1660s	C	23	4	27	1	2	3
	B	13	2	15	6	1	7
	E	6	0	6	0	0	0
	U	7	0	7	8	0	8
	TOTAL	49	6	55	15	3	18
1670s	C	12	2	14	1	1	2
	B	9	1	10	0	0	0
	E	1	0	1	0	0	0
	U	4	0	4	1	0	1
	TOTAL	26	3	29	2	1	3

TABLE IG–3. Service Sector Jobs by Gender

Labor Group		500s			600s		
		Women	Men	Totals	Women	Men	Totals
1680s	C	18	3	21			
	B	25	3	28			
	E	2	0	2			
	U	1	1	2			
	TOTAL	46	7	53			0
1690s	C	10	5	15	1	0	1
	B	12	1	13	0	0	0
	E	1	0	1	0	0	0
	U	3	0	3	0	0	0
	TOTAL	26	6	32	1	0	1
1700s	C	13	2	15	0	0	0
	B	9	1	10	0	0	0
	E	1	0	1	0	0	0
	U	9	0	9	1	0	1
	TOTAL	32	3	35	1	0	1
1710s	C	11	0	11			
	B	7	0	7			
	E	0	0	0			
	U	0	0	0			
	TOTAL	18	0	18			0
TOTALS	C	115	26	141	12	6	18
	B	94	18	112	9	1	10
	E	11	5	16	1	1	2
	U	33	3	36	13	7	20
	TOTAL	253	52	305	35	15	50

TABLE IH. Agricultural Workers' Contracts: "Herders," "Laborers," and "Yanaconas" (Inclusion of Food, Clothing, Land, and Medical Care in the Contracts)

Decade	Food			Clothing		
	HRD	LAB	YAN	HRD	LAB	YAN
1560s	*	*	1	*	*	1
1570s	*	*	1	*	*	1
1600s	*	*	1	*	*	1
1630s	1	1	2	1	0	1
1640s	*	2	3	*	2	2
1650s	1	1	4	1	0	2
1660s	3	5	8	1	3	6
1670s	0	2	1	1	2	1
1680s	1	1	*	0	1	*
1690s	*	2	*	*	2	*
1700s	0	1	*	0	0	*
1710s	0	*	0	1	*	0
Totals	6	15	21	5	10	15

	By Percentages					
	Food			Clothing		
	HRD	LAB	YAN	HRD	LAB	YAN
1560s	*	*	100	*	*	100
1570s	*	*	100	*	*	100
1600s	*	*	100	*	*	100
1630s	100	100	100	100	0	50
1640s	*	50	60	*	50	40
1650s	100	50	100	100	0	50
1660s	75	56	89	25	33	67
1670s	0	67	50	100	67	50
1680s	100	50	*	0	50	*
1690s	*	100	*	*	100	*
1700s	0	100	*	0	0	*
1710s	0	*	0	100	*	0
Totals	60	62	81	50	42	58

* = No entries.

Land			Medical Care			Total N		
HRD	LAB	YAN	HRD	LAB	YAN	HRD	LAB	YAN
*	*	0	*	*	0	0	0	1
*	*	0	*	*	0	0	0	1
*	*	0	*	*	1	0	0	1
1	0	0	0	0	0	1	1	2
*	1	0	*	0	0	0	4	5
0	0	2	1	0	0	1	2	4
0	1	3	0	0	0	4	9	9
0	2	0	0	1	0	1	3	2
0	0	*	0	0	*	1	2	0
*	0	*	*	0	*	0	2	0
0	0	*	0	0	*	1	1	0
0	*	0	*	0	0	1	0	1
1	4	5	1	1	1	10	24	26

By Percentages

Land			Medical Care			Totals		
HRD	LAB	YAN	HRD	LAB	YAN	HRD	LAB	YAN
*	*	0	*	*	0	0	0	1
*	*	0	*	*	0	0	0	1
*	*	0	*	*	100	0	0	1
100	0	0	0	0	0	1	1	2
*	25	0	*	0	0	0	4	5
0	0	50	100	0	0	1	2	4
0	25	33	0	0	0	4	9	9
0	67	0	0	33	0	1	3	2
0	0	*	0	0	*	1	2	0
*	0	*	*	0	*	0	2	0
0	0	*	0	0	*	1	1	0
0	*	0	0	*	0	1	0	1
10	17	19	10	4	4	10	24	26

TABLE II. Laborers from the Exterior: Distribution by Labor Group

	Origin				
	1	2	3	4	5
Labor Group					
100			11	4	4
300	10	14	22	11	6
500–600	2	1	3	6	1
700–800–900	1	1	1	2	2
Totals	13	16	37	23	13
Percentages	8.8	10.8	25.0	15.5	8.8

Key to areas of origin outside of the bishopric of Cuzco, as used in analysis of labor contracts:
1 = Lima and surrounding coast   6 = Bolivian mining area
2 = Northern Sierra   7 = Audiencia de la Plata
3 = Bishopric of Guamanga   8 = Chile, unspecified
4 = Bishopric of Arequipa   9 = Ecuador, unspecified
5 = La Paz and surrounding area

TABLE IJ. Laborers Contracting to Work Within the Provinces of the Bishopric

Destination	310	320	330	340	350	360	370	380
Labor Group								
100	2			4				
300	1						1	
500								
700							1	
Totals	3			4			2	
Percentages	4.0			5.4			2.7	

Origin				Totals	Percentages
6	7	8	9		
	2			21	14.2
10	23	4	2	102	68.9
2	2			17	11.5
	1			8	5.4
12	28	4	2	148	
8.1	18.9	2.7	1.4		

410	420	430	440	450	470	900	Totals	Percentages
		1	46	1	3		57	77.0
				2	1		5	6.8
		1				3	4	5.4
		2				5	8	10.8
		4	46	3	4	8	74	
		5.4	62.2	4.0	5.4	10.8		

TABLE IK. Laborers Contracting to Work Outside the Provinces of the Bishopric

| | | Destination | | | | | | | | | | | |
		I	2	3	4	5	6	7	8	9	A	B	Totals
Origin City	Labor Group												
1630s	100					1	1						2
1640s	100	1					1						2
1650s	700					2							2
1660s	300	1									3		4
Bishopric													
1650s	300	2				1	2						5
1660s	300	1				1					2	4	8
Exterior													
1700s	300	1	(origin #3)										1
Totals													
	100	1				1	2						4
	300	5				2	2				5	4	18
	700					2							2
	TOTALS	6				5	4				5	4	24

Note: See key to TABLE II.
    A = Lima (1) and Potosí (6)
    B = Special trip from Chilques y Masques to Lima (1)

TABLE IL. Skilled Craftsmen Working in Cuzco: Identified Origins by Percentages

Origin	City	Bishopric	Exterior	N
Decade				
1630s	33	33	33	6
1640s	50	50	0	26
1650s	50	38	12	8
1660s	55	36	9	22
1670s	21	71	7	14
1680s	75	12	12	8
1690s	100	0	0	3
1700s	42	50	8	12
1710s	80	20	0	5
Totals	50	42	8	
Total N	52	44	8	104

TABLE IM–I. Labor Contracts with Identified *Fiadores*

Labor Group		100		300		500	
		NU	NT	NU	NT	NU	NT
Decade	Origin						
1630s	C	1	2	3	7	0	1
	B			4	6		
	E			1	1		
	U			0	1	0	1
Total		1	2	8	15	0	2
1640s	C	1	2	6	11	3	7
	B	1	1	10	12	3	4
	E			5	7		
	U			0	1		
Total		2	3	21	31	6	11
1650s	C	0	1	5	7	3	3
	B			5	6	1	3
	E	1	1	0	2		
	U					0	1
Total		1	2	10	15	4	7
1660s	C			13	20	5	7
	B	0	1	20	29	3	4
	E	1	1	13	15		
	U	0	2	1	5	0	1
Total		1	4	47	69	8	12
1670s	C	0	1	0	2	1	2
	B	4	4	5	7	4	5
	E			1	2		
	U			0	1		
Total		4	5	6	12	5	7

NU = number of useful contracts
NT = number of total contracts

| 600 | | 700 | | 800 | | 900 | | Totals | |
NU	NT	NU	NT	NU	NT	NU	NT	NU	NT
								4	10
								4	6
								1	1
								0	2
								9	19
		9	11	0	1			19	32
		7	9	1	1			22	27
								5	7
0	1							0	2
0	1	16	20	1	2			46	68
3	5	2	2					13	18
								6	9
1	1							2	4
0	1							0	2
4	7	2	2					21	33
2	2	0	1					20	30
2	4	1	1					26	39
								14	16
0	3							1	11
4	9	1	2					61	96
1	2							2	7
				1	1			14	17
								1	2
								0	1
1	2			1	1			17	27

TABLE IM–2. Labor Contracts with Identified *Fiadores*

Labor Group		100		300		500	
		NU	NT	NU	NT	NU	NT
Decade	Origin						
1680s	C			3	9	2	5
	B	0	1	9	13	5	6
	E					0	1
	U					0	1
Total		0	1	12	22	7	13
1690s	C	0	1	1	4	2	3
	B			2	3	2	3
	E						
	U					0	1
Total		0	1	3	7	4	7
1700s	C					1	1
	B			1	3		
	E			1	1		
	U	0	1			0	1
Total		0	1	2	4	1	2
1710s	C			1	1	0	2
	B	1	2			0	1
	E						
	U						
Total		1	2	1	1	0	3
1720s							
Total							
1730s	C						
	B					1	1
	E						
	U						
Total						1	1
Totals		10	21	110	176	36	65

600		700		800		900		Totals	
NU	NT	NU	NT	NU	NT	NU	NT	NU	NT
		1	1			1	1	7	16
								14	20
								0	1
								0	1
		1	1			1	1	21	38
								3	8
								4	6
								0	0
		1	2					1	3
		1	2					8	17
		1	1					2	2
				1	1	1	1	3	5
								1	1
0	1					0	1	0	4
0	1	1	1	1	1	1	2	6	12
		1	1					2	4
				0	1			1	4
								0	0
								0	0
		1	1	0	1			3	8
								0	0
								0	0
								1	1
								0	0
								0	0
								1	1
9	20	23	29	3	5	2	3	193	319

TABLE IN. Key to the Nature of the Laborer-*Fiador* Relationship

---

A = *Fiador* and laborer are both contracting to work in identical occupations for the same employer; each Indian guarantees the other's contract. The exact relationship between the two Indians is not given.

B = *Fiador* is a member of the laborer's family

C = *Fiador* is an *indio principal o casique*, but not specifically identified as being from the laborer's home community

D = *Fiador* and laborer have just the same home community

E = *Fiador* and laborer have just the same occupation

F = *Fiador* and laborer have both the same occupation and the same home community

G = *Fiador* and laborer have the same occupation, no matter what other linkages exist; for example, categories A, E, and F, combined

---

TABLE IN-1. Nature of *Fiadores*: Distribution of Select Groups, and Totals

Labor Group:		300						500/600					
	Category:	A	B	C	D	E	F	A	B	C	D	E	F
Decade	Origin												
1630s	C												
	B		2	1	1								
	E				1								
1640s	C			2									
	B	2	3	3	3	2		1			1		
	E	2											
1650s	C		3	1					9				
	B		1		4				1				
	E												
1660s	C	1	4	1	2	2	1	4	1		1		
	B		7	3	6	5			5				
	E	2	2			2	4						

| Totals, Nonartisan Sectors | | | | | | |
A	B	C	D	E	F	Totals
	1	1				2
	2	1	1			4
			1			1
4		3			1	8
4	3	3	4	8	1	23
2						2
	12	1		1		14
	2		4			6
						0
1	8	2	2	3	1	17
	12	3	6	5		26
2	2		1	2	4	11

TABLE IN–I. *Continued*

Decade	Origin	300 A	B	C	D	E	F	500/600 A	B	C	D	E	F
Labor Group:				300						500/600			
1670s	C								3				
	B			1		2	2		3				
	E												
1680s	C		2						1				
	B	1	3	1	3	1			2		2		
	E												
1690s	C		1						2	1			
	B			1	2	1			2		1		
	E												
1700s	C												
	B					1							
	E		1										
1710s	C		1										
	B												
	E												
Totals	C	1	11	4	2	2	1	0	19	2	0	1	0
	B	3	16	10	19	12	2	1	13	0	4	0	0
	E	4	3	0	1	2	4	0	0	0	0	0	0
Totals		8	30	14	22	16	7	1	32	2	4	1	0

| | Totals, Nonartisan Sectors | | | | | |
A	B	C	D	E	F	Totals
	3					3
	5	1	2	3		11
					2	2
	3					3
1	5	1	5	1		13
						0
	3	1				4
	2	1	3	1		7
						0
						0
				1		1
	1					1
	1				1	2
			2			2
						0
5	31	8	2	4	3	53
5	31	10	27	19	3	95
4	3	0	2	2	4	15
14	65	18	31	25	10	163

TABLE IN−2. Nature of *Fiadores* for Nonartisan Sectors

Fiador Category	Percentages of Laborers by Origin Group Linked to *Fiador* Category							
	A	B	C	D	E	F	G	*N*
Origin								
City	9.4	58.5	15.1	3.8	7.5	5.7	22.6	53
Bishopric	5.3	32.6	10.5	28.4	20.0	3.2	28.5	95
Exterior	26.7	20.0	0.0	13.3	13.3	26.7	66.7	15
Totals	8.6	39.9	11.0	19.0	15.3	6.1	30.0	163

Fiador Category	Percentages of *Fiador* Category Linked to Laborers in Each Origin Group							
	A	B	C	D	E	F	G	Totals
Origin								
City	35.7	47.7	44.4	6.4	16.0	30.0	24.5	32.5
Bishopric	35.7	47.7	55.5	87.1	76.0	30.0	55.1	58.3
Exterior	28.6	4.6	0.0	6.4	8.0	40.0	20.4	9.2
N	14	65	18	31	25	10	49	163

TABLE IN−3. Nature of *Fiadores* for Artisan Sector

Fiador Category	A	B	C	D	E	F	G	*N*
Occupation								
700s	14	1	1	2	5		19	23
800s				2	1		1	3
900s	4				3		7	7
Totals	18	1	1	4	9	0	27	33
Percentages	54.5	3.0	3.0	12.1	27.3	0	81.8	

TABLE IP−I. Contracts Creating Apprenticeships: Distribution

Origin	Self-Negotiated				Arranged				Total and % by Self	Total and % Arranged	Totals N
	C	B	E	U	C	B	E	U			
1600s		1	1						2	0	2
									100		
1610s				1					1	0	1
									100		
1620s								1	0	1	1
										100	
1630s		2	2			1	1		4	2	6
									67	33	
1640s	1	4	1		2	1			6	3	9
									67	33	
1650s	1	2	1		1				4	1	5
									80	20	
1660s	3	7	3	1	3	2		5	14	10	24
									58	42	
1670s		4			2				4	2	6
									67	33	
1680s	3	3	1	1	2	1		1	8	4	12
									67	33	
1690s	2	2		1	3	1		3	5	7	12
									42	58	
1700s	1	1	1	1	1	4		3	4	8	12
									33	67	
1710s		1			2	1			1	3	4
									25	75	
Totals	11	27	10	5	14	13	1	13	53	41	94
									56	44	

TABLE IP–2. Summation of Contracts Creating Apprenticeships with Indicated Origin of Indian Laborer

Origin	Self-Negotiated				
	C	B	E	Totals	Percentages
Labor Group					
700	2	11	1	14	29.2
800	4	12	6	22	45.8
900	5	4	3	12	25.0
Totals	11	27	10	48	
Percentages	22.9	56.2	20.8		

Origin	Arranged				
	C	B	E	Totals	Percentages
Labor Group					
700	2	1	0	3	10.7
800	6	10	1	17	60.7
900	5	3	0	8	28.6
Totals	13	14	1	28	
Percentages	46.4	50.0	3.6		

Origin	Totals				
	C	B	E	Totals	Percentages
Labor Group					
700	4	12	1	17	22.4
800	10	22	7	39	51.3
900	10	7	3	20	26.3
Totals	24	41	11	76	
Percentages	31.5	53.9	14.5		

TABLE IP–3. Signer-Apprentice Relationship in Arranged Contracts

| | | Signer | | |
	Father	Mother	Both Parents	Other Relative*	Total N
City	6	4	0	2	
Bishopric	7	6	1	1	
Exterior	1	0	0	0	
Unknown	5	8	0	0	
Totals	19	18	1	3	41
% N	46	44	2	7	

*Includes 1 older brother, 1 older sister, 1 grandmother

TABLE IP–4. Nature of *Fiadores*

| | Self-Negotiated | | | | Arranged | | | | Totals |
	C	B	E	U	C	B	E	U	
Fiador									
Family	4	2	1		1	2			10
Same Labor Group				1					1
Same Home Town					1				1
Unknown	4	2						2	8
Subtotals				14				6	
Total N									20
% N =				70.0				30.0	

| | By Percent | | |
	Self-Negotiated	Arranged	Total
Family	50.0	50.0	50.0
Same Labor Group	7.1	0	5.0
Same Home Town	0	16.7	5.0
Unknown	42.9	33.3	40.0

Entries distribution: 1640s 2 1670s 2
1650s 2 1700s 4
1660s 6 1710s 4

✤ APPENDIX II ✤ ✤

The 1690 Census of the Bishopric of Cuzco

Bishop Don Manuel de Mollinedo y Angulo issued the call for a census of the bishopric of Cuzco in July 1689. During the following year he received a total of 134 reports from the *doctrinas*, or parishes, in his see (table IID). A study of the filing dates of the parish responses shows no correlation between proximity to Cuzco and promptness of reply. The last parish to report, Vellille, Chumbibilcas, was only a few leagues distant from the doctrina of Santo Tomas, which had submitted its accounts one year before.[1]

Although the bishop's letter had listed specific items to be included in each *padrón*, or report, the information sent to Cuzco was neither as standardized nor as complete as ordered. The reports ranged from one to thirty-nine pages[2] and contained such diverse information as a meticulous description of every painting, ornament, and altar cloth in one parish;[3] a carefully drawn map of another parish and its adjacent annexes;[4] and a supplemental list by name of every resident of a third.[5]

Unfortunately the request for essential economic and demographic materials was frequently ignored or misapplied. Parish priests rarely complied with orders to list by name all agricultural units, such as haciendas or *estancias;* each cleric interpreted in his own way the command to enumerate "the people who live in every town, according to the number of Spaniards and Indians present."[6] The resulting raw data required substantial adjustment to insure a correct population count. Table IID indicates the data manipulation performed according to the following code:

o—No manipulation of the undifferentiated data presented in the text, usually in the form of a total population of *almas* or *personas de confesión.* The former term gives the total number of "souls" within the parish; the latter includes only "people capable of making confession," usually Indians over the age of seven. Three parish reports which list "persons other than those of confession" indicate that this additional young population may be as high as 17 percent of the total.[7] Because of the scarcity of available data and the irregularity of the undifferentiated entries, no attempt has been made to amplify the original data. Such totals, however, should be regarded as minimal.

196

1—Regular mathematical calculations and standardization of categories, involving given figures for distinct groups, differentiated by any one or a combination of the following characteristics: gender, age, civil status, tribute obligation, ayllu, origin, or geographic location. This process may include compensation for married women mentioned in the text but not included in numerical data.

2—Additional preliminary calculations required for population listed by family or residence, usually rural agricultural units.

3—Additional preliminary organization, standardization, and calculations required for original data presented in the form of lists of individual Indians.

4—Original data, expressed as the number of tribute-paying Indians in the population, have been amplified through the use of a locally generated multiplier of 4.5806 dependent Indians per tribute payer, based on twenty-five entries.

5—Original data, expressed as the total of adult male Indians in the population, have been amplified through use of a locally generated multiplier of 2.3788 dependent Indians per adult male, based on twenty-three entries.

6—Original data, expressed as a number of Indian families, have been amplified through use of a locally generated multiplier of 3.0837 Indians per family, based on ten entries.

7—Original data, expressed as the number of adult male and female Indians in the population, have been amplified through use of a multiplier of 0.4531 children per adult Indian, based on twenty-four entries. This multiplier was used only in those cases where the text specifically stated that children had not been included in parish totals. The term "children," judged by internal textual evidence, usually included unmarried males and females between the ages of seven and eighteen.

The resulting modified population figures show considerable variation with respect to provincial and parish size. Provincial totals range from 13,374 in Abancay to 973 in Vilcabamba; parish populations fall between 3,211 in Limatambo, ABY-9, and 45 in Vellille, CHMB-6 (tables IIA and IIE). The highest population concentration is found in the provinces making up the Cuzco to Puno corridor—Quispicanche, Chilques y Masques, Canas y Canches, Lampa, and Azángaro—and in the transportation and administrative center of Abancay.

The *forastero* population was well distributed throughout the bishopric of Cuzco. Eight of the nine urban parishes and eighty-five of the 125 provincial doctrinas, an area containing 72.7 percent of the bishopric's population, reported the presence of forastero Indians. In those parishes where forastero and *originario* groups were recorded separately, forasteros totaled 48.4 percent of adult males and 44.6 percent of all Indians. Due to the discrepancy in sample sizes a comparison of the raw data range of the forastero presence in the provincial populations would be somewhat misleading; the numerous parish entries, however, illustrate a wide variation in forastero representation, from the maximum of 100 percent in Chupa, AZG-3, and Challabamba, PCT-5, to a mere 6 percent in Guaquirca, AYM-16 (tables IIB and IIE). Within the city of Cuzco the forastero population ranged from 100 percent of the central Cathedral parish, CUZ-1, to 17 percent of the parishes of San Gerónimo and Hospital de Naturales, CUZ-3 and CUZ-8. Because of repeated reports of a drop in the city's migrant population following a census by the Duque de Palata, these figures represent minimal totals.[8]

The division of the population into originario and forastero groups is of chief interest to this study, but data on the Indian population's geographic origin are not the most commonly supplied secondary characteristic; information on gender composition was more often included in parish reports. Analysis of the male/female ratio in the provincial areas and in the city of Cuzco shows a fairly consistent pattern of a modest female majority, with the variation in the Cotabambas and Vilcabamba totals related to their small sample sizes (table IIC). Most of the individual parish reports reflect this general pattern, with the extremes falling at male/female ratios of 66.0 to 34.0 percent in Las Valles, VLC-2, and 19.0 to 81.0 percent in Aquira, COT-6. Further examination of the small data samples with entries specific to age and family structure reveals a child/adult ratio of approximately one to two and a low average family size of 3.1 Indians.

A consideration of the identical characteristics for the forasteros yields a population profile which contrasts sharply with the traditional view of single males living in isolated, rural conditions or urban centers. Figures from seventeen parishes, primarily from the provinces of Abancay, Aymares, and Chilques y Masques, show a relatively similar male/female composition for the forastero and originario subgroups and for the population as a whole (tables IIC and IIF–1). The percentage of males in the forastero population (48.6) is slightly higher than that in the originario (45.2) and general population (44.3), but the difference is insufficient to support the image of an exclusively male society. Data on the adult/child ratio and family size further discredit the established model for the migrant sector. Both the proportion of children in the population and the average family size are higher for the forasteros than for the originarios (table IIF–2).

The data collected in the 1690 census also contradict the traditional assumption that Indian migrants sought anonymity in urban centers or in rural isolation. The forasteros were a vital presence in intermediary-size parish towns. Although the total figures show a town/rural composition of 34.2 to 65.8 percent for the forastero population, the local distribution is characterized by the extreme dominance of one sector, with only one of the eleven parishes reporting a relatively balanced ratio. In seven doctrinas the majority of the forasteros lived in the rural sector; in three parishes the majority resided in towns (table IIF-3).

In contrast with the internal variation of the forastero data, the total figures for town/rural composition of the originario population, 96.3 to 3.7 percent, reflect the pattern of distribution in the individual parish reports. In only one doctrina did the proportion of the originario population residing in towns fall below 99 percent (table IIF-3).

Adjustment of the entries to show forastero and originario representation in each sector reveals some interesting data patterns. With the exception of two doctrinas in which all Indians were forasteros, the forastero population failed to dominate any one town. However, the forasteros were a substantial subgroup in a few parish towns, and in some cases the majority of the forasteros resided in that sector. In Chupa, AZG-3, and Challabamba, PCT-5, where the entire population was classified as forasteros, the patterns of town/rural distribution present a clear contrast: in the former case, the population is divided evenly between the two sectors; in the latter, an overwhelming majority resides in the rural area (table IIF-3).

Data from those few parish reports which specifically identified town and rural residents by both geographic origin and gender show a relatively even gender distribution in both forastero subgroups. With the exception of the small parish of Colcabamba, AYM-4, none of the eight entries displays a radically skewed gender ratio (table IIF-4).

Obviously, the dynamics of forastero settlement cannot be reduced to a simplistic urban center/rural solitude dichotomy. A closer consideration of area tribute and *mita* obligations, the structure of the productive sector, the availability of land, and local political and religious alliances is essential in order to formulate a total picture of the structure and situation of the forastero population living in the bishopric of Cuzco in the 1690s.

TABLE IIA. Indigenous Population of
the Bishopric of Cuzco in 1690

Provincial Totals	113,565
Abancay	13,734
Aymares	9,540
Azángaro	8,712
Calca y Lares	6,009
Canas y Canches	12,229
Caravaya y Sangaban	4,940
Cotabambas	6,954
Chilques y Masques	11,759
Chumbibilcas	6,434
Lampa	9,390
Marquesado de Oropesa	5,226
Paucartambo	4,668
Quispicanche	12,997
Vilcabamba	973
City of Cuzco Total	8,322
Total, City and Provinces	121,887

TABLE IIB. *Forasteros* in the Population

	Doctrinas Reporting *Forasteros*	Percentage of Population Involved	*Forasteros* Percentage of Adult Males*	*Forasteros* Percentage of All Indios*
Provincial totals	85 of 125	72.0	50.3	43.6
Abancay	9 of 9	100.0	41.2	40.9
Aymares	11 of 16	65.3	26.6	15.2
Azángaro	5 of 9	52.0	100.0	100.0
Calca y Lares	4 of 6	43.2	80.7	—
Canas y Canches	6 of 11	54.2	—	48.7
Caravaya y Sangaban	4 of 6	59.2	—	—
Cotabambas	7 of 13	55.2	72.7	—
Chilques y Masques	8 of 9	93.7	25.8	40.8
Chumbibilcas	7 of 11	68.9	53.8	49.9
Lampa	9 of 13	57.7	36.3	42.8
Marquesado de Oropesa	3 of 4	89.5	87.6	—
Paucartambo	3 of 6	73.0	100.0	100.0
Quispicanche	8 of 10	91.8	47.6	—
Vilcabamba	1 of 2	41.4	—	82.9
City of Cuzco	8 of 9	80.6	33.6	47.6
Total, City and Provinces	93 of 134	72.7	48.4	44.6

*Respective *N* totals available on following pages. For those provinces where no percentages appear, there were no entries.

TABLE IIC. Total Indian Population by Gender

Number of Data Units		Male	Female	Total	Percentages Male	Percentages Female
34	Provincial Totals	15,323	19,290	34,613	44.3	55.7
6	Abancay	4,669	4,919	9,588	48.7	51.3
12	Aymares	2,635	4,525	7,160	36.8	63.2
	Azángaro					
	Calca y Lares					
3	Canas y Canches	988	1,391	2,379	41.5	58.5
	Caravaya y Sangaban					
2	Cotabambas	554	1,465	2,019	27.4	72.6
6	Chilques y Masques	4,099	4,295	8,394	48.8	51.2
2	Chumbibilcas	404	391	795	50.8	49.2
	Lampa					
1	Marquesado de Oropesa	989	1,356	2,345	42.2	57.8
	Paucartambo					
1	Quispicanche	719	811	1,530	47.0	53.0
1	Vilcabamba	266	137	403	66.0	34.0
2	City of Cuzco Total	816	1,043	1,859	43.9	56.1
36	Total, City and Provinces	16,139	20,333	36,472	44.3	55.7

TABLE IID—I. *Doctrinas* of the Bishopric of Cuzco with Their Annexes: Data Manipulation Performed

Province code	Parish	Data Manipulation
CUZ (City of Cuzco)		
CUZ 1	De la Santa Catedral	1
CUZ 2	Santiago	0
CUZ 3	San Gerónimo	2
CUZ 4	San Sebastián	2
CUZ 5	San Cristóbal	1
CUZ 6	Santa Ana˙	2
CUZ 7	Belen	1
CUZ 8	Hospital de Naturales	1
CUZ 9	San Blas	7

TABLE IID-2. *Doctrinas* of the Bishopric of Cuzco with Their Annexes: Data Manipulation Performed

Province code		Parish	Data Manipulation
ABY (Provincia of Abancay)			
ABY 1	Curaguasi	Cachora, Antilla	2
ABY 2	Guarocondo		1
ABY 3	Chinchaypuquio	Sumaro	1
ABY 4	Anta	Puguiura	2
ABY 5	Valle de Abancay	Carbani	1
ABY 6	Zurite		2
ABY 7	Chonta	Pibil, Pantipata	1
ABY 8	Guanipaca	Guayoguayo	2
ABY 9	Limatambo	Pampaconga, Mollepata	2
AYM (Provincia of Aymares)			
AYM 1	Pachaconas	Guancaray, Ayaguaya, Alcopaya	2
AYM 2	Yanaca	Saraica	1
AYM 3	Pocoanca	Pacsica, Pichigua, Checasa	1
AYM 4	Colcabamba	Lucre, Tintay, Chacna, Caracara	2
AYM 5	Lambrama	Caypi	1
AYM 6	Zoraia	Sanayca, Capaia, Foraia	1
AYM 7	Hancobamba	Pampallacta, Chapimarca, Sutcunga, Tiaparo	2
AYM 8	Chalvanca	Caraybamba	1
AYM 9	Pampamarca	Cotarosi, Colca, Caraybamba	1
AYM 10	Totora	Oropesa	0
AYM 11	Chuquinga	Pairaca, Mutca, Guaillarina	1
AYM 12	Mollebamba	Calcauso, Silco, Vito	5

TABLE IID–3. *Doctrinas* of the Bishopric of Cuzco with Their Annexes: Data Manipulation Performed

Province code		Parish	Data Manipulation
(Provincia of Aymares, continued)			
AYM 13	Antabamba		1
AYM 14	Sabayno	Antilla	3
AYM 15	Circa	Uraguacho, Chacochi, Chalguani, Pychiruga	2
AYM 16	Guaquirca	Matara	3
AZG (Provincia of Azángaro)			
AZG 1	Azángaro		0
AZG 2	Arapa	Ventansas	1
AZG 3	Chupa	Putina	1
AZG 4	Pupuja		0
AZG 5	Acillo		0
AZG 6	Pusi		0
AZG 7	Saman		0
AZG 8	Espiritu Santo/ Taraco		0
AZG 9	Caminaca	Achaia, Nicacio	1
CYL (Provincia of Calca y Lares)			
CYL 1	Chinchero	Omasbamba	1
CYL 2	Lares	Choquecancha, Cachin, Gualla	6
CYL 3	Ollantaytambo		0
CYL 4	Lamay	Coya	1
CYL 5	Pisac	Tarai, San Salvador	1
CYL 6	Calca		4

TABLE IID–4. *Doctrinas* of the Bishopric of Cuzco with Their Annexes:
Data Manipulation Performed

Province code		Parish	Data Manipulation
CYC (Provincia of Canas y Canches)			
CYC 1	Pampamarca	Surimana, Sungasuca, San Juan de la Cruz	0
CYC 2	Checasupa		0
CYC 3	Checacupa	Pitomarca	1
CYC 4	Cacha	San Pablo	1
CYC 5	Sicoani	Marangani	1
CYC 6	Yanaoca		0
CYC 7	Langui	Paio	1
CYC 8	Yauri		0
CYC 9	Coporaque		0
CYC 10	Tinta	Combapata	0
CYC 11	Pichigua	Condoroma	1
CYS (Provincia of Caravaya y Sangaban)			
CYS 1	Para	Vicayos, Tiraca, Valle de La Mina	1
CYS 2	Ayapata	Ollacha, Macussani	6
CYS 3	San Juan del Oro	Quiquira, Purumaya	6
CYS 4	Sandia	Guiaca, Patanbuco, Cuyo-cuyo	0
CYS 5	Aporoma		1
CYS 6	Coaza	Ituata	6
COT (Provincia of Cotabambas)			
COT 1	Chirir	Chiquibamba, Corpaguasi	2
COT 2	Curasco	Ayriguanca	1
COT 3	Mara		1

TABLE IID–5. *Doctrinas* of the Bishopric of Cuzco with Their Annexes: Data Manipulation Performed

Province code		Parish	Data Manipulation
(Provincia of Cotabambas, continued)			
COT	4	Tambobamba	Chacaro	2
COT	5	Palcaro	Totorguaillas	2
COT	6	Aquira	Cocha	1
COT	7	Cotabambas	Totora	2
COT	8	Haquira	Patoguasi, Llacva, Cocha	1
COT	9	Cullurqui		1
COT	10	Mamara	Aurpai	1
COT	11	Pinianca	Colpa	1
COT	12	Guayllate	Pallpacacho, Lluchivillca, Corpaguasi	5
COT	13	Picti		1
CHYM (Provincia of Chilques y Masques)			
CHYM	1	Capi	Coyatambo, Tucuyachi	1
CHYM	2	Guanoquite	Corca, Guancaguanca, Coror	1
CHYM	3	Collega	Araypalpa, San Lorenso	1
CHYM	4	Paruro		1
CHYM	5	Omacha	Antapalpa, Quilli, Hacca, Villque	2
CHYM	6	Cuchiriquani	Pacopalta, Panpacucho, Capa	2
CHYM	7	Yaurisque	Pacaritambo	1
CHYM	8	Accha Urinsaya	Guayaconga, Pilpinto	2
CHYM	9	Accha Hanansaya	Parco, Pocoray	2

TABLE IID−6. *Doctrinas* of the Bishopric of Cuzco with Their Annexes: Data Manipulation Performed

Province code		Parish	Data Manipulation
CHMB (Provincia of Chumbibilcas)			
CHMB	1	Quinota	Llusco	1
CHMB	2	Chamaca		0
CHMB	3	Santo Tomas		2
CHMB	4	Capacmarca		2
CHMB	5	Colquemarca	Yanqui	1
CHMB	6	Vellille	Ayacasi	2
CHMB	7	Alca	Puica	1
CHMB	8	Toro	Caspi, Cupi	2
CHMB	9	Tomepampo	Achamba	2
CHMB	10	Cotaguasi		1
CHMB	11	Livitaca	Totora	3
LMP (Provincia of Lampa)			
LMP	1	Lampa	Calapusa	5
LMP	2	Omachiri	Llalli	1
LMP	3	Hatuncolla		0
LMP	4	Hatuncavana		5
LMP	5	Manaso	Vilque	1
LMP	6	Cavanilla		1
LMP	7	Caracoto	Guaca, Iassin	5
LMP	8	Juliaca		1
LMP	9	Horunillo		1
LMP	10	Macari	Cupe	1
LMP	11	Nunoa	Santa Rosa	1
LMP	12	Aiavire		0
LMP	13	Pucara	Vilavila	2

TABLE IID−7. *Doctrinas* of the Bishopric of Cuzco with Their Annexes:
Data Manipulation Performed

Province code	Parish	Data Manipulation
MQO (Marquesado de Oropesa)		
MQO 1 Maras		0
MQO 2 Guaillabamba	Urquillo	1
MQO 3 Yucay		0
MQO 4 Urubamba		1
PCT (Provincia of Paucartambo)		
PCT 1 Paucartambo (or Llaullipata)	Colquepata	2
PCT 2 Coaima		0
PCT 3 Caicai	Guasac	0
PCT 4 Tomopampa		0
PCT 5 Quacanga y Chimor (or Challabamba)		2
PCT 6 Catca	Ocongate	2
QPC (Provincia of Quispicanche)		
QPC 1 Punaqueguar (or Quiguares)	Rontoca, Cunutambo	1
QPC 2 Acos	Acomio, Vaiqui	0
QPC 3 Papres	Pirque, Sanca, Corma	1
QPC 4 Oropesa		1
QPC 5 Andaguailillas		1
QPC 6 Quequijana		0
QPC 7 Urcos	Guaroc	1
QPC 8 Sangarara	Marcaconga, Yanampampa, Acopia	1
QPC 9 Marcapata	Cuchoa	0
QPC 10 Pomacanche	San Juan	0

TABLE IID–8. *Doctrinas* of the Bishopric of Cuzco with Their Annexes: Data Manipulation Performed

			Data Manipulation
VLC (Provincia of Vilcabamba)			
VLC 1	Lucma y Vilcabamba	Acobamba	2
VLC 2	Las Valles de Amay- bamba y Quilla- bamba		2

TABLE IIE–1. Parish Population Totals with Forastero Representation

Province Code	1676	1689–90	Forasteros Cited	Percentages of Forasteros in Identified Population	Percentages of Forasteros Among Adult Males
City of Cuzco					
CUZ 1		535	yes	100	
CUZ 2		300	yes		
CUZ 3		540	yes	16.7	
CUZ 4		512			
CUZ 5		1,900	yes	84.2	
CUZ 6		1,324	yes	47.2	42.4
CUZ 7		88	yes		
CUZ 8		2,610	yes	16.3	
CUZ 9		513	yes		12.7

TABLE IIE−2. Parish Population Totals with Forastero Representation

Province Code	1676	1689–90	Forasteros Cited	Percentages of Forasteros in Identified Population	Percentages of Forasteros Among Adult Males
Abancay					
ABY 1	2,000	1,503	yes		
ABY 2	2,000	947	yes	44.2	
ABY 3	2,000	774	yes	14.6	
ABY 4	5,000	1,334	yes	40.0	38.7
ABY 5	3,500	1,956	yes		
ABY 6	3,000	1,416	yes	54.0	
ABY 7	2,000	1,483	yes	39.8	44.1
ABY 8	200	1,110	yes		
ABY 9	4,000	3,211	yes	48.8	42.6

TABLE IIE−3. Parish Population Totals with Forastero Representation

Province Code	1676	1689–90	Forasteros Cited	Percentages of Forasteros in Identified Population	Percentages of Forasteros Among Adult Males
Aymares					
AYM 1	300	272	yes		41.8
AYM 2	150	488	yes		
AYM 3	350	327	yes	20.8	20.2
AYM 4	1,200	534	yes	13.8	28.0
AYM 5	1,500	600			
AYM 6	1,500	1,413	yes		
AYM 7	800	663	yes	25.6	32.2
AYM 8	600	500	yes		
AYM 9	800	645			
AYM 10	500	520			
AYM 11	1,000	603	yes		31.1
AYM 12	300	615			
AYM 13	1,000	925			
AYM 14	200	251	yes	7.6	13.0
AYM 15	1,000	482	yes		
AYM 16	1,200	702	yes	14.6	6.6

TABLE IIE−4. Parish Population Totals with Forastero Representation

Province Code	1676	1689–90	Forasteros Cited	Percentages of Forasteros in Identified Population	Percentages of Forasteros Among Adult Males
Azángaro					
AZG 1	1,500	1,200			
AZG 2	2,000	900			
AZG 3		1,170	yes	100	
AZG 4	500	680			
AZG 5	2,000	1,400			
AZG 6		500	yes		
AZG 7	500	490	yes		
AZG 8	900	1,015	yes		
AZG 9	2,000	1,357	yes		

TABLE IIE−5. Parish Population Totals with Forastero Representation

Province Code	1676	1689–90	Forasteros Cited	Percentages of Forasteros in Identified Population	Percentages of Forasteros Among Adult Males
Calca y Lares					
CYL 1		983			
CYL 2		472	yes		
CYL 3	2,500	900	yes		
CYL 4	1,500	560	yes		
CYL 5	2,000	2,431			
CYL 6	3,000	663	yes		80.7

TABLE IIE-6. Parish Population Totals with Forastero Representation

Province Code	1676	1689-90	Forasteros Cited	Percentages of Forasteros in Identified Population	Percentages of Forasteros Among Adult Males
Canas y Canches					
CYC 1		1,500			
CYC 2		1,500			
CYC 3	1,500	391	yes		
CYC 4	2,500	360	yes		
CYC 5	2,000	1,628	yes	48.8	
CYC 6		1,000			
CYC 7		1,700	yes		
CYC 8		600			
CYC 9		1,000			
CYC 10		1,550	yes		
CYC 11		1,000	yes		

TABLE IIE-7. Parish Population Totals with Forastero Representation

Province Code	1676	1689-90	Forasteros Cited	Percentages of Forasteros in Identified Population	Percentages of Forasteros Among Adult Males
Caravaya y Sangabán					
CYS 1		515			
CYS 2		1,057	yes		
CYS 3		263	yes		
CYS 4		1,500			
CYS 5		526	yes		
CYS 6		1,079	yes		

TABLE IIE–8. Parish Population Totals with Forastero Representation

Province Code	1676	1689–90	Forasteros Cited	Percentages of Forasteros in Identified Population	Percentages of Forasteros Among Adult Males
Cotabambas					
COT 1		239			
COT 2	300	197	yes		72.8
COT 3	600	700			
COT 4	1,100	1,175			
COT 5	150	305			
COT 6	1,200	1,087	yes		
COT 7		135	yes		
COT 8	300	399			
COT 9	100	220	yes		
COT 10	600	300			
COT 11		932	yes		
COT 12		1,115	yes		
COT 13	150	150	yes		

TABLE IIE–9. Parish Population Totals with Forastero Representation

Province Code	1676	1689–90	Forasteros Cited	Percentages of Forasteros in Identified Population	Percentages of Forasteros Among Adult Males
Chilques y Masques					
CHYM 1		2,774	yes	26.1	25.8
CHYM 2		1,913	yes	42.8	
CHYM 3		928	yes		
CHYM 4		1,159	yes	64.0	
CHYM 5		1,467	yes	37.8	
CHYM 6		524	yes		
CHYM 7		1,090	yes	54.4	
CHYM 8		1,166	yes		
CHYM 9		738			

TABLE IIE–10. Parish Population Totals with Forastero Representation

Province Code	1676	1689–90	Forasteros Cited	Percentages of Forasteros in Identified Population	Percentages of Forasteros Among Adult Males
Chumbibilcas					
CHMB 1		580	yes		
CHMB 2		800	yes		
CHMB 3		758	yes		
CHMB 4		637	yes		
CHMB 5		1,000	yes		
CHMB 6		45			
CHMB 7		580			
CHMB 8		264			
CHMB 9		129	yes		
CHMB 10		1,110			
CHMB 11		531	yes	49.9	53.8

TABLE IIE–11. Parish Population Totals with Forastero Representation

Province Code	1676	1689–90	Forasteros Cited	Percentages of Forasteros in Identified Population	Percentages of Forasteros Among Adult Males
Lampa					
LMP 1	2,500	490	yes		32.4
LMP 2	1,000	750			
LMP 3	200	230	yes		
LMP 4	800	237	yes		28.6
LMP 5	1,000	463	yes		43.4
LMP 6	600	634	yes		
LMP 7	600	669			
LMP 8	1,500	654	yes		
LMP 9	2,000	1,600			
LMP 10	1,000	700	yes		
LMP 11	1,500	950			
LMP 12	1,500	1,200	yes		
LMP 13	1,000	813	yes	42.8	

TABLE IIE–12. Parish Population Totals with Forastero Representation

Province Code	1676	1689–90	Forasteros Cited	Percentages of Forasteros in Identified Population	Percentages of Forasteros Among Adult Males
Marquesado de Oropesa					
MQO 1	3,000	1,485	yes		
MQO 2	2,000	550			
MQO 3	1,500	846	yes		
MQO 4	4,000	2,345	yes		87.6

TABLE IIE–13. Parish Population Totals with Forastero Representation

Province Code	1676	1689–90	Forasteros Cited	Percentages of Forasteros in Identified Population	Percentages of Forasteros Among Adult Males
Paucartambo					
PCT 1		2,491	yes		
PCT 2		60			
PCT 3		1,000			
PCT 4		200			
PCT 5		315	yes	100	
PCT 6		602	yes		

TABLE IIE−14. Parish Population Totals with Forastero Representation

Province Code	1676	1689–90	Forasteros Cited	Percentages of Forasteros in Identified Population	Percentages of Forasteros Among Adult Males
Quispicanche					
QPC 1		410	yes		
QPC 2		2,500	yes		
QPC 3		866			
QPC 4	1,500	1,350	yes		
QPC 5	1,000	1,530	yes		47.6
QPC 6	1,000	1,500	yes		
QPC 7	1,800	2,147	yes		
QPC 8		894	yes		
QPC 9		200			
QPC 10		1,600	yes		

TABLE IIE−15. Parish Population Totals with Forastero Representation

Province Code	1676	1689–90	Forasteros Cited	Percentages of Forasteros in Identified Population	Percentages of Forasteros Among Adult Males
Vilcabamba					
VLC 1		570			
VLC 2		403	yes	82.9	

TABLE IIF–I. Comparison of the Male/Female
Composition of the Originario and Forastero
Populations

Parish	Originario		Forastero	
	Male	Female	Male	Female
ABY 2	252	276	204	215
ABY 4	360	454	233	287
ABY 6	294	323	350	345
ABY 7	449	444	305	285
ABY 9	92	100	86	97
AYM 3	97	162	26	42
AYM 4	168	292	53	21
AYM 7	206	287	83	87
AYM 14	83	149	10	9
AYM 16	237	419	23	23
CYC 5	324	510	328	466
CHYM 1	1,082	969	347	376
CHYM 4	149	268	346	396
CHYM 5	414	498	272	283
CHYM 7	218	279	280	313
CHMB 11	131	135	133	132
VLC 2	47	22	219	115
Totals	4,603	5,587	3,298	3,492
N	10,190		6,790	
%N	45.2	54.8	48.6	51.4

TABLE IIF-2. Comparison of the Adult/Child Composition of the Originario and Forastero Populations

Parish	Originario		Forastero	
	Adults	Children	Adults	Children
ABY 4	696	118	327	193
ABY 7	456	437	306	284
ABY 9	130	62	112	71
AYM 3	180	79	42	26
AYM 14	146	86	13	6
AYM 16	478	178	34	12
CHMB 11	198	68	220	45
Totals	2,284	1,028	1,054	637
N	3,312		1,691	
%N	69.0	31.0	62.3	37.7

TABLE IIF−3. Town/Rural Distribution of the Forastero Population

Parish	Town	Rural	Total	Town Percentages	Rural Percentages
ABY 2	0	419	419	0	100
ABY 4	0	520	520	0	100
ABY 6	0	724	724	0	100
AYM 4	10	64	74	13.5	86.5
AYM 7	147	23	170	86.5	13.5
AZG 3	545	625	1,170	46.6	53.4
CYC 5	779	15	794	98.1	1.9
CHYM 5	91	464	555	16.4	83.6
CHMB 11	218	47	265	82.3	17.7
PCT 5	38	277	315	12.1	87.9
VLC 2	0	334	334	0	100
Totals	1,828	3,512	5,340	34.2	65.8

Town/Rural Distribution of the Parallel Originario Population

Parish	Town	Rural	Total	Town Percentages	Rural Percentages
ABY 2	528	0	528	100	0
ABY 4	814	0	814	100	0
ABY 6	617	0	617	100	0
AYM 4	460	0	460	100	0
AYM 7	384	109	493	77.9	22.1
CYC 5	828	6	834	99.3	0.7
CHYM 5	910	2	912	99.8	0.2
CHMB 11	266	0	266	100	0
VLC 2	0	69	69	0	100
Totals	4,807	186	4,993	96.3	3.7

TABLE IIF-4. Originario/Forastero Composition of Town and Rural Sectors

	Town			Rural		
Parish	Percent-ages of Originarios	Percent-ages of Forasteros	N	Percent-ages of Originarios	Percent-ages of Forasteros	N
ABY 2	100	0	528	0	100	419
ABY 4	100	0	814	0	100	520
ABY 6	100	0	617	0	100	724
AYM 4	97.9	2.1	470	0	100	64
AYM 7	72.3	27.7	531	82.6	17.4	132
AZG 3	0	100	545	0	100	625
CYC 5	51.5	48.5	1,607	28.6	71.4	21
CHYM 5	90.9	9.1	1,001	0.4	99.6	466
CHMB 11	55.0	45.0	484	0	100	47
PCT 5	0	100	38	0	100	277
VLC 2	—	—	0	17.1	82.9	403
Totals	72.4	27.6	6,635	5.0	95.0	3,698

TABLE IIF-4. *(continued)*

Parish	Percent-ages of Originarios	Percent-ages of Forasteros	Percent-ages Town	Percent-ages Rural	N
Composition of the Parishes Cited					
ABY 2	55.7	44.2	55.7	44.2	947
ABY 4	61.0	39.0	61.0	39.0	1,334
ABY 6	46.0	54.0	46.0	54.0	1,341
AYM 4	86.1	13.9	88.0	12.0	534
AYM 7	74.4	25.6	80.1	19.9	663
AZG 3	0	100	46.6	53.4	1,170
CYC 5	51.2	48.8	98.7	1.3	1,628
CHYM 5	62.2	37.8	68.2	31.8	1,467
CHMB 11	50.1	49.9	91.1	8.9	531
PCT 5	0	100	12.1	87.9	315
VLC 2	17.1	82.9	0	100	403
Totals	48.3	51.7	64.2	35.8	10,333

TABLE IIF–5. Town/Rural Comparison of the
Forastero Community Distribution by Gender

	Town		Rural	
Parish	Male	Female	Male	Female
ABY 2	0	0	204	215
ABY 4	0	0	233	287
ABY 6	0	0	350	345
AYM 4	10	0	43	21
AYM 7	70	77	13	10
CHYM 5	46	45	226	238
CHMB 11	108	110	25	22
VLC 2	0	0	219	115
Totals	234	232	1,313	1,253
N	466		2,566	
%N	50.2	49.8	51.2	48.8

Town		Rural	
Percentages of Males	Percentages of Females	Percentages of Males	Percentages of Females
0	0	49.9	50.1
0	0	44.8	55.2
0	0	50.4	49.6
100	0	67.2	32.8
47.6	52.4	56.5	43.5
50.5	49.5	48.7	51.3
49.5	50.5	53.2	46.8
0	0	65.6	34.4

✤ APPENDIX III ✤ ✤

The Ayllu Forastero in the Parish Records of Yucay

Working with Latin American parish records is a rewarding but frustrating process. Inherent problems with loose folios, irregular notations, and erratic formats have been compounded by decay, neglect, and periodic politically motivated destruction.[1] Latin American demographers have been known to regard Western European data runs with awe and envy.

Researchers seeking to consult Peruvian parish records face yet another problem: control of these *registros*, or registers, remains in the hands of ecclesiastical authorities, and access to the documents is both highly restricted and capricious.[2] In the late 1970s the situation was further complicated by political and religious repercussions from the extensive microfilm project conducted in southern Peru for the genealogical program of The Church of Jesus Christ of Latter-day Saints, and parish registers in the Archbishopric of Cuzco were closed. Fortunately, baptismal and matrimonial registers from the parish of Yucay, Marquesado de Oropesa, were located at the Archivo Arzobispal del Cusco, buried in a pile of early-twentieth-century catechisms. These registros provided the data entries analyzed below.

The parish records of Yucay were subdivided by *ayllu*, or kin-group, with events from various years included in each section. Local priests identified an interesting and important *ayllu forastero*, literally a "kin-group of the foreign-born," and clearly distinguished between the ayllu forastero and the town's *indios forasteros*. In many colonial documents the notation "ayllu forastero" after an individual's name merely indicated that the Indian involved was not a native of his current place of residence. Other references to similar groups failed to discuss their origin or function. The ayllu forastero of Yucay, however, was a cohesive, complex social group with tribute and labor obligations and access to local lands. Related documents from the Archivo Arzobispal de Lima describing the formation and composition of the Yucay ayllu are discussed in the text. These supporting materials and the data summaries presented below depict an artificially created but self-perpetuating unit with economic functions and internal organization identical to those of the traditional Yucay ayllus.

Entry into the ayllu forastero was not universally granted to all non-native Indians, and although a number of foreign-born men married into the ayllu a

224

majority of the group's males were descendants of ayllu members (tables IIIA and IIIB). These Yucay natives outnumbered foreign-born Indians until the period from 1710 to 1719, when a large number of migrants fled to the Cuzco area from plague-infested northern Peru. From 1720 to 1724, when disease ravaged the Cuzco area, no foreign-born males were reincorporated into Yucay[3] (table IIIA). Some newcomers sought access to community lands and labor assistance by marrying into existing Yucay ayllus. No foreign-born male residing in Yucay married a foreign-born female. A plurality of these migrants entered the *yanacona* group, and the remainder split equally between the ayllu forastero and the traditional ayllus. Members of the Yucay ayllus, the yanacona group, and the ayllu forastero most frequently married within their ayllu, and the couple usually joined the groom's ayllu (tables IIIB and IIIC). This consistency of matrimonial patterns among the Yucay ayllus attests to the relatively equal status enjoyed by the ayllu forastero and its members.

Data from the baptismal records, particularly strong for the period from 1675 to 1704, are presented in table IIID, which summarizes the origin of foreign-born parents of children baptized in Yucay.[4] During the mid- and late seventeenth century, relocation within the rural sector resulted from short-range migration; an overwhelming majority of the foreign-born parents were natives of neighboring provinces or of the city of Cuzco. The consistently high proportion of Yucay residents of Cuzqueño origins indicates a significant and interesting reversal of generally acknowledged rural-to-urban migration patterns. This movement of urban natives into the depleted rural sector is one of the more intriguing aspects of the rich demographic data found in the fragmented parish records of Yucay.

TABLE IIIA. Origin of Males in the Ayllu Forastero:
Yucay, 1680–1724

Years	Ayllu Forastero	Foreign-Born	Total N
1680–84	62.5	37.5	8
1685–89	69.2	30.8	39
1690–94	47.6	52.4	42
1695–99	65.0	35.0	20
1700–04	57.7	42.3	26
1705–09	85.7	14.3	21
1710–14	40.0	60.0	5
1715–19	57.1	42.8	7
1720–24	100.0	0.0	17
1725–29	92.3	7.7	13
1730–34	75.0	25.0	8
1735–39	66.7	33.3	9

TABLE IIIB. Marriage Patterns in Yucay, 1680–1739: Percentage of Males for Each Social Group Marrying into a Particular Group

| | | Female | | | |
		Yucay Ayllu	Yanacona	Ayllu Forastero	Foreign-Born	Total N
	Male					
1680–99	Yucay Ayllu	58.7	25.4	7.9	7.9	63
	Yanacona	36.2	34.5	29.3	0.0	58
	Ayllu Forastero	36.7	22.0	37.6	3.7	109
	Foreign-Born	36.3	45.4	18.2	0.0	11
						241
1700–19	Yucay Ayllu	53.2	15.6	19.5	11.7	77
	Yanacona	34.2	26.3	15.8	23.6	38
	Ayllu Forastero	13.6	28.8	33.9	23.7	59
	Foreign-Born	16.7	50.0	33.3	0.0	12
						186
1720–39	Yucay Ayllu	68.2	13.6	4.5	13.6	66
	Yanacona	34.1	48.8	2.4	14.6	41
	Ayllu Forastero	21.3	10.6	57.4	10.6	47
	Foreign-Born	—	—	—	—	0
						154
Totals	Yucay Ayllu	59.7	18.0	11.2	11.2	206
	Yanacona	35.0	36.5	17.5	10.9	137
	Ayllu Forastero	27.0	21.4	40.9	10.7	215
	Foreign-Born	26.1	47.8	26.1	0.0	23
						581

TABLE IIIC. Percentage of Matrimonios Entering the Groom's Ayllu: Yucay, 1680–1735

Years	ANCA*	COSCO	GUARAC	LIBRE*	PACA	YANAC*	FORST*
1680–84	—	—	—	—	67	100	100
N	(0)	(0)	(0)	(0)	(3)	(6)	(6)
1685–89	100	100	100	100	100	100	100
N	(3)	(4)	(1)	(1)	(7)	(15)	(26)
1690–94	100	100	100	67	100	100	96
N	(4)	(7)	(2)	(3)	(6)	(14)	(23)
1695–99	100	100	100	100	—	77	100
N	(2)	(9)	(2)	(7)	(0)	(13)	(10)
1700–04	100	100	100	100	91	100	94
N	(7)	(6)	(3)	(8)	(11)	(10)	(16)
1705–09	100	—	100	100	—	87	100
N	(2)	(0)	(2)	(6)	(0)	(15)	(18)
1710–14	—	90	75	100	80	59	100
N	(0)	(10)	(4)	(1)	(5)	(17)	(2)
1715–19	0	33	—	100	33	46	83
N	(4)	(18)	(0)	(5)	(6)	(13)	(6)
1720–24	50	100	100	83	92	78	94
N	(6)	(3)	(7)	(12)	(12)	(27)	(17)
1725–29	0	—	75	100	100	87	92
N	(9)	(0)	(12)	(3)	(5)	(15)	(13)
1730–34	0	—	80	20	100	78	100
N	(2)	(0)	(5)	(5)	(1)	(9)	(6)

*ANCA, Ancaypura
LIBRE, Libre Canari Ynga
YANAC, Yanacona
FORST, Ayllu Forastero

TABLE IIID. Parents of Children Baptized in Yucay: 1675–1735
Identified Origins, by Percentages

	City of Cuzco	Neighboring Provinces*	Other Areas of Bishopric	Exterior	N
1675–79	52	21	24	3	29
1680–84	43	30	23	4	70
1685–89	53	21	25	1	95
1690–94	45	37	16	1	86
1695–99	54	31	10	6	52
1700–04	42	26	23	8	47
1705–09	14	43	28	14	7
1710–14	0	67	33	0	3
1715–19	—	—	—	—	0
1720–24	14	57	28	0	7
1725–29	—	—	—	—	0
1730–34	60	40	0	0	5
Total	47	30	20	3	
N	187	120	81	13	401

*Includes Calca y Lares, 72 entries; Marquesado de Oropesa, 47 entries; Vilca-
bamba, 1 entry

✤ NOTES ✤ ✤

CHAPTER 1: "Innumerable Indians"

1. The description of Toledo's entry into Cuzco is by Arthur F. Zimmerman, *Francisco de Toledo: Fifth Viceroy of Peru, 1569–1581* (New York: Greenwood Press, 1968), p. 101. Originally published in Caldwell, Idaho, by Caston Printers, 1938. A note about the spelling of Cusco" and "Cuzco": I have consistently used the colonial-era spelling, "Cuzco," to refer to both the city and the bishopric, except in those cases where I refer to institutions, such as regional archives, whose names use the modern spelling, "Cusco."

2. This broad survey of pre-Incan and Incan society is based on my own reading of primary documents and on the work of many Andeanists, particularly Brooke Larson, John Murra, Franklin Pease, Irene Silverblatt, Karen Spalding, Steve J. Stern, and Nathan Wachtel. Their works are cited below and listed in the bibliography. Throughout this study the term "traditional" should be considered as indicating the persistence of preconquest values, in the context developed by Eric Wolf: "Persistence, like change, is not a cause—it is an effect," a mechanism which explains "why tradition persists, [and] why people cleave to it." *Peasants* (Englewood Cliffs, N.J.: Prentice-Hall, 1966), p. viii.

3. The report from Toledo's assistant is found in Testimonio de visita, Cuzco, 17-VIII-1571. Quoted in AGI, Escribanía 506A. Martín Garcia de Loyola contra el Fiscal de la encomienda de Yndios del Repartimiento de Yucay, 1633, ff. 3V–4. Many of these Indians claimed to be yanaconas. Toledo's regulations on yanacona status are discussed in detail in chapter 2. The viceroy's comments are from AGI, Lima 1623. Auto del Virrey Don Francisco de Toledo, 3-XII-1571. Unless otherwise indicated, all translations of primary documents and passages from secondary works are my own. The titles of documents are recorded as entered in archival indices or as written on opening folios. After the first citation, documents are identified by their archival codes.

4. The summary of Toledo's findings is drawn from the primary documents cited above and from: AAC, Unmarked boxes B-5. Carta del Virrey Don Francisco de Toledo al Rey, Cuzco, 11-VIII-1572; AGI, Lima 1623. La ordinaria que nuevamente mandó y orderar [*sic*] Su. Exc^a. para sacar guacas, sin fecha. The decree was signed "in Cuzco, the tenth day of this month and this year"; the author was definitely Toledo. The general order to confiscate all guacas cited one particular guaca which he had been told was buried somewhere

in Lima. Any valuables found hidden with the guaca were to be confiscated in the name of the King. It should be remembered that this depiction of the indigenous community was Toledo's. For example, the indigenous community was skilled at manipulating the colonial judicial system, as Steve J. Stern has shown in his *Peru's Indian Peoples and the Challenge of Spanish Conquest: Huamanga to 1640* (Madison: University of Wisconsin Press, 1982). The story of the last Incan uprising is a controversial one and the rumors cited may have been started by Spaniards. Zimmerman defends Toledo's conduct, but other historians have blamed the viceroy for the capture and execution of Tupac Amaru in Cuzco in 1571.

5. This definition of the term is based on specific materials from the Cuzco zone. The term "forastero" could have other or additional meanings in different regions of the Viceroyalty.

6. The original phrase is, of course, from Woodrow Borah, *New Spain's Century of Depression* (Berkeley: University of California Press, 1951). John J. TePaske and Herbert S. Klein use seventeenth-century treasury accounts from New Spain to reconsider the issue in "The Seventeenth-Century Crisis in New Spain: Myth or Reality?," *Past and Present*, no. 90, February 1981, pp. 116–35. See also the "Introduction" in Kenneth J. Andrien's *Crisis and Decline: The Viceroyalty of Peru in the Seventeenth Century* (Albuquerque: University of New Mexico Press, 1985). Immanuel Wallerstein discusses the European "Crisis of the Seventeenth Century?" in his *The Modern World-System II: Mercantilism and the Consolidation of the European World-Economy, 1600–1750* (New York: Academic Press, 1980), pp. 2–11. Mario Góngora, among others, has urged recognition of the increasing diversification and continued development of the Viceroyalty of Peru throughout the seventeenth century, when "the centralist ideal gave way to factional interests and regional demands." *Encomenderos y estancieros: Estudios acerca de la Constitución social aristocrática de Chile después de la Conquista, 1580–1660* (Santiago de Chile: Editorial Universitaria, 1970), p. vii. Karen Spalding's work has been instrumental in creating a new awareness of the transformation of indigenous society during this period. Among her many publications, see *De indio a campesino* (Lima: Instituto de Estudios Peruanos Ediciones, 1974), and *Huarochirí: An Andean Society Under Inca and Spanish Rule* (Stanford: Stanford University Press, 1984).

7. The phrase "classic colonialism" was used to characterize Peru during the period from 1560 to 1700 in the most widely read one-volume textbook of Peruvian history: Henry F. Dobyns and Paul L. Doughty, *Peru: A Cultural History* (New York: Oxford University Press, 1976), chapter 4, title, and passim. Peruvianists have not yet fully discredited James Lockhart's assertion that "all the main population centers of Peru, all the main economic and social trends, had taken shape by 1545 or 1550 and in many cases much earlier, in the course of a spontaneous, undirected development concurrent with the conquest and

civil wars." James Lockhart, *Spanish Peru, 1532–1560: A Colonial Society* (Madison: University of Wisconsin Press, 1968), p. 6. Mexicanists have been more successful at refuting Robert Ricard's bluntly deterministic conclusion that "the sixteenth century was the important period, the period in which Mexico was created, and of which the rest of her history has been only the almost inevitable development," in *The Spiritual Conquest of Mexico*, Lesley Byrd Simpson, trans. (Berkeley: University of California Press, 1966), p. 295. See, for example Richard Boyer's assertion that "historians must view seventeenth-century New Spain not as a century of depression, but as one of transition to capitalism, economic diversification, and vigorous regional economies," in "Mexico in the Seventeenth Century: Transition of a Colonial Society," *Hispanic American Historical Review* (cited hereinafter as *HAHR*) 57, no. 3, August 1977, p. 478.

8. Spalding, *De indio a campesino*. The phrase can be roughly translated as "from Indian to peasant" but loses significant meaning and subtlety in the process. Rolando Mellafe, "The Importance of Migration in the Viceroyalty of Peru," in *Population and Economics. Proceedings of Section V of the Fourth Congress of the International Economic History Association, 1968* (Winnipeg: University of Manitoba Press, 1970), pp. 303 and 311. This quotation is from Karen Spalding, "The Colonial Indian: Past and Future Research Perspectives," *Latin American Research Review* (cited hereinafter as *LARR*) 7, no. 1, Spring 1972, p. 48. Also, see Franklin Pease G. Y., *Del Tawantinsuyu a la historia del Perú* (Lima: Instituto de Estudios Peruanos Ediciones, 1978). See, in particular, pp. 200, 211.

9. Mellafe, *Population and Economics*, pp. 306–9, passim.

10. John H. Rowe offered one of the earliest versions of this model in 1957; the most recent depiction, by Irene Silverblatt, differs only in its gender-specific analysis. See John H. Rowe, "The Incas Under Spanish Colonial Institutions," *HAHR* 37, no. 2, May 1957, pp. 175, 181. Silverblatt maintains that "While indigenous men often fled the oppression of mita and tribute by abandoning their communities and going to work as *yanaconas* (quasiserfs) in the emerging haciendas, women fled to the *puna* (High tablelands)." (Irene Silverblatt, " 'The Universe has turned inside out . . . There is no justice for us here': Andean Women Under Spanish Rule," in *Women and Colonization: Anthropological Perspectives*, Mona Etienne and Eleanor Leacock, eds. [New York: J. F. Bergin, 1980], p. 177.)

11. This depiction of migrants is by Elman R. Service, "Indian-European Relations in Colonial Latin America," *American Anthropologist* 57, 1955, pp. 417–18. For additional examples, see Robert G. Keith, *Conquest and Agrarian Change: The Emergence of the Hacienda System on the Peruvian Coast* (Cambridge: Harvard University Press, 1976), pp. 30–31. Nicolás Sánchez-Albornoz cites new evidence of migration by women, children, and the elderly, but he still concludes that the adult forastero males usually came alone. "In the adopted

community, the male representation and the age distribution patterns were altered by their presence, at least for the first generation." (*Indios y tributos en el Alto Perú* [Lima: Instituto de Estudios Peruanos Ediciones, 1978].)

12. Ann Zulawski summarized this in the Alto Perú area in "*Forasteros* and *Yanaconas:* The Work Force of a Seventeenth Century Mining Town" (paper presented at the 1986 annual meeting of the American Historical Association, New York City).

13. Woodrow Borah, "Demographic and Physical Aspects of the Transition from the Aboriginal to the Colonial World," *Comparative Urban Research* 8, no. 1, 1980, pp. 41–70. Linda A. Newson, "Indian Population Patterns in Colonial Spanish America," *LARR* 20, no. 3, 1985, pp. 41–99. In his review of "The Social and Ethnic Historiography of Colonial Latin America: The Last Twenty Years" (*William and Mary Quarterly* 45, no. 3, July 1988, pp. 453–88), John E. Kicza notes that "The important subject of migration has been so far under-researched" (p. 488). As Kicza notes, the forthcoming *Migration in Colonial Latin America*, edited by David J. Robinson, will address this key theme.

14. For most of the period under study, the bishopric of Cuzco consisted of the city and fourteen provinces. This is the area included in my usage of the term. A list of those provinces and a discussion of the 1690 census can be found in Appendix II. For an account of the conquest and civil wars in Cuzco, see Dobyns and Doughty, *Peru*, chapter 3.

15. For a depiction of the impact of the conquest and an analysis of change in pre-Toledo Peru, see Wachtel, *The Vision of the Vanquished*, and chapters 2 and 3 of Stern's *Peru's Indian Peoples*. Historians who "have assumed that real development of the society and economy began later, either with the rule of Viceroy Toledo in the 1570s, or at the earliest in the later 1560s after the end of the civil wars" have been denounced by Lockhart, *Spanish Peru, 1532–1560*, pp. 7–8. As examples of this approach, he cites Guillermo Lohmann Villena in *El corregidor de indios en el Perú bajo los Austrias* (Madrid: Ediciones Cultura Hispanica, 1957); and George Kubler, "The Neo-Inca State, 1537–1572," *HAHR* 27, no. 2, May 1947, pp. 189–203.

16. Spalding believes that "the process of differentiation of access to re-sources within Indian society had gone relatively far in [southern Peru and Bolivia] by the eighteenth century." (Karen Spalding, "Hacienda-Village Rela-tions in Andean Society to 1830," *Latin American Perspectives* II, no. 1, Issue 4, Spring 1975, p. 117.) In contrast, Richard Adams believes that the transforma-tion dates from the late nineteenth century. (Richard N. Adams, "A Change from Caste to Class in a Peruvian Town," *Social Forces* 31, no. 3, March 1953, passim.)

17. I have chosen this dialectical interpretation over the extreme demo-graphic-structural determinism utilized in Françoise Lautman's study of the way in which "industrial society became possible as a result of modifications in

family organization." (Françoise Lautman, "Differences or Changes in Family Organization," in *Family and Society: Selections from the Annales: Economies, Sociétés, Civilisations.* Robert Forster and Orest Ranum, eds.; Elborg Forster and Patricia M. Ranum, trans. [Baltimore: Johns Hopkins University Press, 1976], p. 252.)

CHAPTER 2: The Failure of the Reducciones

1. The literature on Spanish-American imperial administration is extensive. In *Crisis and Decline* Kenneth J. Andrien identifies and analyzes two major cycles in seventeenth-century Peruvian colonial administration: "The Failure of Arbitrismo, 1607–1664" and "The Visita General, 1664–1690." Because migration policy was usually generated by a combination of local and peninsular circumstances, it does not directly correlate with these trends, but Andrien's work is extremely useful in understanding colonial government. Kendall W. Brown provides an extensive bibliography of sources on colonial administration and a detailed study of the implementation and impact of the Borbón reforms in *Bourbons and Brandy: Imperial Reform in Eighteenth-Century Arequipa* (Albuquerque: University of New Mexico Press, 1986). Jeffrey A. Cole presents a detailed study of the regulations governing the mita to Potosí and its administration in *The Potosí Mita, 1573–1700: Compulsory Indian Labor in the Andes* (Stanford: Stanford University Press, 1985). Because mita labor policy is not the same as migration policy—the two themes were frequently the subject of conflicting proposals—Cole's analysis provides another perspective on the bureaucratic practices and administrative framework governing Indian society under Spanish rule.

2. For details of the disease transfer and mortality rates, see Alfred W. Crosby, Jr., *The Columbian Exchange: Biological and Cultural Consequences of 1492* (Westport, Conn.: Greenwood Press, 1972), chapters 2 and 4; and Nicolás Sánchez-Albornoz, *The Population of Latin America: A History.* W. A. R. Richardson, trans. (Berkeley: University of California Press, 1974), chapter 3.

Peruvian migration is discussed below. For accounts of population dispersal and migration in other areas of Spanish America, see the following sources: Franklin W. Knight, *The Caribbean: The Genesis of a Fragmented Nationalism* (New York: Oxford University Press, 1978), chapters 1 and 2; the Aztec dispersal is described by François Chevalier, *Land and Society in Colonial Mexico: The Great Hacienda.* Lesley B. Simpson, ed.; Alvin Eustis, trans. (Berkeley: University of California Press, 1963), p. 201. See also David Brading, *Miners and Merchants in Bourbon Mexico, 1763–1810* (Cambridge: Cambridge University Press, 1971), p. 5. For case studies from Central America, see W. George Lovell, "The Historical Demography of the Cuchumatán Highlands of Guatemala, 1500–1821," and Linda A. Newson, "Demographic Catastrophe in Sixteenth-

Century Honduras," in *Studies in Spanish American Population History,* David J. Robinson, ed. (Dellplain Latin American Studies, No. 8 [Boulder, Colo.: Westview Press, 1981], pp. 195–216 and 217–42, respectively.

3. Sánchez-Albornoz, *The Population of Latin America,* p. 77.

4. Lewis Hanke has written extensively on the Great Debate. For example, see his *The Spanish Struggle for Justice in the Conquest of America* (Boston: Little, Brown, 1965). For a discussion of the Black Legend and the White Legend, see Benjamin Keen, "The Black Legend Revisited: Assumptions and Realities," *HAHR* 44, no. 4, November 1969, pp. 703–21; Lewis Hanke, "A Modest Proposal for a Moratorium on Grand Generalizations: Some Thoughts on the Black Legend," *HAHR* 51, no. 1, February 1971, pp. 112–27; and Charles Gibson, ed., *The Black Legend: Anti-Spanish Attitudes in the Old World and the New* (New York: Knopf, 1971).

5. For a description of the instructions to Ovando, see Clarence Haring, *The Spanish Empire in America* (New York: Harcourt Brace and World, 1947), p. 10. The instructions to later viceroys can be found in *Colección de las Memorias o Relaciones que escribieron los Virreys del Perú.* Ricardo Beltrán y Rózpide, ed. (Madrid: Biblioteca de historia Hispano-Americana, 1921), passim.

6. Mario Góngora called pre-Toledo Peru "a prime example of an anarchic Hispanic political milieu . . . an epitome of the era of conquistadores, excessively turbulent and violent," in *Studies in the Colonial History of Spanish America.* Richard Southern, trans. (Cambridge: Cambridge University Press, 1975), p. 21.

7. Mellafe, *Population and Economics,* p. 307.

8. This citation is from Cédula Reál, Valladolid, 26-II-1538. AGI, Guatemala 393. Published in *Colección de Documentos para la Historia de la Formación Social de Hispanoamérica, 1493–1810,* vol. I, Richard Konetzke, ed. (Madrid: Consejo Superior de Investigaciones Científicas, 1953), pp. 182–83. For another expression of the Church's concern, see BNP, B347, Expediente sobre la petición presentada por Juan Lorenzo de Zela para que los indios Huaylas sean reducidos para que pueden asistir a los oficios religiosos, 28-IV-1628. See the general discussion of the reducciones by Borah, "Demographic and Physical Aspects," which emphasizes that most existing studies of the reducciones are based on documentation from Mexico. An exception to this trend is Alejandro Málaga Medina's discussion of the formation of the Peruvian settlements in "Las reducciones en el Virreinato del Perú (1532–1580)," *Revista de historia de América* 80, July–December 1975, pp. 9–42.

9. Cédula Reál, Cigales, 21-III-1551. (Published in *Colección de Documentos para la Historia,* vol. I, pp. 283–85.)

10. Cédula Reál, Cigales, 21-III-1551. (*Recopilación de leyes,* vol. II [Madrid: Consejo de la Hispanidad, 1943]. Libro VI, Título III, ley i, pp. 207–8.)

11. Franklin Pease G. Y. has noted that "until the time of Viceroy Toledo, the

reducciones not only were tentative and inconsistent efforts but also were being instituted progressively southward." (Pease, *Del Tawantinsuyu*, p. 190). For details of the early efforts, see Málaga Medina, "Las Reducciones." Thierry Saignes describes the impact of the reducciones on pp. 321–25 of "The Ethnic Groups in the Valleys of Larecaja: From Descent to Residence," in *Anthropological History of Andean Polities*, John V. Murra, Nathan Wachtel, and Jacques Revel, eds. (Cambridge: Cambridge University Press, 1986), pp. 311–41.

12. Cédula Reál, 18-II-1555. (Published in *Colección de Documentos para la Historia*, vol. I, pp. 328–29.) This cédula paraphrases the colonists' complaints.

13. Carta del Rey al Virrey del Perú, 11-VII-1552, AGI, Lima 567. (Published in *Colección de Documentos para la Historia*, vol. I, pp. 306–7.) Carlos V quotes earlier reports from the colonies in this depiction of the Indians.

14. Juan de Matienzo, *Gobierno del Perú* (Buenos Aires: Companía Sudamericana de billetes de banco, 1910), capítulo 4, pp. 14–15.

15. Ibid., capítulo 14, p. 31.

16. Guillermo Lohmann Villena, *Juan de Matienzo, Autor del "Gobierno del Perú": Su personalidad y su obra* (Sevilla: Publicaciones de la Escuela de Estudios Hispano-Americanos, 1966), pp. 61 and 39.

17. Francisco de Jeréz, "Conquest of Peru and the Province of Cuzco," in Augustín de Zarate, *The Discovery and Conquest of Peru*. J. M. Cohen, trans. and ed. (Baltimore: Penguin Books, 1968), pp. 83–84. Other chroniclers and travelers to the Andes were similarly affected by changes in altitude. See chapter I, "Evidence of Climatic Aggression," in Carlos Monge, *Acclimatization in the Andes*. Donald F. Brown, trans. (Baltimore: Johns Hopkins University Press, 1948). See also Cédula Reál, Talabera, 18-I-1541. *Recopilación*, Libro VI, Título I, ley xiii. Tomo II, p. 192. For an example of compliance with this provision, see the "expediente de los Indios de Guarac," AHC, Caja 22, Protocolo 22-517. Registro 4. Awareness of the impact of the dramatic changes in altitude did not always result in compliance with the law. Traveling in Peru in 1802, Alexander Von Humboldt denounced the relocation of Indian laborers to hostile environments and observed, "the constant change of climate—not the work itself—is what makes the mita so dangerous." (*El Perú en la obra de Alejandro de Humboldt* Estuardo Nuñez y Georg Petersen G., eds. [Lima: Libería Studium, 1971], p. 158.)

18. This apt phrase—"un decenio de expectante incertidumbre"—is the title of one of the chapters in Lohmann Villena's study, *Juan de Matienzo.*

19. This definition of the encomienda is from Keith, *Conquest and Agrarian Change*, p. 36. The peninsular encomienda is described by Haring, *The Spanish Empire*, pp. 39ff. For a discussion of administration on the peninsula, see J. H. Elliott, *Imperial Spain, 1469–1716* (New York: St. Martin's Press, 1963), chapters 3 and 5. For a case study of the consulado in Spain and the Americas, see Ann M. Wightman, "The *Consulado* of Lima and the *Meridionalización* of the

Pacific Trade." (Unpublished ms., prepared in seminar for Professor Karen Spalding, June 1975.)

20. The European corregimiento is described in Elliott, *Imperial Spain, 1469–1716*, chapter 3. Its colonial counterpart is defined by Robert G. Keith, "Encomienda, Hacienda, and Corregimiento in Spanish America: A Structural Analysis," *HAHR* 51, no. 3, August 1971, pp. 431–46.

21. This thesis is central to Keith's work.

22. The description of the Toledo residencia is from Lewis Hanke, personal communication, December 1977. For a favorable biography, see Zimmerman, *Francisco de Toledo.*

23. Memoria de Francisco de Toledo, 1581. (*Colección de las Memorias*, pp. 82–83.)

24. Ibid., p. 84.

25. For a summation of the Toledo regulations issued at various times throughout his visita of the sierra, see the *Ordenanzas del Virrey Don Francisco de Toledo*, Copia del 14-VIII-1604, BNP, B511. Additional details are found in *Tasa de la visita general de Francisco de Toledo*, Noble David Cook, ed. and introd. (Lima: Universidad Nacional Mayor de San Marcos, 1975).

26. Local exemptions to these tribute patterns and the relevant regulations are found in *Ordenanzas del Virrey Don Francisco de Toledo*, ff. 79V-82V.

27. Ibid., ff. 435–38. The administration of the mita is analyzed in detail by Cole, *The Potosí Mita*, and by Peter Bakewell, *Miners of the Red Mountain: Indian Labor in Potosí, 1545–1650* (Albuquerque: University of New Mexico Press, 1984).

28. For details of the religious organization of the reducciones, see Memoria de Francisco de Toledo, p. 74. The privileges and responsibilities of the kurakas are discussed below.

29. Kubler, "The Quechua in the Colonial World," in *Handbook of South American Indians*, vol. 11 (Washington, D.C.: Government Printing Office, 1964), p. 379. For studies which emphasize the slavery approach, see Louis Baudin, *Daily Life in Peru Under the Last Incas.* Winifred Bradford, trans. (New York: Macmillan, 1962), p. 107; and Thomas M. Davies, Jr., *Indian Integration in Peru* (Lincoln: University of Nebraska Press, 1970), p. 11. The linkage with serfdom is discussed in Mellafe, *Population and Economics*, p. 306, and Silverblatt, *Women and Colonization*, p. 177.

30. Nathan Wachtel raises the major questions concerning yanacona status in *The Vision of the Vanquished*, pp. 73–75. John H. Rowe summarizes the debate over the yana in "Inca Policies and Institutions Relating to the Cultural Unification of the Empire," in George A. Collier, Renato I. Rosaldo, and John D. Wirth, eds., *The Inca and Aztec States, 1400–1800: Anthropology and History* (New York: Academic Press, 1982), pp. 93–118.

31. Rowe, citing the chronicler Santillán, argues that the yana were chosen to

be "personal retainers who performed honorable service and might be rewarded with responsible administrative posts," ibid., p. 100. Early scholars argued that yana were the descendants of communities which had rebelled against the empire: Philip C. Means, *Ancient Civilizations of the Andes* (New York: Scribner's, 1931), p. 297 and Baudin, *Daily Life in Peru*, p. 107. John Murra summarizes this argument before denouncing it in "The Economic Organization of the Inca State," (Ph.D. dissertation, University of Chicago, 1956), pp. 275–77. Murra has linked the position of the yana within the empire to the role of herders in pre-Incan societies and has emphasized the diversity of origin and occupation within the yana sector. See his "An Aymaran Kingdom in 1567," *Ethnohistory* 15, no. 2, Spring 1968, pp. 115–51; and "New Data on Retainer and Servile Populations in Tawantinsuyu," *Actas y memorias*, vol. II, XXVI Congreso Internacional de Americanistas, Sevilla, 1966, pp. 35–44.

32. Rowe concludes that "service to the Inca ruler was the one thing [the yana] had in common" in *The Inca and Aztec States, 1400–1800*, p. 102. Karen Spalding emphasizes that the yana were "divorced from the kin-group of their birth," in "Social Climbers: Changing Patterns of Mobility among the Indians of Colonial Peru," *HAHR* 50, no. 4, November 1970, p. 651. Also, see Murra, "The Economic Organization of the Inca State," pp. 176–77, 251, 288; and Pease, *Del Tawantinsuyu*, pp. 76, 99.

33. See Murra, "The Economic Organization of the Inca State," p. 270. Wachtel makes a similar point in *The Vision of the Vanquished*, p. 75.

34. Murra, "The Economic Organization of the Inca State," p. 291.

35. This formal definition of the yanacona is found in Cédula Reál, Fuensalida, 26-X-1541. AGI, Lima 556. Published in *Colección de Documentos para la Historia*, vol. I, p. 205. The conquistadores' responses are reported in Lockhart, *Spanish Peru, 1532–1560*, p. 219, and in John Hemming, *The Conquest of the Incas* (New York: Harcourt Brace Jovanovich, 1970), p. 136.

36. Ibid. See also Cédula Reál, 11-III-1550 and Cédula Reál, 23-XI-1566. (Published in *Colección de Cédulas Reales dirigidas a la Audiencia de Quito, 1538–1600* [Publicaciones del Archivo Municipal, Vol. IX, Quito, 1935], pp. 136–37.) Matienzo, *Gobierno del Perú*, pp. 19–22, passim.

37. *Ordenanzas del Virrey Don Francisco de Toledo*, ff. 227–34V, 74-74V. BNE, 20.065. "Noticia del origen de los Yndios llamados Yanaconas del Perú," sin fecha. The regulations quoted within the document are definitely from 1574.

38. AGI, Lima 126, Vol. IV. Carta al Rey, 25-II-1583, f. 1.

39. Ibid.

40. ANP, Superior Gobierno, Legajo II, Cuaderno 16. Autos Seguidos ante el superior Gobierno, Carta del Corregidor del Cuzco, 11-XI-1597, f. 27.

41. AGI, Contaduría General 1826. Libros del Cusco, 10-II-1629, f. 116. Information on the 1659 and 1728 visitas is found in ANP, Tributos, Legajo 2, Cuaderno 22. Tributos de los indios de la Pa. de Chumbibilcas, 1-VIII-1728, ff.

4–7 and 20–24. See chapter 3 for a discussion of pan-Andean demographic patterns.

42. AGI, Lima 158, No. II. Carta del Protector General de los Yndios del Perú, Lima, 9-III-1627, ff. 1–1V.

43. Regulations governing forasteros can be found in AGI, Charcas 271, No. V, ff. 353–53V. The term "forastero" had different meanings throughout the viceroyalty, and a complete definition of the term as applied in the Cuzco area appears in chapter 3. The varying degrees to which migrants escaped their home communities' obligations will be discussed in chapter 6.

44. Max Weber, *The Theory of Social and Economic Organization*. Talcott Parsons, ed.; A. M. Henderson and Parsons, trans. (New York: Oxford University Press, 1947), sections II and IV.

45. For a detailed description of the imposition of the Toledo reducciones, see Málaga Medina, "Las Reducciones," and Rowe, "The Incas Under Spanish Colonial Institutions," pp. 155–59. The description of preconquest living patterns is by Francisco de Toledo, as translated and presented by Woodrow Borah. (Borah, "Demographic and Physical Aspects," p. 43.) Borah's subsequent characterization of the reducciones emphasizes Mexican pre- and postconquest urbanization. In a study of societal development on the eastern side of the Andes, Thierry Saignes has shown that Incan political domination and colonization in some instances initiated population resettlement. The impact of the Toledo reducciones in the valleys of Larecaja complicated this process of community redefinition. See Saignes's "The Ethnic Groups in the Valleys of Larecaja," in *Anthropological History*.

46. Murra, "The Economic Organization of the Inca State," p. 54. For specific studies, see ANP, Real Audiencia, Causas Civiles, Legajo 15, Cuaderno 77. Autos seguidos por Diego Lopez de Olibares, Cuzco, 1576, f. 31; and Enrique González Carré and Virgilio Galdo Gutiérrez, "Supervivencias prehispánicas en la etapa colonial: Ayacucho, Siglos XVII-XVIII." III Congreso Peruano del hombre y la cultura andina. Universidad Nacional Mayor de San Marcos, Lima, 1977.

47. AGI, Lima 123, No. I. Carta al Rey de Don Xptobal Guacaí, 26-IV-1572, f. 1.

48. AGI, Lima 124, No. I. Carta al Rey de Fiscal de la Audiencia de Lima, 7-V-1576, f. 4V.

49. AGI, Lima 124, No. III. Carta del Lizdo. Ramirez de Cartagena, Lima 7-III-1577, f. 1.

50. AGI, Lima 124, No. I, f. 4V. A supporting opinion can be found in AGI, Lima 124, No. II. Carta al Rey de Lizdo. Recalde, 1-III-1577, f. 2.

51. The irregularity of assessments is denounced in AGI, Lima 126, No. IV. Carta al Rey de Lzdo. Falcón, 25-II-1583, f. 1. The impact of the tribute

assessments can be found in AGI, Lima 124, No. IV. Carta al Rey de Lzdo. Ramirez de Cartagena, Lima 6-V-1576, ff. 2–2V.

52. AGI, Lima 123, No. II. Carta al Rey de Juan de Vera, Cuzco, 24-III-1572, f. 1.

53. This quotation is from Reál Cédula, Valladolid, 1536. *Recopilación*, Libro VI, Título I, ley xii. Tomo II, p. 192. Pre-1570 migration policy is discussed in Málaga Medina, "Las Reducciones" and in Charles Gibson, *The Aztecs Under Spanish Rule* (Stanford: Stanford University Press, 1964), p. 150.

54. Reáal Cédula, Valladolid, 13-II-1544. AGI, Indiferentes 423. Published in *Colección de Documentos para la Historia*, Vol. I, pp. 228–30.

55. Reál Cédula, Madrid, 31-III-1583. AGI, Mexico 2999. Published in *Colección de Documentos para la Historia*, Vol. I, pp. 547–48.

56. The movement of mestizo children was approved in Reál Cédula, Burgos, 21-V-1524. *Recopilación*, Libro VI, Título I, ley viii. Tomo II, p. 191. For legal relocation within Indian society, see Reál Cédula, Madrid, 10-X-1618. *Recopilación*, Libro VI, Título I, ley x. Tomo II, pp. 191–92. The Chilean Indians are discussed in Reál Cédula, Madrid, 17-VII-1622. *Recopilación*, Libro VI, Título XVI, ley xi. Tomo II, p. 318.

57. For the debate on residency requirements, see BNP, B1176. Memorial. 20-X-1692. The requirements for relocation within rural areas are merely described as "prolonged." The residency requirements specifically governing urban migrants will be discussed in chapter 5.

58. Murra, "The Economic Organization of the Inca State," pp. 199–200.

59. ANP, Derecho Indígena, Legajo 4, Cuaderno 61. Revista y padrón de los indios del Repartimiento de Parinacochas, 1616, ff. 87V–88. It should be remembered that population data compiled for the assignment of Indian lands were usually distinct from census figures for tribute and mita purposes.

60. These fraudulent padrones are described in AGI, Lima 471. Relación de la doctrina de Pocoanca, s.f., c. 1690. Of course, the kurakas could have been defending the community's interests as well as their own. The Omacha renumeration is discussed in ANP, Derecho Indígena, Legajo 4, Cuaderno 66. Auto original del Excel. Sr. Príncipe de Esquilache, 9-IV-1620, f. 1. For a similar case of tax fraud, see BNP, B1030. Expediente sobre la petición presentada por el Lic. Luis Enrique, Cuzco, 3-II-1629, ff. 71–72V.

61. AGI, Charcas 266, No. II. Carta de Don Juan de Carbajál, 18-III-1636, f. 1.

62. This practice is denounced in BNP, B516, and Reál Cédula, Madrid, 22-III-1680. AGI, Charcas, 416. Published in *Colección de Documentos para la Historia*, Vol. II, p. 699.

63. Relación de Luis de Velasco, 28-XI-1604. *Colección de las Memorias*, Vol. I, pp. 118–19.

64. These observations and commands appear in Reál Cédula, Tordesillas, 12-VII-1600. AGI, Lima 570, Libro 16. Published in *Colección de Documentos para la Historia*, Vol. II, p. 63.

65. Cédula Reál a la Audiencia de los Charcas, Valladolid, 29-IX-1602. AGI, Buenos Aires 5. Published in *Colección de Documentos para la Historia*, Vol. II, pp. 88–89.

66. Decreto, Madrid, 4-II-1604. *Recopilación*, Libro VI, Título III, ley xviii. Tomo II, p. 211.

67. *Anales del Cuzco*, f. 26.

68. Quoted in AGI, Lima 154, No. IV. Carta al Rey de Jorge Fonseca, procurador de Guancabelica, 20-IV-1623.

69. Memoria de Juan de Mendoza y Luna, Marqués de Montesclaros, 12-IX-1615. *Colección de las Memorias*, Vol. I, pp. 166–68.

70. Ibid., p. 168.

71. Ibid., p. 206, pp. 167–68.

72. Ibid., p. 206.

73. AGI, Charcas 270, No. XXIV, ff. 47–47V.

74. Memorial del marqués de Montesclaros, p. 167.

75. ANP, Derecho Indígena, Legajo 4, Cuaderno 65. Testimonio de los documentos relativos a la visita y reducción, 1619, f. 1.

76. Ibid., f. 2V.

77. Memoria de Francisco de Borja y Aragón, Príncipe de Esquilache, 1621. *Colección de las Memorias*, Vol. I, p. 238.

78. Reál Cédula, Madrid, 10-X-1618. *Recopilación*, Libro VI, Título I, ley xx. Tomo II, p. 194.

79. Reál Cédula, Madrid, 10-X-1618. *Recopilación*, Libro VI, Título III, ley xii. Tomo II, p. 210.

80. AGI, Charcas 266, No. XII. Autos sobre que no se entienda con Yndios de la mita las provisiones de los diez años, 1654, f. 6.

81. Memoria del Príncipe de Esquilache, pp. 217–18.

82. AGI, Charcas 266, No. IV. Testimonio de Cédula del Rey, 28-IV-1650, f. 1V.

83. AGI, Charcas 266, No. XII-30D. Carta del Virrey Conde de Salvatierra al Rey, 2-IX-1651, f. 1V.

84. AGI, Charcas 266, No. XIIII, ff. 1V, 7V–8.

85. The church's opposition is presented in AGI, Charcas 266, No. XXIII. Carta del Fray Fco. de la Cruz, 14-IV-1660, f. 1. The miners' objections are found in AGI, Charcas 266, No. XIII, ff. 7–7V.

86. ANP, Juicios de Residencias, Legajo 28, Cuaderno 81, f. 183.

87. This incident is recounted in AGI, Charcas 266, No. XIII, ff. 1–5.

88. AGI, Charcas 270, No. X-16. Carta del Virrey Duque de Palata al Rey, 21-VIII-1683, f. 2.

89. AGI, Charcas 270, No. VI. Carta y enforme del Arcobispo de la Plata, 28-II-1682, ff. 2V–3. A half-century earlier, Guaman Poma de Ayala had proposed a similar solution to the labor crisis which involved an alternative form of forced service. See Felipe Guaman Poma de Ayala, *La nueva crónica y buen gobierno del Perú*, Vol. III, Luis F. Bustios Galvéz, ed. (Lima: Editorial Cultura, 1956), p. 123.

90. Lima 471. Relación de la doctrina de Anta, Abancay, 20-IV-1690.

91. BNP, B1504-VII. Provisión del Duque de Palata, 1683, f. 143.

92. AGI, Charcas 270, No. X-16, f. 2V.

93. AGI, Charcas 270, No. X-16. Palata's observations on the size of the Indian population are found in BNP, B1504-VII, f. 143. Palata's commitment to a visita general of the Indian community was part of his larger efforts to reform Peruvian government. See Kenneth J. Andrien's description of the role of the visita general in late-seventeenth-century colonial administration. Andrien, *Crisis and Decline*, particularly chapter 7, "The Visita General, 1664–1690."

94. For various reports on the Palata reforms, see AGI, Charcas 270, No. XVII. Decretos del Duque de Palata, copia del 15-II-1689, f. 38; BNP, B1504-VII, f. 143V; AGI, Charcas 270, No. XV. Carta al Rey del Duque de Palata, 18-III-1688, f. 1; and AGI, Charcas 271, No. V, passim. Brian M. Evans has summarized the instructions governing the Palata census and has characterized the migrant community of Alto Perú in "Census Enumeration in Late Seventeenth-Century Alto Perú: The Numeración General of 1683–84," *Studies in Spanish American Population History*, pp. 25–44. Jeffrey A. Cole has discussed the Palata administration in "Viceregal Persistence Versus Indian Mobility: The Impact of the Duque de la Palata's Reform Program on Alto Perú, 1681–1692," *LARR* 19, no. 1, 1984, pp. 37–56.

95. AGI, Charcas 270, No. XXIV, Carta del Lzdo. Blas Robles de Salzedo, 30-V-1643, f. 15.

96. The October 1683 announcement appears in Josephe and Francisco Mugaburu, *Chronicle of Colonial Lima: The Diary of Josephe and Francisco Mugaburu, 1640–1697*. Robert Ryal Miller, trans and ed. (Norman: University of Oklahoma Press, 1975), p. 277. Labor regulations are discussed in *Aranzel de los jornales que se han de pagar los indios. Mandado ordenar por el Excelentíssimo Señor D. Melchor de Navarra y Rocafull, Duque de Palata, 7 de noviembre, 1687*. Numerous examples of the opposition to Palata's reforms can be found in AGI, Charcas 271 and in AGI, Charcas 270, No. VI, ff. 2V, 4.

97. The bishop's protests are in Carta del obispo de Cusco, 19-III-1691. AGI, Charcas 171, No. V, ff. 381V–82. The kurakas' complaints appear in AGI, Lima 471. (Relación de la doctrina de Pucara, Lampa, 12-IX-1689.)

98. AGI, Charcas 270, No. XVI. Carta del Rey al Virrey, 18-II-1697, ff. 3–3V.

99. Ibid. The moratorium is announced in Cédula Reál, 10-VI-1685. AGI, Charcas 271, No. V, ff. 452–59V. This citation appears on f. 459.

100. This quotation is from AGI, Charcas 270, No. XII. Carta al Rey, 6-IV-1686, f. 1. The corregidores' actions are described in AGI, Charcas 271, No. V, f. 41V. AGI, Charcas 270, No. XI, f. 5.

101. AGI, Charcas 271, No. V, ff. 95–96, 151–52, 216V–17V, 230–32, 303–5, 311V–12V.

102. Informe de Tribunal de Cuentas, 1-VII-1689. AGI, Charcas 271, No. V, ff. 89V–92.

103. Ibid., ff. 89V–90, 91V. Franklin Pease reports that there was a substantial increase in state revenue after the Palata renumeration. (Pease, *Del Tawantinsuyu*, pp. 208, 216.) Because reassessments were never completed in the Cuzco area, the revenue increases must have been in other administrative zones.

104. Carta del obispo de Lima, 1-IX-1692. AGI, Charcas 271, No. V, f. 3V.

105. AGI, Charcas 271, No. V, f. 460.

106. AGI, Charcas 271, No. XXII-33. El Virrey Conde de Monclova a V.M., 15-III-1690, ff. 5–6. Emphasis in the original.

107. Ibid., f. 6.

108. For the reduced labor allocations, see BNE, No. 6225. Materiales que yo iba juntando para formar el extracto de la mita a Potosí, rúbrica (sin otra firma), 1743, f. 195. The *Aranzel* is described in *Anales del Cuzco, 1600–1750*. Compiled by Don Diego de Esquivel y Navia, Museo Arqueológico del Cusco, f. 180.

109. AGI, Lima 431, No. III. Decreto del Conde de la Monclova, 27-IV-1692, passim. Some of these regulations appear in ANP, Derecho Indígena, Legajo 39, Cuaderno 811. Provisión original dictada por el Virrey Marqués de Castelfuerte, 1720, passim.

110. AGI, Charcas 271, No. IV. Carta al Rey, 10-XII-1692, ff. 1–1V.

111. AGI, Charcas 271, No. 1. Carta al Rey, 1-IX-1692, ff. 1–1V.

112. AGI, Charcas 271, No. V. Carta del Casique de Nicassio, 11-IX-1689, ff. 214–15.

113. AGI, Charcas 271, No. V. Carta al rey del Obispo del Cuzco, 10-IV-1689, ff. 67V–69V. The Corregidor of Lampa agreed with this estimate. AGI, Charcas 271, No. V. (Carta de Don Pedro Merino de Hereda, Corregidor de Lampa, 30-III-1689, f. 211V.)

114. AGI, Charcas 271, No. V. Carta del Obispo del Cusco, 19-III-1691, f. 382V.

115. Reál Cédula, al Virrey del Perú, Madrid, 10-IV-1609. AGI, Lima 570. Published in *Colección de Documentos para la Historia*, Vol. II, p. 148.

116. Aprobación, 10-X-1618. AGI, Buenos Aires 2. Published in *Colección de Documentos para la Historia*, Vol. II, p. 202. Consulta del Consejo de Indias, 29-IV-1703. AGI, Chile 67. Published in *Colección de Documentos para la Historia*, Vol. III, pp. 89–92.

117. AGI, Lima 45, No. I. Carta al Rey del Conde de Chinchón, 21-III-1634, ff. 39–39V. AGI, Lima 471. Relación de la doctrina de Aiabire, 20-X-1689.

118. Memoria de Diego Fernández de Cabera, Marqués de Guadalcázar, 14-XII-1628. *Colección de las Memorias*, Vol. II, p. 13.

119. ANP, Juicios de Residencias, Legajo 11, Cuaderno 27. Autos que promovió Don Diego García de Paredes, enero 1593, ff. 40–109, passim. BNP, C1861. Expediente sobre el juicio de residencia, 6-XI-1714, ff. 182ff.

120. AHC, Provincia de Urubamba, Legajo 1. Repartación de tierras, Valle de Urubamba, 1595. AGI, Lima 138, No. X. Carta al Rey del Doctor Perez Merchán, 20-V-1607, ff. 2–2V.

121. ANP, Juicios de Residencias, Legajo 11, Cuaderno 27, f. 40. Additional confirmation, ff. 45–46.

122. BNP, B1497. Expediente sobre la residencia, 17-VII-1609, f. 104.

123. BNP, B347. Expediente sobre la petición presentada por Juan Lorenzo de Zela, Lima 28-IV-1628, f. 2.

124. ANP, Juicios de Residencias, Legajo 28, Cuaderno 77. Juicio de Residencia que promovió el Capitán Dr. Gabriel Parraga y Rojas, 30-VIII-1627, f. 40. Additional confirmation on ff. 48, 56.

125. *Anales del Cuzco*, f. 69. For the corregidores' responses, see: ANP, Juicios de Residencias, Legajo 29, Cuaderno 82. Autos de Residencia y cuentas, Cotabambas, 1634; ANP, Juicios de Residencias, Legajo 33, Cuaderno 96. Autos promovidos por Don José de Carbajál Manrique, Aymares, 1657; BNP, B1154. Autos y residencias, Chumbibilcas, Cuzco, 5-VI-1658; and BNP, B1177. Expediente de los autos seguidos entre Juan Francisco, indio, y Luís Macas, Cacique Principal. Lima, Mayo, 1692.

126. BNP, B1063. Expediente sobre la petición presentada por Miguel Gutiérrez, Cuzco, 16-VII-1686.

127. BNP, B516, f. 1V.

128. AGI, Lima 162, No. V. Carta del Capitán Juan Serrano de Almagro al Rey, 1634, f. 6.

129. AGI, Lima 168, No. IIA. Carta de Ayudante Hernando Gomez Boza a su Magestad, 3-IV-1653, ff. 5–5V.

130. BNP, B516, f. 4V.

131. For details of these plans, see Ibid., ff. 3 and 4V; AGI, Charcas 270, No. VIII-10, f. 5; ANP, Superior Gobierno, Legajo 4, Cuaderno 61. Testimonio de las diligencias que practicó Dn. Francisco de Tosas y de Valle, Chilques y Masques, 1651, f. 7V; and AGI, Lima 168, No. IIA, f. 6V. This specific quotation is from AGI, Lima 168, No. IIa, f. 4. The plans are denounced by the Protector General in AGI, Lima 162, No. II. Carta al Rey, 18-VII-1635, f. 4V.

132. BNP, B516, f. 4. Only a few of these proposals deplored the great deal of damage being done to Indians.

133. AGI, Charcas 270, No. XXII-33. El Virrey Conde de la Monclova a V.M., 15-III-1690, f. 4V.

134. Reál Cédula, 1637, copied in AGI, Lima 163, No. III. Carta de Juan de Porras Vallejo a S.M., 27-V-1637.

135. Memoria de Luís Fernández de Cabrera, Conde de Chinchón, 26-I-1640. *Colección de las Memorias,* Vol. II, p. 85.

136. For the Marqués's terse comment, see Memoria de Pedro de Toledo y Leiva, Marqués de Mancera, 8-X-1648. *Colección de las Memorias,* Vol. II, p. 133. The order for a reducción is quoted in AGI, Charcas 266, No. IV. Testimonio de Cédula del Rey, 28-IV-1650, f. 1V.

137. AGI, Lima 168, No. VIIA. Carta de Don Francisco Henrique de Sanguesa al Rey, 15-IX-1651. Marginalia, 1-IX-1653. Note the delay before this proposal was considered by the Consejo de Indias.

138. Henry F. Dobyns believes that this *fiebre,* or fever, was probably small-pox or influenza, or a succession of the two diseases. See his "An Outline of Andean Epidemic History to 1720," *Bulletin of the History of Medicine* 37, no. 6, November–December 1963, p. 513. The mortality data for the viceroyalty and bishopric are found in AGI, Lima 437, No. I. Petición de Don Vicente de Mora Chimo Capac, sin fecha, c. 1727, f. 2V, and *Anales del Cuzco,* ff. 249–50. The priest was careful to note that "because this epidemic began before August 15, 1719, it can not be a consequence of the eclipse experienced that date." The total population of the bishopric at this time was approximately 130,000.

139. *Anales del Cuzco,* ff. 246–47. For details of medical techniques used during the epidemic, see AGI, Lima 411. Relación informativa de la peste, que se remitió del Cuzco, c. 1720. Published in Michèle Colin, *Le Cuzco à la fin du XVIIe et au début du XVIIIe siècle* (Paris: Institut des Hautes Etúdes de l'Amérique Latine, 1966), pp. 189–93.

140. *Anales del Cuzco,* ff. 248–49. For the suspension of the mita, see Noble David Cook, "La población indígena en el Perú colonial," *America Colonial: Población y economía, Anuario* (Instituto de Investigaciones Históricas, Universidad Nacional de Litoral, Rosario, Argentina, 1965), p. 100. For the impact on Cuzco's agricultural production, see AHC, Beneficencia 15, Legajo 54. Expedientes de ventas, 1682–1725, ff. 43V–44 and *Anales del Cuzco,* f. 251.

141. ANP, Derecho Indígena, Legajo 39, Cuaderno 811, ff. 1–2.

142. Specific instructions to the corregidores of Abancay and Quispicanche are repeated in BNP, C1956. Provisión de Retassa del Tributo que deven pagar los Yndios originarios y forasteros del Repartimiento y Pueblos de Ocongate y Marcapata Concuchoa, Provincia de Quispicanche, 6-VII-1725. This citation is from f. 3V.

143. ANP, Informes de Tributos, Legajo 1, Cuaderno 13. Provisión Reál, Lima, 23-II-1772, ff. 5, 8, 14. AGI, Lima 1172, No. II. Informe del Visitador General del Perú, Lima, 20-IV-1780, f. 3V.

CHAPTER 3: The Forasteros of Cuzco

1. Rolando Mellafe has characterized this period as one of "constant movement of people in all senses of the term," in *Population and Economics*, p. 303. This chapter deals with demographic change; the following chapters will focus on the consequences of widespread indigenous migration.

2. Pease describes the depopulation of the lower Andes in *Del Tawantinsuyu*, p. 200. Hernando de Santillán, *Relación del Origen, Decendencia, Política, y Gobierno de los Incas (1563–1564)*, is quoted in George Kubler, "The Quechua in the Colonial World," in *Handbook of South American Indians*, p. 379. John Murra has a substantially different interpretation of Incan restrictions on travel and migration. See "The Economic Organization of the Inca State," p. 195.

3. Matienzo, *Gobierno del Perú*, p. 191.

4. This practice is denounced in the Cédula Reál de 19-XI-1539. (Published in *Colección de documentos para la Historia*, Vol. I, pp. 194–96.)

5. Crosby, *The Colombian Exchange*, chapters 2 and 4. Dobyns, "An Outline of Andean Epidemic History to 1720," passim. Nicolás Sánchez-Albornoz discusses this issue in *The Population of Latin America*, chapter 3. Even before the arrival of the Spaniards in Peru, European diseases had attacked the Andean populations. For example, the smallpox epidemic that broke out in Mexico in 1519 struck Peru in 1524. Dobyns and Doughty, *Peru: A Cultural History*, p. 61 and Crosby, *The Columbian Exchange*, p. 39. Juan Friede issues the following caveats concerning the interpretation of "plague data" in his study of "Demographic Changes in the Mining Community of Muzo after the Plague of 1629," *HAHR* 47, no. 3, August 1967, pp. 338–43: "1. Data on plagues given by contemporary chroniclers must be used cautiously when not corroborated by reliable documents. 2. When there were epidemics in Spanish America, these were neither general nor of identical consequences throughout the regions affected." Crosby, Dobyns, and Sánchez-Albornoz are aware of these pitfalls and provide a variety of documentation to support their assertions concerning the nature and impact of epidemics in Spanish South America. However, Dobyns's use of evidence in *Their Number Become Thinned* (Knoxville: University of Tennessee Press in Cooperation with the Newberry Library Center for the History of the American Indian, 1983), has been criticized by David Henige in "Primary Source by Primary Source? On the Role of Epidemics in New World Depopulation," *Ethnohistory* 33, no. 3, Summer 1986, pp. 293–312.

6. Dobyns, "An Outline of Andean Epidemic History to 1720," passim.

7. AHC, Cabildo del Cuzco, Tomo 6, 1573–1578. El cabildo del 19 de julio, 1577, f. 188.

8. Dobyns, "An Outline of Andean Epidemic History to 1720," p. 507.

9. Ibid. Noble David Cook, "La población indígena," in *America Colonial*,

p. 98. AHC, Cabildo del Cuzco, Tomo 11, 1613–1618. El cabildo del 27 de junio, 1614, f. 58.

10. Dobyns, "An Outline of Andean Epidemic History to 1720," p. 511.

11. Ibid., p. 513. Cook, *America Colonial*, p. 99.

12. The mortality rates are described in the *Anales del Cuzco, 1600–1750*. Compiled by D. Diego de Esquivel y Navia, ff. 243–49. Dobyns suggests that the impact of this epidemic was intensified by the denser concentration of the recovering Indian population. See his "An Outline of Andean Epidemic History to 1720," p. 514. Sánchez-Albornoz cites the spread of disease throughout the viceroyalty in *The Population of Latin America*, p. 93. The epidemic is discussed in greater detail in chapter 2. For the events of 1726, see the *Anales del Cuzco*, f. 267.

13. The drought of 1592 is described in AGI, Lima 131, No. III. Carta del cabildo de Potosí, 2-II-1592, f. 1. For the crisis of 1657, see ANP, Juicios de Residencias, Legajo 33, Cuaderno 95. Autos que promovió Don José de Carbajál Manrique, 1657, f. 1.

14. BNE, No. 2381. Del notable teremoto que huvo en la Ciudad del Cuzco, 1650. PTT, Ynforme individual que al Excmo. Sr. Virrey se le hizo sobre el estrago que causaron en esta ciudad los temblores grandes, Cuzco 1650.

15. *Anales del Cuzco*, ff. 221–22.

16. Relocation as a form of punishment is described by Rowe, "The Incas Under Spanish Colonial Institutions," p. 185. An example of the Church's concern over the spiritual consequences of migration is found in AGI, Lima 149, No. V. (Carta del Dr. Alberto de Acuña al Rey, 20-IV-1619, ff. 2–2V.)

For a discussion of the relationship between an ayllu, its lands, and its earth shrines, see Joseph W. Bastien, *Mountain of the Condor: Metaphor and Ritual in an Andean Ayllu* (New York: West Publishing, 1978). For a parallel, contemporary account of a community's attachment to its ancestral lands, see Anthony Oliver-Smith's depiction of local resistance to government resettlement programs following the destruction and demographic collapse brought on by the earthquake and avalanche that leveled Yungay, Peru, on May 31, 1970. (*The Martyred City: Death and Rebirth in the Andes* [Albuquerque: University of New Mexico Press, 1986].)

The survival of indigenous religious practices will be discussed in chapter 4.

17. See, for example, Robert Keith's discussion of economic change in coastal Peru, particularly in the Ica and Nazca regions, where the formation of the wine industries brought new opportunities for small-scale cultivators, including some Indian kurakas and communities. (*Conquest and Agrarian Change*, pp. 101–2.) Keith A. Davies traces the expansion of wine production in "Wine Estates and Landowners," chapter 3 of *Landowners in Colonial Peru* (Austin: University of Texas Press, 1984).

18. AGI, Lima 471. Relación de la doctrina de Aiabire, Lampa, 20-X-1689.

19. AGI, Lima 471. Relación de la doctrina de Horunillo, Lampa, 15-VIII-1689. Further evidence of the impact of the loss of community resources is found in AGI, Lima 132. Carta del Doctor Alberto de Acuña, 20-XI-1593. Doctor de Acuña reported that many Indians abandoned their hometowns after the seizure of community assets increased members' tax burdens.

20. Reál decreto, 25-VIII-1681. AGI, Indiferentes 430. Published in *Colección de documentos para la Historia*, Vol. II, p. 729.

21. See, for example, Memoria de Luís Fernández de Cabrera, conde de Chinchón, in the *Colección de las Memorias*, Vol. II, p. 85.

22. Cédula Reál, Madrid, 5-XI-1540. AGI, Indiferentes 423. Cédula Reál, Madrid, 11-I-1541. AGI, Indiferentes 423. (Published in *Colección de documentos para la Historia*, Vol. I, pp. 197–98.) Cédula Reál, Madrid, 8-XI-1539. AGI, Panama 235. (Published in *Colección de documentos para la Historia*, Vol. I, p. 194.)

23. Cédula Reál, Granada, 9-XI-1526. Repeated on 2-VIII-1530, 13-I-1532, 5-XI-1540, 21-V-1542, and 24-X-1548. *Recopilación*. Libro VI, Título II, ley i. Vol. II, p. 201. A similar Cédula Reál, Madrid, 22-IX-1667, was proclaimed on 25-I-1670 in Lima, as quoted by Josephe and Francisco Mugaburu, in *Chronicle of Colonial Lima*, p. 153.

24. Cédula Reál, Madrid, 7-VI-1618. AGI, Buenos Aires 2. (Published in *Colección de documentos para la Historia*, Vol. II, p. 201.) Cédula Reál, Madrid, 8-X-1681. AGI, Buenos Aires 5. (Published in *Colección de documentos para la Historia*, Vol. II, p. 732.)

25. AGI, Lima 141, No. I. Relación de Joan de Belvede, 1611, f. 9V. AAC, Legajo 307, Protocolo 38, No. 11. Autos contra Joseph de Avila, 1684–1700.

26. ANP, Juicios de Residencias, Legajo 35, Cuaderno 103. Incidente de carácter penál dentro del juicio de Residencia y Reducción de Cuentas, Quispicanche, 1670, f. 70. Another example of Indians fleeing obraje labor can be found in BNP, B1095. Títulos y demás documentos del obraje de Ragua, 16-V-1672, f. 18.

27. Some Indian men—kurakas, village officials, and church wardens—were excused from mita duty. Local regulations and practices allowed for additional, specific exemptions. The mita is discussed in greater detail in chapter 6.

28. This citation is from AGI, Lima 471. Relación de la doctrina de Pachaconas, Aymares, 4-X-1689. Also, see Las relaciones de las doctrinas de Yanaca, Aymares; Colcabamba, Aymares; Hancobamba, Aymares; Pampamarca, Aymares; Antabamba, Aymares; Arapa, Azángaro; Cacha, Canas y Canches; Sandía, Carabaya y Sangabán; Aquira, Cotabambas; Cotabambas, Cotabambas; and Vellille, Chumbibilcas. Additional information can be found in AAC. Paquete V. Autos de capítulo contra Don Felipe Ramires de Arellano, 28-VI-1673, f. 2; and ANP, Juicios de Residencias, Legajo 29, Cuaderno 96, f. 113.

29. BNE, No. 3040. Carta del Protector de Potosí, Diego Nuñez, al Virrey, 12-VII-1582, f. 152.

30. AGI, Charcas 266, No. 37-A. Travajos que padecen los Indios, 20-VII-1657, f. 5V. With respect to infant mutilation and murder, Irene Silverblatt states that "Sometimes women became so desperate at seeing their culture destroyed that they preferred to commit infanticide than allow a new generation to suffer." Citing Guaman Poma, Silverblatt argues that women "killed only their male children. Perhaps revealing their complete despair at seeing themselves abused not only by male representatives of colonial authority, but by male members of their own culture, women attempted to recreate the 'female component' of Andean institutions." Silverblatt, *Women and Colonization*, p. 179.

31. AGI, Lima 154, No. I. Servicios de Don Francisco Fernández de Cordova, Lima, 1623, f. 1V.

32. AHC. Cabildo del Cuzco, Tomo 12, 1623–1627. El cabildo del 17 de enero, 1626, f. 182V.

33. AGI, Lima 471. Relación de la doctrina de Arapa, Azángaro, 9-IX-1689, y la de la doctrina de Sicoani, Canas y Canches, 19-IX-1689. For an example of such land transfers within one community, see AGI, Lima 471. Relación de la doctrina de Hatuncolla, Lampa, 12-IX-1689. The ways in which assimilated migrants gained access to natives' lands are described in chapters 4 and 6.

34. The linkage between migration and the repartimiento is found in AGI, Lima 471. Relación de la doctrina de Colcabamba, Aymares, 15-XI-1689. Additional citations for the flight from the repartimiento de bienes, all from the 1690 census of the bishopric of Cuzco, can be found in AGI, Lima 471. Las relaciones de las doctrinas de Anta, Abancay; Guanipaca, Abancay; Colcabamba, Aymares; Hancobamba, Aymares; and Catca, Paucartambo. For a description of the flooding of the Peruvian market, see Wightman, "The *Consulado* of Lima."

35. AGI, Lima 471. Relación de la doctrina de Hancobamba, Aymares, 27-IX-1689. An excellent description of the abuses of the repartimiento de bienes can be found in Jorge Juan and Antonio de Ulloa, *Noticias Secretas de América* (c. 1735) (Madrid: Editorial-America, 1918), pp. 261–75.

36. The proceedings of the Audiencia are summarized in Lohmann Villena, *El corregidor de indios*, pp. 569–73, passim. The death of the corregidor is described in *Anales del Cuzco*, f. 268. For descriptions and analyses of the eighteenth-century rebellions, see Ward Stavig, "Ethnic Conflict, Moral Economy, and Population in Rural Cuzco on the Eve of the Thupa Amaro II Rebellion," *HAHR* 68, no. 4, November 1988, pp. 735–70; Steve J. Stern, ed., *Resistance, Rebellion, and Consciousness in the Andean Peasant World, 18th to 20th Centuries* (Madison: University of Wisconsin Press, 1987); Carlos Daniel Valcarcel, *Rebeliones coloniales sudamericanas* (Mexico City: Fondo de cultura eco-

nómica, 1982); Leon G. Campbell, "Recent Research on Andean Peasant Revolts, 1750–1820," *LARR* 14, no. 1, 1979, pp. 3–49; Oscar Cornblit, "Society in Mass Rebellion in Eighteenth-Century Peru and Bolivia," in Latin American Affairs, Raymond Carr, ed., Saint Anthony's College Papers, No. 22. (London: Chatto and Windus, 1970); and Manuel Burga and Alberto Flores Galindo, "La producción agrícola y las sublevaciones durante el siglo XVIII: Apuntes Metodológicos," Private Issue, Huancayo, 1975.

37. ANP, Juicios de Residencias, Legajo 35, Cuaderno 103, f. 20. The abuse of Indian women is also discussed by Silverblatt, *Moon, Sun, and Witches: Gender Ideologies and Class in Inca and Colonial Peru* (Princeton: Princeton University Press, 1987), pp. 125–47, and by Felipe Guaman Poma de Ayala, *La nueva crónica y buen gobierno del Perú* (Lima, Editorial Cultura, 1956), Vol. III, pp. 107–8.

38. ANP, Juicios de Residencias, Legajo 29, Cuaderno 82. Residencia Tomada al corregidor de la provincia de Cotabambas, 1634, f. 289.

39. Complaints against priests can be found in ANP, Juicios de Residencias, Legajo 11, Cuaderno 27. Autos que promovió Don Diego Garcia de Paredes, Cotabambas, 30-I-1593, f. 112; AGI, Lima 134, No. VII. Carta de Diego de Figueroa al Rey, sin fecha; en el Consejo, 7-X-1598, f. 1; AAC, XXXIX, 2, 31. Información sobre las quejas del gobernador del Collana Aimarán, contra el licenciado Don Francisco Xaques de Ayala, cura interino, 1665; and BNP, C1883. Expediente sobre la queja interpuesta por Pascual Coyca, Andahuayles, 18-III-1716, passim. In 1629 the visiting inspector Domingo de Luna wrote that if the Indians question the priests' demands for goods or services "they are seized and tested for their knowledge of the catechism—even though they know it—until they miss a word, so that they can be stripped and whipped," in AGI, Lima 160, Carta de Domingo de Luna, 23-V-1629.

40. BNP, B744. Expediente de los autos seguidos entre Don Felipe Guayca, Curaca Principal de Totopón, y el Padre Mateo Quijada, 15-IV-1608, ff. 32–33.

41. AGI, Lima 305, No. II. Carta del Obispo del Cusco al Rey, 24-II-1635, ff. 1–1V.

42. Two accounts of Indian women fleeing their husbands are found in AAC, Paquete L. Auto contra Theresa Sisa, 1698 and AAC, Unmarked boxes, our #7. Auto contra Maria Sisa, 1700. The identical surnames are definitely coincidental. For the story of two Indians escaping arranged marriages, see AAC, Unmarked boxes, our #8. Criminal contra Augustín Ypi y María Pocochiclla, 15-II-1683.

43. David Brading and Harry E. Cross, "Colonial Silver Mining: Mexico and Peru," *HAHR* 52, no. 4, November 1972, p. 559. There is no one answer to their question, but the mita is discussed in chapter 6.

44. Confusion over the nature of the yanacona persisted throughout the colonial period. See the discussion below.

45. The Toledo settlements are described in chapter 2. For the two categories developed by Toledo, see AGI, Charcas 271, No. V, ff. 353–53V. The term "originario" had a distinct meaning in the special structure of the communities of Paraguay. See Elman Service, "The *Encomienda* in Paraguay," *HAHR* 31, no. 2, May 1951, pp. 230–52.

46. Karen Spalding offered this broadest definition of the word "forastero" in her "Social Climbers," pp. 662–63.

47. BNP, B516. Memorial acerca de las Mitas de los Indios del Perú, 10-XI-1664, f. 1V. For a discussion of forastero contributions, see AGI, Charcas 270, Libro XXIV. Carta de 8-VII-1677, ff. 21–21V.

48. AGI, Charcas 270, No. VIII-10. Carta de Contador Sebastián del Collado de Potosí, 11-V-1682, f. 4. Also, see AGI, Lima 471. Relación de la doctrina de Chupa, Azángaro, c. 1690 y la de la doctrina de Quacanga y Chimor, Paucartambo, c. 1690, for two case studies.

49. AGI, Lima 471. Relación de la doctrina de San Cristóbal, Cuzco, 3-VII-1690. Emphasis in the original.

50. AGI, Lima 167, No. III-b. Ynforme de Don Diego Perez Gallego, Corregidor de Cañete, 20-VI-1648, f. 1V.

51. AGI, Lima 471. Relación de la doctrina de San Marcos de Alcopaya, Aymares, c. 1690.

52. AGI, Lima 471. Relación de la doctrina de Calca, Paucartambo, 7-IX-1689. Ayllu identification in contemporary Andean communities continues to reflect the special status of descendants of migrants. Oscar Núñez del Prado reported in his study of Kuyo Chico that "Although there is a fair degree of social homogeneity in Kuyo Chico, some very subtle differences in the prestige of certain families can be noted. More esteem is accorded to those families whose roots are local and go back very far in the history of the community. . . . The foreign origin of other families, even some which have been in the community for several generations is not forgotten." (Oscar Núñez del Prado, *Kuyo Chico: Applied Anthropology in an Indian Community*. With the collaboration of William Foote Whyte. Lucy Whyte Russo and Richard Russo, trans. [Chicago: University of Chicago Press, 1973], p. 27.)

53. AGI, Charcas 270, No. XXIV. Libro y relación sumaria del Exmo. Señor Duque de Palata, 1690, f. 48V.

54. AGI, Lima 471. Relación de la doctrina de Paruro, Chilques y Masques, 1-IX-1689. These terms are used in a similar way, but not defined, in other parish reports. See, for example, AGI, Lima 471. Relación de la doctrina de Guanoquite, Chilques y Masques, sin fecha, c. 1690.

55. These transients were a persistent problem for administrators, particularly those at Potosí, who were constantly ordered to "clear the land of these vagrants." AGI, Lima 136, No. IV. Carta de Pedro de Cordova, 16-III-1603, f. 1V.

56. AGI, Charcas 270, No. XI-20A. Ynforme de Don Joseph de Villegas, Contador de Retassas, 12-VI-1685, ff. 8–8V.

57. Magnus Mörner, *Race Mixture in the History of Latin America* (Boston: Little, Brown, 1967), p. 75.

58. This quotation is from the Reál Cédula al Virrey del Perú, Madrid, 19-XI-1551. AGI, Lima 567. (Published in *Colección de documentos para la Historia*, Vol. I, pp. 289–90.) See also Reál Cédula, Madrid, 2-V-1563. Cedulario de Ayala, Tomo 107. (Published in *Colección de documentos para la Historia*, Vol. I, p. 400); and Reál Cédula al Virrey del Perú, Valladolid, 30-VIII-1603. AGI, Lima 570. (Published in *Colección de documentos para la Historia*, Vol. II, pp. 97–98.)

59. The fate of transients sent to the Philippines, Florida, and northern Mexico is not clear. Exile to the Philippines is described in Reál Cédula al Virrey de Nueva España, Madrid, 1-X-1626. AGI, Mexico 1006. (Published in *Colección de documentos para la Historia*, Vol. II, p. 290.) For the provisions concerning the Florida settlements, see Reál Cédula al Virrey de Nueva España, Madrid, 9-III-1718. Cedulario de Ayala, Tomo 57. (Published in *Colección de documentos para la Historia*, Vol. III, pp. 143–44); and Reál Cédula, al Virrey de Nueva España, Madrid, 20-XI-1700. Cedulario de Ayala, Tomo 57. (Published in *Colección de documentos para la Historia*, Vol. III, pp. 83–84.)

60. Reál Cédula, Madrid, 11-IV-1661. AGI, Quito 209. (Published in *Colección de documentos para la Historia*, Vol. II, p. 488.)

61. One official in Charcas thought that all Indian vagrants should be called "yanaconas." AGI, Charcas 270. Libro XXIV. Carta al rey, 8-VII-1677, f. 21V.

62. AGI, Lima 471. Relación de la doctrina de San Sebastián de Livitaca, Chumbibilcas, 1690.

63. See Appendix II and the discussion of the 1690 census results below in this chapter. For the local officials' belief that the numeration had cleared the bishopric of most of its transient population, see AGI, Lima 471. Relación de la doctrina de Juliaca, Lampa, 22-VIII-1689, y la de la doctrina de Lampa, Lampa, sin fecha, c. 1690.

64. BNP, Z763. Expediente sobre la petición presentada por Pedro de Azana, Lima 26-III-1716. The formal structure of colonial law and its impact on the issue of Indian identity were discussed in chapter 2. The changes within indigenous society which predate and mandate the redefinition of the forasteros are described in detail in chapter 4.

65. BNP, C2323. Autos que siguió [*sic*] los indios forasteros de la ciudad de Chachapoyas, 7-XII-1750, passim.

66. Magnus Morner, "Tenant Labour in Andean South America Since the Eighteenth Century, A Preliminary Report," XIII International Congress of Historical Sciences, Moscow, August 15–23, 1970. Reprinted by Nauka Publishing House, Moscow, 1970, p. 1.

67. Ibid., p. 5.

68. Magnus Mörner, "The Spanish Hacienda: A Survey of Recent Research and Debate," *HAHR* 53, no. 2, May 1973, pp. 183–216. Herbert S. Klein, "Hacienda and Free Community in Eighteenth-Century Alto Peru: A Demographic Study of the Aymara Population of the Districts of Chulumaní and Pacajes in 1786," *Journal of Latin American Studies* 7, part 2, November 1975, pp. 193–220. Oscar Cornblit, in "Society and Mass Rebellion," p. 26, states that in the eighteenth century "authorities classified [migrants] in the census as 'foreign Indians with land' and 'foreign Indians without land' (*forasteros con tierras,* and *forasteros sin tierras*)." (Emphasis in the original). However, Cornblit does not discuss the meaning or the significance of these two categories of forasteros. Mörner cites the use of the category "indios forasteros sin tierra" in the late eighteenth century, but fails to distinguish between these Indians and the forasteros of 1690. (Magnus Mörner, *Perfil de la sociedad rural del Cuzco a fines de la colonia* [Lima: Universidad del Pacífico, 1978], pp. 49–50, passim.) A similar approach is taken by Sánchez-Albornoz in *Indios y tributos en el Alto Perú,* pp. 35–67, passim, and by Noble David Cook, *Demographic Collapse: Indian Peru, 1520–1620* (Cambridge: Cambridge University Press, 1981), pp. 85–87. Burga and Flores Galindo actually equate the two groups in "La producción agrícola," p. 174.

69. For a discussion of these revolts, see Stavig, "Ethnic Conflict"; Stern, *Resistance, Rebellion, and Consciousness;* and Cornblit, "Society and Mass Rebellion," p. 43.

70. This characterization of the late-eighteenth-century transients is from Burga and Flores Galindo, "La producción agrícola," p. 176.

71. For a description of the ecclesiastical census, see Appendix II. The reports of parish priests throughout the area describe the flight of the transients. See, for example, AGI, Lima 471. Relación de la doctrina de Lampa, sin fecha, c. 1690, y las de las doctrinas de Juliaca, Lampa, 22-VIII-1689, y Horunillo, Lampa, 15-VIII-1689.

72. See Appendix II for a discussion of the manipulation and generation of data from the 1689–1690 census of the bishopric of Cuzco. The statistics in this paragraph are all from Appendix II, tables IIB and IIE. The extremes of forastero representation in individual parishes are AYM-16, 6 percent, and AZG-3 and PCT-5, both 100 percent. The urban-to-rural migration will be discussed later in this chapter and below. For comparative figures from other areas of the Viceroyalty of Peru, see Cook, *Demographic Collapse,* pp. 85–87 and Zulawski, *"Forasteros* and *Yanaconas."*

73. The provinces of the bishopric of Cuzco which supplied Indian labor to Guancavelica were Aymares, Cotabambas, and Chumbibilcas. Those in the mita to Potosí were Azángaro, Canas y Canches, Lampa, and Quispicanche. Local mitas prevailed in Abancay, Calca y Lares, Carabaya y Sangabán, Chil-

ques y Masques, Marquesado de Oropesa, and Vilcabamba. The cultivation of coca is discussed below.

74. See Appendix II, tables IIF–3.

75. In the undifferentiated format, the reports on the originario group showed a consistent town majority: in only one doctrina did the proportion of the originario population residing in town fall below 99 percent. The extreme distribution polarity of individual entries in the forastero category, however, displayed a confusing and contradictory alternative dominance by one locale or the other. Supporting data entries are found in Appendix II, tables IIF–3.

76. See, for example, AGI, Lima 471. Relación de la doctrina de Chupa, Azángaro, y la de la doctrina de Challabamba, Paucartambo.

77. See Appendix II, table IIC and table IIF–1.

78. See Appendix II.

79. See Appendix II, table IIF–4.

80. See Appendix II, table IIF–2.

81. BNP, B1479, passim. See also, AGI, Lima 471. Relación de la doctrina de Guaquirca, Aymares, 26-IX-1689.

82. AGI, Lima 471. Relación de la doctrina de Pampamarca, Aymares, 9-IX-1689. The autonomy of these forasteros is in sharp contrast to developments in the Yucatan, where the formation of satellite communities through the dispersal of population from established towns preserved community linkages between the two settlements. (Nancy M. Farriss, "Nucleation versus Dispersal: The Dynamics of Population Movement in Colonial Yucatan," *HAHR* 58, no. 2, May 1978, pp. 187–216. Farriss's interesting model of "flight, drift, and dispersal" migration patterns in the Yucatan cannot be successfully applied to the Cuzco zone, in which a strong urban core and mining poles influence population movement.

83. AGI, Lima 471. Relación de la doctrina de Chonta, Abancay, 5-V-1690.

84. See Appendix I.

85. See the discussion of these records in Appendix III and the treatment of the ayllu forastero in chapter 4.

86. Yucay's proximity to the city of Cuzco produced an unusually high representation of urban natives within the 97 percent of forasteros from within the bishopric, but urban Indians were slightly outnumbered by those from area provinces (50 percent to 47 percent). Towns surrounding Cuzco were not the only areas in which urban natives resettled: the parish priest of Chonta, in the province of Abancay, reported that among the established forastero community in his district were natives of parishes in the city of Cuzco, in AGI, Lima 471. Relación de la doctrina de Chonta, 5-V-1690. The significance of this urban outflow will be discussed below. Internal evidence clearly demonstrates that Yucay forasteros born in nearby towns were independent of their ancestral

communities. Data from Appendix III, table IIID are the source for all these statistics.

87. Cook, *Demographic Collapse*, p. 114. See also Sally Falk Moore, *Power and Property in Inca Peru* (New York: Columbia University Press, 1958), p. 1; Cook, "La población indígena," passim; and Sánchez-Albornoz, *The Population of Latin America*, pp. 32–36 and 38–39.

88. Cook, "La población indígena," passim; Sánchez-Albornoz, *The Population of Latin America*, chapter 3; and Crosby, *The Columbian Exchange*, chapters 2 and 4. Sánchez-Albornoz stated that "the 1719 epidemic, together with later, localized outbreaks, reduced the Indian population to the minimum" (p. 91). Cook, in a widely accepted and frequently cited graphic representation of the size of the Indian population of colonial Peru, dipped his population curve to an unspecified data point at an unidentified date in the early 1700s (p. 93). Both analyses compared population estimates from the 1620s with the data compiled by the Conde de Superunda in 1754, and postulated a regular rate of decline throughout the seventeenth and early eighteenth centuries. Although both demographers have amended these models in later works, the depiction of continuous decline to a 1720s nadir has yet to be replaced by a model which allows for regional variation and reflects the importance of indigenous migration as a force in that variation. For an example of their later work, see Cook's *Demographic Collapse* and Sánchez-Albornoz's "Mita, migraciones y pueblos. Variaciones en el espacio y en el tiempo," *Revista boliviana* III, no. 1, 1983, pp. 31–59. Although Linda A. Newson does not consider the important role which indigenous migration played in demographic change, she does recognize some regional population variations within the Indian community in "Indian Population Patterns," pp. 42–46.

89. Some of the decline may be attributed to the inclusion of transients in the 1676 census and their exclusion from the 1690 tally, but not all of the decrease can be explained by bureaucratic procedures: the 1687 smallpox epidemic was also responsible for significant population losses. Rather than assuming a rapid population recovery from 1652 to 1676 and an equally rapid reversal from 1676 to 1690, it is more accurate to note both the incomplete nature of the first sample and the omission of the transient population from the second.

90. The figure of 82,367 for the maximum originario population of 1690 was achieved by multiplying the total population by the percentage of the population with forasteros present in order to obtain a figure of 88,612 for the population containing both forasteros and originarios. The number of forasteros in that pool (39,520) was obtained by use of the average percentage of forasteros throughout the bishopric and was subtracted from the total. The remaining number of originarios (49,092) was added to 33,275 (the population of those parishes which may or may not contain forasteros) for a maximum of 82,367 originarios. Simply applying the average rate of forastero presence to the entire

population would yield an even lower originario population of 68,282, but I have adopted the first, more cautious, manipulation. In either case, the population nadir is obvious. Data entries and subtotals are in Appendix II, tables IIA and IIE.

91. AGI, Lima 471. Padrón del obispado del Cuzco, 1690, passim.

92. See the discussion of administrative practices in chapter 2. Forasteros are described as "numerous," without any specific figures being given, in ANP, Superior Gobierno, Legajo II, Cuaderno 16. Autos seguidos ante el Superior Gobierno por Don Hernan Gonzalez de Vargas, Yucay, 11-XI-1597, f. 27; AHC, Cabildo del Cuzco, Tomo 11, 1613–1618. El cabildo del 7 de agosto, 1617, ff. 166V–67; BNP, B144. Para que el Corregidor de Yucay cumpla la provisión que aquí se refiere, 27-III-1618, f. 1; AGI, Lima 55, Libro IV, No. 2. Carta del Virrey, 20-IX-1651, f. 128; and AGI, Charcas 270, No. V-16. El virrey Duque de Palata al Rey 21-VIII-1683, f. 2V.

93. AHC, Cabildo del Cuzco, Tomo 11, 1613–1618. El cabildo del 7 de agosto, 1617, ff. 166V–67.

94. AGI, Charcas 270, No. V-16, f. 2V.

95. AGI, Charcas 266, No. II. Carta de Don Juan de Carvajál, 18-III-1636, f. 1.

96. The definition of the "homicide" theory is from Sánchez-Albornoz, *The Population of Latin America*, pp. 51–66, passim. Cook presents a similar analysis in "La población indígena," passim. Kubler's famous statement that "not until 1720 did any great losses through pestilence occur in Peru" (*Handbook of South American Indians*, p. 334), has been totally discredited by the work of Sánchez-Albornoz, Cook, Dobyns, and others.

97. Indian claims to mestizo status were in direct violation of Spanish law, which stipulated that "sons of married Indian women should be considered to be sons of the husbands, with no contradictory opinion allowed . . . and sons of unmarried Indian women should follow the lineage of the mother." Reál Cédula, Madrid, 10-X-1618. *Recopilación*, Libro VI, Título I, ley x. Vol. II, pp. 191–92. Mario Góngora cites the numerical importance of the "biological and legal assimilation to the white sector of Indians and *mestizos*" in his *Studies in the Colonial History*, p. 160. Sánchez-Albornoz mentions the growth of the mestizo sector in *The Population of Latin America*, p. 104.

98. Sánchez-Albornoz, *The Population of Latin America*, p. 104.

99. Ibid., p. 92. Sánchez-Albornoz does identify the migrant group as an essential element in the recovery of the Indian population in Upper Peru, but he dates that recovery from a later period, when transients were finally included in census data; he also fails to differentiate between the alienated forasteros sin tierra of the eighteenth century and the assimilated forasteros of the seventeenth. Ibid., p. 93. Sánchez-Albornoz, *Indios y tributos en el Alto Perú*, pp. 35–67, passim.

CHAPTER 4: The Ayllu and Community Structure

1. For a theoretical discussion and case study of the shift from tribal-communal to tribal-tributary structure, see Francisco Moscoso, "Tributo y Formación de Clases en la Sociedad de los Tainos de las Antillas." Ponencia, VII Congreso Internacional para el Estudio de las Culturas Pre-Colombínas de las Antillas Menores. Caracas, 1977.

2. The description is from George Kubler's influential study, "The Quechua in the Colonial World," in *Handbook of South American Indians*, p. 409. Kubler prefers the term "communes" over "ayllus."

3. Means, *Ancient Civilizations of the Andes*, p. 286.

4. See, for example, John H. Rowe's landmark study, "Incan Culture at the Time of the Spanish Conquest," in *Handbook of South American Indians*, Vol. 11, p. 253.

5. Karen Spalding, *De indio a campesino*, p. 103. For this single quotation, I have not translated directly from the Spanish text. Rather, I have used Spalding's own words, contained in a preliminary manuscript, "Web of Production," p. 21, read in a seminar she taught at Yale University in the spring of 1975. Spalding also discusses the ayllu in "Kurakas and Commerce: A Chapter in the Evolution of Andean Society," *HAHR* 53, no. 4, November 1973, pp. 581–99. For an alternative definition, see Douglas Gifford and Pauline Hoggarth, *Carnival and Coca Leaf: Some Traditions of the Peruvian Quechua Ayllu* (Edinburgh: Scottish Academic Press, 1976).

6. Kubler, "The Quechua in the Colonial World," *Handbook of South American Indians*, p. 49, and Nathan Wachtel, "La reciprocidad y el Estado Inca: de Karl Polanyi a John V. Murra," in *Sociedad e Ideología* (Lima: Instituto de Estudios Peruanos Ediciones, 1973), p. 63.

7. This definition of the ayllu is used by both Steve J. Stern, in *Peru's Indian Peoples*, p. 261, and Brooke Larson, *Colonialism and Agrarian Transformation in Bolivia: Cochabamba, 1550–1900* (Princeton: Princeton University Press, 1988), p. 333. Bernard Mishkin makes this suggestion in "The Contemporary Quechua," in *Handbook of South American Indians*, Vol. II, p. 441. For this study I have presented the ayllu within a context which emphasizes essential structural features and the role of indigenous migration in their transformation under Spanish rule. For an alternative approach, see Karen Spalding's excellent study of *Huarochirí*.

8. Harry Tschopik, Jr., "The Aymara," in *Handbook of South American Indians*, Vol. II, p. 571.

9. See, for example, Giorgio Alberti and Enrique Mayer's "Reciprocidad andina: ayer y hoy," in *Reciprocidad e intercambio en los Andes peruanos*, Alberti and Mayer, eds. Perú Problema 12. (Lima: Instituto de Estudios Peruanos, 1974).

10. The pioneering work on the theme of verticality in Andean communities is John V. Murra's "El contról verticál de un máximo de pisos ecológicos en la economía de las sociedades andinas." (Private issue, 1956.)

11. Larson, Stern, and Spalding have all discussed the role of the kuraka.

12. The legendary origins of the Incas are described in detail in Bernabé Cobo's *History of the Inca Empire*, Roland Hamilton, trans. and ed. (Austin: University of Texas Press, 1979). Hamilton's translation of this work is based on the recently recovered manuscript version of Cobo's work, found in the Biblioteca Capitular y Colombiana de Sevilla, and appears to be the most complete edition of this important seventeenth-century text. Means's *Ancient Civilizations of the Andes*, p. 206, and Rowe's "Incan Culture at the Time of the Spanish Conquest," *Handbook of South American Indians* (p. 317), also describe the legend in detail.

13. María Rostorowski de Diéz Canseco identified the specific characteristics of the royal ayllus and described the formation of new lineages by descendants of reigning monarchs, whose siblings and other kin-members remained within existing groups, in "Succession, Co-option to Kingship, and Royal Incest Among the Inca" in the *Southwestern Journal of Anthropology* 16, 1960, pp. 417–27.

14. Murra, "The Economic Organization of the Inca State," p. 277.

15. See Catherine J. Julien's description of "Incan Decimal Administration in the Lake Titicaca Region," in *The Inca and Aztec States, 1400–1800*, George A. Collier, Renato I. Rosaldo, and John D. Wirth, eds. (New York: Academic Press, 1982), pp. 119–51. For details of the legal system, see Moore, *Power and Property*.

16. For contrasting views of the degree to which imperial administration altered pre-Incan societies, see Julien, *The Inca and Aztec States, 1400–1800;* and John V. Murra, "The *Mit'a* Obligations of Ethnic Groups to the Inka State," and Franklin Pease G.Y., "The Formation of Tawantinsuyu: Mechanisms of Colonization and Relationship with Ethnic Groups" in *The Inca and Aztec States, 1400–1800*, pp. 237–62 and 173–98, respectively.

17. As noted above, endogamy is a key feature of the ayllu. Rowe considers this control over marriage linkages so important that he makes it the basis for his definition of the ayllu: "the social group which restricted marriage on a broader basis was the ayllu (aylyo), a kinship group," in "Incan Culture at the Time of the Spanish Conquest," *Handbook of South American Indians*, p. 252.

18. Cobo, *History of the Inca Empire*, pp. 211 and 212.

19. Ibid., p. 211.

20. Murra, "The Economic Organization of the Inca State," p. 155. Also, see his discussion of "The *Mit'a* Obligations," in *The Inca and Aztec States, 1400–1800*.

21. Pedro Sarmiento de Gamboa. *History of the Incas* (1572). (Preserved, translated, and published for the Hakluyt Society by Sir Clements Markham. [London: The Hakluyt Society, 1907], p. 46.)

22. For a case study which describes these practices, see Ann Wightman, "Diego Vasicuio: Native Priest," in *Struggle and Survival in Colonial America: Lives of Women and Men who Coped.* Gary B. Nash and David G. Sweet, eds. (Berkeley: University of California Press, 1981).

23. Spalding, "Kurakas and Commerce."

24. This law is cited in BNP, B454. Autos y diligencias hechas de oficio de la real justicia, Oropesa, 27-V-1621. For a case study, see BNP, B815. Legajos de documentos [de] Juan Guallerto Chiquihuanca, Arequipa, 30-VIII-1614.

25. The claims of a competent younger son are presented in BNP, B1872. Probanza hecha por parte de Don Antonio Caxapaico, Carrión de Velasco, 28-II-1679.

26. See Appendix III and table III B, below.

27. AGI, Lima 333. Título a Bachiller Don Francisco de Grado, Collao, 12-V-1648, f. 1V.

28. AAC. Unmarked box, our #8. Crimināl contra Augustín Ypi Curaguasi, 13-XII-1694. When further testimony revealed that the elopement was actually a forced abduction, the cabildo ordered that the conveniently absent groom be given one hundred lashes and that the "young and simple" bride become a "perpetual recluse" in one of the convents of Lima.

29. AGI, Charcas 270, No. XI, f. 9.

30. The priest's report is found in AGI, Lima 471. Relación de la doctrina de Urubamba, 1690. Evidence of continuing ayllu identification is found in AHC, Provincia de Urubamba, Legajo C-2. Informe de Don Pascual Yaainlloclla, Urubamba, 15-IX-1690, f. 1.

31. AGI, Lima 471. Relación de la doctrina de Chinchaypuquio, Abancay, sin fecha, c. 1690.

32. Memoria del Marqués de Mancera, p. 166. Additional details on the number of illegal yanaconas are found in BNP, B516, ff. 1V–2V, passim. For a retrospective denunciation of the evils of the increase in the yanacona sector, see Reál Cédula, Madrid, 15-VIII-1685. AGI, Charcas 410. Published in *Colección de documentos para la Historia,* Vol. II, pp. 771–72.

33. This citation is from AGI, Charcas 270, f. 17. See also ANP, Derecho Indígena, Legajo 4, Cuaderno 65, ff. 2V, 10; AGI, Charcas 270, No. X. Carta del Contador Sebastian del Callado de Potosí, 11-V-1682, ff. 4, 5V.

34. The legal definition of yanacona status has been discussed in chapter 2. See also Memoria del Marqués de Montesclaros, *Colección de las Memorias,* p. 210; and Memoria del Príncipe de Esquilache, p. 37. Even as Esquilache denounced the practice, new grants of yanaconas were being assigned in Paraguay and the Río de la Plata basin in Reāl Aprobaciōn de las ordenanzas,

Madrid, 10-X-1618. AGI, Buenos Aires 2. Published in *Colección de documentos para la Historia*, Vol. II, pp. 202–28.

35. For the petition of the involuntary yanacona, see AAC, Paquete XLIII. Carta de Andrés Chancas, 18-XI-1705, f. 1. For examples of yanaconas who sought that status, see ANP, Derecho Indígena, Legajo 4, Cuaderno 65, ff. 15V–17; AGI, Lima 123, No. IX. Carta de los indios yanaconas de Juan Arias Maldonado y otros del Cuzco, 11-I-1575, passim.

36. See Appendix I for the data base of this description of yanacona labor. In this analysis the yanaconas were not coded as agricultural workers unless clearly identified as such by information in the contracts.

37. See the data in Appendix I, below. Yanaconas were not the only workers vulnerable to debt peonage, as will be discussed in chapter 6.

38. Góngora, *Studies in the Colonial History*, p. 151. Yanaconas could be the beneficiaries of such wills as well. See the bequests of Pedro Fernández Freisancho to his yanaconas cited in AAC, Archivo de Urubamba, Paquete V, Legajo 190, No. 8. Juicio seguido y ganado por el Bachiller Eugenio Gomez de la Baquera, 1607–1642, f. 14.

39. BNP, B1504, No. III. Copia de Reál Cédula, Madrid, 22-II-1680, f. 117V.

40. *Aranzel*, Capítulo V. See Appendix I for details of the contracts.

41. In support of this point, see Magnus Mörner, *Perfil de la sociedad rural*.

42. Matienzo, *Gobierno del Perú*, p. 18. For an example of this trend, see Góngora, *Studies in the Colonial History*, p. xi.

43. The quote is from Mellafe, *Population and Economics*, p. 311. For works linking yanaconas and migration, see Silverblatt, *Women and Colonization*, p. 177, and Rowe, "The Incas Under Spanish Colonial Institutions," pp. 175, 191.

44. ANP, Derecho Indígena, Legajo VII, Cuaderno 129. Testimonio de la visita . . . a los yndios de septima y yanaconas que sirvan en la hacienda denominada Huaraypata, 20-III-1653, passim.

45. Keith, *Conquest and Agrarian Change*, p. 45. For details of the yanacona contracts, see Appendix I.

46. AGI, Charcas 266, No. XIII, f. 10V.

47. Murra, "El contról verticál." Pre-Incan resource colonies are identified by Dobyns and Doughty, *Peru: A Cultural History*, p. 38; Murra, "The Economic Organization of the Inca State," p. 292; and Cobo, *History of the Inca Empire*, p. 192.

48. For a study of mitimas under the Incan state, see Nathan Wachtel, "The *Mitimas* of the Cochabamba Valley: The Colonization Policy of Huayna Capac," in *The Inca and Aztec States, 1400–1800*, pp. 199–235.

49. For a discussion of the two types of mitmaq, see Cieza de León, *La crónica del Peru* (c. 1570), Edición Biblioteca Peruana (Lima: Editorial Universo S.A., 1973), pp. 68–69. Franklin Pease presents a much more diversified view of the

mitimas in "The Formation of Tawantinsuyu." The political position of the mitmaq is recorded by Cieza de León in *La crónica del Peru*, pp. 68–69 and by Marvin Harris, *Patterns of Race in the Americas* (New York: Walker and Company, 1964), pp. 9–10. Cobo describes this resettlement process and cites six or seven thousand families as the usual number exchanged. (Cobo, *History of the Inca Empire*, pp. 189–91.)

50. For the cultivation of maize, see Cieza de León, *La crónica del Peru*, p. 69. For a definition implying forced relocation, see Sarmiento de Gamboa, *History of the Incas*, p. 121. For the "newcomer" identification, see Cobo, *History of the Inca Empire*, p. 189.

51. For the Europeans' definition of the mitmaq, see Sarmiento de Gamboa, *History of the Incas*, p. 121. The flight of the mitmaq is described in ANP, Causas Civiles de la Real Audiencia, Legajo 15, Cuaderno 77. Autos seguidos por Diego Lopez de Olivares, 8-II-1576.

52. Cobo, *History of the Inca Empire*, p. 193. Cobo uses the Spanish "mitimaes"; this study uses the term "mitmaq."

53. Cobo, *History of the Inca Empire*, p. 190.

54. Memoria del príncipe de Esquilache, *Colección de las Memorias*, p. 239.

55. The early distinction is recorded in BNP, A499. Tasa de repartimiento de mitmaes de la Nasca, 3-VIII-1580. For the Indians' perspectives, see BNP, B614. Relación de los indios mitimaes de Huarochirí, 3-XII-1642; AAC, Unmarked box, our No. 20. Petición, 8-VII-1647, suelta.

56. Two examples of such second flights are AAL, Legajo X, No. 1. Información, 1651; and AAC, Paquete V, No. 2. Criminál contra Lzdo. Alonso de Ocón, 1672. In both instances forasteros fled when a priest and a kuraka, respectively, tried to collect more money than had originally been demanded of the migrants.

57. ANP, Derecho Indígena, Legajo 6, Cuaderno 119. Revista y Padrón, San Juan de los Sancos, 15-V-1645. AGI, Lima 471. Relación de la doctrina de Nuñoa, 11-IX-1689.

58. Forasteros filling political offices are described in BNP, B575. Paucarcolla: Autos sobre el despacho de la mita de Potosí, Villa de Concepción, 24-X-1669. The musicians appear in BNP, B1030. Expediente sobre la petición presentada por el Lic. Luis Enrique, Cuzco, 3-II-1629.

59. AAL, Legajo XI, No. I. Sin título, 1653, ff. 105, 123, 153. For a study of pre-1570 change in Yucay, see Wachtel's *The Vision of the Vanquished*, pp. 109–14.

60. Ibid., ff. 126V–27.

61. Ibid., f. 166.

62. Ibid., ff. 153, 159.

63. AAC. Unmarked box, our #18. Autos seguidos por los curas de Urubamba y Yucay, 1653, f. 2V.

64. AAL, Legajo XI, No. I, ff. 157V, 159.

65. Ibid., ff. 175–75V, 127, 153V, 154.

66. Ibid., f. 165V.

67. Ibid., ff. 151V–52, 164V.

68. Ibid., f. 175V. AAC. Autos seguidos por los curas de Urubamba y Yucay, f. 2V.

69. AAC. Autos seguidos por los curas de Urubamba y Yucay, f. 68.

70. AAL, Legajo XI, No. I, sin título, ff. 23–24.

71. AAL, Legajo I, No. I. Suelto.

72. Detailed accounts of the parish records are given in Appendix III, tables B and C. N. David Cook's demographic analysis of the parish of Yanque traces the relationship between marriage patterns and migration, but his analysis emphasizes moiety status, not ayllu identity, because of weakened ayllu linkages within the community. Cook, "Eighteenth-Century Population Change in Andean Peru: The Parish of Yanque," in *Studies in Spanish American Population History*, pp. 243–70.

73. Spalding, "Social Climbers."

74. Karen Spalding has described other factors contributing to the emergence of this "system of social differentiation that only marginally reflected Spanish laws or attitudes." Ibid., p. 649.

75. Ibid. For details of the cultural transformation, see the work of Karen Spalding, Luis Millones, John Murra, Franklin Pease, Irene Silverblatt, and Steve J. Stern. Two earlier studies are George Kubler's "The Quechua in the Colonial World," and Charles Gibson's "The Problem of the Impact of Spanish Culture on the Indigenous American Population," in *Latin American History: Select Problems* (New York: Harcourt Brace and World, 1969), p. 649.

76. Frank Tannenbaum, *Ten Keys to Latin America* (New York: Vintage Books, 1960), p. 37.

77. Henry F. Dobyns, *The Social Matrix of Peruvian Indigenous Communities* (Cornell Peru Project Monograph, Department of Anthropology, Cornell University, Ithaca, N.Y., 1964), pp. 13, 15. Marvin Harris, *Patterns of Race*, p. 27.

78. Seminario de Ideología y Religión, Primera Jornada del Museo Nacional de Historia, Lima, Peru, November 1977. Silverblatt, passim. I have tried to convey this sense of fusion in "Diego Vasicuio: Native Priest." The work of Irene Silverblatt has been critical in identifying and articulating cultural resistance. See her *Moon, Sun, and Witches*. Deborah A. Poole and Penelope Harvey consider Silverblatt's work and its impact on theories of resistance in "Luna, sol y brujas: Estudios andinos e historiografía de resistencia," *Revista Andina* 6, no. 1, July 1988, pp. 277–95.

79. Tannenbaum, *Ten Keys to Latin America*, p. 38.

80. Elman Service attributed acculturation patterns to the economic and social structures of the preconquest societies. (Service, "Indian-European Relations," p. 424.) Service also cited the isolating nature of postconquest administrative procedures, particularly the encomienda which, except in Paraguay,

"tended to isolate the indigenes from acculturative influences." (Service, "The encomienda in Paraguay," p. 252.) In contrast, George Kubler maintained that the switch from encomienda to corregimiento actually increased Indian autonomy by removing the community from direct contact with the encomendero and his household. (Kubler, *Handbook of South American Indians*, pp. 346–47.) Mario Góngora agreed with Service that the switch from encomienda to corregimiento played an important part in increased Indian-European exchange, but Góngora argued that the most significant consequence of this administrative change was a diminution in the role of the Indian councils and the "deculturation" and fall of the indigenous elite. (Góngora, *Studies in the Colonial History*, p. 119.) Julian H. Steward contrasted the "radical changes in the national institutions" with the diminished impact at "the lower levels of the native sociocultural system." (Steward, "Levels of Sociocultural Integration: An Operational Concept," *Southwestern Journal of Anthropology*, 1951, p. 386.) Recently, Silverblatt has argued that the male-dominated structures of both Hispanic and indigenous colonial societies alienated Indian women and produced gender-specific acculturation patterns. (Silverblatt, *Women and Colonization*.)

81. The three-step acculturation of the Quechua proposed by Kubler in 1946 has been modified by subsequent regional studies, but these analyses have generally accepted Kubler's basic periodization: 1532–1572, Conquest Quechua, with tensions between pacified and separatist groups; 1572–1650, Early Colonial Quechua, with an "unprecedented conflict and disturbance" in Quechua culture, "matching the disorder introduced into their economic and social lives"; and 1650–1750, Mature Colonial Quechua, with the survival of individual communities contingent upon their successful adaptation of European doctrines, practices, and commodities. (Kubler, "The Quechua in the Colonial World," passim.) Some of the area studies are of limited use for a history of the Cuzco region. For example, Thomas R. Ford's claim that thousands of Indians were unaware of the shift from Incan to Spanish rule has little relevance for most of the Cuzco zone, the center of the conflict of the 1530s and 1540s. (Ford, *Man and Land in Peru* [Gainesville: University of Florida Press, 1955], p. 21.) However, Charles Gibson's analyses of the varied cultural change in distinct regions of Mexico are directly applicable to the eastern provinces of the bishopric of Cuzco. (Gibson, *Tlaxcala in the Sixteenth Century* [New Haven: Yale University Press, 1952], p. 156.)

82. These principles are exemplified in the Laws of Burgos. See the version in Charles Gibson, ed., *The Spanish Tradition in America* (New York: Harper and Row, 1968), pp. 61–82.

83. The bishop's letter is contained in AGI, Lima 305, No. DII. Carta al Rey, 24-II-1635, ff. 1–1v. Steve Stern discusses the ambivalent position of the indigenous elite in "The Tragedy of Success," chapter 7 in his *Peru's Indian Peoples*.

84. Morner, *Race Mixture*, p. 75. Of Eric Wolf's many works, see *Sons of the Shaking Earth* (Chicago: University of Chicago Press, 1959), pp. 238ff.

85. For the isolation of the Indian parishes, see Cédulas Reales of 8-VIII-1577, 25-XI-1578, 23-IX-1580, etc., published in *Colección de documentos para la Historia*, Vol. I, pp. 504, 513, 527–28. The Reál Cédula of 10-X-1618, *Recopilación*, Libro VI, Título I, ley x. Vol. II, pp. 191–92, which ordered that illegitimate children with claims to Spanish parentage remain with their mothers did not contradict these provisions. Such "casta" children were legally defined as Indians. The mestizos were kept from public office by the Reál Cédula, Madrid, 11-I-1576. *Recopilación*, Libro VI, Título VII, ley vi. Vol. II, p. 246. Repeated in 1656, 1664, 1680.

86. See Appendix I.

87. For data on the Yucay forasteros, see Appendix III, table IIID. The survey of the parish of Santiago is found in BNP, B853. Lista de los indios tributarios y viejos que hay en la parroquia de Santiago de la ciudad del Cuzco. Cuzco, 27-VII-1645.

88. Female mayors are described in AGI, Lima 168, No. IIA, f. 4V. For the most recent summary of women's roles in preconquest society, see Irene Silverblatt's "'The universe has turned inside out,'" and *Moon, Sun and Witches*.

89. Silverblatt, "'The universe has turned inside out,'" in *Women and Colonization*, pp. 175–76.

90. Ibid., p. 176.

91. BNP, B1176. Memorial, 20-X-1692, passim.

92. AGI, Charcas 270, No. XXV. Carta del Protector de Naturales de Lima, 26-XI-1690, f. 3.

93. Juan and Ulloa, *Noticias Secretas*, p. 300. I am grateful to John J. TePaske for bringing this passage to my notice.

94. For a theoretical discussion of this process, see Jack Godoy, "The Evolution of the Family," in *Household and Family in Past Time* (Cambridge: Cambridge University Press, 1972), p. 119.

95. The specific terms "originario" and "forastero" were, of course, developed by the Spaniards, but colonial documents contain repeated instances in which Indians used those terms to describe distinctions which may have been expressed in different words within indigenous society.

96. Bautista Saavedra, *El Ayllu* (Paris: P. Ollendorff, 1913), p. 520. Mellafe, *Population and Economics*, p. 311. For the complaints of the repartimiento de los Hacas, see BNP, B1095, f. 18. For the details of the assault and subsequent investigation, see ANP, Reál Audiencia, Causas Criminales, Legajo 1, Cuaderno 4. Autos seguidos por el Corregidor de la Provincia de Andahuaylas, 1703.

97. Charles Gibson writes that "The Church, in pursuing its own ends, nurtured and preserved communal forms of life among Indians." (*The Aztecs Under Spanish Rule*, pp. 134–35.)

98. Baudin, *Daily Life in Peru*, p. 43. See the discussion of "Idolos y Uacas del Inca" in Guaman Poma de Ayala, *La nueva crónica*, Vol. I, pp. 185–95. For a description of the royal guauqui, see Sarmiento de Gamboa, *History of the Incas*, p. 61.

99. See the Spaniards' interpretation of guacas in Sarmiento de Gamboa, *History of the Incas*, p. 61. For details of the campaigns against idolatry, see Pablo Joseph de Arriaga, *Extirpación de la idolatría en el Perú*. (Lima, 1621.) For an example of this practice of hiding guacas, see Wightman, "Diego Vasicuio: Native Priest," passim. For details of ceremonial functions, see John Murra's "Cloth and Its Functions in the Inca State," *American Anthropologist* 64, 1962, pp. 710–28, and his "Rite and Crop in the Inca State," in *Culture in History, Essays in Honor of Paul Radin* (New York: Columbia University Press, 1960).

100. For the manipulation of indigenous religion for political purposes, see Luis Millones, "Religión y poder en los Andes: Los Curacas Idólatras de la Sierra Central" (Seminario de Ideología y Religión, Primera Jornada del Museo Nacional de Historia, Lima, Perú, November, 1977); and Wightman, "Diego Vasicuio: Native Priest."

101. Wightman, "Diego Vasicuio: Native Priest."

102. AGI, Lima 149, No. V, f. 3.

103. This quotation is from BNP, B1683. Carta de Fray Antonio de Villabona, 20-II-1684, f. 99. The more observant priest's report is found in BNP, B1715. Informe contra Andrés Caya, 1638, f. 2V. *Cuy* are an Andean relative of the guinea pig.

104. The regulations are found in Rowe, "The Incas Under Spanish Colonial Institutions," p. 185. The priest's opinion is in AGI, Lima 471. Relación de la doctrina de San Pedro, Cotabambas, 30-VIII-1690. The attachment to ancestral lands is also discussed in chapter 3.

105. AGI, Lima 149, No. V, f. 2.

106. BNP, B1683. Carta de 23-XII-1684, Lima, sin firma, f. 1. The contents of this letter identify its author as a priest. Supporting testimony can be found in AGI, Charcas 266, No. XVIII. Carta del Fray Francisco de la Cruz, Potosí, 14-II-1660, ff. 1V–2. Silverblatt, *Women and Colonization*, passim.

107. Wightman, "Diego Vasicuio: Native Priest."

108. Arriaga, *Extirpación*, Capítulo 14.

109. Various cases are found in the AAC, the AAL, and the BNP.

CHAPTER 5: The Urban Migrant in Cuzco

1. Cobo, *History of the Inca Empire*, p. 185. Joseph Bastien writes that "[t]he geography of Cuzco is another pre-Columbian example of sacredly organizing space by earth shrines." Bastien, *Mountain of the Condor*, p. 61. For a theoretical approach to "the city as symbol," see chapter 1, "The City at the Center of the

World," in James Dougherty, *The Five Square City: The City in the Religious Imagination* (Notre Dame, Ind.: University of Notre Dame Press, 1980). For details of the physical and spiritual organization of preconquest Cuzco, see B. C. Brundage, *Lords of Cuzco: A History of the Inca People in Their Final Days* (Norman: University of Oklahoma Press, 1967) and R. T. Zuidema, *The Ceque System of Cuzco: The Social Organization of the Capital of the Inca* (Leiden: E. J. Brill, 1964).

2. Cobo, *History of the Inca Empire*, pp. 187, 251–52. The school for the sons of regional kurakas is described by Dobyns and Doughty, *Peru: A Cultural History*, p. 48. J. H. Rowe discusses the role of Cuzco as a political unit and ceremonial center in "What Kind of Settlement was Inca Cuzco?" *Ñawpa Pacha*, no. 5, 1967, pp. 59–77.

3. Pedro Pizarro, *Relation of the Discovery and Conquest of the Kingdoms of Peru*, Vol. I. Philip A. Means, trans. (New York: The Cortés Society, 1921), pp. 272, 273–74.

4. Cieza de León, *La crónica del Peru*, p. 214.

5. For details, see Ibid., pp. 215ff.

6. For a more detailed account of Cuzco's economic growth, see Michèle Colin's *Le Cuzco*.

7. *Anales del Cuzco*, ff. 99–109. The compiler's informants were either confused by the earthquake or bad mathematicians: the various subtotals they give for the number of aftershocks and temblors during certain time spans are self-contradictory; the final total was 823 disturbances between March 31, 1650, and January 1, 1651. The authors of various sections of the *Anales* are unknown, but its compiler was a canon of the cathedral of Cuzco (1725–1750) who gathered materials from various ecclesiastical records. The topics included range from a total eclipse of the sun (21-VII-1637, f. 73) to the price of official notarial paper (28-XII-1638) to a blind woman's miraculous recovery (10-VIII-1614, f. 22). The rather dramatic accounts of the residents' behavior during the earthquake are found in BNE, 2381, Folio 124. Del notable terremoto que huvo en la Ciudad de Cuzco el año de 1650, ff. 125, 124.

8. The higher casualty figures and the higher damage estimate are from BNE, 2381, Folio 124, "Del notable terremoto," f. 127. See chapter 2 for population data and a discussion of the seventeenth-century decline in the indigenous sector. The detailed report of property damage and the lower damage estimate are from PTT, Ynforme individual que al Exmo. Señor Virrey se le hizo sobre el estrago que causaron en esta ciudad los temblores grandes. (Cuzco, 1650, f. 1 and passim.) For the priests' reaction, see *Anales del Cuzco*, f. 108.

9. The damage to Indian towns is described in BNE, 2381, Folio 124, "Del notable terremoto," f. 126V. The disaster relief deliberations appear in AGI, Lima 8. Consulta de la Cámera de Indias, 12-X-1652. (Published in *Colección de Documentos para la Historia*, Vol. II, Part I, pp. 451–52.) Some of the Cuzco

encomenderos had asked that their grants be awarded in perpetuity. The deliberations of the Cámera say specifically that "for six years no tributes or taxes will be collected." However, other documents indicate that at least some Cuzco-area Indians paid tribute during this period. Perhaps they were defrauded by local officials or their kurakas.

10. The forced resettlement is described in AGI, Indiferentes Generales 1660. Ynforme de Juan de Moreyra, 18-XI-1654.

11. James Lockhart describes the impact of "tribute-bearing migrations" and the subsequent migration to urban zones in his analysis of *Spanish Peru*, p. 207. Lockhart believes that "by 1550 this movement had already reached major proportions." John Murra has asked, "Is it possible that the last decades before 1532 saw the development in Cuzco of a floating urban population, free of tribal and kin ties, who looked for a patron and undertook servile duties of a semi-religious, semi-state nature to avoid other, more strenuous responsibilities?" Murra, "Economic Organization of the Inca State," p. 273. The priest's complaint is in AGI, Lima 471. Relación de la doctrina de San Pedro de Aquira, Cotabambas, 30-VIII-1689.

12. N. David Cook begins his discussion of the population of Cuzco by noting that "There is no definite agreement on the size and nature of Cuzco when the Europeans first reached it in 1533." (*Demographic Collapse*, p. 212.) Cook concludes that "a range between 150,000 and 200,000 is feasible" (p. 219). The population of the city fell dramatically during the conquest and the civil wars: the Indian population around 1561 was between 12,100 and 13,300 (p. 215). With the exception of the period immediately following the earthquake of 1650 the city's Indian population, sustained by a steady influx of migrants, probably hovered in the 10,000 range throughout the mid-colonial period. Regarding the statement I just made, I can only repeat Cook's caveat: "until [a thorough study] is completed the present generalizations must be taken as tentative" (p. 212). For this particular study of indigenous migration to Cuzco, the proportion of migrants in the population is of greater importance.

13. The labor contracts which form the data base for these figures are discussed in detail below and in Appendix I. Migrants from Lima, Northern Peru, Ecuador, and Chile played a very minor role in the Cuzco labor force (table II). The representation of short-range migrants is much higher than that found by Claude Mazet in his study, "Population et Société à Lima aux XVIe et XVIIe Siècles: La Paroisse San Sebastián (1562–1689)," *Cahiers des Amériques Latines* 13/14, 1976, pp. 51–101. Mazet found that 30.8 percent of identified migrants were from the Lima region and 54.25 percent were from the area included in present-day Peru (pp. 75–76). For an analysis of the migrant community in Lima in 1613, see N. David Cook, "Les Indiens immigrés à Lima au début du XVIIe siècle," *Cahiers des Amériques Latines* 13/14, 1976, pp. 33–50.

14. For the data on migrants to Cuzco, see Appendix I. The reports of the parish priests are contained in AGI, Lima 471. Relación de la parroquia de la ciudad, 16-VII-1690 and Relación de la doctrina de San Cristobal, 3-VII-1690.

15. These percentages are based on data from the five city parishes—of a total of nine—whose priests gave specific totals for forastero and originario populations. An additional three parishes reported the presence of forasteros but did not record how many; the last two parishes failed to comment on migrants in the total population (see Appendix II). The transient population was undoubtedly a smaller percentage of the total Indian population: these percentages are slightly skewed by the fact that the one parish which was 100 percent foreign-born, the "parish of the city," was the one which was 100 percent transients. Ann Zulawski has compiled a demographic profile for Oruro, a city founded by Spaniards, where by definition the entire Indian population, except the yanaconas, was of foreign ancestry. See her "Mano de obra y migración en un centro minero de los Andes: Oruro, 1683," in *Población y mano de obra en América Latina*. Nicolás Sánchez-Albornoz, ed. (Madrid: Alianza Editorial, S.A., 1985), pp. 95–114, particularly pp. 96, 104.

16. See the detailed discussion of these themes in chapter 2.

17. For a discussion of Stadtluft macht's frei, see Henri Pirenne, *Economic and Social History of Medieval Europe* (New York: Harcourt, Brace, and World, 1937), pp. 50–51. The length of time that a migrant had to have spent in a city in order to be exempt from the mita varied during the colonial period. For the debate on urban residency requirements, see BNP, B1176. Memorial. 20-X-1692. Of course, such regulations could not and did not guarantee that an individual would totally escape the demands of a persistent kuraka, particularly if the migrant's native community was close to the urban zone.

18. AGI, Indiferentes Generales 1660. Carta de Don Pedro Vásquez de Velasco, 15-X-1648. Vásquez was more concerned with denouncing corrupt officials who used migrants to file grievances and initiate lawsuits than with protecting the Indians' rights.

19. Gabriel Haslip-Viera, "The Underclass," in *Cities and Society in Colonial Latin America*. Louisa S. Hoberman and Susan M. Socolow, eds. (Albuquerque: University of New Mexico Press, 1986), p. 288. Haslip-Viera does not estimate the size of the underclass but asserts that "unemployment and crime were relatively predictable in those urban centers which were economically more stable, such as Cuzco, Guatemala City, and Querétaro." Given the rate at which forasteros appear in ecclesiastical and criminal litigation, however, a modern reader might almost be justified in accepting the colonial authorities' condemnation of migrants. Much more research on the underclass in Cuzco and in other colonial cities is needed. Haslip-Viera's own work is based on data from Mexico City during the late colonial period, where "the disproportionately greater number of migrants arrested by the municipal authorities was the result

of police procedures and the widespread belief that migrants were responsible for the majority of day-to-day crimes" (p. 290).

20. ADC, Corregimiento, Causas Criminales, Legajo 72, 1582–1693. Diego Guaman Topa, maestro sastre, natural del pueblo de Urcos contra Miguel Hilaguita, maestro sastre, y su hijo Bernabe Hilaguita, 1664.

21. AAC, Causas Matrimoniales, 17-234-2. Querella contra Diego Quispe, 1646. Bernard Lavallé uses causas matrimoniales to depict "Divorcio y nulidad de matrimonio en Lima (1650–1700): La desavenencia conyugal como indicador social," *Revista Andina*, Año 4, no. 2, December 1986, pp. 427–62.

22. See, for example: AAC, Liturgia 21.1, LXXV, 2, 30. Auto, cabeza de proceso y comisión contra una india nombrada Teresa Sisa, casada dos veces en Urcos y Guanta, 1698 and AAC, Liturgia 21.1, XLIV, 5, 96. Expediente contra Maria Sisa, natural de Combapata, por haberse casado dos veces, 1700.

23. AAC, Causas Matrimoniales, 17-236-1. Querella contra Juan Poma, 1698. The document ends with this punishment, which probably did not resolve Sisa's and Poma's problems.

24. For a discussion of efforts to control migrants, see BNP, C2323. Autos que siguió [*sic*] los indios forasteros de la ciudad de Chachapoyas, 7-XII-1750, ff. 15–16. The most noted example of the attempt to concentrate urban migrant populations into special zones was the community of Santiago, on the outskirts of Lima. In 1589 an anonymous informant who described himself as "one who has been in this country for a long time" wrote Philip II that the Jesuits who were responsible for the spiritual guidance of the resettled Indians had built a vacation retreat in Santiago where all sorts of "illicit acts" occurred. AGI, Lima 130. Carta, sin firme, de 20-IV-1589. The viceroy sent a follow-up letter to the King the next year. AGI, Lima 32. Libro I, No. 36, ff. 178–79V. Carta del Virrey al Rey, 27-XII-1590.

25. Velasco's earlier statements are repeated in a preface to one copy of the "Cédula Reál, su fecha en Aranjuéz a 26 de mayo de 1609" found in BNP, B1674. This cédula, without supporting documentation, appears in the *Recopilación*, Libro VI, Título XV, ley x. Tomo 2, pp. 313–14.

26. Cédula Reál, Valladolid, 24 de noviembre, 1601. *Recopilación*, Libro VI, Título III, ley x. Tomo 2, p. 209.

27. Cédula Reál, Aranjuéz, 26 de mayo, 1609. *Recopilación*, Libro VI, Título XV, ley xviii. Tomo 2, p. 313.

28. Ibid., pp. 313–14.

29. Ibid., p. 313.

30. BNP, B1674, copia de Cédula Reál de 26-V-1609.

31. Davies, *Landowners in Colonial Peru*, p. 7.

32. AAC, Unmarked box, our #10. Ordenanza, Don Andrés Ygnacio en nombre de Don Constantino de Basconselos, 12-XII-1650, f. 2.

33. Migrants also affected the economy of the communities they had de-

serted, attempting to sell lands they had abandoned to Spaniards or other urban residents. These activities will be discussed in more detail in chapter 6. The migrant's will can be found in ADC, Archivo Notarial, Protocolo 49-461, Francisco Maldonado. Testamento, 28-VII-1715, f. 775.

34. Patricia Seed, "Social Dimensions of Race: Mexico City, 1753," *HAHR* 62, no. 4, 1982, pp. 569–606. Comparisons between Cuzco and Mexico City are necessarily limited by the differences in data bases and the contrasting racial composition of the two work forces. For example, the service sector in Mexico City showed a high mulatto presence, a group virtually unrepresented in the Cuzco data. The 1690 census of the city of Cuzco included only forty-five "Negros and Mulattos," less than 1 percent of the population; from AGI, Lima 471. Padrón del obispado del Cuzco, 1689–1690.

35. For specific figures and variation by decade, see tables IB and IC. The verbs "negotiated" and "arranged" must be used advisedly. In theory, Indians were "voluntarily" and "freely" entering employment; in practice, circumstances limited—or eliminated—some individuals' options. Although migrants negotiated a majority of these contracts, they were a minority of the city's indigenous population. Their disproportionate representation in the conciertos reflects both the migrants' need for guaranteed employment and their isolation from less formal labor relationships among native Cuzqueños.

36. The foreign-born contractees ranged from 62 to 80 percent of all transport workers, with the exception of the 1690s. In the smaller data samples the figure rose to 100 percent. The comparable range for agricultural workers was 50 to 80 percent foreign-born workers, with occasional decades at 100 percent. The service categories show a 35 to 59 percent range for the foreign-born, with the low point falling in the decade following the devastating earthquake of 1650. Specific data entries can be found in tables ID, IE, and IF. Occupational patterns among immigrants to San Salvador and Guatemala City during the 1960s show parallel distribution concentrations in the transport and service sectors. (Jorge Balán, "Migrant-Native Socioeconomic Differences in Latin American Cities: A Structural Analysis," *LARR* IV, no. I, 1969, pp. 3–29.)

37. Wightman, "The *Consulado* of Lima." For details of specific aspects of this shift in trade patterns, see Armando de Ramón, "Grupos elitarios chilenos y su vinculación con la metrópoli peruana a fines del siglo XVII, 1681–1695," XXXIX Congreso Internacional de Americanistas, Lima, August 1970, and Demetrio Ramos, "Trigo chileno, navieros del Callao y hacendados limeños entre la crisis agrícola del siglo XVII y la comercial de la primera mitad del XVIII," *Revista de Indias* XXVI, no. 105–6, 1966, pp. 209–321. The shift in prevailing trade routes is consistent with data from the conciertos which explicitly stated a convoy's destination. For a discussion of eighteenth-century trade patterns in the Arequipa zone, see Brown, *Bourbons and Brandy,* chapter 4, "Commerce in Southern Peru." Carlos Sempat Assadourian discusses regional

markets and exchange in *El sistema de la economía colonial: Mercado interno, regiones y espacio económico.* Lima: Instituto de Estudios Peruanos Ediciones, 1982.

38. ADC, Archivo Notarial, Protocol 553, Box 71, Alonso Calvo. Concierto, 22-IX-1640, ff. 1347V–48.

39. Contracts involving agricultural workers were divided into three main categories: herders, yanaconas, and general laborers. These detailed contracts were analyzed for length of contract, wage rate, cash advance, access to land, promised medical care, and food and clothing allotments. Because the specific terms of these agreements are essential to the analysis of rural labor patterns, these conciertos will be discussed more fully in chapter 6. See Appendix I for specific figures.

40. Both J. H. Rowe, in "Incan Culture" and George Kubler, in "The Quechua in the Colonial World" emphasized that coca was used only by the upper classes in preconquest society. Later studies have amended that view. For various studies on the use and impact of coca, see Deborah Pacini and Christine Franquemont, eds., *Coca and Cocaine: Effects on People and Policy in Latin America,* Cultural Survival Report No. 23 (Peterborough, N.H.: Transcript Printing Company, 1986). For the use of coca at Andean festivals, see Gifford and Hoggarth, *Carnival and Coca Leaf.* Thomas M. Davies, Jr., summarizes the arguments for and against trying to control the use of coca in contemporary Peru in *Indian Integration in Peru,* pp. 6–7. Cieza de León wrote about coca consumption in his *La crónica del Perú,* pp. 220–21. The first quote is from p. 220, the second from p. 221.

41. AGI, Lima 471. Padrón de la doctrina de Tomopampa, 12-XII-1689.

42. Toledo's regulations on coca labor are found in BNP, B511. Ordenanzas del Virrey Don Francisco de Toledo, Lima, copia del 14-VIII-1604. The rules regarding the seizure of Indians' blankets, the cash advances, and the twenty-four-day time limit are restated in BNP, A17. Disposiciones dictadas por el Cabildo y Regimiento de la ciudad del Cuzco sobre su mejor administración y normas que deben regir el trabajo particular y colectivo de los indios, 18-X-1573. As the index states, this document is "Missing its opening and closing pages. Damaged by fire." Toledo's regulations were the most comprehensive effort to control abuses in the coca zone, but they were certainly not the first such attempt. Cédulas Reales insisting that the Indians "not be forced into coca labor" were issued on 23-XII-1560 and 2-XII-1563. *Colección de Cédulas Reales,* pp. 76–77.

43. AAC, Legajo 221, No. 7. Juicio, 1821, ff. 35ff. The document contains Esquilache's pronouncement on coca labor, dated 1-XII-1618. Further testimony on the perils of coca labor can be found in BNP, B147. Duplicado de la provisión en que se da licencia para que los 10 indios del trajen [*sic*] de la coca sirvan en la estancia de Chingara y se les confirman otros que tienen los señores marqueses de Oropesa, Lima, 20-VIII-1619. For an investigation of abuses in

the coca zone, see AGI, Escribanía 534B. Residencias de tres Corregidores de la Provincia de Paucartambo en el Perú. Vista y sentenciada, 8-VIII-1680.

44. Although families frequently accompanied male Indians to their mita service in the mines, the practice was not common among hired agricultural workers. These are the only two contracts with such provisions; see ADC, Archivo Notarial, Protocolo 590, Caja 83, Juan Flores Bastides. Concierto, 12-II-1646, f. 774 and Concierto, 16-II-1646, f. 778. The coca workers' contracts are drawn from this register and from Protocolo 591, Caja 83, Juan Flores Bastids.

45. Additional data and specific figures can be found in table IE. In the service sector, the high proportion of laborers of unknown origins—13.3 percent—may slightly distort the actual relationship between native and foreign-born service workers. Contracts involving women workers more often failed to include the worker's origin. Officials probably considered it more important to identify the home community of a male tribute payer. This service category is dominated by women workers, a feature which will be discussed in detail below (table IG).

46. See tables IC and IF for details. The consistent patterns of service-sector increase and transport-sector decrease are too pervasive to be the result of sampling irregularities.

47. Tucra's contract is found in ADC, Archivo Notarial, Protocolo 473, Caja 155, Pedro de Cáceres. Concierto, 30-IX-1683, f. 507. The married migrants' contracts are located in ADC, Archivo Notarial, Protocolo 14, Caja 136, Lorenzo Meza de Andueza. Concierto, 18-IV-1668, f. 914; and Protocolo 94A-284, Pedro Fernández de Mosquera. Concierto, 24-V-1708, f. 20.

48. Several contracts from the 1660s and 1670s reveal these wage differences. For the pastry makers' contracts, see ADC, Archivo Notarial, Protocolo 675, Caja 136, Lorenzo Meza de Andueza. Concierto, 26-II-1669, f. 425; and Protocolo 585, Caja 138, Martín Lopez de Pardes. Concierto, 12-II-1670, f. 788. Contracts for two cooks, who also had to serve as laundresses, are found in ADC, Archivo Notarial, Protocolo 674, Caja 133, Lorenzo Meza de Andueza. Concierto, 3-VI-1668, f. 928; and Protocolo 675, Caja 136, Lorenzo Meza de Andueza. Concierto, 12-VI-1669, ff. 796–97. In addition to higher wages the pastry makers were given cash to buy their own food supplies; cooks received "regular food." The notarial contracts did not yield enough data to make a statement about "equal pay for equal work," but two additional contracts are particularly interesting. In 1655 a man was hired to sell bread at twenty-five pesos per year; in 1663 a woman with the same job earned twelve pesos. ADC, Archivo Notarial, Protocolo 654, Caja 105, Lorenzo Meza de Andueza. Concierto, 29-X-1655, ff. 2164–65V; and Protocolo 579, Caja 125, Martín López de Pardes. Concierto, 15-IX-1663, f. 802.

49. ADC, Archivo Notarial, Protocolo 674, Caja 133, Lorenzo Meza de

Andueza. Concierto, 5-VII-1668, f. 932. Failure to mention a salary could, of course, have been a scribe's error, but wages should have been mentioned in various places in the document. If Ynquillay received a large cash advance that, too, would have been noted.

50. The nature of this job may have affected its high representation in the documentation. See Appendix I for details.

51. Josepha Mallqui's contract is described in ADC, Archivo Notarial, Protocolo 493, Caja 157, Pedro López de la Cerda. Concierto de Ama, 27-IV-1684, f. 1050. That same register contains a variety of such contracts, including one in which an Indian wet nurse was hired by a Spanish woman to care for a mulatto infant, the son of her slave. Concierto de Ama, 3-IV-1684, f. 1038. A more typical contract, complete with the standard provisions and stipulations, can also be found in that register: Concierto de Ama, 13-III-1684, f. 1004.

52. The pair's contract is described in ADC, Archivo Notarial, Protocolo 568, Caja 92, Martín López de Paredes. Concierto, 2-III-1650, f. 863V–64. For an example of pay based on volume of chicha produced, see the contract issued to a migrant from Anta, Abancay, recorded in ADC, Archivo Notarial, Protocolo 578, Caja 123, Martín López de Pardes. Concierto, 28-II-1662, f. 886. For a more standard contract, issued to a Cuzco native, see ADC, Archivo Notarial, Protocolo 579, Caja 125, Martín López de Pardes. Concierto, 8-X-1663, f. 824. The documentation indicates that migrants were more likely than urban natives to be paid by volume produced, but the sample size is too small to form any firm conclusions.

53. The practice of guaranteeing contracts will be discussed in detail below. For specific figures, see tables IM and IN. Guild activity among urban food producers is discussed in Lyman Johnson's "Artisans," in *Cities and Society in Colonial Latin America* (Albuquerque: University of New Mexico Press, 1986), pp. 227–50. On pp. 251–83 of that volume, Mary Karasch discusses "Suppliers, Sellers, Servants, and Slaves," based chiefly on data from late-eighteenth-century Brazil.

54. For a detailed discussion of the formation of guilds in Iberia and Spanish America, see Johnson, "Artisans." (His characterization of production and markets is from p. 234.) The guilds' increased representation in the work force reflects the decline in other occupations but also indicates an expansion of the artisan sector in the late seventeenth century. Mario Góngora has argued that this period of expansion was also one of declining prosperity for guild members. (Mario Góngora, "Urban Social Stratification in Colonial Chile," *HAHR* 55, no. 3, 1975, p. 443.) Johnson notes that the guilds' acceptance of Indian members should not be considered a sign of racial mobility: "It would be a gross misrepresentation of colonial social reality to suggest that these changes in the racial characteristics of artisan trades meant that racism and discrimination had been overcome." ("Artisans," p. 238.) The following discussion concentrates on

Indian craftsmen. Much more work must be done on the number of mestizo and mulatto craftsmen in the Cuzco area, their role in local production, and their involvement in the apprenticeship system. Slaves, too, could be trained as craftsmen. For a contract in which a Spaniard arranged for his slave to be apprenticed to a master carpenter, see ADC, Archivo Notarial, Protocolo 764, Caja 2, Cristobal Lucero. Concierto de Aprendís, 12-II-1600, f. 78.

55. Felipe Guanca's contract is found in ADC, Archivo Notarial, Protocolo 535, Caja 49, Domingo de Oro. Concierto, 4-XI-1632, ff. 1447V–48.

56. Johnson, "Artisans," p. 244. The contract involving Lucas Corimanya and his anonymous wife is found in ADC, Archivo Notarial, Protocolo 94A-284, P. F. de Masquera. Concierto de 28-XI-1707, f. 5.

57. An interesting contract from the beginning of this period indicates this trend: a woman identified elsewhere in the documentation as the owner of a silver shop apprenticed her son to a master craftsman, a silverworker. The shopowner was probably the wife, widow, or daughter of another master craftsman; she may have started the silver shop independently, but given the general patterns of guild membership in Cuzco, this seems very unlikely; see ADC, Archivo Notarial, Protocolo 579, Caja 125, Martín López de Pardes. Concierto de Aprendís, 27-X-63, f. 731. The contract in which the silver shop owner hires a new employee is in the same register: Concierto, 12-IV-1663, f. 713.

58. Two of the women identified were widows; the third was described as the wife of an absent husband: "mujer con marido ausente." The resulting data gap prevents an accurate assessment of the role of female heads of households.

59. Contracts did not always contain the specific obligations of the fiadores, who often pledged that they would "fulfill the usual duties" of a guarantor. In cases where workers were advanced part of their salaries, fiadores were clearly responsible for compensating the employer if the worker departed before the advance had been repaid. For a specific example, see ADC, Archivo Notarial, Protocolo 284, Caja 94A, Jerónimo de Meza. Concierto, 27-VI-1705, f. 1. See Appendix I for a discussion of the data source for fiadores.

60. Thirty-three contracts involving craftsmen contained useful material on fiadores. See tables IM and IN–3. The low number of conciertos de aprendís which fully identified both the contractee and fiador (only twelve of ninety-four contracts) severely limits the usefulness of the data in table IP–4.

61. See Appendix I, tables IM and IN. Of the 1,167 general labor contracts, only 196 completely identified both the contractee and the guarantor involved; 12 of the 94 agreements creating apprenticeships supplied similar information (tables IM, IN, and IP–4). Nevertheless, the conciertos with identified fiadores provide some interesting information on the ties between Indian laborers, their families, and their home communities.

62. ADC, Archivo Notarial, Protocolo 629, Caja 128, Diego de Quiñonez. Concierto, 14-IV-1664, f. 1282, and Concierto, 25-IV-1664, f. 1283.

63. Charles Gibson and James Lockhart, among others, have identified a higher rate of acculturation among Indian migrants to urban centers due to the "strength of the Spanish influence" and the disorientation and "fragmentation of the displaced . . . Indians." This quotation is from Lockhart, *Spanish Peru, 1532–1560*, p. 218. See also Gibson, "The Problem of the Impact of Spanish Culture on the Indigenous American Population," p. 71. For an excellent study of the impact of urban migration on kin ties, see Michael Anderson, *Family Structure in Nineteenth Century Lancashire* (Cambridge: Cambridge University Press, 1971), particularly Part II: "Theory and Method." The role of migration in a number of Peruvian communities is discussed in Henry F. Dobyns and Mario C. Vázquez, eds., *Migración e integración en el Perú*. Monografías andinas, No. 2 (Lima: Editorial Estudios Andinos, 1963). For a discussion of urban migration and its impact on kinship patterns in contemporary Lima, see Susan Lobo, *A House of my Own: Social Organization in the Squatter Settlements of Lima, Peru* (Tucson: University of Arizona Press, 1982).

CHAPTER 6: The Transformation of Production

1. For example, see Karen Spalding's assertion that forasteros "were consigned to the margins of the Indian productive sector by their lack of access to the goods and resources held by the village community." ("Exploitation as an Economic System: The State and the Extraction of Surplus in Colonial Peru," in *The Inca and Aztec States, 1400–1800*, pp. 335–36.) As will be argued below, that disrupted access to resources often forced migrants to participate directly in production.

2. Spaniards were aware that the demand for cash violated Incan tradition. José de Acosta discussed the Incan and Spanish value systems, with particular regard to gold and silver, in his *Historia*, p. 189. See the related comments in AGI, Lima 123. Carta del Lzdo. Falcon, 15-III-1575. For the earlier view of the cash economy, see George Kubler's comment that an Indian entitled to be paid in Spanish currency "never saw it, but if he were remunerated, it was in bullion or in goods." (*Handbook of South American Indians*, p. 373.) Marvin Harris claimed that "it was to the economic advantage of everybody except the Indians . . . that the Indians enter the market economy." (Harris, *Patterns of Race*, p. 21.) These generalizations have been contradicted by much more detailed and diverse views of indigenous participation in the cash economy in the works of Karen Spalding, among others. In particular, see her "Exploitation as an Economic System."

3. The urban kurakas' abuse of forastero vendors is described in ADC, Cabildo del Cuzco, Tomo 12, 1623–1627. El cabildo del 17 de julio de 1623, f. 40. In Guamanga, Indian women purchased forasteros' produce and resold it at a substantial profit, much to the annoyance of local officials supervising the city's

markets; see ANP, Juicios de Residencia, Legajo 11, Cuaderno 29. Autos promovidos por Don Salvador Salas y de Valdéz, Corregidor y Justicia Mayor de la ciudad de Huamanga, 1593, f. 69. I want to thank Steve J. Stern for bringing this document to my attention. For an example of the ways in which corregidors defrauded Indian communities by inflating the cash value of goods, see ANP, Juicios de Residencia, Legajo 29, Cuaderno 82, 1634, ff. 555–58, passim and AGI, Lima 138. Carta del Doctor Don Gonzalo Pedro de Herrera, 29-VII-1607.

In 1662 the Corregidor of Quispicanche refused a request from the Protector de Naturales that the Indians of the town of Oropesa be exempted from paying their assessed goods because after a series of poor harvests even the seed crops had been eaten and village residents had gone to work on local haciendas in order to feed themselves and their families. ADC, Corregimiento, Causas Ordinarias, Provincias, Legajo 60. El Protector de Naturales en nombre de los indios del pueblo de Oropesa, 19-VIII-1662. Indian communities located near market centers could sell their goods and offer the corregidors cash, but officials would probably raise the conversion figures to reflect the market price of commodities. The Indians were not the only potential losers in the sale of assessed goods. In 1611 the King demanded that Viceroy Montesclaros investigate charges that local authorities had sold tribute goods cheaply to merchants for resale at Potosí; if profits were being made, the King wanted the Crown to make them. The viceroy reported that some resale was occurring, but chiefly in rural provinces rather than in the mining zones; see AGI, Lima 36, No. 1, Libro IV, ff. 59–62. Carta del Virrey a Su Magestad, 30-III-1611, f. 59V.

4. The Toledo regulations which allowed a community to satisfy mita obligations in cash are cited in AGI, Charcas 226. Carta del Corregidor de Potosí, 31-V-1655, f. 1. Magnus Mörner argues that by the late eighteenth century "As far as the mita was concerned, it certainly constituted much less of a hardship for Cuzco Indians than it used to do. Widespread commutation made it at the most an added economic obligation." (*The Andean Past*, p. 91.) Involvement in the cash economy was intensified in the mid-eighteenth century, when the repartimiento de bienes, or forced sale of goods, increased the demand for cash. Karen Spalding described this change in "Hacienda-Village Relations," p. 112–13. For a contemporary description of the repartimiento de bienes, see AGI, Indiferentes General 318. Ynstrucción. Por parte del Capitán J. de Salzedo, c. 1703, ff. 2–2V.

5. The Emperor's early statement, issued in Valladolid, 26-VI-1523, is contained in *Recopilación*, Libro VI, Título V, ley i. Tomo II, p. 225. The regulation governing mitimaes, dated Madrid, 18-X-1539, is found in Libro VI, Título V, ley iiii. Tomo II, pp. 225–26. The Toledo regulations were discussed at length above. Philip II issued a cédula confirming the tribute obligations of the yanaconas del Rey in Madrid, 30-XII-1571; it appears in Libro VI, Título V, ley v.

Tomo II. p. 226. The justification for the lower taxes assessed migrants is summarized in AGI, Charcas 271, No. V. Carta del Obispo de la Paz, 9-IV-1691, ff. 401–1V.

6. The Spaniards' employees are discussed in two provisions of the *Recopilación*, Libro VI, Título V, leyes viiii and x. Tomo II, p. 227. A decree of 15-II-1575 covered Indians working in mines, extensive gardens, and "other haciendas"; a subsequent provision, dated 4-VII-1593, expanded the requirements to include Indians working in estancias, obrajes, and "other activities." The regulations exempting forasteros are reported in Libro VI, Título V, ley xiiii. Tomo II, p. 228.

7. Philip's decree, pronounced in Madrid on 9-IV-1628, appears in the *Recopilación*, Libro VI, Título V, ley vi. Tomo II, p. 226. For an example of the King's concern that an ayllu not pay the tribute of its missing members, see AGI, Lima 35, No. 35, Libro III, f. 13. Reál Cédula a la Audiencia de Lima para que informe si los indios presentes pagan el tributo por los ausentes y muertos and AGI, Lima 36, No. 1, Libro IV, ff. 194–97. Carta del Virrey a Su Magestad, 13-IV-1611, f. 97. The provision governing tributes, issued in San Lorenzo on 6-VI-1609, appears in *Recopilación*, Libro VI, Título XV, ley xv. Tomo II, p. 228. Excessive labor demands were forbidden in a pronouncement of 10-XII-1618, Libro VI, Título XV, ley vi. Tomo II, p. 310. These regulations are cited in an extensive correspondence contained in AGI, Lima 35 and Lima 36. See, for example, Lima 35, No. 35, Libro III, ff. 14–15V. Copia de un capítulo de Carta de la Audiencia de Lima escrita a Su Magestad, 13-V-1606; and Lima 36, No. 1, Libro IV, ff. 201–2V. El Virrey a Su Magestad, 17-III-1610. The Audiencia of Quito claimed that no communities under *its* jurisdiction had paid tribute for absent or dead members, but that these abuses certainly occurred throughout the rest of Peru; see AGI, Lima 36, No. 1, Libro IV, ff. 198–99. Capítulo de la Audiencia de Quito sobre la paga de tributos de los indios por los ausentes y muertos. Quito, 22-III-1611.

8. For a general description of the confusion and chaos characterizing tribute collection, see AGI, Lima 35, No. 35, Libro III, ff. 16–16V. [Copia de carta en que] el Consejo da por arbitrio que se quite del cuidado de los indios la cobranza de los tributos, 28-I-1609. For the Aymares situation, see ANP, Juicios de Residencia, Legajo 33, Cuaderno 96, 1656, f. 48. The Quispicanche data are contained in ANP, Juicios de Residencia, Legajo 35, Cuaderno 98. Autos que promovió Don Pedro de Rubalcaba por especial comisión del Gobierno, Quispicanche, 1660, ff. 15–31. The longevity of the 1720s retasas—which may have helped a few communities with recovering populations—is recorded in ANP, Tributos, Legajo 1, Cuaderno 13. Legajo en que contiene 14 instrumentos, 1724–1736 [contains documentation through the 1780s], passim; and AGI, Lima 1172. Carta del Visitador General del Perú, 20-IV-1780, ff. 3V–4.

9. Toledo's opinions on the natural replacement of the tributary pool are

summarized in AGI, Lima 126. Carta del Lcdo. Falcon, 25-II-1583. For one example of the many communities where originarios paid the tribute of ausentes, see AGI, Lima 134. Retassa de indios, 22-I-1596. In 1690 the parish priest of Coaza, Caravaya y Sangabán, conveyed the community's complaint that the corregidor's most recent tribute and mita lists included transients as well as forasteros and originarios. AGI, Lima 471. Relación de la doctrina de Coaza, 1690. The characterization of the kurakas is from AGI, Lima 35, No. 35, Libro III, ff. 7–12V. Carta del Virrey a Su Magestad, 17-III-1610, f. 8. Kurakas who hid tributaries or lied about their community's population were subject to loss of office and other penalties described in ANP, Derecho Indígena, Legajo 4, Cuaderno 61. Revista y padrón de los indios del Rto. de Parinacochas, encomienda del Marqués de Oropesa, 1616.

10. ANP, Superior Gobierno, Legajo 8, Cuaderno 146. Canas y Canches, 1729, ff. 13–14. The 1725 report is contained in BNP, C1956. Memorial é informe, 6-VII-1725, f. 6. The notarial registers described in Appendix I contained only one authorization for collecting tribute from ausentes. In 1571 four principales from Haquiqura empowered an unidentified individual to collect tribute owed them by Indians in Potosí; see ADC, Archivo Notarial, Protocolo 8-777, A. Sánchez. Concierto, 4-V-1571, ff. 747V–48.

11. The priest's complaints are in AGI, Lima 471. Relación de Nuñoa, 11-IX-1689. For an inquiry into the illegal assessment of fees, see AAL, Legajo VIII, No. I. Sin título, [missing opening page], Antabamba, 1648. Details of fees charged, particularly for burials, are found in AGI, Lima 17, Carta de Don XPoval Yamque al Rey, 29-XI-1662, ff. 1V–2. The complaints from Potosí are contained in AGI, Charcas 270, No. 10. Carta del Contador Sebastián del Collado de Potosí, 11-V-1682, f. 4. The Cédula Reál of 14-V-1680 is quoted in AGI, Charcas 270. Carta y Aviso del Rvo. de la Cédula, La Plata, 20-VI-1681, ff. 1–1V. Palata's regulations, dated 20-II-1684, are quoted in BNP, B1504, ff. 122–22V. In 1690 a Cuzco priest complained that his urban parish was poor because there were no fee-paying forasteros within the district; see AGI, Lima 471. Relación de la doctrina de Belén, Cuzco, 1690. Collecting fees from forasteros was only one of the charges filed against the incumbent of Andarapa in BNP, C1883. Expediente sobre la queja interpuesta por Pascual Coyca, Cacique y Gobernador del pueblo de Andarapa contra el cura Juan de Medrano, por maltratos, Andahuaylas, 18-III-1716.

12. Among the various comments by officials who thought that the failure to collect tribute from forasteros would ruin the colony, see AGI, Charcas 266, No. I. Consulta del Don Joan de Luaravia, 1-III-1636, ff. 1–1V.

13. Few colonial observers believed that royal officials were diligently tracing forasteros. For example, see BNP, B516, ff. 1V–2. The denunciation of Spaniards accused of "helping Indians in order that they not pay tribute" appears in AGI, Charcas, Legajo 270. Libro XXIV, ff. 45V–46. For an example of an

employer who claimed that he had paid his forastero workers' tribute, see ADC, Benificencia, Legajo 4. Expediente, fragment, internal date of 1607, ff. 60–62V, passim.

14. Examples of kurakas collecting tribute from absent community members are found in BNP, B1079. Expediente sobre la petición presentada por el Procurador de Naturales de la villa de Acobamba, 20-II-1629, f. 71V and ANP Juicios de Residencia, Legajo 32, Cuaderno 89. Autos promovidos por Dr. Juan Ortiz de Chavez contra el Capitán Don Juan de Molina Guzman, Paucartambo, 1639, f. 15. For the 1690 responses, see AGI, Lima 471. Relaciones de las doctrinas de Pocoanca, Horunillo, Pucara, Savayno, and Guaquirca. Diligent kurakas are depicted in Relación de la doctrina de Savayno, 16-IX-1689; the wary residents appear in Relación de la doctrina de Guaquirca, 26-IX-1689. Both of these parishes are in the province of Aymares, which was not obligated to send mita laborers to either mining zone.

15. Testimony by the kurakas' agent from Belén is recorded in BNP, B1537. Títulos de Román de Baños, hijo de Dª Leonor Palla Inguilla, compuso con el Lic. Alonso Maldonado de Torres y su comisario Juan de Salas y Valdés en Guaylla, Camatai, y Quincoro . . . Cuzco, 1-VIII-1606; the relevant section of the document is from 1633. In 1690 151 tributarios were present in San Blas; 154 were listed as "ausentes," in AGI, Lima 471. Relación de la doctrina de San Blas, Cuzco, 1690.

16. Regulations governing migrants to the urban zone were discussed in chapter 2. Individuals with ten years' residency in urban centers were exempt from their home community's obligations, but this does not mean that all Indians abandoned their kin-members. Nor does it mean that all urban residents es-caped tribute payments: in 1692 a forastero who had been living in Lima for twenty years promised to pay the taxes his kurakas claimed he owed if the kurakas would abandon their attempts to return him to his reducción. Writing in the 1690s, one parish priest insisted that all of "his" forasteros paid tribute to their kurakas who came to Cuzco specifically to find missing tributarios but, like most officials, he was probably trying to avoid being entangled in the compli-cated issue of forastero tribute; see AGI, Lima 471. Relación de la doctrina del Hospital de Naturales, Cuzco, 1690.

17. The three contracts which stated that wages would cover current tribute obligations involved a male migrant who agreed to serve as a yanacona, a migrant arranging an apprenticeship, and a woman whose agreement to work as a wet nurse included a six-peso advance to pay her husband's tribute. The documents are found, respectively, in ADC, Archivo Notarial, Protocol 591, Caja 83, J. Flores Bastids. Concierto, 27-II-1646, f. 796; Protocol 578, Caja 123, Martín López de Pardes. Concierto, 9-VIII-1662, f. 956; and Protocol 53–310, Melias Jiménez O. Concierto de Ama, 7-IX-1717, ff. 320V–22V. The two contracts in which cash advances are to be applied to tax debts cover a married couple who

would work as household servants in order to pay off the husband's back taxes and an Indian who was going to work as a yanacona in Quillabamba. In this last contract the total wages to be paid equaled the cash advance, which was given to the alcalde mayor to whom the worker owed thirty pesos in back taxes. These contracts, particularly the second one, demonstrate an increasing tendency toward debt peonage, which will be discussed below. The two contracts are found, respectively, in the ADC, Archivo Notarial, Protocol 18, Caja 142, Martín López de Pardes. Concierto, 11-VI-1672, f. 775; and Protocol 1, Caja 70, Alonso Calvo y Arturo Montoya. Concierto, 10-IV-1638, f. 304.

18. My understanding of the nature of property owes much to Karl Marx, particularly his treatment of the "Asiatic" societies, in *Pre-capitalist Economic Formations* (New York: International Publishers, 1964), pp. 69–70, 83, 89–99, and to the application of that concept in the work of Karen Spalding. See also Wachtel's description of the nature of property in preconquest society in *The Vision of the Vanquished*, pp. 65–70.

19. The disputed estate is described in AAC, Legajo 173. Testamento de Juan Gaspar, Cuzco, 22-VI-1655. For an example of forastero holdings, see BNP, C4213. Sobre la querella instaurado por Juan Gerónimo Alejo Paullo y Sebastián Puma, San Pedro de Calca, 18-II-1719.

20. For an example of a rental arrangement which paid a priest's salary, see Lima 471. Relación de la doctrina de Capacmarca, 8-X-1689. The Tinta community is described in BNP, B1479. The complaints of the Indians of Checacupe and Pitomarca are reported in ANP, Derecho Indígena, Legajo 6, Cuaderno 125. Sin título (missing opening folios), 1650. Forasteros were not the only renters of Indian-owned lands, but judging from the trouble one community had in collecting from a Spaniard, kurakas may have found the forasteros to be more vulnerable, if not more reliable, tenants; see BNP, B771. Enplazamiento en forma para notificar a Diego de Salas, hacendado, en la Pa. de Andahuaylas La Grande el estado de la causa que contra él siguen el governador é indios de los pueblos de Piscobamba y Callara, 9-I-1647.

21. The Viceroy's letter is found in AGI, Lima 45, Libro I, ff. 39–39V. Carta del conde de Chinchón al Rey, 21-III-1634. Reál Cédula al Virrey del Perú, Madrid, 16-III-1642. Published in *Colección de documentos para la Historia*, Vol. II, Tomo I, pp. 380–81.

22. BNP, B1030. The kuraka's absence is noted on f. 60V. The witness's testimony appears on f. 62V. The judge's decision and the final disposition of the land are described on ff. 80, 227, 242, 270. A *topo* is approximately one and one-half leagues, squared.

23. BNP, B1479. La causa que sigue por parte de los indios del pueblo de Combapata, Tinta, 27-IX-1647.

24. Ibid., f. 25.

25. Ibid.

26. Ibid.

27. Toledo had hoped that his regulations would eliminate the need for Indians to engage in frequent court action, not only because such litigation was costly, but also because "many Indians had died in traveling to and from the Audiencia of Lima" to pursue their cases; see AGI, Lima 1623. Ynforme de Don Francisco de Toledo, 5-II-1572.

28. The use of land and the distribution of goods within preconquest ayllus were described in chapter 4. For additional details, see Polo de Ondegardo, pp. 155–57, and Murra, "The Economic Organization of the Inca State," p. 126. For copies of the correspondence between the King and Viceroy Toledo affirming the Crown's rights to property used for the support of guacas, the Sun God, and the Inca, see AGI, Lima 132. Carta y informe del Don Alberto Acuña, 29-IV-1593. The Spaniard's claim against Incan lands is reported in ANP, Derecho Indígena, Legajo 1, Cuaderno 12. Testimonio de los autos que siguió don Hernando Alvarez Azevedo, como procurador de don Pedro Atahualpa, cacique principal del pueblo Urco-Urco o Chuquimatuo en el valle de Quispi-canchis y de los demás indios de aquella parcialidad contra el Capitán Diego Maldonado, quien usando de violencia se apoderó de ciertas tierras propias de los dichos indios de Urco-Urco é hizo en ellas unos bohios y puso unos yanaconas, 1571. The Indian church warden of the parish of Abancay asked for and received a private title for lands assigned to him by local kurakas "because I serve the church" in ADC, Corregimiento, Causas Ordinarias, Provincias, Legajo #60. Testamento y títulos de tierras de Don Fernando Quispe, 1656. Case histories of individuals using Spanish law to advance their private claims to ayllu lands are contained in BNP, B1858. Expediente sobre la petición presentada por un indio tributario del pueblo de Huacho, 26-X-1685; and AGI, Charcas 270, No. 5. Carta del Corregidor Don Pedro Luis Enrriquez, 24-I-1682. A kuraka claimed community lands as his own in ADC, Benificencia, Legajo 29. Expediente, 11-X-1594. For an example of the ways in which a community resisted the usurpation of its lands by local kurakas, see BNP, B701. Expediente sobre la petición presentada por Francisco Roldán para que se le ampara en la posesión de unas tierras de su propiedad. Cuzco, 4-III-1666.

29. The Cabildo's grant is found in ADC, Cabildo de Cuzco, Tomo 11, 1613–1618, f. 33V, Acta, 8-XI-1613.

30. For a detailed study of the formation of haciendas in the Cuzco zone, see Luis Miguel Glave and María Isabel Remy, *Estructura agraria y vida rural en una región andina: Ollantaytambo entre los siglos XVI y XIX* (Cuzco: Centro de estudios rurales andinos "Bartolomé de las Casas," 1983). Manuel Burga discusses the relationship between the declining indigenous population, the composiciones de tierras, and the formation of haciendas in northern coastal Peru in *De la encomienda a la hacienda capitalista: El valle del Jequetepeque del siglo XVI al XX* (Lima: Instituto de Estudios Peruanos, 1976). For additional studies, see Lar-

son, *Colonialism and Agrarian Transformation;* Davies, *Landowners in Colonial Peru;* Keith, *Conquest and Agrarian Change;* and Nicholas P. Cushner, *Lords of the Land: Sugar, Wine, and Jesuit Estates of Coastal Peru, 1600–1767* (Albany: State University of New York Press, 1980).

31. The preconquest population is cited in BNP, B1605. Ejecutoria de las sentencias de visita y revisita y autos pronunciadas por esta Real Audiencia en la causa que en ella han tratado el cacique é indios de Laupaca reducidos en Huarmey. The priest's letter is found in BNP, B1442. Expediente sobre la petición presentada por el Cacique Juan Gabriel . . . Sin otra fecha, 1619. Throughout the seventeenth century, the clergy continued to urge that vacant Indian lands be sold to pay tribute, which included their salaries; see AAC, Box D–5, Calca y Lares, 1698.

32. Chinchón's comments are in his *Colección de las Memorias,* p. 85. He obviously had second thoughts about the forasteros by the time he left office. For an example of the royal instructions governing composiciones, see BNP, B1063. Recurring composiciones de tierras are described in BNP, B1606. Expediente sobre la visita de tierras practicada en la zona de Abancay, Cuzco, 1682. One visitor to the sierra thought that Indians were usually left with the poorest lands; see AGI, Lima 133, Carta de Alonso Garcia Ramon al Rey, Lima, 1-VII-1597. Keith explains how the composiciones functioned on the Peruvian coast in *Conquest and Agrarian Change,* p. 121.

33. Steve J. Stern gives an excellent account of the Indians' use of the colonial court system in "The Indians and Spanish Justice," chapter 5 of *Peru's Indian Peoples.* See also Stern's "The Social Significance of Judicial Institutions in an Exploitative Society: Huamanga, Peru, 1570–1640" and Woodrow Borah's "The Spanish and Indian Law: New Spain," both in *The Inca and Aztec States, 1400–1800,* pp. 289–320 and 265–88, respectively.

34. The first case involving disputed Quiquijana lands is reported in ANP, Derecho Indígena, Legajo 5, Cuaderno 85. Autos que siguieron los indios del ayllo Sailla . . . 1630, ff. 40, 43, and passim and in Legajo 5, Cuaderno 86. Títulos de las tierras que los indios del Ayllo Sailla reducidos en la paroq. de San Gerónimo de la ciudad del Cuzco poseían en la comarca del pueblo de Quiquijana . . . 1631, passim. The second is in AGI, Indiferentes General 1660. Ynforme de Juan de Moreyra, 18-XI-1654, f. 1. These are three distinct documents from two different archives, and the timing of the various sales is not clear. It is tempting to speculate, however, that the forastero was sued first because he was the more vulnerable target. For an example of the kind of forastero actions which provoked land disputes, see the case in which an Indian widow, born in the town of Coya, Calca y Lares, but living in Cuzco, sold land she had inherited in Coya to a sacristan of the Cuzco cathedral; see ADC, Archivo Notarial, Protocolo 58-256, A. F. Escudero. Concierto, 13-I-1719, f. 802.

35. The absentee's lands are contested in BNP, B1878. Expediente sobre la petición presentada por Juan Pizarro, indio natural de Huacho y principal de los aillus de Carquín, Vilcahuaura, y Lachay, para que Antonio Peréz deje las tierras de Lachay, cuya posesión debe darse a Juan de Guzman, 1673. The occupied lands in the province of Lampa are described in AGI, Lima 471. Relación de la doctrina de San Andrés de Hatuncolla, 12-IX-1689.

36. For an example of an urban resident selling property he could not defend, see ANP, Legajo 12, Cuaderno 345. Testimonio de la escritura de compra-venta que Bartolomé Quispe indio natural del pueblo de Oropesa en la provincia de Quispicanche, otorgó a favor del Cap. Miguel de Mendoza, 1698. For a contested title, see ANP, Derecho Indígena, Legajo 4, Cuaderno 58. Autos que Francisco Inga-yupanqui, indio de la parcialidad de Guaraypata en terminos y jurisdicción de la ciudad del Cuzco, y nieto de don Antonio Tito-yupanqui, siguió contra Juan Guamán Sauñi, principal del ayllo denominado Sayba, sujeto al pueblo de Quiquijana, sobre propiedad de las tierras que se decían Haguacullaypata, en terminos del dicho pueblo de Quiquijana, 1612. When migrants residing in Cuzco sold property within the urban zone, the transfer was usually uncontested; see ANP, Títulos de Propiedad: Cuaderno 640. Títulos de casas y solares en Cusco, 1626; Cuaderno 84, Testimonio de compra y venta, 1632.

37. Forasteros were used to occupy disputed lands in ANP, Derecho Indígena, Legajo 1, Cuaderno 12. They were involved in a dispute between two groups of Indians in BNP, B1514. Cuaderno 2º de documentos presentados por el Procurador Pablo Garcias nombre [sic] del comun de indios del pueblo de San Juan Bautista de Huchumarca con los de la estancia de Longotea, Los Reyes, 2-XI-1608. Forasteros are mentioned in intriguing but ultimately frustrating ways in a badly fragmented and deteriorated account of a composición de tierras in ADC, Provincia de Urubamba, M. Ochoa, No. 2. Cuaderno de Repartición y venta de solares y composición de tierras del valle de Urubamba-Yucay-Huayllabamba y Maras entre todos los Ayllos, 1595.

38. The inability of ayllus to absorb returning members is discussed in AGI, Charcas 270, No. XXIV, 30-VI-1646, ff. 15V–16.

39. Cédula Reál, Madrid, 24-IX-1648. Published in *Colección de documentos para la Historia*, Vol. II, Tomo I, pp. 435–36. Memorial del conde de Salvatierra, 22-III-1651, p. 254. The colonist's suggestions are found in AGI, Indiferentes General 1660. Carta del Dr. Don Francisco Valencuela, 26-VIII-1652, ff. 1, 1V.

40. The hacienda owners' requests are denied in AGI, Indiferentes General 1660. Memorial del Capitan Don Lorenzo de Avendaño y Cuniga, 8-XI-1650.

41. The kurakas' complaints are recorded in BNP, B1479. The Protector's letter appears in AGI, Charcas 270, No. 34. Carta del Protector de Naturales de Lima, 26-XI-1690. The relationship between the composiciones de tierras and the mita to Potosí is also discussed in AGI, Charcas 271, No. V, ff. 8V–9. In a cédula dated 24-IX-1648 the King insisted that the mita be filled despite the

impact of the composiciones de tierras; see AGI, Charcas 416. (Published in *Colección de Documentos para la Historia*, Vol. II, Tomo I, pp. 435–36.)

42. The Toledo exemptions are lamented in AGI, Charcas 226. Carta del Fray Francisco de la Cruz, 14-IV-1660. In 1604 Viceroy Velasco deplored the failure of the mita system, established just thirty years earlier. Memorial del Virrey Luis de Velasco, *Colección de las Memorias*, 1604, p. 109. Opinions differed as to who was responsible for shortfalls in the mita, but Viceroy Esquilache, writing in 1621, knew who to blame. He condemned the kurakas who, he claimed, knew exactly where to find their missing laborers but ignored the absentees' mita obligations in return for collecting their taxes "and a lot more money." (Memorial del Príncipe de Esquilache, *Colección de las Memorias*, 1621, p. 238.) For further comments by Velasco, Esquilache, and other colonial officials, see the discussion in chapter 2.

In 1669 the kurakas of Paucarcolla explained that they could not meet their mita quota because the only Indians in their jurisdiction were forasteros; see BNP, B575. Paucarcolla. Autos sobre el despacho de la mita de Potosí, 24-X-1669. Kurakas in Puno faced the same problem in 1673 and satisfied their mita obligations in cash; see BNP, B585. Despacho de la mita de Potosí. Puno. 2-XI-1673. In some instances unmarried women were forced to serve in local mitas, but I have found no evidence that Cuzco-area women served mita duty in Potosí. For an example of a community in which unmarried women served local mita duty, see AGI, Lima 471. Relación de la doctrina de San Salvador de Antabamba, Aymares, 27-IX-1689.

43. That "stabilization" was, of course, due to the influx of migrant workers and laborers who remained at the mines after completing their mita duty because by 1650 the mita to Potosí was yielding only about one-fifth of the required number of workers. See Peter Bakewell's description of this process in *Miners of the Red Mountain;* the specific data are from p. 106. Not all of the Cuzco-area workers who remained at the mines did so voluntarily. Some could not afford the journey home; others were forcibly kept in Potosí by employers or officials; see AGI, Lima 471. Relación de la doctrina de Arapa, Azángaro, s.f., c. 1690, y la de la doctrina de Sicoani, Canas y Canches, 19-IX-1689.

44. Sánchez-Albornoz has cautioned against interpreting the decline in the tributario-mitayo sector as indicative of the total population loss for the originario sector in his *Indios y tributos en el Alto Perú*, pp. 18–34. The previous discussion of the size of the forastero population in the bishopric of Cuzco in 1690 provides specific evidence to support his general caveat (see chapter 3).

45. The few surviving data from the 1685 survey of the Cuzco area show a tributario sector only 3.9 percent larger than the labor pool of 1725. Although the dependent population might have been more vulnerable to the epidemics of 1719–1721, the post-1690 tributario-mitayo increase of 53.6 percent cannot be attributed to sex- or age-specific mortality.

46. Ann Zulawski's assessment of the Oruro work force is found in "Mano de obra y migración en un centro minero de los Andes: Oruro, 1683," in *Población y mano de obra en América Latina*. Nicolás Sánchez-Albornoz, ed. (Madrid: Alianza Editorial, 1985), p. 113. In that same article she shows that approximately 80 percent of the tributarios living in Oruro paid taxes, even those from the Cuzco-area provinces of Canas y Canches, Azángaro, and Lampa (pp. 110–11). However, in 1690 a parish priest from San Andres de Hatuncolla, Lampa, protested that no tribute could be collected from Lampa originarios in the mining zone in spite of the fact that the town officials had journeyed to Upper Peru; see AGI, Lima 471. Relación de la doctrina de San Andres de Hatuncolla, Lampa, s.f., c. 1690. Potosí is the subject of excellent studies by Peter Bakewell and Jeffrey Cole, whose work shows clearly that the survival of the mita depended on the availability of non-mita labor.

47. Restrictions on the "voluntary" laborers are found in AGI, Lima 271. Reglamentos. Guancavelica, 6-IX-1645, ff. 20V–21. The report of the visiting inspector is found in AGI, Lima 145. Carta del Lcdo. Canseco, 10-V-1615. Solórzano's efforts are described in AGI, Lima 38, Libro IV, ff. 494–94V. Carta del Virrey a Su Magestad, 27-III-1619. Later conditions are described in AGI, Lima 271. Informe de Bartolome de Salazar, 4-XI-1662, f. 3V and AGI, Lima 171. Testimonio de los mineros de Guancavelica, 11-XI-1666. Monclova's complaints are found in AGI, Lima 90. Despacho del Virrey, Conde de la Monclova, 15-VIII-1695.

48. Complaints about shortfalls in local mita services are found in ANP, Superior Gobierno, Legajo 2-37. Autos seguidos ante el Corregidor don Felipe Manrique, Corregidor de la ciudad del Cuzco, 29-VII-1627 and AGI, Lima 306. Carta del obispo Manuel al Rey, 28-II-1695. Robert G. Keith describes the early failure of coastal agricultural mitas in *Conquest and Agrarian Change*, p. 96. The Protector's denunciation is found in ADC, Corregimiento. Causas Criminales, Legajo 72. El Protector de Naturales contra Francisco Alarcón, 25-XI-1650. The document ends with the case unresolved. Landowners who tried to sell their Indian laborers are described in AGI, Lima 126. Carta del Lcdo. Falcón, 25-II-1583 and ANP, Juicios de Residencia, Legajo 32, Cuaderno 89. Autos promovidos por Don Juan Ortíz de Chavez . . . Paucartambo, 1639, f. 1785.

49. The importance of the Cuzco obrajes and their exports to Upper Peru are described by Fernando Silva Santistéban. *Los obrajes en el Virreinato del Perú* (Lima: Publicaciones del Museo Nacional de Historia, 1964), pp. 150–51. He describes the unhealthy conditions within the Urcos obraje on pp. 154–55 but says on p. 101 that workers in the obrajes of Cuzco were the best-paid and the least-abused in the viceroyalty; he revises this position on p. 155, where he describes how poorly paid workers from Cuzco obrajes robbed travelers on the bishopric's highways because their wages were not paid during the late-

eighteenth-century depression, when exports to Upper Peru declined. Oscar Cornblit also discusses the Cuzco obrajes, drawing chiefly on Silva Santistéban's work. (Cornblit, "Society and Mass Rebellion," pp. 21–22.) A royal cédula issued on 31-XII-1671 demanded a thorough investigation of the Urcos workshop; see AGI, Lima 574. Published in *Colección de Documentos para la Historia*, Vol. II, Tomo II, pp. 571–73.

50. The changing policies governing obraje labor are described by Silva Santistéban on pp. 22–38 of *Los obrajes*. The assessment of the composition of the obraje work force is on p. 53. The various decrees forbidding involuntary labor in obrajes are listed in the cédula of 12-X-1670; see AGI, Lima 574. Published in *Colección de Documentos para la Historia*, Vol. II, Tomo II, p. 559. The forced detention of Indians in Cuzco obrajes is described in BNE, Papel de Don Sancho de Arévalo Briceño sobre la visita de los obrajes de los diez leguas de la jurisdición del Cuzco, 1662–1663. The Abancay obraje is described in ANP, Derecho Indígena. Legajo 6, Cuaderno 123, Visita del Obraje y trapiche de Ylianya en el Valle de Abancay, 28-IV-1649. Silva Santistéban accepts the official argument that many Indians worked in obrajes "voluntarily" and that those who were there against their will were criminals or debtors (*Los obrajes*, pp. 38–39). We need to know much more about specific labor relationships in the obrajes throughout Peru.

51. The Toledo statements supporting and regulating individual labor arrangements are found in BNP, Ordenanzas de Toledo, f. 85V. Confirmation of this practice by Viceroy Marqués de Cañete (1589–1596) and Viceroy Marqués de Monstesclaros (1607–1615) is cited in a labor contract in which a migrant was hired to work on estates owned by Cuzco's Jesuits; see ADC, Archivo Notarial, Protocolo 731, Caja 51, Luis Díaz Morales. Concierto, 6-V-1633, ff. 980–80V.

52. One of the clearest statements regarding the communal nature of the Incan mita and tribute structures is by John Murra, who says that "Liability was not individual." ("The Economic Organization of the Inca State," p. 169.) The special status of surviving Incan elites is the basis for a 1585 petition in which the husband of Doña Beatriz Coya cited her noble heritage and claimed the services and taxes owed by 563 "Indios tributarios yanaconas"; AGI, Escribanía 506A. Memorial del Pleito, 30-IV-1585.

53. The kurakas' responsibilities for community obligations were clear in 1710, when the kurakas of two ayllus based in San Sebastian, Cuzco, sold land to pay their communities' tribute debts and to release their ayllus' principales from jail. The land seems to have been the kurakas' personal property, but unfortunately the phrasing of the document is ambiguous; see ADC, Archivo Notarial, Protocolo 35-304, Gregorio V. Serrano, 5-VI-1710, f. 587. The position of early-eighteenth-century Cuzco kurakas was ambivalent in more ways than one: the four kurakas from Maras, Marquesado de Oropesa, who

signed a formal pledge to pay delinquent tribute to the Marqués offered as security houses in Cuzco owned by the head kuraka and valued at 5,000 pesos; see ADC, Archivo Notarial, Protocolo 58-256, A. F. Escudero, 11-I-1719, ff. 798–801V. The three labor contracts negotiated by kurakas—two of which were signed after Toledo had arrived in Cuzco in June, 1571, but before he outlawed the practice—are found in ADC, Archivo Notarial, Protocolo 8-777, Antonio Sánchez. Contrato de 3-IV-1571, ff. 819–19V; Contrato de 30-VII-1571, ff. 1089–89V; Contrato sin fecha, f. 1,092. (The last page of this contract has been cut from the volume; judging by internal evidence and its placement within the volume, the document was signed in July 1571.)

The Cabildo's regulations are found in BNP, A17, folios sueltos. Private agents are authorized to hire Indians in ADC, Archivo Notarial, Protocolo 13-793, Caja 9, Juan de Quiroz y Luís de Quesada. Concierto de 20-III-1579, f. 17V and ADC, Archivo Notarial, Protocolo 9-798, Caja 5. Concierto de 5-X-1573, ff. 195–98. The Corregidor of Cuzco scrutinized an informal labor relationship between a Spanish hacendado and the kurakas of Surite, Guarocondo, and Anta, in the province of Abancay, in ADC, Corregimiento. Causas Ordinarias, Provincias, Legajo 60. Carta de Román de Baños Osorio, 5-X-1601.

54. The transfer of the repartimiento of Pitic Caica y Guasac is recorded in ADC, Archivo Notarial, Protocolo 695, Caja 14, Pedro de la Cavera, 8-I-1609, f. 479. The contract of the Indian who worked for his own kuraka is recorded in Protocolo 604, Caja 131, J. Flores Bastids. Concierto, 27-V-1666, f. 15.

55. Seasonal laborers were described by the parish priest of Ayapata, who carefully distinguished them from established forasteros; see AGI, Lima 471. Relación de la doctrina de Ayapata, Caravaya y Sangabán, 8-IX-1689. Thierry Saignes discusses seasonal and temporary migration in "The Ethnic Groups in the Valleys of Larecaja," p. 325. For an analysis of the structure and impact of seasonal migration in a later period, see the chapter on "Migration and the Peasant Community" in Florencia E. Mallon, *The Defense of Community in Peru's Central Highlands: Peasant Struggle and Capitalist Transition, 1860–1940* (Princeton: Princeton University Press, 1983). Many features of this later migration can be compared to or directly traced to similar patterns in and consequences of colonial-era migration.

56. Employers in the Paucartambo coca fields, as seen above, were forced into early and periodic reliance on the urban labor pool in order to satisfy labor demands due to low mita compliance and high mortality rates. See Appendix I for a discussion of the labor contracts.

57. See the discussion of sources, sampling techniques, and data in Appendix I.

58. The migrant muleteer's complicated contract is found in ADC, Archivo Notarial, Protocolo 679, Caja 140, Lorenzo Meza de Andueza. Concierto, 10-

XI-1671, ff. 1099–101. The contract in which an employer paid "damages" for a migrant is in Protocolo 14, Caja 136, Lorenzo Meza de Andueza. Concierto, 9-IV-1668, ff. 379–80V. Indians who agreed to work until they had paid their debts appear in Protocolo 547, Caja 56, L. Jaimes. Concierto, 20-I-1696, f. 10 and Concierto, 20-II-1696, f. 29 and in Protocolo 94A-284, Pedro Fernández de Mosqueria. Concierto, 23-V-1707, f. 34.

CHAPTER 7: "All the Indians Have Died"

1. Guaman Poma de Ayala's description of Toledo is in Vol. II, p. 72, of his *La nueva crónica*. Guaman Poma blames King Philip II's refusal to receive Toledo for the viceroy's death.

The changes in community structure stemming from indigenous migration which have been depicted in this study clearly contradict Eric Wolf's image of the "closed corporate peasant community" as "a creature of the Spanish Conquest." ("Closed Corporate Peasant Communities in Mesoamerica and Central Java," *Southwestern Journal of Anthropology* 13, no. 1, Spring 1957, p. 7.) Indigenous communities under Spanish rule were not isolated elements within colonial society, and migration played a major role in social interaction. Moreover, one key feature of Wolf's definition of the contemporary peasant community— that "[t]he community is territorial, not kinship-based"—is actually the result of social changes related to widespread indigenous migration. Wolf's model has been criticized by David J. Robinson, "Indian Migration in Eighteenth-Century Yucatán: The Open Nature of the Closed Corporate Community," in *Studies in Spanish American Population History*, pp. 149–73.

2. Data from the Cuzco zone support this statement, which N. David Cook believes is true for the viceroyalty as a whole. See his *Demographic Collapse*, pp. 86, 210, passim.

3. In *Miners of the Red Mountain*, Peter Bakewell cites a depiction of the viceroy as "el señor Don Francisco de Toledo, que todo lo previno." Bakewell reports that the characterization was made by "Don Juan de Carvajal y Sande, councillor of the Indies and visitor to Potosí, in the preamble to his repartimiento of the mita, Potosí, September 3, 1633—referring specifically to Toledo's regulation on the sale of mita Indian labor. Carvajal was not, moreover, a man to extend undue respect to his predecessors. (AGI, Lima 45, Tomo 1, f. 12V.)" (Bakewell, *Miners of the Red Mountain*, p. 81.)

4. I certainly do not intend to disparage the importance of indigenous resistance to Spanish rule, which I have written about elsewhere. But an individual's act may acquire an alternative significance in a broader structural context. Jeffrey Cole, in *The Potosí Mita*, p. 136, characterizes indigenous migration in response to the mita to Potosí as "passive resistance," but I believe that resistance through migration was definitely an assertive act.

APPENDIX I

1. Personal communication from Jorge Olivera O., Assistant Archivist, Archivo Departamental del Cusco, May 1980. Sometimes even the papel sellado failed. On July 10, 1641, the scribes in Cuzco noted that no papel sellado was available and asked the government to approve their decision to substitute regular paper. The scribes promised that they would be paying the fees as if they were using papel sellado; see ADC, Archivo Notarial, Protocol 588, Caja 77, J. Flores Bastids. Copia de petición, 10-VII-1641, f. 721.

2. One of the 1,167 conciertos was an open-ended agreement: in 1668 Joseph Guaman agreed to accompany a priest collecting charitable offerings in the provinces of Quispicanche and Canas y Canches, pledging to work "as long as necessary" to complete the journey. Three years earlier two Cuzco natives had undertaken a vaguer journey "to go to all the provinces and towns and wherever it might be necessary" in order to collect offerings, but their contract was limited to one year; see ADC, Archivo Notarial, Protocolo 14, Caja 16, Lorenzo Meza de Andueza. Concierto, 13-IV-1668, f. 393; Protocolo 32, Caja 130, Lorenzo Meza de Andueza. Concierto, 1-VII-1665, f. 529V–30V.

3. Cosme Bueno. *Geografía del Perú Virrenial* (siglo XVIII). Publicado por Daniel Valcarcel. Lima, 1951. The 1690 census, discussed at length in Appendix II, is found in AGI, Audiencia de Lima, Legajo 471, Padrón del obispado del Cusco, 1689–1690.

APPENDIX II

1. The parish reports are found in AGI, Audiencia de Lima, Legajo 471, Padrón del obispado del Cusco, 1689–90 (hereafter, Lima 471). The specific reports cited are the relación de la doctrina de Vellille, Chumbibilcas, 28-VII-1690, and la de la doctrina de Santo Tomas, Chumbibilcas, 16-VIII-1689. The names of the principal towns and their annexes appear as they were written by the local parish priests. Reports from adjacent parishes occasionally contain different versions of these names, but the original spellings were regarded as valid.

2. The longest response is the relación de la doctrina de Guaquirca, Aymares. Of the one-page reports the shortest is the relación de Pusí, Azángaro.

3. AGI, Lima 471. Relación de la doctrina de Mamara, Cotabambas.

4. AGI, Lima 471. Relación de la doctrina de Capi, Chilques y Masques.

5. AGI, Lima 471. Relación de la doctrina de Sabayno, Aymares.

6. AGI, Lima 471. Relación de la doctrina de Urcos, Quispicanche.

7. Reports from Chinchaypuquio, ABY 3; Mara, COT 3; and Collega, CHYM 3 show a total population of 2,402; 2,002 "personas de confesión" and 400 "others."

8. The Duque de Palata, viceroy of Peru from 1681 to 1689, conducted a census of the Andean area but was unsuccessful in his attempts to readjust tribute and mita obligations on the basis of existing population distribution. Unfortunately, the census documents relating to the Cuzco area have not yet been located.

APPENDIX III

1. Nicolás Sánchez-Albornoz addressed these problems in his "Los registros parroquiales en America Latina," XXXVII Congreso Internacional de Americanistas, Mar de Plata, Argentina, 1966. John V. Lombardi discussed population records in "Population Reporting Systems: An Eighteenth-Century Paradigm of Spanish Imperial Organization," in *Studies in Spanish American Population History*, pp. 11–23. Marcello Carmagnani discussed the use of parish materials from the eighteenth century in his "Colonial Latin American Demography: Growth of Chilean Population, 1700–1830," *Journal of Social History* 1, no. 2, 1967–68, pp. 179–91. Pierre Chaunu deals primarily with Mexican data in his "La population de l'Amérique indienne (Nouvelles recherches)," *Revue Historique* 232, no. 1, 1964, pp. 111–18. The use of emigration documents and official reports is discussed in Richard Konetzke's "Las fuentes para la historia demográfica de Hispano-America durante la época colonial," *Anuario de estudios americanos* 5, 1948, pp. 267–323. For a more general discussion, see Woodrow Borah's "The Historical Demography of Latin America," in *Population and Economics: Proceedings of Section V of the Fourth Congress of the International Economic History Association*, 1968. Paul Deprez, ed. (Winnipeg: University of Manitoba Press, 1970).

2. In December 1977 Lewis Hanke assured me that the question of access to parish records would soon be resolved. Although Dr. Hanke and other scholars from both North and South America have held repeated discussions with the ecclesiastical authorities, they have reached no final conclusions on this issue. In the interim several researchers have obtained access to varying amounts of material, chiefly through individual agreements with local authorities.

3. See Dobyns, "An Outline of Andean Epidemic History to 1720," passim, and chapters 2 and 3 for a discussion of these epidemics.

4. The term "parents" was consistently used by parish priests who made no distinction between the child's mother and father. A few notations, labeled "Parents unknown, mother native of ———," indicate that clerics may have customarily noted the father's origin.

✦ BIBLIOGRAPHY ✦ ✦

ARCHIVAL ABBREVIATIONS

AAC   Archivo Arzobispal del Cusco
AAL   Archivo Arzobispal de Lima
ADC   Archivo Departamental del Cusco
AGI   Archivo General de Indias, Sevilla
ANP   Archivo Nacional del Peru
BNE   Biblioteca Nacional de España
BNP   Biblioteca Nacional del Perú
PTT   Palacio de Torre Tagle, Archivo del Ministerio de Asuntos Exteriores del Perú. I appreciate the efforts of Guillermo Lohmann Villena in expediting my petition to work in this restricted archive.

The titles of documents are recorded as entered in archival indices or as written on opening folios. The references to "AAC, Unmarked box, our No. ———" are based on a preliminary inventory of unidentified, unsorted materials stored in boxes or bound with string at the Archivo Arzobispal del Cusco.

ADDITIONAL DOCUMENTARY SOURCES

Acosta, José de. *Historia natural y moral de las Indias,* Edmundo O'Gorman, ed. Mexico: Fonda de cultura económica, 1940.
Anales del Cuzco, 1600–1750. Compiled by D. Diego de Esquivel y Navia. Museo arqueológico del Cusco. (An additional copy can be found in BNP, C876.)
Aranzel de los jornales que se han de pagar los indios. Mandado ordenar por el Excelentíssimo Señor D. Melchor de Navarra y Rocafull, Duque de Palata, 7 de noviembre, 1687.
Colección de Cédulas Reales dirigidas a la Audiencia de Quito, 1538–1600. Publicaciones del Archivo Municipal, Vol. IX, Quito, 1935.
Colección de Documentos para la Historia de la Formación Social de Hispanoamérica, 1493–1810. Richard Konetzke, ed. Madrid: Consejo Superior de Investigaciones Científicas, 1953.

Colección de las Memorias o Relaciones que escribieron los Virreys del Perú. Ricardo Beltrán y Rózpide, ed. Madrid: Biblioteca de historia Hispano-Americana, 1921.

Extirpación de la idolatría en el Perú. Pablo Joseph de Arriaga, Lima, 1621.

Laws of Burgos, 1512–1513. Charles Gibson, trans. and ed. *The Spanish Tradition in America.* New York: Harper and Row, 1968, pp. 61–82.

Memorias de los Virreyes que gobernaron el Perú durante el tiempo del colonaje español. Madrid: Biblioteca de la historia Hispano-Americana, 1927.

Recopilación de leyes (1681, 1791). Several volumes. Madrid: Consejo de la Hispanidad, 1943.

Bueno, Cosme. *Geografía del Perú Virrenial* (siglo XVIII). Publicado por Daniel Valcarcel. Lima, 1951.

Cieza de León, Pedro. *La crónica del Peru* (c. 1570). Edición Biblioteca Peruana. Lima: Editorial Universo S.A., 1973.

Cobo, Bernabé. *History of the Inca Empire* (c. 1653). Roland Hamilton, trans. and ed. Austin: University of Texas Press, 1979.

Guaman Poma de Ayala, Felipe. *La nueva crónica y buen gobierno del Perú.* Vols. 1–3 (c. 1613) Luis F. Bustios Galvéz, ed. Lima: Editorial Cultura, 1956.

Humboldt, Alexander von. *El Perú en la obra de Alejandro de Humboldt.* Estuardo Nuñez y Georg Petersen G., eds. Lima: Librería Studium, 1971.

Jeréz, Francisco de. "Conquest of Peru and the Province of Cuzco," in Augustín de Zarate. *The Discovery and Conquest of Peru.* J. M. Cohen, trans. and ed. Baltimore: Penguin Books, 1968.

Juan, Jorge and Antonio de Ulloa. *Noticias Secretas de América* (c. 1735). Madrid: Editorial America, 1918.

Matienzo, Juan de. *Gobierno del Perú* (c. 1567). Buenos Aires: Companía Sudamericana de billetes de banco, 1910.

Molina, Cristóbal de. *Rítos y fábulas de los Incas.* Buenos Aires: Editorial Futuro, 1947.

Mugaburu, Josephe and Francisco. *Chronicle of Colonial Lima: The Diary of Josephe and Francisco Mugaburu, 1640–1697.* Robert Ryal Miller, trans. and ed. Norman: University of Oklahoma Press, 1975.

Pizarro, Pedro. *Relation of the Discovery and Conquest of the Kingdoms of Peru.* Philip A. Means, trans. New York: The Cortés Society, 1921.

Sáncho de Hoz, Pedro. "Descripción de la Ciudad del Cuzco" (c. 1530), in *Crónicas de Indias.* Guillermo Díaz Plaja, ed. Estella, Navarra: Salvat Editores, S.A.—Alianza Editorial, S.A., 1972.

Sarmiento de Gamboa, Pedro. *History of the Incas* (1572). C. R. Markham, trans. London: The Hakluyt Society, 1907.

Toledo, Francisco de. *Tasa de la Visita General.*

Zarate, Augustín de. *The Discovery and Conquest of Peru.* J. M. Cohen, trans. and ed. Baltimore: Penguin Books, 1968.

SECONDARY SOURCES

Adams, Richard N. "A Change from Caste to Class in a Peruvian Town." *Social Forces* 31, no. 3 (March 1953).

Adorno, Rolena. *Guaman Poma: Writing and Resistance in Colonial Peru.* Austin: University of Texas Press, 1986.

———, ed. *From Oral to Written Expression: Native Andean Chronicles of the Early Colonial Period.* Syracuse, N.Y.: Maxwell School of Citizenship and Public Affairs, 1982.

Alberti, Giorgio, and Enrique Mayer. "Reciprocidad andina: ayer y hoy," in *Reciprocidad e intercambio en los Andes peruanos,* Alberti and Mayer, eds. Perú Problema 12. Lima: Instituto de Estudios Peruanos, 1974.

Anderson, Michael. *Family Structure in Nineteenth Century Lancashire.* Cambridge: Cambridge University Press, 1971.

Andrien, Kenneth J. *Crisis and Decline: The Viceroyalty of Peru in the Seventeenth Century.* Albuquerque: University of New Mexico Press, 1985.

Ascher, Marcia and Robert. *Code of the Quipu: A Study in Media, Mathematics, and Culture.* Ann Arbor: University of Michigan Press, 1981.

Assadourian, Carlos Sempat. "La crisis demográfica del siglo XVI y la transición del Tawantinsuyu al sistema mercantil colonial," in *Población y mano de obra en América Latina,* Nicolás Sánchez-Albornoz, ed. Madrid: Alianza Editorial, S.A., 1985, pp. 69–93.

———. *El sistema de la economía colonial: Mercado interno, regiones y espacio económico.* Lima: Instituto de Estudios Peruanos, 1982.

Bakewell, Peter. *Miners of the Red Mountain: Indian Labor in Potosí, 1545–1650.* Albuquerque: University of New Mexico Press, 1984.

Balán, Jorge. "Migrant-Native Socioeconomic Differences in Latin American Cities: A Structural Analysis." *Latin American Research Review* (hereinafter cited as *LARR*) IV, no. I (1969): 3–29.

Bastien, Joseph W. *Mountain of the Condor: Metaphor and Ritual in an Andean Ayllu.* New York: West Publishing Company, 1978.

Baudin, Louis. *Daily Life in Peru Under the Last Incas.* Winifred Bradford, trans. New York: Macmillan, 1962.

Bennett, Wendell C. "The Andean Highlands: An Introduction," in *Handbook of South American Indians,* Vol. II. Julian H. Steward, ed. Washington, D.C.: Government Printing Office, 1964.

Bloch, Marc. *The Historian's Craft.* Peter Purnam, trans. New York: Vintage Books, 1953.

Bolton, Ralph and Enrique Mayer, eds. *Andean Kinship and Marriage.* American Anthropological Association, Special Publication Number 7, 1977.

Borah, Woodrow. "Demographic and Physical Aspects of the Transition from the Aboriginal to the Colonial World." *Comparative Urban Research* 8, no. 1 (1980): 41–70.

———. "The Historical Demography of Latin America." *Population and Economics: Proceedings of Section V of the Fourth Congress of the International Economic History Association,* 1968. Paul Deprez, ed. Winnipeg, Canada: University of Manitoba Press, 1970.

———. *New Spain's Century of Depression.* Berkeley: University of California Press, 1951.

———. "The Spanish and Indian Law: New Spain," in *The Inca and Aztec States, 1400–1800: Anthropology and History,* George A. Collier, Renato I. Rosaldo, and John D. Wirth, eds. New York: Academic Press, 1982, pp. 265–88.

Bowser, Fredrick P. *The African Slave in Colonial Peru, 1524–1650.* Stanford: Stanford University Press, 1974.

Boyer, Richard. "Mexico in the Seventeenth Century: Transition of a Colonial Society." *Hispanic American Historical Review* (hereinafter cited as *HAHR*) 57, no. 3 (August 1977): 455–78.

Brading, David. *Miners and Merchants in Bourbon Mexico, 1763–1810.* Cambridge: Cambridge University Press, 1971.

Brading, David and Harry E. Cross. "Colonial Silver Mining: Mexico and Peru." *HAHR* 52, no. 4 (November 1972): 545–79.

Braudel, Fernand. *La historia y las ciencias sociales.* Josefina Gómez Mendoza, trans. Madrid: Alianza Editorial, S.A., 1968.

Bronner, Fred. "Peruvian Encomenderos in 1630: Elite Circulation and Consolidation." *HAHR* 57, no. 4 (November 1977): 644–59.

Brown, Kendall W. *Bourbons and Brandy: Imperial Reform in Eighteenth-Century Arequipa.* Albuquerque: University of New Mexico Press, 1986.

Brundage, Burr Cartwright. *Lords of Cuzco: A History of the Inca People in Their Final Days.* Norman: University of Oklahoma Press, 1967.

Burga, Manuel. *De la encomienda a la hacienda capitalista: El valle del Jequetepeque del siglo XVI al XX.* Lima: Instituto de Estudios Peruanos, 1976.

Burga, Manuel and Alberto Flores Galindo. "La producción agrícola y las sublevaciones durante el siglo XVIII: Apuntes Metodológicos." Private Issue. Huancayo, 1975.

Burkholder, Mark A. and D. S. Chandler. *From Impotence to Authority: The Spanish Crown and the American Audiencias, 1687–1808.* Columbia: University of Missouri Press, 1977.

Campbell, Leon G. "Recent Research on Andean Peasant Revolts, 1750–1820." *LARR* 14, no. 1 (1979): 3–49.

Carmagnani, Marcello. "Colonial Latin American Demography: Growth of Chilean Population, 1700–1830." *Journal of Social History* 1, no. 2 (1967–68): 170–91.

Céspedes del Castillo, Guillermo. "La Sociead colonial americana en los siglos XVI y XVII," in *Historia de España y América*, J. Vicens Vives, ed. Barcelona: Editorial Vicens Vives, 1961.

Chaunu, Pierre. "La population de l'Amérique indienne (Nouvelles recherches)." *Revue Historique* 232, no. 1 (1964): 111–18.

Chevalier, François. *Land and Society in Colonial Mexico: The Great Hacienda.* Lesley B. Simpson, ed. Alvin Eustis, trans. Berkeley: University of California Press, 1963.

Cline, Howard F. "Civil Congregations of the Indians in New Spain, 1598–1606." *HAHR* 29, no. 3 (August 1949): 349–69.

Cobb, Gwendolin B. "Supply and Transportation for the Potosí Mines, 1545–1640." *HAHR* XXIX, no. 1 (February 1949): 25–45.

Cole, Jeffrey A. *The Potosí Mita, 1573–1700: Compulsory Indian Labor in the Andes.* Stanford: Stanford University Press, 1985.

———. "Viceregal Persistence Versus Indian Mobility: The Impact of the Duque de la Palata's Reform Program on Alto Perú, 1681–1692." *LARR* XIX, no. 1 (1984): 37–56.

Colin, Michèle. *Le Cuzco à la fin de XVIIᵉ et au début du XVIIIᵉ siècle.* Paris: Institut des Hautes Etudes de l'Amérique Latine, 1966.

Cook, N. David. *Demographic Collapse: Indian Peru, 1520–1620.* New York: Cambridge University Press, 1981.

———. "Eighteenth-Century Population Change in Andean Peru: The Parish of Yanque," in *Studies in Spanish American Population History*, David J. Robinson, ed. Dellplain Latin American Studies, No. 8. Boulder, Colo.: Westview Press, 1981, pp. 243–70.

———. "Les indiens immigrés à Lima au début du XVIIᵉ siècle." *Cahiers des Amériques Latines* 13/14 (1976): 33–50.

———. "La población indígena de Vegueta 1623–1683: Un estudio del cambio en la población de la costa central del Perú en el siglo XVII." *Historia y cultura* no. 8 (1975): 81–89.

———. "La población indígena en el Perú colonial." *America Colonial: Población y economía, Anuario.* Instituto de Investigaciones Históricas, Universidad Nacional de Litoral, Rosario, Argentina, 1965.

Cornblit, Oscar. "Society and Mass Rebellion in Eighteenth-Century Peru and Bolivia," in *Latin American Affairs*, Raymond Carr, ed., *Saint Anthony's College Papers*, no. 22. London: Chatto and Windus, 1970.

Cotler, Julio. *Clases, estado, y nación en el Perú.* Perú Problema 17. Lima: Instituto de Estudios Peruanos, 1978.

Cox, Oliver C. *Caste, Class and Race: A Study in Social Dynamics.* New York: Monthly Review Press, 1959.

Crosby, Alfred W., Jr. *The Colombian Exchange: Biological and Cultural Consequences of 1492.* Westport, Conn.: Greenwood Press, 1972.

Cushner, Nicholas P. *Lords of the Land: Sugar, Wine, and Jesuit Estates of Coastal Peru, 1600–1767.* Albany: State University of New York Press, 1980.

Davies, Keith A. *Landowners in Colonial Peru.* Austin: University of Texas Press, 1984.

Davies, Thomas M., Jr. *Indian Integration in Peru.* Lincoln: University of Nebraska Press, 1970.

Dobyns, Henry F. "An Outline of Andean Epidemic History to 1720." *Bulletin of the History of Medicine* 37, no. 6 (November–December 1963): 493–515.

———. *The Social Matrix of Peruvian Indigenous Communities.* Cornell Peru Project Monograph, Department of Anthropology, Cornell University. Ithaca, 1964.

———. *Their Number Become Thinned: Native American Population Dynamics in Eastern North America.* Knoxville: University of Tennessee Press in Cooperation with the Newberry Library Center for the History of the American Indian, 1983.

Dobyns, Henry F. and Paul L. Doughty. *Peru: A Cultural History.* New York: Oxford University Press, 1976.

Dobyns, Henry F. and Mario C. Vázquez, eds. *Migración e Integración en el Perú.* Monografías Andinas, no. 2. Lima: Editorial Estudios Andinos, 1963.

Dougherty, James. *The Fivesquare City: The City in the Religious Imagination.* Notre Dame, Ind.: University of Notre Dame Press, 1980.

Earls, John and Irene Silverblatt. "Ayllus y etnías de la región Pampas-Qaracho," paper presented at the III Congreso Peruano del Hombre y la Cultura Andina, Lima, 1977.

Elliott, J. H. *Imperial Spain, 1469–1716.* New York: St. Martin's Press, 1963.

Evans, Brian M. "Census Enumeration in Late Seventeenth-Century Alto Perú: The Numeración General of 1683–84," in *Studies in Spanish American Population History,* David J. Robinson, ed. Dellplain Latin American Studies, No. 8. Boulder, Colo.: Westview Press, 1981, pp. 25–44.

Farriss, Nancy M. "Nucleation versus Dispersal: The Dynamics of Population Movement in Colonial Yucatan." *HAHR* 58, no. 2 (May 1978): 187–216.

Favre, Henri. "The Dynamics of Indian Peasant Society and Migration to Coastal Plantations in Central Peru," in *Land and Labour in Latin America,* Kenneth Duncan and Ian Rugledge, eds., with the collaboration of Colin Harding. Cambridge: Cambridge University Press, 1977, pp. 253–67.

Fisher, J. R. *Government and Society in Colonial Peru: The Intendant System.* London: University of London's Athlone Press, 1970.

Ford, Thomas R. *Man and Land in Peru.* Gainesville: University of Florida Press, 1955.

Friede, Juan. "Demographic Changes in the Mining Community of Muzo after the Plague of 1629." *HAHR* 47, no. 3 (August 1967): 338–43.

García Gallo, Alfonso. *Metodología del derecho Indiano.* Santiago de Chile: Editorial Juridica de Chile, 1970.

Gibson, Charles. *The Aztecs Under Spanish Rule.* Stanford: Stanford University Press, 1964.

——, ed. *The Black Legend: Anti-Spanish Attitudes in the Old World and the New.* New York: Knopf, 1971.

——, ed. and introduction, "The Problem of the Impact of Spanish Culture on the Indigenous American Population," in *Latin American History: Select Problems,* Frederick B. Pike, ed. New York: Harcourt Brace & World, 1969.

——, ed. *The Spanish Tradition in America.* New York: Harper and Row, 1968.

——. *Tlaxcala in the Sixteenth Century.* New Haven: Yale University Press, 1952.

——. "The Transformation of the Indian Community in New Spain, 1500–1810." *Journal of World History* 2, no. 3 (1955): 581–607.

Gifford, Douglas and Pauline Hoggarth. *Carnival and Coca Leaf: Some Traditions of the Peruvian Quechua Ayllu.* Edinburgh: Scottish Academic Press, 1976.

Glave, Luis Miguel and María Isabel Remy. *Estructura agraria y vida rural en una región andina: Ollantaytambo entre los siglos XVI y XIX.* Cuzco: Centro de estudios rurales andinos "Bartolomé de las Casas," 1983.

Godelier, Maurice. "The Concept of the 'Asiatic Mode of Production' and Marxist Models of Social Evolution," in *Relations of Production: Marxist Approaches to Economic Anthropology,* David Seddon, ed. Helen Lackner, trans. London: Frank Cass and Company, 1978, pp. 209–57.

——. *Perspectives in Marxist Anthropology.* Robert Brain, trans. Cambridge: Cambridge University Press, 1977.

Godoy, Jack. "The Evolution of the Family," in *Household and Family in Past Time,* Peter Laslett, ed. Cambridge: Cambridge University Press, 1972.

Góngora, Mario. *Encomenderos y estancieros: Estudios acerca de la Constitución social aristocrática de Chile después de la Conquista, 1580–1660.* Santiago de Chile: Editorial Universitaria, 1970.

——. *Studies in the Colonial History of Spanish America.* Richard Southern, trans. Cambridge: Cambridge University Press, 1975.

——. "Urban Social Stratification in Colonial Chile." *HAHR* 55, no. 3 (1975): 421–48.

González Carré, Enrique and Virgilio Galdo Gutiérrez. "Supervivencias prehispánicas en la etapa colonial: Ayacucho, Siglos XVII–XVIII." III Congreso Peruano del hombre y la cultura andina. Universidad Nacional Mayor de San Marcos, Lima, 1977.

Hanke, Lewis. "A Modest Proposal for a Moratorium on Grand Generalizations: Some Thoughts on the Black Legend." *HAHR* 51, no. 1 (February 1971): 112–27.

———. *The Spanish Struggle for Justice in the Conquest of America.* Boston: Little, Brown, 1965. (Copyright, American Historical Association, 1959).

Haring, Clarence H. *The Spanish Empire in America.* New York: Harcourt Brace and World, 1947.

Harris, Marvin. *Patterns of Race in the Americas.* New York: Walker and Company, 1964.

Haslip-Viera, Gabriel. "The Underclass," in *Cities and Society in Colonial Latin America,* Louisa Schell Hoberman and Susan Migden Socolow, eds. Albuquerque: University of New Mexico Press, 1986, pp. 285–312.

Hemming, John. *The Conquest of the Incas.* New York: Harcourt Brace Jovanovich, 1970.

Henige, David. "Primary Source by Primary Source? On the Role of Epidemics in New World Depopulation." *Ethnohistory* 33, no. 3 (Summer 1986): 293–312.

Isbell, Billie Jean. "Parentesco andino y reciprocidad," in *Reciprocidad e intercambio en los andes peruanos,* Giorgio Alberti and Enrique Mayer, eds. Lima: Instituto de Estudios Peruanos, 1974, pp. 110–52.

———. *To Defend Ourselves: Ecology and Ritual in an Andean Village.* Austin: University of Texas Press, 1978.

Johnson, Lyman. "Artisans," in *Cities and Society in Colonial Latin America,* Louisa Schell Hoberman and Susan Migden Socolow, eds. Albuquerque: University of New Mexico Press, 1986, pp. 227–50.

Julien, Catherine J. "Incan Decimal Administration in the Lake Titicaca Region," in *The Inca and Aztec States, 1400–1800: Anthropology and History,* George A. Collier, Renato I. Rosaldo, and John D. Wirth, eds. New York: Academic Press, 1982, pp. 119–51.

Karasch, Mary. "Suppliers, Sellers, Servants, and Slaves," in *Cities and Society in Colonial Latin America,* Louisa Schell Hoberman and Susan Migden Socolow, eds. Albuquerque: University of New Mexico Press, 1986, pp. 251–83.

Keen, Benjamin. "The Black Legend Revisited: Assumptions and Realities." *HAHR* 44, no. 4 (November 1969): 703–21.

Keith, Robert G. *Conquest and Agrarian Change: The Emergence of the Hacienda System on the Peruvian Coast.* Cambridge: Harvard University Press, 1976.

———. "Encomienda, Hacienda, and Corregimiento in Spanish America: A Structural Analysis." *HAHR* 51, no. 3 (August 1971): 431–46.

———. "Origen del sistema de hacienda: El valle de Chancay," in *Hacienda, comunidad y campesinado en el Perú,* José Matos Mar, ed. Lima: Instituto de Estudios Peruanos, 1976, pp. 53–104.

———, ed. *Haciendas and Plantations in Latin American History.* New York: Holmes and Meier, 1977.

Kicza, John E. "The Social and Ethnic Historiography of Colonial Latin America: The Last Twenty Years," in *The William and Mary Quarterly* 45, no. 3 (July 1988): 453–88.

Klein, Herbert S. *Bolivia: The Evolution of a Multi-Ethnic Society.* Oxford: Oxford University Press, 1982.

———. "Hacienda and Free Community in Eighteenth-Century Alto Peru: A Demographic Study of the Aymara Population of the Districts of Chulumaní and Pacajes in 1786." *Journal of Latin American Studies* 7, Part 2 (November 1975): 193–220.

Knight, Franklin W. *The Caribbean: The Genesis of a Fragmented Nationalism.* New York: Oxford University Press, 1978.

Konetzke, Richard. "Las Fuentes para la historia demográfica de Hispano-America durante la época colonial." *Anuario de estudios americanos* 5 (1948): 267–323.

Kubler, George. *The Indian Caste of Peru, 1795–1940.* Washington, D.C.: Smithsonian Institute, Institution of Social Anthropology, Publication No. 14, 1952.

———. "The Neo-Inca State, 1537–1572." *HAHR* 27, no. 2 (May 1947): 189–203.

———. "Population Movements in Mexico, 1520–1600." *HAHR* 22, no. 4 (November 1942): 606–43.

———. "The Quechua in the Colonial World," in *Handbook of South American Indians,* Vol. II, Julian H. Steward, ed. Washington, D.C.: Government Printing Office, 1964.

Larson, Brooke. *Colonialism and Agrarian Transformation in Bolivia: Cochabamba, 1550–1900.* Princeton: Princeton University Press, 1988.

Lassegue-Moleres, O. P., Juan Bautista. *Guia del investigador en el Archivo Arzobispal del Cuzco.* Limited Issue, supported by el Fondo del Libro del Banco Industrial del Perú. Cuzco: Centro de estudios rurales andinos "Bartolomé de las Casas," 1981.

Lautman, Françoise. "Differences or Changes in Family Organization," in *Family and Society: Selections from the Annales: Economies, Societés, Civilisations,* Robert Forster and Orest Ranum, eds. Elborg Forster and Patricia M. Ranum, trans. Baltimore: Johns Hopkins University Press, 1976.

Lavallé, Bernard. "Divorcio y nulidad de matrimonio en Lima (1650–1700): La desavenencia conyugal como indicador social." *Revista Andina* 4, no. 2 (diciembre 1986): 427–64.

Lehmann, David, ed. *Ecology and Exchange in the Andes.* Cambridge: Cambridge University Press, 1982.

Lobo, Susan. *A House of my Own: Social Organization in the Squatter Settlements of Lima, Peru.* Tucson: University of Arizona Press, 1982.

Lockhart, James. "Encomienda and Hacienda: The Evolution of the Great Estate in the Spanish West Indies." *HAHR* 29, no. 3 (August 1969): 411–29.

———. *The Men of Cajamarca: A Social and Biographical Study of the First Conquerors of Peru.* Austin: University of Texas Press, 1972.

———. *Spanish Peru, 1532–1560: A Colonial Society.* Madison: The University of Wisconsin Press, 1968.

Lockhart, James and Enrique Otte, trans. and eds. *Letters and People of the Spanish Indies.* Cambridge: Cambridge University Press, 1976.

Lohmann Villena, Guillermo. *El Conde de Lemos.* Madrid: Publicaciones de la Escuela de Estudios Hispano-Americanos de la Universidad de Sevilla, 1946.

———. *El corregidor de indios en el Perú bajo los Austrias.* Madrid: Ediciones Cultura Hispanica, 1957.

———. *Juan de Matienzo, Autor del "Gobierno del Perú": Su personalidad y su obra.* Seville: Publicaciones de la Escuela de Estudios Hispano-Americanos, 1966.

Lombardi, John V. "Population Reporting Systems: An Eighteenth-Century Paradigm of Spanish Imperial Organization," in *Studies in Spanish American Population History,* David J. Robinson, ed. Dellplain Latin American Studies, No. 8. Boulder, Colo.: Westview Press, 1981, pp. 11–23.

Lounsbury, Floyd G. "Some Aspects of the Inka Kinship System," in *Anthropological History of Andean Polities,* John V. Murra, Nathan Watchel, and Jacques Revel, eds. Cambridge: Cambridge University Press, 1986, pp. 121–36.

Lovell, W. George. "The Historical Demography of the Cuchumatán Highlands of Guatemala, 1500–1821," in *Studies in Spanish American Population History,* David J. Robinson, ed. Dellplain Latin American Studies, No. 8. Boulder, Colo.: Westview Press, 1981, pp. 195–216.

Macera, Pablo. *Trabajos de Historia,* Tomos I–IV. Lima: Instituto Nacional de Cultura, 1977.

Málaga Medina, Alejandro. "Las reducciones en el Virreinato del Perú (1532–1580)." *Revista de historia de América* 80 (July–December 1975): 9–42.

Mallon, Florencia E. *The Defense of Community in Peru's Central Highlands: Peasant Struggle and Capitalist Transition, 1860–1940.* Princeton: Princeton University Press, 1983.

Marx, Karl. *Pre-Capitalist Economic Formations.* Eric J. Hobsbawm, ed. Jack Cohen, trans. New York: International Publishers, 1964.

Matos Mar, José. *Yanaconaje y reforma agraria en el Perú: el caso del valle de*

Chancay. Perú Problemas, No. 15, Lima: Instituto de Estudios Peruanos Ediciones, 1976.

Mazet, Claude. "Population et Société à Lima aux XVIᵉ et XVIIᵉ Siècles: La Paroisse San Sebastian (1562–1689)." *Cahiers des Amériques Latines* 13/14 (1976): 51–100.

Means, Philip C. *Ancient Civilizations of the Andes.* New York: Scribner's, 1931.

Mellafe, Rolando. "The Importance of Migration in the Viceroyalty of Peru," in *Population and Economics. Proceedings of Section V of the Fourth Congress of the International Economic History Association, 1968.* Winnipeg: University of Manitoba Press, 1970.

Millones, Luis. "Religión y poder en los Andes: Los Curacas Idólatras de la Sierra Central." Seminario de Ideología y Religión, Primera Jornada del Museo Nacional de Historia, Lima, Perú, November 1977.

Mishkin, Bernard. "The Contemporary Quechua," in *Handbook of South American Indians,* Vol. II., Julian H. Steward, ed. Washington, D.C.: Government Printing Office, 1964.

Monge, Carlos. *Acclimatization in the Andes.* Donald F. Brown, trans. Baltimore: Johns Hopkins University Press, 1948.

Moore, Sally Falk. *Power and Property in Inca Peru.* New York: Columbia University Press, 1958.

Morner, Magnus. "A Comparative Study of Tenant Labor in Parts of Europe, Africa, and Latin America, 1700–1900: A Preliminary Report of a Research Project in Social History." *LARR* 5, no. 2 (1970): 3–15.

———. *The Andean Past: Land, Societies, and Conflicts.* New York: Columbia University Press, 1985.

———. *Perfil de la sociedad rural del Cuzco a fines de la colonia.* Lima: Universidad del Pacífico, 1978.

———. *Race Mixture in the History of Latin America.* Boston: Little, Brown, 1967.

———. "The Spanish Hacienda: A Survey of Recent Research and Debate." *HAHR* 53, no. 2 (May 1973): 183–216.

———. "Tenant Labour in Andean South America Since the Eighteenth Century, A Preliminary Report." XIII International Congress of Historical Sciences, Moscow, August 15–23, 1970. Reprinted by Nauka Publishing House, Moscow, 1970.

Moscoso, Francisco. "Tributo y Formación de Clases en la Sociedad de los Tainos de las Antillas." Ponencia, VII Congreso Internacional para el Estudio de las Culturas Pre-Colombínas de las Antillas Menores. Caracas, 1977.

Murra, John V. "An Aymaran Kingdom in 1567." *Ethnohistory* 15, no. 2 (Spring 1968): 115–51.

———. "Cloth and Its Functions in the Inca State." *American Anthropologist* 64 (1962): 710–28.

———. "El contról verticál de un máximo de pisos ecológicos en la economía de las sociedades andinas." Private issue, 1956.

———. "The Economic Organization of the Inca State." Ph.D. dissertation. University of Chicago, 1956.

———. *Formaciones económicas y políticas del mundo andino.* Lima: Instituto de Estudios Peruanos, 1975.

———. "The *Mit'a* Obligations of Ethnic Groups to the Inka State," in *The Inca and Aztec States, 1400–1800: Anthropology and History,* George A. Collier, Renato I. Rosaldo, and John D. Wirth, eds. New York: Academic Press, 1982, pp. 237–62.

———. "New Data on Retainer and Servile Populations in Tawantinsuyu." *Actas y memorias,* XXVI Congreso Internacional de Americanistas, Seville, 1966, Vol. II, pp. 35–44.

———. "Rite and Crop in the Inca State," in *Culture in History, Essays in Honor of Paul Radin,* Stanley Diamond, ed. New York: Columbia University Press, 1960.

Murra, John V. and Nathan Wachtel. "Introduction," in *Anthropological History of Andean Polities,* John V. Murra, Nathan Watchel, and Jacques Revel, eds. Cambridge: Cambridge University Press, 1986, pp. 1–8.

Newson, Linda A. "Demographic Catastrophe in Sixteenth-Century Honduras," in *Studies in Spanish American Population History,* David J. Robinson, ed. Dellplain Latin American Studies, No. 8. Boulder, Colo.: Westview Press, 1981, pp. 217–42.

———. "Indian Population Patterns in Colonial Spanish America." *LARR* XX, no. 3 (1985): 41–99.

Núñez del Prado, Oscar. *Kuyo Chico: Applied Anthropology in an Indian Community.* With the collaboration of William Foote Whyte. Lucy Whyte Russo and Richard Russo, trans. Chicago: University of Chicago Press, 1973.

Oliver-Smith, Anthony. *The Martyred City: Death and Rebirth in the Andes.* Albuquerque: University of New Mexico Press, 1986.

Pacini, Deborah and Franquemont, Christine, eds. *Coca and Cocaine: Effects on People and Policy in Latin America.* Cultural Survival Report No. 23. Peterborough, N.H.: Transcript Printing Company, 1986.

Parejas, Alcides. *Historia de Moxos y Chiquitos a fines del siglo XVIII.* La Paz: Instituto Boliviano de Cultura, 1976.

Parry, J. H. *The Spanish Seaborne Empire.* New York: Knopf, 1966.

Pease G. Y., Franklin. *Del Tawantinsuyu a la historia del Perú.* Lima: Instituto de Estudios Peruanos Ediciones, 1978.

———. "Etnohistoria andina: un estado de la cuestión." Private issue, Lima, 1977.

———. "The Formation of Tawantinsuyu: Mechanisms of Colonization and Relationship with Ethnic Groups," in *The Inca and Aztec States, 1400–*

1800: Anthropology and History. George A. Collier, Renato I. Rosaldo, and John D. Wirth, eds. New York: Academic Press, 1982, pp. 173–98.

————. "Las visitas como testimonio andino." Preliminary version, private issue, Lima 1977.

Phelan, John L. *The Kingdom of Quito in the Seventeenth Century: Bureaucratic Politics in the Spanish Empire.* Madison: University of Wisconsin Press, 1967.

Pirenne, Henri. *Economic and Social History of Medieval Europe.* I. E. Clegg, trans. New York: Harcourt Brace and World, 1937.

Platt, Tristan. "Acerca del sistema tributario pre-Toledano en el Alto Perú." *Avances,* no. 1 (1978): 33–44.

————. "Mirrors and Maize: The Concept of *yanantin* Among the Macha of Bolivia," in *Anthropological History of Andean Polities,* John V. Murra, Nathan Watchel, and Jacques Revel, eds. Cambridge: Cambridge University Press, 1986.

Poole, Deborah A. and Penelope Harvey. "Luna, sol y brujas: Estudios andinos e historiografía de resistencia." *Revista Andina* 6, no. 1 (July 1988): 277–95.

Prescott, William H. *The Conquest of Peru.* Victor W. von Hagen, ed. New York: New American Library, 1961.

Ramón, Armando de. "Grupos elitarios chilenos y su vinculación con la metrópoli peruana a fines del siglo XVII, 1681–1695," XXXIX Congreso Internacional de Americanistas, Lima, August 1970.

Ramos, Demetrio. "Trigo chileno, navieros del Callao y hacendados limeños entre la crisis agrícola del siglo XVII y la comercial de la primera mitad del XVIII." *Revista de Indias* XXVI, no. 105–6 (1966): 209–321.

Ricard, Robert. *The Spiritual Conquest of Mexico.* Lesley Byrd Simpson, trans. Berkeley: University of California Press, 1966.

Robinson, David J. "Indian Migration in Eighteenth-Century Yucatán: The Open Nature of the Closed Corporate Community," in *Studies in Spanish American Population History,* David J. Robinson, ed. Dellplain Latin American Studies, No. 8. Boulder, Colo.: Westview Press, 1981.

Rosenblat, Angel. *La población indígena y el mestizaje en América.* Buenos Aires, 1945.

Rostorowski de Diéz Canseco, María. *Etnía y sociedad: Costa Peruana prehispánica.* Lima: Instituto de Estudios Peruanos, 1977.

————. "Succession, Co-option to Kingship, and Royal Incest Among the Inca." *Southwestern Journal of Anthropology* 16 (1960): 417–27.

Rowe, John H. "Inca Policies and Institutions Relating to the Cultural Unification of the Empire," in *The Inca and Aztec States, 1400–1800: Anthropology and History.* George A. Collier, Renato I. Rosaldo, and John D. Wirth, eds. New York: Academic Press, 1982, pp. 93–118.

———. "Incan Culture at the Time of the Spanish Conquest," in *Handbook of South American Indians*, Vol. II, Julian H. Steward, ed. Washington, D.C.: Government Printing Office, 1964.

———. "The Incas Under Spanish Colonial Institutions." *HAHR* 37, no. 2 (May 1957): 155–99.

———. "El movimiento Nacional Inca del Siglo XVIII." *Revista Universitaria del Cusco* XLIII, no. 107 (1954): 17–47.

———. "What Kind of Settlement was Inca Cuzco?" *Nawpa Pacha*, no. 5, (1967): 59–77.

Ryder, James W. "Internal Migration in Yucatán: Interpretation of Historical Demography and Current Patterns," in *Anthropology and History in Yucatán*, Grant D. Jones, ed. Austin: University of Texas Press, 1977.

Saavedra, Bautista. *El ayllu*. Paris: P. Ollendorff, 1913.

Saignes, Thierry. "Ayllus, mercado y coacción colonial: el reto de las migraciones internas en Charcas (siglo XVII)," in *La participación indígena en los mercados surandinos: Estrategias y reproducción social, siglos XVI a XX*, Olivia Harris, Brooke Larson, and Enrique Tandeter, eds. La Paz: Centro de Estudios de la Realidad Económica y Social, 1987.

———. "The Ethnic Groups in the Valleys of Larecaja: From Descent to Residence," in *Anthropological History of Andean Polities*, John V. Murra, Nathan Wachtel, and Jacques Revel, eds. Cambridge: Cambridge University Press, 1986, pp. 311–41.

Salomon, Frank. *Native Lords of Quito in the Age of the Incas: The Political Economy of North Andean Chiefdoms*. Cambridge: Cambridge University Press, 1986.

———. "Vertical Politics on the Inka Frontier," in *Anthropological History of Andean Polities*, John V. Murra, Nathan Wachtel, and Jacques Revel, eds. Cambridge: Cambridge University Press, 1986, pp. 89–117.

Sánchez-Albornoz, Nicolás. *Indios y tributos en el Alto Perú*. Lima: Instituto de Estudios Peruanos Ediciones, 1978.

———. "Migración rural en los Andes: Sipesipe, 1645." *Revista de historia económica* 1 (1983): 13–36.

———. "Mita, migraciones y pueblos. Variaciones en el espacio y en el tiempo." *Revista boliviana* III, no. 1 (1983): 31–59.

———. *The Population of Latin America: A History*. W. A. R. Richardson, trans. Berkeley: University of California Press, 1974.

———. "Los registros parroquiales en America Latina," XXXVII Congreso Internacional de Americanistas, Mar de Plata, Argentina, 1966.

———, ed. *Población y mano de obra en América Latina*. Madrid: Alianza Editorial, 1985.

Seed, Patricia. "Social Dimensions of Race: Mexico City, 1753." *HAHR* 62, no. 4 (1982): 569–606.

Service, Elman R. "The *Encomienda* in Paraguay." *HAHR* 31, no. 2 (May 1951): 230–52.

———. "Indian-European Relations in Colonial Latin America." *American Anthropologist* 57 (1955): 411–25.

Shea, Daniel E. "A Defense of Small Population Estimates for the Central Andes in 1520," in *The Native Population of the Americas in 1492*, William M. Denevan, ed. Madison: University of Wisconsin Press, 1976.

Sherman, William L. *Forced Labor in Sixteenth-Century Central America*. Lincoln: University of Nebraska Press, 1979.

Silva Santistéban, Fernando. *Los obrajes en el Virreinato del Perú*. Lima: Publicaciones del Museo Nacional de Historia, 1964.

Silverblatt, Irene. *Moon, Sun, and Witches: Gender Ideologies and Class in Inca and Colonial Peru*. Princeton: Princeton University Press, 1987.

———. "'The Universe has turned inside out . . . There is no justice for us here': Andean Women Under Spanish Rule," in *Women and Colonization: Anthropological Perspectives*, Mona Etienne and Eleanor Leacock, eds. New York: J. F. Bergin, 1980.

Smith, C. T. "Depopulation of the Central Andes in the 16th Century." *Current Anthropology* 11, no. 4–5 (October–December 1970): 453–64.

Spalding, Karen. "The Colonial Indian: Past and Future Research Perspectives." *LARR* VII, no. 1 (Spring 1972): 47–76.

———. *De indio a campesino*. Lima: Instituto de Estudios Peruanos Ediciones, 1974.

———. "Exploitation as an Economic System: The State and the Extraction of Surplus in Colonial Peru," in *The Inca and Aztec States, 1400–1800: Anthropology and History*, George A. Collier, Renato I. Rosaldo, and John D. Wirth, eds. New York: Academic Press, 1982, pp. 321–42.

———. "Hacienda-Village Relations in Andean Society to 1830." *Latin American Perspectives* II, no. 1, Issue 4 (Spring 1975): 107–22.

———. *Huarochirí: An Andean Society Under Inca and Spanish Rule*. Stanford: Stanford University Press, 1984.

———. "Indian Rural Society in Colonial Peru." Ph.D. dissertation. University of California at Berkeley, 1967.

———. "Kurakas and Commerce: A Chapter in the Evolution of Andean Society." *HAHR* 53, no. 4 (November 1973): 581–99.

———. "Social Climbers: Changing Patterns of Mobility among the Indians of Colonial Peru." *HAHR* 50, no. 4 (November 1970): 645–64.

Stavig, Ward. "Ethnic Conflict, Moral Economy, and Population in Rural Cuzco on the Eve of the Thupa Amaro II Rebellion." *HAHR* 68, no. 4 (November 1988): 735–70.

Stern, Steve J. *Peru's Indian Peoples and the Challenge of Spanish Conquest: Huamanga to 1640*. Madison: University of Wisconsin Press, 1982.

———, ed. *Resistance, Rebellion, and Consciousness in the Andean Peasant World, 18th to 20th Centuries.* Madison: University of Wisconsin Press, 1987.

———. "The Social Significance of Judicial Institutions in an Exploitative Society: Huamanga, Peru, 1570–1640," in *The Inca and Aztec States, 1400–1800: Anthropology and History,* George A. Collier, Renato I. Rosaldo, and John D. Wirth, eds. New York: Academic Press, 1982, pp. 289–320.

Steward, Julian H. "Levels of Sociocultural Integration: An Operational Concept." *Southwestern Journal of Anthropology,* VII (1951): 374–90.

Tandeter, Enrique. "Forced and Free Labour in Late Colonial Potosí." *Past and Present,* no. 93 (1981): 98–136.

Tannenbaum, Frank. *Ten Keys to Latin America.* New York: Vintage Books, 1960.

TePaske, John J. and Herbert S. Klein. "The Seventeenth-Century Crisis in New Spain: Myth or Reality?" *Past and Present,* no. 90 (February 1981): 116–35.

Tschopik, Harry Jr. "The Aymara," in *Handbook of South American Indians,* Vol. II, Julian H. Steward, ed. Washington, D.C.: Government Printing Office, 1964.

Valcarcel, Carlos Daniel. *Rebeliones coloniales sudamericanas.* Mexico City: Fondo de cultural económica, 1982.

Wachtel, Nathan. "The *Mitimas* of the Cochabamba Valley: The Colonization Policy of Huayna Capac," in *The Inca and Aztec States, 1400–1800: Anthropology and History,* George A. Collier, Renato I. Rosaldo, and John D. Wirth, eds. New York: Academic Press, 1982, pp. 199–235.

———. *Sociedad e Ideología.* Lima: Instituto de Estudios Peruanos Ediciones, 1973.

———. *The Vision of the Vanquished: The Spanish Conquest of Peru through Indian Eyes, 1520–1570.* Ben and Siân Reynolds, trans. Sussex, England: Harvester Press, 1977.

Wallerstein, Immanuel. *The Modern World-System. Volume I: Capitalist Agriculture and the Origins of the European World-Economy in the Sixteenth Century.* New York: Academic Press, 1974.

———. *The Modern World-System. Volume II: Mercantilism and the Consolidation of the European World-Economy, 1600–1750.* New York: Academic Press, 1980.

Weber, Max. *From Max Weber: Essays in Sociology.* H. H. Gerth and C. Wright Mills, trans. and eds. Oxford: Oxford University Press, 1946.

———. *The Theory of Social and Economic Organization.* Talcott Parsons, ed. A. M. Henderson and Parsons, trans. New York: Oxford University Press, 1947.

Whitaker, Arthur P. *The Huancavelica Mercury Mine.* Cambridge: Harvard University Press, 1941.

Wightman, Ann M. "The *Consulado* of Lima and the *Meridionalización* of the Pacific Trade." Unpublished ms., prepared in seminar for Professor Karen Spalding, June 1975.

———. "Diego Vasicuio: Native Priest," in *Struggle and Survival in Colonial America: Lives of Women and Men Who Coped,* Gary B. Nash and David G. Sweet, eds. Berkeley: University of California Press, 1981.

———. "From Caste to Class in the Andean *Sierra:* the *Forasteros* of Cuzco." Ph.D. dissertation, Yale University, 1983.

Wolf, Eric. "Closed Corporate Peasant Communities in Mesoamerica and Central Java." *Southwestern Journal of Anthropology* 13, no. 1 (Spring 1957).

———. *Europe and the People Without History.* Berkeley: University of California Press, 1982.

———. *Peasants.* Englewood Cliffs, N.J.: Prentice Hall, 1966.

———. *Sons of the Shaking Earth.* Chicago: University of Chicago Press, 1959.

Zimmerman, Arthur Franklin. *Francisco de Toledo: Fifth Viceroy of Peru, 1569–1581.* New York: Greenwood Press, 1968.

Zuidema, R. T. *The Ceque System of Cuzco: The Social Organization of the Capital of the Inca.* Leiden: E. J. Brill, 1964.

———. "The Inca Kinship System: A New Theoretical View," in *Andean Kinship and Marriage,* Ralph Bolton and Enrique Mayer, eds. American Anthropological Association, Special Publication Number 7, 1977, pp. 240–81.

Zulawski, Ann. "*Forasteros* and *Yanaconas:* The Work Force of a Seventeenth Century Mining Town." Paper presented at the 1986 Annual Meeting of the American Historical Association, New York City.

———. "Mano de obra y migración en un centro minero de los Andes: Oruro, 1683," in *Población y mano de obra en América Latina,* Nicolás Sánchez-Albornoz, ed. Madrid: Alianza Editorial, S.A., 1985, pp. 95–114.

✤ Index ✤ ✤

Library of Congress Cataloging-in-Publication Data
Wightman, Ann M.
Indigenous migration and social change: the forasteros of Cuzco,
1570–1720/Ann M. Wightman.
p. cm.
Bibliography: p.
Includes index.
ISBN 0-8223-1000-7
1. Indians of South America—Peru—Cuzco—Social conditions.
2. Rural-urban migration—Peru—Cuzco. 3. Incas—Tribal government.
4. Incas—Social conditions. 5. Colonial administrators—Peru—
Cuzco. 6. Peru—History—1548–1820. I. Title.
F3429.3.S59W54 1989
985'.3700498—dc20   89-33443